# EXPLORING LITERACY

## The Nineteenth Yearbook
## A Peer Reviewed Publication of
## The College Reading Association
## 1997

### EDITORS

**Wayne M. Linek**
Texas A&M University-Commerce

**Elizabeth G. Sturtevant**
George Mason University

### EDITORIAL ASSISTANTS

**Charlene Fleener**
Texas A&M University-Commerce

**Cathy Zeek**
Texas Woman's University

**Syamsundar Uppuluri**
Texas A&M University-Commerce

**Juliana Tiss**
George Mason University

**Janice Winters**
George Mason University

ISBN 1-883604-03-6

Printed at Texas A&M University-Commerce

Cover Design: Jonathan Sampson

# COLLEGE READING ASSOCIATION BOARD MEMBERS 1997-1998

## Executive Officers

*President,* Marino Alvarez, Tennessee State University
*President-Elect & Program Chair,* Timothy Rasinski, Kent State University
*Past President & Awards Chair,* Judy Richardson, Virginia Commonwealth University
*Second Past President,* Betty Heathington, University of Tennessee
*Executive Secretary,* Ora Sterling King, Coppin State College
*Treasurer,* Gary L. Shaffer,University of Wisconsin-Platteville

## Directors

James King, University of South Florida
Barbara Walker, Montana State University-Billings
Nancy J. Padak, Kent State University
Robert B. Cooter, Jr., Dallas Independent School District
Jon Shapiro, The University of British Columbia
Jack Cassidy, Millersville University
D. Ray Reutzel, Brigham Young University
Victoria J. Risko, Vanderbilt University
Patricia Koskinen, University of Maryland
Wayne M. Linek, Texas A&M University-Commerce
Donna Alvermann, University of Georgia

## Division Chairs

*Teacher Education,* Arthur Smith, SUNY-Brockport
*College Reading,* Cathy Leist, University of Louisville
*Clinical,* Diane Allen, University of North Texas
*Adult Learning,* Laurie Elish-Piper, Northern Illinois University

## Editors

*Reading Research and Instruction,* D. Ray Reutzel (Editor), Brigham Young University
*The Reading News,* Ellen Jampole (Editor), SUNY-Cortland
*CRA Monographs,* Barbara Martin Palmer (Editor), Mount St. Mary's College
*CRA Yearbook,* Wayne Linek (Co-Editor), Texas A&M University-Commerce and
    Elizabeth Sturtevant (Co-Editor), George Mason University

## Committee Chairs And Co-Chairs

*Conferences,* Maria Valeri-Gold, Georgia State University
*Membership,* Robin Erwin, Jr., Niagra State University; Susan Davis Lenski, Illinois State
    University
*Professional Affairs,* Gwendolyn Turner, University of Missouri-St. Louis
*Public Information,* Jane Matanzo, Florida Atlantic University
*Media,* Nancy Bertrand, Middle Tennessee State University; John Bertrand, Tennes-
    see State University
*Historian,* J. Estill Alexander, University of Tennessee; Susan Strode, Jefferson City
    Public Schools
*Photographer,* Frederick Fedorco, East Stroudsburg University
*Research,* Evangeline Newton, Unviersity of Akron; Steven Rinehart, West Virginia University
*Elections,* Betty Heathington, University of Tennessee
*Resolutions and Rules,* Patricia Linder, Texas A&M University-Commerce
*Publications,* Michael McKenna, Georgia Southern University
*Legislative and Social Issues,* Sherry Kragler, Ball State University
*Ad Hoc Technology,* Carolyn Andrews-Beck, Miami University

Marilyn Saunders, University of California-Bakersfield
Barbara K. Schneider, Purdue University-North Central
Joan Simmons, University of Wisconsin-Green Bay
Barbara Smukler, College of Mount St. Vincent
Mary W. Spor, Decatur, AL
Toni K. Stiefer, Southeastern Oklahoma State University
Sandra M. Stokes, University of Wisconsin-Green Bay
Denise Stuart, Cleveland State University
Beverly Tully, Southeastern Oklahoma State University
Carole Walker, Texas A&M University-Commerce
Carolyn A. Walker, West Virgina University
Mary A. Wham, University of Wisconsin-Whitewater
Katherine D. Wiesendanger, Alfred University
J.M. Wile, Miami University
Catherine K. Zeek, Texas Woman's University

# TABLE OF CONTENTS

# INTRODUCTION

Where in the human psyche do we find the catalyst for "Exploring Literacy?" We believe the driving force that provides fuel for individual and collaborative explorations into the nature of literacy is grounded in a stimulating interplay among a variety of factors. Collegial relationships in professional organizations like CRA provide an impetus, a forum, and a means for clarification of, and reflection upon, our explorations into literacy.

As we reflect on the title for the Nineteenth Yearbook of the College Reading Association, "Exploring Literacy," we first think of the 1996 CRA conference in Charleston, South Carolina. The annual conference provides a professional and social impetus for getting scholarly papers written while we anticipate the opportunity to see old friends and make new acquaintances. Second, we recognize the forum CRA provides for sharing our work with others who explore literacy through their own researching, teaching, and learning. Third, we appreciate the opportunity for discourse and perception checking that challenges us to clarify what we have done while logically discussing and defending our interpretations. Finally, we are thankful for the reflective fuel that this process provides. Sharing and discussing creates the mindset for reflection while the prospect of publishing provides the cognitive energy necessary for progress in our field. Overall, this synergistic process provides the basis, not only for this Yearbook, but for all of our ongoing inquiries into literacy.

Thus, as the final year of our first editorial term closes, we would like to dedicate this volume to the College Reading Association. The members of this extraordinary organization provided us the opportunity to serve as Yearbook Editors very early in our academic careers and have supported us immeasurably in this and other endeavors. Throughout our extensive interactions with the CRA officers, board members, and the general membership, we have encountered not only outstanding scholarship and professionalism, but also a genuine kindness and patience. We hope we can give back at least a part of what we have gained.

As always, this publication was the product of many hands and minds. First thanks go to all authors who submitted papers. While space allowed us to accept only about half of the papers submitted, we commend all authors, both published and unpublished, for their support of CRA. Their efforts helped to build a strong Yearbook.

Second, thanks go to the reviewers. Every peer-reviewed publication relies on thoughtful reviewers to provide advice and feedback, yet only authors and editors actually see a reviewer's anonymous work. CRA reviewers this year prepared careful, thoughtful reviews which were extremely helpful to authors and editors alike. Support in the review selection process and in other editorial matters was provided by the CRA Publications Committee, chaired by Mike McKenna of Georgia Southern University.

Third, thanks go to our hard-working, behind-the-scenes editorial assistants. At Texas A&M University—Commerce, Syamsundar Uppuluri assisted with sending manuscripts for review and tracking the review process, while Charlene Fleener and Cathy Zeek communicated with authors, sent galley proofs, and assisted extensively with reading and editing. At George Mason University, Julianna Tiss worked on the development of the Editorial Review Board last fall, while Janice Winters assisted with manuscript editing in the spring and summer.

We also greatly appreciate the support our universities have provided for this project throughout the years of our editorship. At Texas A&M University-Commerce, President Jerry Morris, Academic Vice President Donna Arlton, Dean Donald Coker, Assistant Dean Jerry Hutton, and former Department Head Michael Sampson granted financial assistance and time while the faculty members in the Department of Elementary Education rendered ongoing moral support. Vivian Freeman and Lyndal Burnett contributed their support and expertise in the production of the book, Frances Norman and Jan Hazelip furnished expert secretarial assistance, Jonathan Sampson created the cover design, while Carol Adams and Kenneth Edwards assisted with mailing. At George Mason University, President Alan Merten, Provost David Potter, Dean Gustavo Mellander, Dean Gary Galluzzo, Associate Dean Martin Ford, and the faculty of the Graduate School of Education provided continuing encouragement and support for this project. In addition, Firzana Ahmad and Ly-Cheng Mosier provided superb secretarial assistance.

WML & EGS
Fall 1997

# AWARDS IN
# LITERACY RESEARCH

# Patterns of Response: Struggling Readers Respond to a Real Book During Transactional Literature Discussions

## Dissertation Award

### JoAnn Rubino Dugan

Texas A&M University-Commerce

## Abstract

*This study is part of a larger case study that investigated how six struggling readers constructed meaning while reading, writing about, and discussing a full-length novel. Transactional Literature Discussions, a response-based approach, was used to support the social construction of meaning through shared literacy events. Students met as a small group twice a week for eight weeks to read and discuss the story. Sessions were audio and video taped. Discussions were categorized as teacher-led, collaborative, or student-led. A qualitative analysis of student dialogue about the story during small group discussions revealed eight types of response: predicting events, resolving misunderstandings, understanding text language, envisioning possibilities, identifying personally, understanding characters, voicing opinions, and retelling. Although individual responses varied greatly in both frequency and quality, envisioning possibilities and understanding characters were predominant responses. High levels of response were found during the middle segment of discussions. Students appeared to benefit from the collaborative dialogue and interaction during discussions. They grew more confident in their ability to discuss their responses and made sense of the story themselves.*

In the following dialogue, four struggling readers respond to the first chapter of the book, *Shiloh* (Naylor, 1991). Allison initiates the discussion by wondering what motivated the character's thinking and other students respond by suggesting possible reasons. Later during the same talk session, Roy returns to this discussion to extend his response.

Allison: I wonder why Marty thinks the dog was getting beat.

George: Probably because he's bruised or something.

Nicole: Maybe he doesn't listen.

Teacher: Because the dog doesn't listen.

Roy: Maybe he's a hunting dog. (a little later) I think if it was a hunting dog, and you know how beagles hunt for ducks, and the guy that owned the dog, well, was hunting ducks, the dog didn't go find the ducks, he might have beat him for that.

Students were actively engaged in meaning-making. They realized that there was no single correct answer, only possibilities that might change as the story unfolded. Discussion was an opportunity for students to explore multiple responses and broaden their perspectives, as well as a chance to reflect and elaborate on initial responses as Roy did.

Reader response theory holds that readers actively construct meaning by responding to a text for a range of aesthetic and efferent purposes (Rosenblatt, 1978). Aesthetic reading is essential for readers to become personally involved in the appreciation and exploration of literature. However, some poor readers have trouble becoming actively involved in the meaning-making process (Johnston & Winograd, 1985). They've been found to use comprehension strategies ineffectively (Brown, 1980; Torgesen, 1982; Winograd, 1984) and experience feelings of low self-esteem and helplessness (Abramson, Garber, & Seligman, 1980; Diener & Dweck, 1978, 1980). When reading literature, poor readers tend to focus on surface information, struggle with implicit meanings, and build simple and incomplete understandings (Langer, 1990; Purcell-Gates, 1991). Their difficulties appear to be augmented by remedial instruction that limits reading of whole texts and emphasizes low-level skills (Allington, 1983; Bean, McDonald, & Fotta, 1990; Johnston & Allington, 1991; Stanovich, 1986).

A social constructivist view (Vygotsky, 1986) of reading offers support for creating learning environments where readers can learn from each other and share responsibility for learning. Literature discussions are a time and place for teachers and students to scaffold learning. Scaffolding is a collaborative process in which teachers and students build on each other's responses to make sense of the story. It involves demonstration by the teacher of ways to respond, wonder, and question the text as well as each other within the group setting (Tharp & Gallimore, 1988; Wood, Bruner, & Ross, 1976). Communication centered around a piece of literature helps students reconstruct individual interpretations to appropriate meaning or develop shared understandings (Stone, 1993). With practice, students learn to hold the discussions themselves and become independent learners (Pearson & Gallagher, 1983).

To investigate how struggling readers would jointly construct understandings about a whole book during literature discussions, scaffolded instruction was used to help six struggling readers participate in small group discussions to construct more elaborate and complex understandings. I facilitated the discussions with students. To gain insight about the development of students' responses during discussions, one of the questions raised was: How do individual students' responses toward literature vary during Transactional Literature Discussions? A multiple case study design was used to study students' responses as individuals and as members of the group. Qualitative analyses of audio-taped discussions permitted detailed descriptions of individual responses and identification of response patterns.

### *Students*

Six low-achieving fifth graders, four boys and two girls ranging from 10 to 12 years of age, were selected to participate in this study. Students attended a rural public school where they were receiving instructional support for their reading difficulties and overall low performance. Students showed little interest in reading and rarely read an entire book on their own. Their classroom was self-contained. Whole group reading instruction consisted of basal selections read silently followed by written answers to comprehension questions. It was determined that students had sufficient decoding skills based on two decoding assessments: the *Names Test* (Cunningham, 1990; Dufflemeyer, Kruse, Merkley, & Fyfe, 1994) and a 200 word passage from the book *Shiloh* (Naylor, 1991) that students had selected to read during the study. A minimum score of 90% accuracy on each assessment was considered sufficient for the purposes of this study (see Table 1). Students' names are pseudonyms.

**Table 1. Baseline Data for Students**

| Student | CA | Gender | Decoding Assessments | |
| | | | Names Test | Passage |
| --- | --- | --- | --- | --- |
| Donald | 11.4 | M | 90 | 94 |
| John | 11.11 | M | 96 | 95 |
| George | 11.4 | M | 97 | 94 |
| Allison | 10.7 | F | 99 | 99 |
| Nicole | 10.8 | F | 94 | 96 |
| Roy | 11.9 | M | 90 | 94 |

*Note. Assessment values represent percentages of correctly identified words. CA=Chronological age in years and months.*

### Instructional Approach

The instructional approach used in this study was Transactional Literature Discussions (TLD) (Dugan, 1996). TLD consists of a cycle of contiguous literacy events in which the goal is to understand the story (see Figure 1). Meaning-making strategies are demonstrated and practiced in the process of reading and discussing a whole book.

Beginning with *getting ready,* students are involved in previewing and selecting a book as well as predicting or anticipating events when beginning a new section or chapter of the book. Students in this study browsed through a collection of books recommended by their classroom teacher and me. They read the book covers, chapter headings, author notes, and skimmed some of the text. After some discussion and negotiation they agreed on *Shiloh* (Naylor, 1991) because it was a book about a boy and a dog.

*Reading and thinking aloud* involves students in pausing and express-

**Figure 1. Transactional Literature Discussions (TLD)**

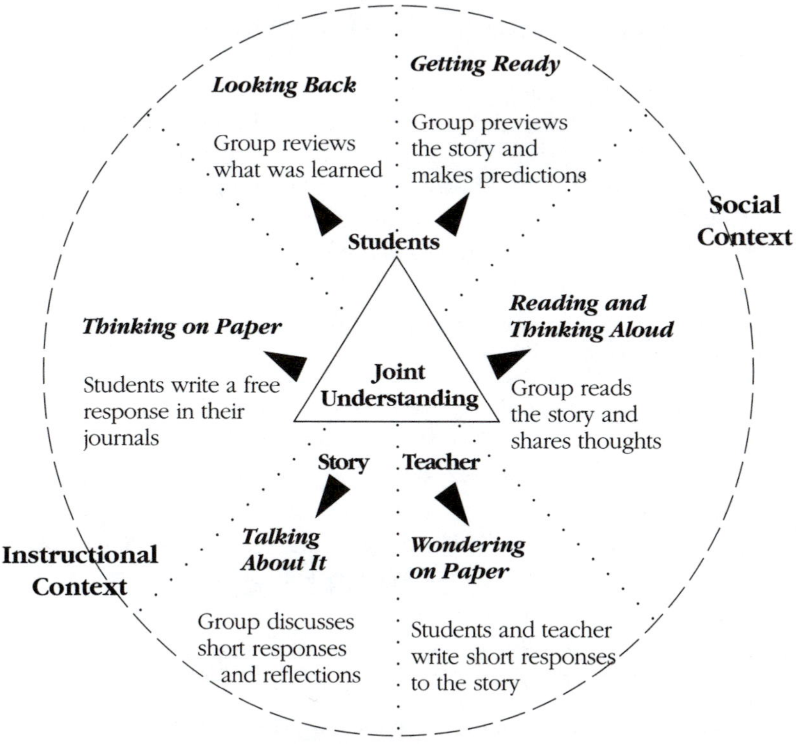

*A framework for holding small group discussions about a whole book.*

ing spontaneous thoughts during reading. Points at which students pause to think aloud are not predetermined, but depend on their response to the story.

*Wondering on paper* is a short written response that students record on a sticky note shortly after reading. Wonderings may include both questions and comments about the story. Students' wonderings provide a springboard for discussion and an opportunity for all to initiate discussion.

*Talking about it* is a time for sharing, reflecting, and developing deeper understandings. As students read their wonderings aloud, the group takes time to discuss them during talk sessions. Sometimes this also involves questioning and rereading a portion of text to explore its meaning in depth.

*Thinking on paper* is a free writing experience that builds on the discussion and gives students a chance to respond personally. Students write for a few minutes in their journals, exploring ideas pertaining to the story or discussion.

*Looking back* encourages students to summarize discussions, evaluate their performance, and predict future events. This may be done orally or in writing.

To help students participate in the talk sessions, $RQL_2$, a cognitive structure, is used to raise a mental awareness of how students can participate (Dugan, 1996) (see Figure 2). $RQL_2$ is an acronym for Respond, Question, Listen, and Link. In this study, students were introduced to $RQL_2$ during lesson two. We discussed what it means to respond, question, listen, and link. A piece of thermal cloth was used to illustrate the notion of weaving our thoughts about the story to form stronger understandings. Occasionally, I referred to $RQL_2$ to remind students to respond, question, listen, and link.

**Figure 2. $RQL_2$: A cognitive structure for helping students talk about a story.**

| | | |
|---|---|---|
| 1. | ***Respond*** | Tell what you liked or disliked. |
| | | Tell about your favorite part. |
| | | Tell how the story makes you feel. |
| 2. | ***Question*** | Ask questions about the story. |
| | | Ask your classmates and teacher questions. |
| | | Ask questions the whole group can answer. |
| 3. | ***Listen*** | Listen to what your classmates say. |
| | | Listen and respond to the questions. |
| | | Listen and join in the discussion. |
| 4. | ***Link*** | Link events in the story. |
| | | Link your experiences with the story. |
| | | Link your ideas with the ideas of your classmates. |

Both the teacher and students were instrumental in the scaffolding process. Scaffolding occurred in the form of teacher modeling and demonstration of activities such as *thinking aloud* and *wondering on paper* and instructions about procedures for working with partners and in the group. Discussions about the story also provided students with many examples of responses as well as ways to express and elaborate on these. Students' own wonderings served as examples for responding spontaneously to the story, and their own questions about the story prompted them to clarify, reread, and explore it in ways that they might not have considered independently. In noting different perspectives and modeling how to disagree without arguing, the teacher showed students how to express and explore multiple perspectives. By listening and then responding to a specific aspect of the story, teacher and students together demonstrated how to stay on the topic to construct a mutual understanding.

### Procedures

After reviewing a collection of children's books, students chose to read *Shiloh* (Naylor, 1991), a story about a boy, Marty, who wants to save a beagle from its abusive owner, Judd. *Shiloh* was awarded the 1992 John Newberry Medal for the most distinguished contribution to American literature for children.

For a period of eight weeks, the group met in a room separate from their regular classroom for fifteen lessons lasting forty-five minutes each. Students were given more support initially, so lessons 1-5 were more teacher-directed. As more responsibility for reading and discussing the book was shared with students, lessons 6-10 became more collaborative. Lessons 11-15 were student-led since students were assigned roles as discussion leaders. Lessons were video and audio taped by the researcher and later transcribed for analysis.

To describe patterns of student responses that focused on making sense of the story during the talk sessions, a discourse analysis was conducted. A coding scheme was developed recursively by reading transcripts of four lessons selected at random and describing responses with a phrase that best described the focus of meaning-making (Guba & Lincoln, 1981). These responses were recorded and sorted to form categories of response based on similar focus. Similar responses were clustered in each category and were given headings that best described the characteristics of the responses in each cluster. Initially, seven response categories were formed. After coding all transcripts, an eighth category was added (see Appendix). Of 764 total student responses, 722 that focused on the story were coded and each was assigned to only one category. Responses not coded were those that focused on procedures (i.e, "Should we read the first page?") or were nongenerative (i.e,

"Can I get a drink of water?"). Discrepancies were resolved through discussion with a research advisor. Twenty-five percent of the transcripts were coded by a graduate student researcher. Interrater reliability was found to be 91%.

The frequency of response patterns was determined by tallying the total number of responses across all talk sessions and the number of responses made by individual students for each response category. Also, to note changes over time in relation to the teacher-led (lessons 1-5), collaborative (lessons 6-10), and student-led discussions (lessons 11-15), responses were tallied within each group of lessons for individual students.

## Findings
### *Patterns of Student Response*

Eight response patterns that varied widely in quality and frequency were found (see Table 2). Predominant responses were *envisioning possibilities* and *understanding characters. Resolving misunderstandings* was the least frequent response followed by *identifying personally* and *predicting events.*

**Table 2. Frequency of Response Patterns**

| Pattern | Code | n | % |
|---|---|---|---|
| Envisioning Possibilities | EP | 260 | 36 |
| Understanding Characters | UC | 161 | 22 |
| Voicing Opinions | VO | 70 | 10 |
| Understanding Text Language | UT | 67 | 09 |
| Retelling | RT | 65 | 09 |
| Predicting Events | PE | 43 | 06 |
| Identifying Personally | IP | 47 | 07 |
| Resolving Misunderstandings | RM | 9 | 01 |
| Total Responses | | 722 | 100 |

Individual response patterns also varied greatly in both frequency and quality (see Table 3). Roy contributed the highest number of responses. Next to Roy, Donald, George, and Nicole contributed similar numbers of responses, while Allison and John contributed fewer responses. Approximately 40% of the responses made by Roy, Nicole, and John focused on *envisioning possibilities,* while one-third of George's responses and slightly more than one-fourth of Donald's responses focused on *envisioning possibilities.* Next to *envisioning possibilities, understanding characters* was the most frequent response, accounting for one-fifth to one-fourth of individual students' responses. Other types of response varied from low frequency to none.

**Table 3. Frequency of Response Patterns for Individual Students**

| Student | | Response Patterns | | | | | | | | Total |
|---|---|---|---|---|---|---|---|---|---|---|
| | | *PE* | *RM* | *UT* | *EP* | *IP* | *UC* | *VO* | *RT* | |
| Roy | n | 14 | 2 | 20 | 83 | 7 | 38 | 13 | 19 | 196 |
| | % | 7 | 1 | 10 | 42 | 4 | 19 | 7 | 10 | |
| Donald | n | 6 | 3 | 15 | 39 | 8 | 33 | 22 | 7 | 133 |
| | % | 5 | 2 | 11 | 29 | 6 | 25 | 17 | 5 | |
| George | n | 8 | 4 | 22 | 41 | 6 | 25 | 8 | 9 | 123 |
| | % | 7 | 3 | 18 | 33 | 5 | 20 | 7 | 7 | |
| Nicole | n | 5 | — | 6 | 47 | 7 | 25 | 14 | 13 | 117 |
| | % | 4 | — | 5 | 40 | 6 | 21 | 12 | 11 | |
| Allison | n | 3 | — | 4 | 22 | 9 | 23 | 8 | 15 | 84 |
| | % | 4 | — | 5 | 26 | 11 | 27 | 10 | 18 | |
| John | n | 7 | — | — | 28 | 10 | 17 | 5 | 2 | 69 |
| | % | 10 | — | — | 41 | 14 | 25 | 7 | 3 | |

Changes in response patterns over time varied from student to student (see Table 4). For example, Donald's responses gradually decreased across lessons. This was accompanied by a noticeable change in behavior from dominator and competitor to collaborator and facilitator. By contrast, John and Allison, both shy, quiet students, responded less frequently in teacher-led lessons but more frequently during student-led lessons. Nicole's responses more than doubled during collaborative lessons and remained stable during the final lessons. George's responses steadily increased across the lessons. Roy, considered the least proficient reader in the group, dominated the teacher-led and collaborative lessons, but responded less frequently during student-led lessons.

In the next section, qualities and changes in responses unique to individual students are discussed.

**Donald.** Early on, Donald dominated the group. He was outspoken, initiated frequently, asserted his position, and often volunteered to read aloud. Next to Roy, he had the highest total number of responses. At first Donald was concerned with procedures and inquired if we would "go around and read one page" and if they would "be tested on the story." Once we began reading, he shifted his attention to the story and raised questions about the language of the text such as, "Why is this word printed like that? C'mon. It says See-mon." This encouraged discussion about the spelling and pronunciation of words and the dialogue. Donald sometimes focused on superficial and minute details rather than implicit meanings. For instance he noted, "I

**Table 4. Frequency of Response Patterns for Individual Students During Teacher—Led, Collaborative, and Student—Led Lessons**

| Student | | Teacher—Led | | | | | | | | Collaborative | | | | | | | Student—Led | | | | | | | | |
|---|---|---|---|---|---|---|---|---|---|---|---|---|---|---|---|---|---|---|---|---|---|---|---|---|---|
| | | PE | RM | UT | EP | IP | UC | VO | RT | PE | RM | UT | EP | IP | UC | VO | RT | PE | RM | UT | EP | IP | UC | VO | RT |
| Roy | n | 6 | — | 9 | 38 | 1 | 13 | 3 | 8 | 4 | 2 | 9 | 33 | 6 | 13 | 8 | 6 | 4 | — | 2 | 12 | — | 12 | 2 | 5 |
| | % | 8 | — | 12 | 49 | 1 | 17 | 4 | 10 | 5 | 2 | 11 | 41 | 7 | 16 | 10 | 7 | 11 | — | 5 | 32 | — | 32 | 5 | 14 |
| | Total | | | | 78 | | | | | | | | 81 | | | | | | | | 37 | | | | |
| Donald | n | 2 | 2 | 6 | 14 | 5 | 11 | 8 | 2 | 1 | 1 | 6 | 14 | 2 | 12 | 7 | 3 | 3 | — | 3 | 11 | 1 | 10 | 7 | 2 |
| | % | 4 | 4 | 12 | 28 | 10 | 22 | 16 | 4 | 2 | 2 | 13 | 30 | 4 | 24 | 14 | 6 | 8 | — | 8 | 30 | 3 | 27 | 19 | 5 |
| | Total | | | | 50 | | | | | | | | 46 | | | | | | | | 37 | | | | |
| George | n | 3 | 3 | 12 | 11 | 2 | 3 | 1 | 1 | 3 | 1 | 5 | 12 | — | 10 | 4 | 5 | 2 | — | 5 | 18 | 4 | 12 | 3 | 3 |
| | % | 8 | 8 | 33 | 31 | 6 | 8 | 3 | 3 | 8 | 3 | 13 | 30 | — | 25 | 10 | 13 | 4 | — | 11 | 38 | 9 | 26 | 6 | 6 |
| | Total | | | | 36 | | | | | | | | 40 | | | | | | | | 47 | | | | |
| Nicole | n | 4 | — | 3 | 6 | 2 | 5 | — | 3 | — | — | 3 | 22 | — | 11 | 5 | 7 | 1 | — | — | 19 | 5 | 9 | 9 | 3 |
| | % | 17 | — | 13 | 26 | 9 | 22 | — | 13 | — | — | 2 | 46 | — | 23 | 10 | 15 | 2 | — | — | 41 | 11 | 20 | 20 | 7 |
| | Total | | | | 23 | | | | | | | | 48 | | | | | | | | 46 | | | | |
| Allison | n | 2 | — | — | 7 | 4 | 11 | 1 | 3 | 1 | — | 2 | 9 | — | 4 | 1 | 2 | — | — | 2 | 6 | 5 | 8 | 6 | 10 |
| | % | 7 | — | — | 25 | 14 | 39 | 4 | 11 | 5 | — | 11 | 47 | — | 21 | 5 | 11 | — | — | 5 | 16 | 14 | 22 | 16 | 27 |
| | Total | | | | 28 | | | | | | | | 19 | | | | | | | | 37 | | | | |
| John | n | 2 | — | — | 5 | 4 | 1 | 1 | — | 4 | — | — | — | 14 | 2 | 12 | 1 | 1 | 1 | — | — | 9 | 4 | 4 | 3 | 1 |
| | % | 15 | — | — | 38 | 31 | 8 | 8 | — | 12 | — | — | — | 41 | 6 | 35 | 3 | 3 | 5 | — | — | 5 | 18 | 18 | 14 | 5 |
| | Total | | | | 13 | | | | | | | | 34 | | | | | | | | 22 | | | | |

think on page 26 they're talking about a garden 'cause they said stuff about vegetables." Nevertheless, this was an opportunity for the group to explore deeper meanings with the guidance of the teacher. In time, Donald became more collaborative, listened to other students, and gave them a chance to respond. While facilitating a final talk session, Donald encouraged students to elaborate by asking, "What made you write that?" and "Does anyone have anything else to say?"

**John.** The quietest student in the group, John made the least number of responses. Nevertheless, he was an active listener, quick to identify inconsistencies in discussions. John's responses were brief at first, but became more elaborate during the middle and final groups of discussions. During the student-led talk sessions, John facilitated by asking students to share their wonderings. He also became more assertive in voicing his own opinion. For example, during discussion about whether Marty was to blame for the attack on Shiloh, John stated, "It wasn't Marty's fault (that the German shepherd got inside the fence) cause any dog could jump over the fence and attack another dog." John appeared to have grown more confident and secure with himself and his ability to make sense of the story.

**George.** George eagerly participated in the talk sessions and his responses consistently increased in number across sessions. Thirty-three percent of his responses were coded as *envisioning possibilities*. However, during the first five talk sessions, George focused mostly on *understanding text language*. For example, he wondered about the meaning of the phrase, "I decided to wait the dog out." Other students suggested that the dog wouldn't come to Marty because it was tired, but George still seemed puzzled. When I asked students to describe what had happened in this scene, George himself responded, "He (Marty) was sitting on a log waiting for the dog to come." Being able to talk about the language of the text in his own words seemed to help him and the others understand it. With a little encouragement to "say why", he began to justify his thinking. For example, when a student asked "Why does Marty keep Shiloh a secret?", George responded, "So his mom won't find out, because if his mom finds out, he knows he'll have to give Shiloh back." During the final talk sessions, he openly disagreed with other students by saying, "I disagree because . . ." At times, George was rigid in his thinking and grew impatient when other students thought differently. Other times, after students explained themselves, George would change his mind and agree.

**Allison.** Allison was very shy and soft-spoken. At the outset, she seemed to lack confidence in herself and hesitated to express her ideas, even asking at one point if she could say what she was thinking. Allison had next to the least number of total responses, but responded more frequently during the talk sessions. She also seemed more confident and demonstrated that she could lead a discussion. More than one fourth of her responses were coded as *envisioning possibilities* or *understanding the characters*. As the group explored what would happen to Shiloh if he was returned to Judd, Allison suggested, "He'll probably sell Shiloh because he's just sick of him." Later, she again stressed, "I think he'll give it (Shiloh) back to him *for money*." When Donald said he thought Judd would kill the dog, Allison disagreed: "I don't think he's that cruel." However, after reading more of the story, she changed her mind, telling the group, "I think Judd Travers is a really bad person now because he said he would break Shiloh's four legs." Allison related the story to her personal experiences, commenting that her family "gave scraps to the dog in the yard next door." Allison noticed the authentic dialogue and used an accent when reading aloud with her partner and during a readers theater that the group held. Upon finishing the story, Allison commented, "I enjoyed reading the story, and I think Judd was nice in the end."

**Nicole.** During the first few sessions, Nicole focused on *understanding text language* asking questions such as, "Why does it say take 'em?" But soon she turned her attention to the abuse of Shiloh and the conflict between Marty and Judd, stating that, "Marty doesn't like Judd. Marty thinks it's not right to kick a dog." Occasionally, Nicole volunteered to summarize the story, usually constructing detailed retellings. She became more outspoken, responded more frequently to other students' questions and comments, and appeared more confident as she asserted herself. She explained that Marty didn't tell his parents about the dog "because maybe his parents would give Shiloh back to Judd." She asked *why* questions that encouraged students to think and explore possibilities: "Why would a German Shepherd attack Shiloh? Why does Marty blame himself for what happened to Shiloh?" As students discussed Marty's decision not to tell his parents about Shiloh, Nicole asserted, "Keeping a secret is not lying." In the beginning, Nicole was sometimes quick to give up and say she did not know, but grew more confident over time. For example, she defended her position, insisting that "Judd could break a promise" when other students argued otherwise. During the final segment of lessons, Nicole demonstrated that she was able to lead the discussion.

**Roy.** Roy made the highest number of total responses (196). Most of these were expressed during the first and second segments of talk sessions. However, the frequency of his responses decreased considerably during the last segment. Forty-two percent of his total responses dealt with *envisioning possibilities*. Although Roy was perceived as the student struggling the most in the classroom, his responses often helped clarify questions for other students, and were well stated and usually consistent with the story line. He helped students understand the meaning of words they had questioned. For instance, when Donald questioned the word "plumped," Roy used the word in several meaningful contexts: "He (Shiloh) isn't chubby. He's not real fat. He doesn't have a lot of meat on him." Roy also helped the group understand why Judd was abusing the dog, explaining, "He (Judd) got child abuse." When a student challenged Roy because the story did not explicitly state this, Roy defended his reasoning: ". . . if Judd had that problem, he should give the dog the problem. He's taking out his anger on the dog." Roy also voiced his opinion about characters' actions. He argued that Marty was "just keeping a secret" when he did not tell his father about Shiloh. Although he thought Marty "shouldn't have did that," Roy admits "I wouldn't have told the truth (either)." In the last segment of talk sessions, Roy responded less frequently, but he continued to focus on the characters, envisioning possible solutions to Marty's problem and reasons for characters' actions. For instance, he explained why Judd wanted to give some deer meat to Marty's mother: "So Marty wouldn't tell the game warden. He was being nice to him." Roy also led a talk session in which he routinely asked students "why" and gave them opportunities to respond.

## Discussion

The multiplicity of responses found in this study is evidence that meaning is not fixed and singular, but a dynamic interplay of individual interpretations that evolve as the story evolves and as the reader transacts with the text (Langer, 1994; Rosenblatt, 1978). Students appeared to find wondering about the story easy to do. Wondering empowered them to express their ideas and respond to what they thought was important rather than what the teacher expected. Students' responses were not limited to answering questions or making predictions, but depended on what students found significant. Furthermore, students were flexible in their meaning-making as they constantly moved back and forth between the story and their own interpretations, checking and revising their responses as the story unfolded. Consequently, these struggling readers went beyond the surface of the text to construct their understandings. Thus, understanding was not limited to literal, single right and wrong answers or to ideas the teacher had previously identified, but emerged from students' background knowledge, experiences, and responses to the story.

This study shows that struggling readers can learn to hold sophisticated discussions about literature when provided with the necessary support. Small group discussions gave students a time and place to share their spontaneous responses where they could model and practice different ways of responding, hear various perspectives, and socially construct meaning. Individual responses were a springboard for students to begin constructing meaning, while talk about the story broadened their understandings. As Nystrand and Gamoran (1993) found, student performance improves in "classes characterized by higher levels of student participation and higher-quality instructional discourse . . ." (p. 106). As students engaged in the flow of conversation, they acknowledged each other, respected their right to particular points of view, and listened with genuine interest. When students disagreed, they did so diplomatically, which encouraged even more dialogue. Such engagement involving both individual experiences and social interchanges is crucial to the development of self-determined readers (Guthrie, 1996).

## Conclusion

This case study demonstrated that a small group of struggling readers could become active readers when placed in a social situation that supported response and shared meaning-making (Vygotsky, 1986). TLD gave students a framework for reading and understanding a story as a group. By modeling how to think aloud and wonder, incorporating their ideas into the discussion, then inviting students to participate, the teacher placed students in the teaching role so they would take ownership for the discussions (Palincsar & Brown, 1984). Activities such as *thinking aloud* and *wondering on paper* encouraged spontaneous responses that opened the door for exploration of multiple responses and reflection (Rosenblatt, 1938). By shifting the focus from correct answers to the process of responding, exploring, and understanding the story, students could read to appreciate (Langer, 1994). No longer did they rely on the teacher to tell them what the story meant or expect the teacher to ask the questions. As their confidence grew, they took risks with their thinking and looked to each other for support. The teacher was then able to take advantage of students' ideas to guide them to see the significance of an event and take them beneath the surface to deepen the level of understanding. As Stone (1993) points out, adults who place little value on a child's learning are "unlikely to provide the finely tuned directives necessary to encourage the child's inferences. Similarly, if children place little value on the activity . . . , they are not motivated to engage in inferential interactions" (p. 180). During discussions, collaboration between students and teacher in the form of dialogue and interaction about the process played a powerful role in mediating understanding (Palincsar, 1986). If teachers wish to help their students become active meaning-makers, they must not only create contexts for social interchanges. They must truly value what students think and say and in turn help students value themselves and one another.

---

# References

Abramson, L.Y., Garber, J., Seligman, M.E. (1980). Learned helplessness in humans: An attributional analysis. In J. Garber & M.E. Seligman (Eds.), *Human helplessness: Theory and applications* (pp. 3-34). New York: Academic Press.

Allington, R.L. (1983). The reading instruction provided readers of differing ability. *Elementary School Journal, 83,* 548-559.

Bean, R.M., McDonald, L., & Fotta, B. (1990). *A joint survey: KSRA, PAFPC, PDE, Nature of Chapter I reading programs in the state of Pennsylvania.* Pittsburg, PA: University of Pittsburgh.

Brown, A.L. (1980). Metacognitive development and reading. In R. Spiro, B. Bruce, & W.F. Brewer (Eds.), *Theoretical issues in reading comprehension* (pp. 453-481). Hillsdale, NJ: Erlbaum.

Cunningham, P.M. (1990). The Names Test: A quick assessment of decoding ability. *The Reading Teacher, 44,* 124-129.

Diener, C., & Dweck, C. (1978). An analysis of learned helplessness: Continuous changes in performance, strategy, and achievement cognitions following failure. *Journal of Personality and Social Psychology, 36,* 451-462.

Diener, C.I., & Dweck, C.S. (1980). An analysis of learned helplessness: II. The processing of success. *Journal of Personality and Social Psychology, 39,* 940-952.

Duffelmeyer, F.A., Kruse, A.E., Merkley, D.J., & Fyfe, S.A. (1994). Further validation of the Names Test. *The Reading Teacher, 48,* 118-128.

Dugan, J.R. (1996). *Enhancing less-proficient readers' literary understanding through transactional literature discussions.* Unpublished doctoral dissertation. University of Pittsburgh.

Guba, E.G., & Lincoln, Y.S. (1981). *Effective evaluation.* San Francisco: Jossey Bass Publishers.

Guthrie, J.T. (1996). Educational contexts for engagement in literacy. *The Reading Teacher, 49,* 432-445.

Johnston, P., & Allington, R. (1991). Remediation. In R. Barr, M.L. Kamil, P.B. Mosenthal, & P.D. Pearson (Eds.), *Handbook of reading research: Vol. II* (pp. 984-1012). New York: Longman Publishing Group.

Johnston, P.H., & Winograd, P.N. (1985). Passive failure in reading. *Journal of Reading Behavior, 27,* 279-301.

Langer, J.A. (1990). The process of understanding: Reading for literary and informative purposes. *Research in the Teaching of English, 24,* 229-257.

Langer, J.A. (1994). Focus on response-based approach to reading instruction. *Language Arts, 71,* 203-211.

Naylor, P.R. (1991). *Shiloh.* New York: Dell Publishing.

Nystrand, M., & Gamoran, A. (1993). From discourse communities to interpretive communities. In R.K. Durst & G.E. Newell (Eds.), *Exploring texts* (pp. 91-111). Norwood, MA: Christopher Gordon Publishers.

Palincsar, A.S. (1986). The role of dialogue in providing scaffolding instruction. *Educational Psychologist, 21*(1&2), 73-98.

Palincsar, A.S., & Brown, A.L. (1984). Reciprocal teaching of comprehension-fostering and comprehension-monitoring activities. *Cognition and Instruction, 1,* 117-175.

Pearson, P.D., & Gallagher, M.C. (1983). The instruction of reading comprehension. *Contemporary Educational Psychology, 8,* 317-344.

Purcell-Gates, V. (1991). On the outside looking in: A study of remedial readers' meaning-making while reading literature. *Journal of Reading Behavior, 23,* 235-253.

Rosenblatt, L.M. (1938). *Literature as exploration* (4th ed.). New York: Modern Language Association.

Rosenblatt, L.M. (1978). *The reader, the text, the poem: The transactional theory of the literary work.* Carbondale, IL: Southern Illinois University Press.

Stanovich, K.E. (1986). Matthew effects in reading: Some consequences of individual differences in the acquisition of literacy. *Reading Research Quarterly, 21,* 360-407.

Stone, C.A. (1993). What is missing in the metaphor of scaffolding? In E.A. Forman, N. Minick, & C.A. Stone (Eds.), *Contexts for learning: Sociocultural dynamics in children's development* (pp. 169-183). New York: Oxford University Press.

Tharp, R.G., & Gallimore, R. (1988). *Rousing minds to life: Teaching, learning, and schooling in social context.* New York: Cambridge University Press.

Torgesen, J.K. (1982). The learning disabled child as an inactive learner. *Topics in Learning and Learning Disabilities, 2,* 45-52.

Vygotsky, L. (1986). *Thought and language.* Cambridge, MA: MIT Press.

Winograd, P. (1984). Strategic difficulties in summarizing texts. *Reading Research Quarterly, 19,* 404-425.

Wood, D., Bruner, J.S., & Ross, G. (1976). The role of tutoring in problem solving. *Journal of Child Psychology and Psychiatry, 17,* 89-100.

## Appendix: Types of Student Responses

### Predicting Events (PE)
Stating what might occur before reading a portion of the story.
**Example.** *I think in the next chapter, Marty will not find Shiloh and Judd will help Marty look for Shiloh, and they will still not find Shiloh.*

### Resolving Misunderstandings (RM)
Identifying and clarifying confusions.
**Example.** *What does he mean when he's talking about Heaven and Shiloh?*

### Understanding Text Language (UT)
Questioning the meaning of words and phrases in the text.
**Example.** *What is a **bag swing?** What does **wooee** mean?*

### Envisioning Possibilities (EP)
Exploring the meaning of past story events; looking beyond the text and drawing inferences.
**Example.** *They're having a party because they all want Shiloh back. They missed him and they're glad he's back.*

### Identifying Personally (IP)
Relating personal experiences that are similar to or connected with story events and characters.
**Example.** *I think Marty's mad just like I'm mad right now because something happened to my cat. She climbed up a tree and she's been there for two days.*

### Understanding Characters (UC)
Focusing on the behavior and motives of the characters.
**Example.** *I want to know why Marty blames himself for what happened to Shiloh.*

### Voicing Opinions (VO)
Expressing a like or dislike for the story or characters; making judgments based on attitudes or beliefs.
**Example.** *I thought these were really good because they show how Marty stood up to Judd.*

### Retelling (RE)
Paraphrasing or summarizing events after reading the story.
**Example.** *And then Judd just walked in the house without knocking and bent over to pet Shiloh and Shiloh crouched down. And then he said he could keep him till Sunday.*

# Literacy Behaviors in the Spontaneous Play of a Multi-national Group of First Graders in a Small Overseas School

## Thesis Award

### Karen Schroeder
John Carroll University

## Abstract

*This paper reports a part of a larger study of the effect of print-enriched play centers on the literacy behaviors of a group of children in an overseas school. The researcher developed play centers stocked with real-world literacy tools for first graders. She then observed the children during their daily free play time for 7 weeks, recording their literacy behaviors and examples of their play. Results indicate that the intervention led to substantial increases in literacy behaviors for children whose literacy skills were initially less well-developed.*

Many children enter school with an awareness of the functions and uses of print, which may predispose them to school literacy and later to conventional literacy activities as adults. These children may have had experiences with such real tools of literacy as paper, pencils, crayons, markers, and computers. They may also have had the opportunity to observe parents, older siblings, and others modeling literacy behaviors of reading and writing, so they may have an awareness of tools and behaviors beyond their five and six-year-old capabilities. Other children enter school without a strong awareness of written language. For various reasons, they have not had meaningful contact with either the tools or the uses of literacy. My experience as a teacher in overseas schools suggests that children living in other countries are often not exposed to the tools of literacy to the same extent and in the same contexts as are children living in the United States. For instance, the quantity and quality of environmental print available to children overseas seems to be less. Based on my experience, I believed that these children could benefit from opportunities to use literacy tools in school settings. Therefore, my study examined the effects of print-enriched play centers on young children in an overseas school.

## Background

Children may develop both speech and the use of literacy tools most effectively through interaction with other persons in their environment (Vygotsky, 1978). They learn by experimentation, by observation, and by transforming social interactions, including play, with adults and peers. Through these ongoing interactions, children become effective users of literacy tools, including reading and writing, both individually and for the purpose of communicating with others. Researchers working with preschool and kindergarten children (Morrow, 1989; Neuman & Roskos, 1990) have created print-enriched play centers which provide materials and contexts to encourage the collaboration with more capable peers suggested by Vygotsky. Their results indicate that using these enhanced play centers leads to increases in children's literacy behaviors (Morrow, 1989; Neuman & Roskos, 1990, 1991). My study extended the design developed by Neuman & Roskos (1989, 1990 ,1991) to first grade children in an overseas classroom to investigate whether enriched play areas would help these slightly older children develop their print awareness. As part of my study, I asked two questions:

1. How would the children's literacy behaviors change during and after play-center interventions patterned after Neuman & Roskos (1990)?
2. How would children with minimal print awareness compare, after intervention, with children having a more developed awareness of print?

## Intervention

This study was conducted in the American Cooperative School of Tunis, Tunisia. Originally designed as a 12-week intervention, it was cut to 7 weeks by the evacuation that resulted from the Gulf War. Although I was not able to administer the planned posttests, my results demonstrate the children's growth over the 7 weeks of the intervention.

### *Participants*

The 8 boys and 6 girls who participated in the study were all first graders in my class, with a mean age of 6.9 years. As a baseline measure, the Concepts About Print (CAP) Test, Sand booklet (Clay, 1972), was given to each child to assess familiarity with print. Based on the results of the CAP, the children fell naturally into two groups (see Table 1), which I called "Standard Players" and "Super Players."

Of the 9 "Standard Players," 6 read comfortably at the pre-primer level or higher as the study began, and all showed early writing behaviors, either writing or pretending to write for communication. The Standard Players used materials as an adult might in every day life, even at the beginning of the study. For instance, one of these children might take a paper, draw or write on it, fold it, put it an an envelope, put a postage stamp on it, and "send" it to someone. These children drew meaning from the materials and situations they saw before them. Their play tended to be materials-oriented or center-oriented; that is, play was suggested by the materials themselves, wherever they were found, or by the theme suggested by a center and its related materials. One child, for instance, wrote letters on paper wherever she found it in the room. Others in the kitchen area would say, "Let's play kitchen today."

The 6 "Super Players" had less well developed literacy skills. Only one of them read at the pre-primer or higher level, and none of them showed early writing behaviors. The Super Players generally did not draw meaning in the standard way from the materials or play areas. While they might explore the paper, envelope, and postage stamps, they did not respond as the Standard Players did. In addition, the Super Players tended to engage in center-oriented

## Table 1. Initial Play Styles and Reading and Writing Behaviors by Group

| Name | Play Style | Reading at Entry | Early Writing Behaviors |
|------|------------|------------------|-------------------------|
| *Standard Players* | | | |
| Cheyenne | M | Yes | Yes |
| Femke | M | Yes (Dutch) | Yes |
| Jay | M+I | No | Yes |
| Katrina | C+M | Yes | Yes |
| Lindsay | C | Yes | Yes |
| Maik | M | No | Yes |
| Michael | M+I | Yes | Yes |
| Nikki | M | No | Yes |
| *Super Players* | | | |
| Ben | C+I | No | No |
| Charlie | I | No | No |
| Christopher | C+I | No | No |
| Jacob | I | No | No |
| Max | I | Yes | No |
| Rami | C+I | No | No |

*Note. C=Center-oriented play; M=Materials-oriented play; I=Imaginative play*

or imaginative play. Imaginative players generally had an idea of what they wanted to play before the session began or thought up things as they went along, rather than responding to materials or to scenarios suggested by the play areas. "Cops and Robbers," for instance, would be decided upon some-times before the session began and it might be played in any of the areas.

### Classroom Setting

Before the intervention, the classroom was divided into four distinct sections: the desk and central teaching area; the carpeted free reading area;

**Figure 1. Clasroom Before Intervention.**

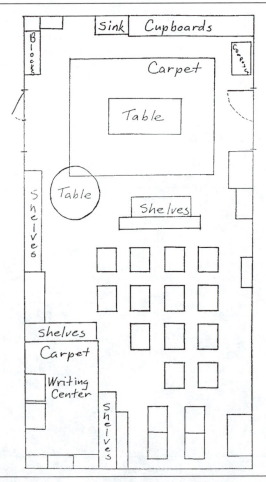

the "teaching reading" area; and the play, display, and activity area (see Figure 1). As the intervention began, 4 play centers were developed—library, kitchen, office, and post office (see Figure 2). These centers represented real-life scenes which might be familiar to the children, but were non-specific enough that each could be used for a variety of play scenarios. Centers were

**Figure 2. Clasroom After Intervention.**

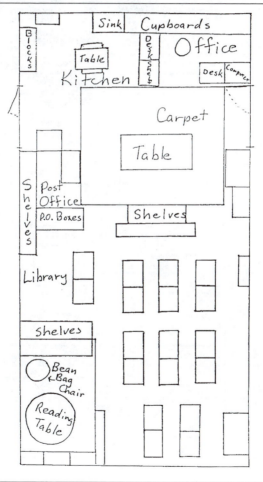

stocked with materials that might be found in each of the real world environments represented. Table 2 summarizes the materials found in each center.

**Table 2. Literacy Materials Used to Stock Play Areas**

| Kitchen | Post Office | Office | Library |
|---|---|---|---|
| table and benches | pens, pencils, markers | disk for each child | carded books |
| dishes | paper and envelopes | calendar | big books |
| flatware | stamps, stars, stickers | appointment books | libary cards and file |
| empty food, toiletry, cleaning containers | canvas mail bag | Apple II computer with Magic Slate | pens, pencils, markers |
| coupons | post office box | message pads | stamps, stamp pad |
| telephone | labeled mail boxes | open/closed sign | stapler and staples |
| telephone book | calendar | pencils, pens, markers | books |
| cookbooks | telephone | business catalogs | newspapers |
| recipe box and cards | telephone book | in/out box | magazines |
| stationery, note paper, and envelopes | post office, mail box signs, posters, etc. | large file box and file folders | book marks |
| magazines | open/closed sign | business size paper | stickers and labels |
| catalogs | lables | business envelopes | telephone |
| play money | stamps/stamp pads | file drawers | telephone book |
| menus | bag of junk mail | 3x5 cards and box | open/closed sign |
| "guest checks" | stapler and staples | business cards | typewriter |
| pens, pencils, markers | calculator | receipt forms | |
| note pads | clipboard | date and other stamps | |
| styrofoam fast food containers | | stamp pads | |
| fast food place mats | | stapler and staples | |
| open/closed sign | | play money | |
| calculator | | Post-it notes | |
| | | calculator | |
| | | clipboard | |
| | | check files | |
| | | reinforcements, labels | |
| | | calculator | |
| | | scissors | |

The children were allowed to play freely in the centers for 35 minutes at the end of each school day. During weeks 2 and 7 I collected the data for this study, observing each child for 2 10-minute periods and recording their literacy behaviors on the Literacy in Play Observation Form (see Figure 3) for later analysis. This form (adapted from Neuman & Roskos, 1989) allowed me to record 4 types of literacy behaviors. *Handling* behaviors are those in which a child picks up, touches, or explores an object without using it. *Reading* behaviors are those in which a child reads or pretends to read a text, assigning meaning to it. *Writing* behaviors are those in which a child uses a tool to make marks intended to communicate meaning to himself/herself or some other person. *Stamping* behaviors are those in which a child uses stamps on paper or other surface with intended meaning. This last category was added because many of the children in this class used all kinds of stamps purposefully, for more than artwork. In addition to recording frequency of these literacy behaviors, I used the back of the form to keep anecdotal notes about the children's play.

**Figure 3. Literacy in Play Observation Form (Adapted from Neuman & Roskos, 1989).**

Child's name _____

Date _____

Play area/center _____

Time _____

- Look for examples of handling, reading, writing, and stamping behaviors.

- Make a tally mark in the appropriate column for each literacy behavior observed.

- Summarize your observation into brief written statements. Continue on reverse if needed.

| Handling | Reading | Writing | Stamping |
|---|---|---|---|
|  |  |  |  |

Summary:

## Results

The results are reported for each research question.

*Question 1: How would the children's literacy behaviors change during and after play-center interventions patterned after Neuman & Roskos (1990)?*

My anecdotal notes indicated that, during the intervention, many children moved from aimless handling of literacy objects to more purposeful interactions with reading and writing. This shift was seen most clearly among the Super Players, who initially displayed fewer literacy behaviors and had an imaginative play style that was independent of the play centers and materials. As the intervention progressed, however, the Super Players incorporated the materials and contexts into their own play sets.

Tabulating the frequency of the children's literacy behaviors indicated that these behaviors increased during the intervention. From Week 2 to Week 7, the frequency of all literacy behaviors per child rose from 20.91 to 24.80, an increase of 18.49% (see Table 3). During the intervention, the greatest increase for the class as a whole was in reading behaviors per child, which rose from 4.6 in Week 2 to 7.2 in Week 7. These increases indicated that the class as a whole had greater involvement with the tools of literacy during the intervention.

**Table 3. Average Frequency Change in Literacy Behaviors from Week 2 to Week 7 for Whole Class.**

| Literacy Behavior | Mean | | % Increase |
|---|---|---|---|
| | Week 2 | Week 7 | |
| Handling | 12.85 | 13.47 | 4.80 |
| Reading | 4.64 | 7.20 | 55.00 |
| Writing | 2.92 | 2.93 | 0.30 |
| Stamping | .50 | 1.20 | 140.00 |
| Totals | 20.91 | 24.80 | 18.49 |

*Question 2: How would children with minimal print awareness compare, after intervention, with children having a more developed awareness of print?*

The Super Players showed an even more dramatic increase in literacy behaviors than the class as a whole. During the observations in Week 2, the Super Players demonstrated only 34% as many literacy behaviors as the Standard Players (75 literacy behaviors compared to 218) (see Table 4). The Super Players' average frequency of literacy behaviors was 12.50, or 45.9% of the Standard Players' average, 27.25 (see Table 5). By Week 7, the Standard Players' average frequency of literacy behaviors had actually declined slightly (see Table 5), while the Super Players' average frequency of literacy behaviors had increased dramatically, by 94.60% (see Table 5).

**Table 4. Frequency of Literacy Behaviors by Group: Week 2**

| Name | Frequency | | | | |
|---|---|---|---|---|---|
| | Handling | Reading | Writing | Stamping | Totals |
| | | Standard | Players | | |
| Cheyenne | 16 | 0 | 8 | 0 | 24 |
| Femke | 23 | 7 | 6 | 2 | 38 |
| Jay | 11 | 2 | 4 | 1 | 18 |
| Katrina | 16 | 3 | 1 | 0 | 20 |
| Lindsay | 18 | 1 | 5 | 0 | 24 |
| Maik | 13 | 16 | 7 | 0 | 36 |
| Michael | 7 | 4 | 0 | 0 | 11 |
| Nikki | 24 | 13 | 7 | 3 | 47 |
| Totals | 128 | 46 | 38 | 6 | 218 |
| | | Super | Players | | |
| Ben | 11 | 7 | 0 | 0 | 18 |
| Charlie | 12 | 1 | 2 | 1 | 16 |
| Christopher | 1 | 2 | 0 | 0 | 3 |
| Jacob | 9 | 4 | 1 | 0 | 14 |
| Max | 4 | 5 | 0 | 0 | 9 |
| Rami | 15 | 0 | 0 | 0 | 15 |
| Totals | 52 | 19 | 3 | 1 | 75 |

The Super Players also showed a substantial increase in each category of literacy behaviors. Their average incidents of handling rose by 53%, reading behaviors rose by 136%, and writing events rose by 300% from Week 2 to Week 7 (see Table 5). Further, the Super Players' average frequency of literacy behaviors in Week 7 (24.33) almost equaled the average frequency of the Standard Players (25.11) (see Table 5). These children apparently benefited from the intervention.

**Table 5. Average Frequency Change in Literacy Behaviors from Week 2 to Week 7 by Group**

| Category | Week 2 Mean | Week 7 Mean | % Change |
|----------|-------------|-------------|----------|
| | | Standard Players | |
| Handling | 16.00 | 13.55 | -15.00 |
| Reading | 7.00 | 6.80 | -2.90 |
| Writing | 4.75 | 3.55 | -25.00 |
| Stamping | .70 | 1.20 | +71.00 |
| Totals | 27.25 | 25.11 | -7.80 |
| | | Super Players | |
| Handling | 8.70 | 13.33 | +53.00 |
| Reading | 3.30 | 7.80 | +136.00 |
| Writing | .50 | 2.00 | +300.00 |
| Stamping | .20 | 1.16 | +480.00 |
| Totals | 12.50 | 24.33 | +94.60 |

## Discussion and Conclusion

Although this was study was limited to 14 children in one school, similar increases in average frequencies of literacy behaviors have been noted by other researchers using similar interventions (Morrow, 1989; Neuman & Roskos, 1990, 1991). The results of this study are promising, both for the class as a whole and for those with less well-developed literacy skills. More frequent and more purposeful interactions with the tools of literacy suggest a broader base of familiarity and a larger framework of information from which a child can learn about reading and writing. Children entering school without extensive schemata for reading and writing seemed to benefit most from exposure to the materials and the centers and from interactions with the materials and their more capable peers (Vygotsky, 1978). These results suggest that children in overseas settings could benefit from opportunities to experiment imaginatively with the materials presented in these literacy-enriched play centers. Teachers who serve this population and who are concerned with finding ways to enrich the print consciousness of these students may wish to replicate this study themselves, or at least develop similar play settings for their classes. Researchers may wish to replicate the study in similar settings or with similar populations to compare results.

# References

Clay, M. (1972). *SAND, the concepts about print test.* Auckland, New Zealand: Heinemann Educational Books.

Morrow, L.M. (1989). *Literacy development in the early years.* Englewood Cliffs, NJ: Prentice Hall.

Morrow, L.M. (1989). Designing the classroom to promote literacy development. In D.S. Strickland & L.M. Morrow (Eds.), *Emerging literacy: Young children learn to read and write.* Newark, DE: International Reading Association.

Neuman, S.B., & Roskos, K. (1989). Preschoolers' conceptions of literacy as reflected in their spontaneous play. In S. McCormick & J. Zutell (Eds.), *Cognitive and social perspectives for literacy research and instruction* (pp. 87-93). Chicago: National Reading Conference.

Neuman, S.B., & Roskos, K. (1990). Play, print, and purpose: Enriching play environments for literacy development. *Reading Teacher,* .

Neuman, S.B., & Roskos, K. (1991). The influence of literacy-enriched play centers on preschoolers' conceptions of the functions of print. In J.F. Christie (Ed.), *Play and early development* (pp. 167-187). Albany, NY: State University of New York Press.

Vygotsky, L. (1978). *Mind in society.* Cambridge, MA: Harvard University Press.

# KEYNOTE
# ADDRESSES

# THOSE WONDERFUL TOYS:
# READ-ALOUDS FROM THE CLASSICS
# AND ASSORTED LITERATURE

### Judy S. Richardson
Virginia Commonwealth University
Presidential Address
College Reading Association
November, 1996

*Since joining CRA in 1979, Judy Richardson has served as Chair of the Adult Learning Division and on the Awards, Nominating, and Publications Committees. She has contributed to several studies and presentations for both the Teacher Education and Adult Learning Divisions, reviewed program proposals, and served on the Board of Reviewers for several Yearbooks and for* Reading Research and Instruction.

*Judy has spent more than 30 years in the teaching field, with experiences in English, reading and special education. She has taught at Virginia Commonwealth University for 17 years,* both undergraduate and graduate level courses in Reading and related areas.

*Judy's publications include the textbook,* Reading to Learn in the Content Areas *(Wadsworth, 1990; 1994; 1997); the teacher text,* The English Teacher's Survival Guide, *articles in several International Reading Association and College Reading Association monographs and yearbooks; chapters in CRA's monograph* Adult Beginning Readers: To Reach Them My Hand; *articles in* Journal of Adolescent and Adult Literacy, Reading Today, Adult Literacy and Basic Education, Lifelong Learning, CARE, The Reading Professor, Reading News, Virginia English Bulletin, and Reading in Virginia. *Judy has presented at numerous national, regional, state and local conferences.*

*Judy has also contributed to the International Reading Association as Chair of the Affective Domain and of the Adult Literacy Special Interest Groups; member of the Adult Literacy Committee; conference arrangements commit-*

*tee member for the Third and Fourth IRA Adolescent and Adult Literacy Conference; and reviewer for* Journal of Reading.

---

Thirty years ago I was awarded a sizable fellowship to pursue graduate studies in English literature. Personal difficulties sidetracked me to a high school where I taught ninth and twelfth graders for a year. I was hooked! Here were rapscallions who did not appreciate literature—some could not read well enough and others did not want to read—but whose appreciation for life seduced me! I wanted my students to discover the satisfaction of learning.

I abandoned my plans to become an English scholar and fell into teaching positions across the United States and on Okinawa during the Vietnam War. The more I interacted with learners of all kinds—special needs, elementary, middle, high, and adult—the more I knew my heart belonged to the teaching of reading. However, my brain has never forgotten its original plan. I retain a deep appreciation for good literature. I pursue my study of Flannery O'Connor. I take courses. I read voraciously, as I am sure you do.

And sometimes I wonder what my professional life would have been like had I taken the other road of which Robert Frost writes:

> . . . Knowing how way leads on to way,
> I doubted if I should ever come back . . .

But I have found a way to travel a double path. While my heart lies with students, and my profession requires me to keep abreast, I also make time to read for pleasure. Now I *explore* rather than *deeply study* literature. I read many genres, from classics to light fantasies. And I think about learners *always* as I read.

So, when asked recently where I got all of those great ideas for my "Read It Aloud" column in the *Journal of Adolescent and Adult Literature* (JAAL), I was reminded of the Joker's line in *Batman, The Movie*. Batman has just rescued his girlfriend by employing a series of marvelous tricks. The Joker expresses his admiration for "those wonderful toys." This address is a series of stories to illustrate my parallel travels in the lands of literature and the teaching of reading, finding wonderful toys from literature to use in instruction. I have selected a slice of time, from July and August of 1996, for my stories.

My husband, son—Andrew was fifteen—and I toured Great Britain in the summer of 1996. We stayed in Stratford-Upon-Avon for several nights because we wanted to see a Royal Shakespearean play. To appease Andrew as he stoically indulged us in our enthusiasm for Shakespeare, I took him shopping for souvenirs. Andrew found a crossbow; he had to have it! The shopkeeper told me that if I purchased ten pounds more, I could avoid the tax and qualify for direct shipping to my home. So of course I looked around and found a wonderful toy. The figurine I bought is "The Intellectual Witch." She is staggering under a load of several books. I loved her immediately. And when the shopkeeper told me that she is modeled after a Terry Pratchett character, I had to read about this character.

Terry Pratchett is the popular writer of a fantasy series, The Discworld, in Great Britain. The shopkeeper could not remember in which of his books I would find The Intellectual Witch. So I was bound to read until I found her. I started with *The Colour of Magic* (1983). I did not find the Intellectual Witch. However, I did find the circumfence! And this passage became the topic of my March 97 column for JAAL:

". . . So why aren't we going over the edge, then?" asked Rincewind with glassy calmness.

"Because your boat hit the circumfence," said the voice behind him (in tones that made Rincewind imagine submarine chasms and lurking Things in coral reefs).

"The Circumfence?" he repeated.

"Yes, it runs along the edge of the world," said the unseen troll. Above the roar of the waterfall Rincewind thought he could make out the splash of oars. He *hoped* they were oars.

"Ah, you mean the *circumference*," said Rincewind. "The circumference makes the edge of things."

"So does the Circumfence," said the troll.

"He means this," said Twoflower, pointing down. Rincewind's eyes followed the finger, dreading what they might see . . .

Hubwards of the boat was a rope suspended a few feet above the surface of the white water. The boat was attached to it, moored yet mobile, by a complicated arrangement of pulleys and little wooden wheels. They ran along the rope as the unseen rower propelled the craft along the very lip of the Rimfall. That explained one mystery—but what supported the rope?

Rincewind peered along its length and saw a stout wooden post sticking up out of the water a few yards ahead. As he watched the boat neared it and then passed it, the little wheels clacking neatly around it in a groove obviously cut for the purpose . . .

"All things drift into the Circumfence in time," said the troll, gnomically, gently rocking in his chair. "My job is to recover the flotsam. Timber, of course, and ships. Barrels of wine. Bales of cloth. You."

Light dawned inside Rincewind's head.

"It's a net, isn't it? You've got a net right on the edge of the sea!"

"The Circumfence," nodded the troll. Ripples ran across his chest. Rincewind looked out into the phosphorescent darkness that surrounded the island, and grinned inanely.

"Of course," he said. "Amazing! You could sink piles and attach it to reefs and —good grief! The net would have to be *very* strong."

"It is," said Tethis.[1]

[1]*From* The Colour of Magic *(pp. 164-165), by T. Pratchett, 1983, Buckinghamshire, England: Colin Smythe Ltd. Copyright 1983 by Colin Smythe Ltd. Reprinted with permission.*

Terry Prachett has written many Discworld novels. Next, I selected *Witches Abroad* (Pratchett, 1993), thinking it a likely title in which to find my intellectual witch. I could see her there; it must be Magrat, I reasoned, but I was not yet completely satisfied. However, here is one "toy" I found, excellent for a read-aloud whenever I am teaching about the importance of spelling or about homophones:

Local people called it the Bear Mountain. This was because it was a *bare* mountain, not because it had a lot of bears on it. This caused a certain amount of profitable confusion, though; people often strode into the nearest village with heavy duty crossbows, traps and nets and called haughtily for native guides to lead them to the bears. Since everyone locally was making quite a good living out of this, what with the sale of guide books, maps of bear caves, ornamental cuckoo-clocks with bears on them, bear walking-sticks and cakes baked in the shape of a bear, somehow no one had time to go and correct the spelling.*

*Bad spelling can be lethal. For example, the greedy seriph of Al-Ybi was once cursed by a badly-educated deity and for some days everything he touched turned to Glod, which happened to be the name of a small dwarf from a mountain community hundreds of miles away who found himself magically dragged to the kingdom and relentlessly duplicated. Some two thousand Glods later the spell wore off. These days, the people of Al-Ybi are renowned for being unusually short and bad-tempered.[2]

[2]*From* Witches Abroad *(pp. 11-12), by T. Pratchett, 1993, Buckinghamshire, England: Colin Smythe Ltd. Copyright 1993 by Colin Smythe Ltd. Reprinted with permission.*

Next, I went to *Wyrd Sisters* (Pratchett, 1990), and here I found my Intellectual Witch described:

"Magrat had learned a lot of witchcraft from books" (p. 16).

But her sister witches, Nanny Ogg and Granny Weatherwax, do not necessarily take to books:

"It's all these books they read today." said Granny. "It overheats the brain. You haven't been putting ideas in her head, have you?"

(p.117). . . . Granny had never had much time for words. They were so insubstantial. Now she wished that she had found the time. Words were indeed insubstantial. They were soft as water, but they were also powerful as water and now they were rushing over the audience, eroding the levees of veracity, and carrying away the past" (p. 271).[3]

[3]*From* Wyrd Sisters *(pp. 16, 117, 271), by T. Pratchett, 1990, Buckinghamshire, England: Colin Smythe Ltd. Copyright 1990 by Colin Smythe Ltd. Reprinted with permission.*

Also in *Wyrd Sisters,* I have found a wonderful introduction to theatre for language arts classes. In this novel, the witches "hide" the crown prince from an evil duke who has usurped the throne; they place the prince with a company of actors. TomJohn becomes one of the best actors in the troupe. Ironically, his company is commissioned by the duke to stage a play in which the witches are portrayed as evil hags. Why do people enjoy plays? What happens when we watch a play? Here is Granny's impression:

Granny subsided into unaccustomed, troubled silence, and tried to listen to the prologue. The theatre worried her. It had a magic of its own, one that didn't belong to her, one that wasn't in her control. It changed the world, and said things were otherwise than they were. And it was worse than that. It was magic that didn't belong to magical people. It was commanded by ordinary people, who didn't know the rules. They altered the world because it sounded better."[4]

[4]*From* Wyrd Sisters *(p. 265), by T. Pratchett, 1990, Buckinghamshire, England: Colin Smythe Ltd. Copyright 1990 by Colin Smythe Ltd. Reprinted with permission.*

After three Terry Prachett fantasies, I switched to reading another genre when Andrew began his summer reading requirements—the last three weeks before school was to start. I read along with him, to sustain him, through Flaubert's *Madame Bovary* (1857). Emma is a romantic. She is a reader. Leon is also a reader, and certainly a romantic at the start of the novel. The following passage foreshadows their relationship, as well as painting for the reader an early portrait of Emma. This passage was the subject of my May 1997 Read It Aloud column.

"—My wife doesn't care much for it," said Charles; "she'd rather, even though she's been recommended to take exercise, stay in her room the whole time, reading."

"—That's like me," remarked Leon; "what could be better, really, than an evening by the fire with a book, with the wind beating on the panes, the lamp burning? . . ."

"—I do so agree," she said, fixing on him her great black eyes open wide.

"—Your head is empty," he continued, "the hours slip away. From your chair you wander through the countries of your mind, and your thoughts, threading themselves into the fiction, play about with the details or rush along the track of the plot. You melt into the characters; it seems as if your own heart is beating under their skin."

"—Oh, yes, that is true." she said.

"—Has it ever happened to you," Leon went on, "in a book you come across some vague idea you once had, some blurred image from deep down, something that just spells out your finest feelings?"

"—I have," she answered.

"—That" he said, "is why I particularly love the poets. I find verse more tender than prose, and it brings more tears to the eye."

"—Though rather exhausting after a while," Emma went on; "and at the moment, you see, I adore stories that push on inexorably, frightening stories. I detest common heroes and temperate feelings, the way they are in life."[5]

[5]*From* Madame Bovary: Provincial Lives *(p. 66), by G. Flaubert (G. Wall, Trans.), 1857/1992, New York: Penguin Books. Copyright 1992 by Penguin Books.*

I will think of this passage when I want to talk with students about the reasons we might read, the way reading can carry us away. And I might use this passage also as a way to segue into a discussion of some of the differences between poetry and prose.

To initiate a discussion about poetry, always a challenging topic for secondary English teachers, I discovered a wonderful story by Fred Chappell. I could use the following excerpt in an English class when introducing a poetry unit: What is a poem? What does a poem look like? How do poems get made? Who is a poet? Fred Chappell (1991), noted author and master of the short story, encourages readers to explore these questions in his short story "Mankind Journeys Through the Forest of Symbols" in his collection *More Shapes Than One.* Sheriff Balsam needs to clear a major highway of a fog so dense that motorists cannot drive through it. The fog turns out to be an unwritten poem disturbing someone's unconscious so greatly that it has caused the unwitting poet to create a fog. This clouded thinking has settled on the highway. Balsam calls in the expert Dr. Litmouse to help find a way to dissolve it:

> Dusk had come to the mountains like a sewing machine crawling over an operating table, and Dr. Litmouse and Hank and Bill and Balsam were back in the sheriff's office. Balsam sat at his desk, the telephone receiver still off the hook. Bill and Hank had resumed their corner chairs. The three lawmen were listening to the scientist's explanation.
>
> 'Basically, it's the same problem as a dream, so it's mostly out of

our hands. Somebody within a fifty-mile radius is ripe to write a symbolist poem but hasn't gotten around to it yet. As soon as she or he does, then it will go away, just as the usual dream obstructions vanish when the dreamers wake.' He took off his glasses and polished them with his handkerchief. His eyes looked as little and bare as shirt buttons and made the others feel queasy. They were glad when he replaced his spectacles.

'It's worse than a dream, though, because we may be dealing with a subconscious poet. It may be that this person never writes poems in the normal course of his life. If this poem originated in the mind of someone who never thinks of writing, then I'm afraid your highway detour will have to be more or less permanent.' (pages 160-161)

The sheriff picked up a ballpoint pen and began clicking it. 'Well, let's see . . . There it is, and it'll go away if somebody writes it down on paper.'

'Correct.' (page 162)

'Well, what we got to do then is just get as many people as we can out there writing poems. Community effort. Maybe we'll luck out.'

'How?' asked Dr. Litmouse.

He clicked his ballpoint furiously. He got a sheet of department stationery and began printing tall uncertain letters. The other three watched in suspense, breathing unevenly. When he finished, Balsam picked up the paper and held it at arm's length to read. His lips moved slightly. Then he showed them his work. 'What do you think?' he asked.

THE SHERIFF'S DEPARTMENT
OF OSGOOD COUNTY
in cooperation with the
NORTH CAROLINA STATE HIGHWAY DEPARTMENT
announces
A POETRY CONTEST
$50 first prize
Send entries to SHERIFF ELMO BALSAM
OSGOOD COUNTY COURTHOUSE
EMBER FORKS, N. C. 26816
SYMBOLISM PREFERRED!!!

'I suppose it's worth a try,' Dr. Litmouse said, but he sounded dubious. (pp. 162-163)[6]

[6]*From "Mankind Journeys Through Forests of Symbols" in* More Shapes Than One *(p. 160-163), by Fred Chappell, 1991, New York: St. Martin's Press Incorporated. Copyright 1991 by Fred Chappell. Reprinted by permission of St. Martin's Press.*

The poet, incidentally, turns out to be Sheriff Balsam's deputy, Bill. Bill sweats out his poem, which clears his head, and thus the road clears, and everyone goes back to a normal life. Adolescents are bound to have fun thinking about unwritten poems fogging up unsuspecting minds and creating all kinds of havoc in one's community. Why, anyone might write a poem, even a sheriff's deputy!

To conclude my stories, I want to take you back with me to Haworth, near the Lake Country of England. My husband and I spent three hours wandering through Haworth, in the home of the Bronte sisters. Our son sat outside and fumed in the hot sun; this was not his most exciting part of our trip! When we returned to the car, he spewed at us,

"They're just dead people! You're worshipping dead people!"

And to him I respond,

"Ah, yes, my son, the Brontes are dead. But they have left us such wonderful toys."

---

## References

Chappell, F. (1991). *Mankind journeys through forests of symbols. More Shapes Than One.* New York: St. Martin's Press.

Flaubert, G. (1992). *Madame Bovary: Provincial lives.* (G. Wall, Trans.) New York: Penguin Books. (Original work published 1857).

Frost, R. The road not taken. In E. C. Lathem (Ed.), *The Poetry of Robert Frost* (p. 105). NY: Holt Rinehart and Winston, Inc.

Pratchett, T. (1983). *The colour of magic.* Buckinghamshire, England: Colin Smythe Ltd.

Pratchett, T. (1990). *Wyrd sisters.* Buckinghamshire, England: Colin Smythe Ltd.

Pratchett, T. (1993). *Witches abroad.* Buckinghamshire, England: Colin Smythe Ltd.

Richardson, J. S., & Gross, E. (1997). A read-aloud for mathematics. *Journal of Adolescent and Adult Literacy, 40,* 492-494.

Richardson J. S., Wimer, D. B., & Counts, J. (1997). A read-aloud for romantics and realists. *Journal of Adolescent and Adult Literacy, 40,* 658-661.

# IF THE HORSE IS DEAD, GET OFF

**Wayne Otto**

Professor Emeritus
University of Wisconsin

Keynote Address
College Reading Association
November, 1996

*Wayne Otto, a former US Marine and high school English teacher, earned his doctorate from the University of Wisconsin-Madison in 1961. He taught at the University of Oregon for three years, the University of Georgia for one year, then joined the faculty of the Department of Curriculum and Instruction at the University of Wisconsin-Madison and served there until 1995. He coauthored several books, one which was moderately successful* (Corrective and Remedial Teaching, *three editions), and contributed to the development of instructional materials including the* Wisconsin Design for Reading Skill Development. *He wrote a monthly column for the* Journal of Reading *(which is now called something else) from 1985 to 1995, when he retired at the end of the spring semester. He was the major professor of 62 doctoral students, a few of whom have subsequently become good friends, and a whole bunch of master's degree students, some of whom still send an occasional Christmas card. As a Professor Emeritus he now spends his time watching tapes of* Northern Exposure, *live trapping raccoons, raising hostas and lilies, reading lots of really good books, and wondering why we keep making this learning-to-read-thing so difficult for kids.*

Used to be that all I had to do is walk across the street when troubles troubled me. Over to the Old Style place. There amongst frosty mugs of diet Dr Pepper, Willie singing sad songs soft and sweet, and dreamy ambiance, I'd spend a couple hours telling Jimmy and be healed. Go in with blue eyes cryin' in the rain and come out back on the road again.

But now that I'm retired, living in the country, the Old Style place and Jimmy are a trip to town away. Out of sight and almost out of mind because out here the closest thing to trouble is when the heifers get out and trample the lilacs. Excitement is maybe burning some brush in the driveway. But that was before I heard from Marino.

When I heard from Marino, what I told him was that, sure, I could be at the next College Reading Association meeting and how pleased I was to be asked. It seemed like an okay idea at the time, there at the American Reading Forum annual meeting on Sanibel Island in December. Must have been the surfeit of sunshine, Dove bars, and grits that had got me feeling so euphoric. Besides, who could pass up a trip to Charleston, jewel of the Atlantic seaboard?

Of course I was feeling different by the time I got back to the cold reality of December in Wisconsin, after the customary delays at the Detroit airport. I've always looked forward to making formal presentations with about as much gusto as cleaning behind the kitchen stove or passing a kidney stone, so the prospect of coming out of retirement for a rare public appearance made me wish I'd asked Doc Crocker to renew my Prozac prescription. I asked Diane if she thought Marino would believe it if I told him my Pacemaker was on the blink and just didn't show up.

She said I could suit myself, but she was going to Charleston. Not only that, she said, but she'd be taking a side trip to Savannah to check out that garden of good and evil that's been haunting the best seller list for the past three years or so.

So I did what I'd always done when troubles troubled me. I waited until the township's crack snow removal team had knocked over our mailbox, I blew the biggest drifts out of the driveway, and then I drove to town.

Jimmy seemed a little bit distracted when he slid my diet Dr. Pepper down the bar, kept edging over toward the book he'd just put down. But true to the high traditions of the fraternity of barkeeps, he pulled up a stool when I started pouring out my pitiful tale of woe. When I got to the part where I wondered what I could say to such a distinguished group of colleagues, he stopped me with a gesture and he said, "Don't you big shot perfessers ever read any books?"

He popped me another diet Dr Pepper and he showed me his book. It was Kinky Friedman's *Elvis, Jesus, and Coca Cola* (1993). (I knew about Kinky Friedman. I'd seen him on the Stephanie Miller Show. He's not merely a guitar playing country and western singer and band leader of considerable repute;

he is also the author of quite an impressive string of mystery novels that have earned him more than just passing critical acclaim. And he earned my admiration and respect after Stephanie schmeikled him about all the subtle meaning his fans keep finding in his works. Kinky replied that people seem to be able to get a lot more out of his books than he puts into them. That's a degree of insight and candor seldom seen in my line of work.) I leaned forward in anticipation.

Jimmy opened his book, told me listen to this, and quoted me a line where Kinky is addressing his associate, Ratso, as follows: "We have another wise old saying in Texas, Ratso . . . When the horse is dead, get off" (Friedman, 1993, p. 36).

Jimmy let that sink in for a while. Then he said, "You reading people got lotsa dead horses cluttering up your field. That's bad. What's worse is that you people just keep on riding the dead ones."

After he'd let that sink in for a while, he said, "Talk about the horses." And then, before I could ask which horses looked deadest to him, he said, "Now get outta here; I gotta finish this book before the after-work crowd comes barging in." He smiled when he said it.

Naturally, I called Fats Grobnik, my confidant and seer, to see what he might say about the dead hoses. Seemed like a good idea to him, he said, but he couldn't talk because he just happened to be right in the middle of *Armadillos and Old Lace* (Friedman, 1994), another of Kinky's creations, and he had to find out if the butler did it, and he hung up.

Which was okay with me, because I was pretty sure by then that there would be enough dead horses out there to last me at least an hour. I pawed the turf and got set to break out of the starting gate.

But then I remembered a little ritual that Diane started years ago. On Derby Day she always makes us a couple of mint juleps and we watch the annual running of the Kentucky Derby. It isn't the race, it's the juleps that bring me back year after year; but I have learned one thing from watching. And that's that picking the right horses is no easy task.

So I got to thinking that I'd better be careful not to talk about just any old horses—not sick ones or wounded ones or three legged ones, not even little dead ones. I should talk about the really big ones—Morgans and Clydesdales—and the really dead ones. I reined in my urge for a quick breakaway and e-mailed out a call for help.

I told a very select few of my most trusted colleagues about Kinky's words to the wise and I asked them to tell me about their dead horses. I told them that I wanted to know what reading practices and programs and rituals and tribal behaviors they thought were the biggest and the deadest of the dead horses that reading professionals continue to ride.

My esteemed colleagues' responses were enthusiastic, even passionate. They told me they were seeing lots of dead horses being ridden out there;

and judging from their language, some of them were pretty upset about it. It was reassuring to know that it isn't just Jimmy, Fats, and me who see dead horses when we survey the field of reading. And it was challenging to see that their responses were diverse—they were seeing some horses that I'd missed. And they were calling some horses that I HAD seen by entirely different names. That was disconcerting.

I could see that I'd need to do some serious sifting and winnowing in order to find the biggest and deadest horses that reading professionals continue to try to ride. What I finally came up with is my personal Top Ten list of dead horses, which I shall momentarily submit for your scrutiny. But first, take that moment to think what horses would be on your personal list if you were, perchance, to make one. My guess is that your list wouldn't be very different from mine. We'll see. Meanwhile, no wagering, please.

## Top Ten

10. **Early, Intensive Teaching of Phonics**. If this horse isn't dead, it ought to be; but what with people like Phyllis Schlafly glued to the saddle, I doubt that the people who are riding it can be persuaded to get off. I think it was Mike Royko who called Schlafly "the national nag." Which brings to my mind an intriguing picture: the national nag riding the national nag.

I truly believe that some people are born with a phonics gene and some are not. People with the phonics gene are irrefutably convinced that they themselves can recognize words effortlessly, spell flawlessly, and understand perfectly everything ever written by Plato, Shakespeare, and Newt Gingrich because they were taught (they never say they learned, they always say they were taught) phonics early and well. And they all believe that everyone else should be—or should have been—taught the same phonics in the same way that they themselves were taught.

People without the phonics gene generally seem to think that a little phonics isn't likely to do serious harm; and many of them actually think a balanced diet that includes some phonics can be quite nutritious.

I place myself in the latter group, the balanced diet group. So while I'm hoping that the phonics nag will finally be abandoned, I'm also hoping that it manages to leave a few of its genes behind to enrich the pool.

Now let me add another short parenthetical observation. When I read E. D. Hirsch's new book, *The Schools We Need and Why Don't We Have Them* (1996), I sort of expected him to be an early, intensive phonics nut. So I was pleased when he took what I just called a balanced diet position instead. Hirsch laments the unproductive polarization that results when the "phonics approach" is characterized as "conservative, hickory stick and Republican" and the "whole language approach"—generally identified as the antithesis of phonics—is characterized as "liberal, wishy washy, and Democratic." And then he says that in the heat of battle, few have wanted to listen to Chall and Adams, who found that middle of the road approaches, including  phonics and whole-language, are the most effective. I'm not sure I agree with his choice of exemplary middle-of-the-roaders, but I can't hate a guy who is willing to take a balanced, commonsense position regarding phonics instruction.

Which brings me to my next dead horse. . . .

9. **(Capital W) Whole (Capital L) Language**. This was a pretty good horse until it got the big WL branded on its flank. After that, lots of folks apparently failed to notice that what had been a perfectly sensible collection of ideas had deteriorated into effete rhetoric and bumper sticker slogans, so they continued to climb onto that poor horse until it died. Died of mismanagement and abuse. And that's a crying shame, because a dead horse makes an awfully easy target for all the slings and arrows that professional education critics care to hurl its way.

Again, I think we had a good horse here before it got branded and ridden to death by people who lacked the good sense to keep it up and running. Like the phonics horse, I hope it left some genes in the pool.

8. **Explicit Instruction Is Bad**. I approach this horse with some trepidation; I'm not so sure I want to declare it dead. No doubt about it, there's a lot of ill-conceived and poorly-executed explicit instruction going on out there, and it's bad. Still, on the other hand, there is a widely held belief in certain education circles that any and all explicit instruction is bad—that it's unnatural. I'm not certain where such a belief originated, but in reading education it has been broadcast and strengthened by pronouncements from WL gurus. To be fair, some of those pronouncements have been vastly over interpreted by zealous disciples, but that only adds to the mystique.

Personally, I'm satisfied with the abundance of common sense evidence to show that while some learning occurs as a function of holistic activity, other learning does indeed proceed from direct instruction. I have heard that Courtney Cazden, for example, talks about the "Peekaboo" and "Bye-Bye" metaphors for learning (and teaching). Infants learn to play peekaboo by playing it. On the other hand, most parents spend a fair amount of time and effort teaching their children the appropriate way, place, and time to say bye-bye. I think if we'd introspect for a moment, each of us could think of some instances where *Holistic Learning* and other instances where *Direct Instruction* is the more effective in helping people learn to read.

So do you see what I mean about approaching this horse with trepidation? To declare *Explicit Instruction is Bad* a dead horse is to suggest that explicit instruction is good. Which it is—sometimes. But other times it isn't. So there's your dilemma. Of course it could easily be resolved with the application of a little common sense. But ours is a field where the application of common sense is singularly uncommon. Hence, my trepidation.

7. **Programs and Models**. This is the Wonder Horse. It's the deadest of the lot, so I wonder why so many people keep trying to ride it. I wonder why well read, deeply insightful, perfectly sensible people keep skulking around publishers' displays and rushing off to visit far-away sites in search of better ways to teach reading. That the horse is dead is amply demonstrated by the fact that programs and models for teaching reading come and go as regularly as the seasons change. Yet multitudes keep to the saddle, looking to strangers for answers to questions that only they, themselves, can answer.

Personally, I'm convinced that the Programs and Models Horse has always been propped up mainly by charlatans and self-serving schemers—and, yes, a few sincere but misguided dreamers. I'm in no position to cast stones because I, myself, have—in a previous incarnation—participated in a large scale program/model development project. I, of course, see myself as one of the few misguided dreamers; but the fact is that the Wisconsin Design for Reading Skill Development, in spite of (or possibly to a great extent because of) good intentions, proved to be a dismal failure. As I experienced it, the failure wasn't due to shoddy construction; it was due to the fact that the people who attempted to adopt the developed program hadn't had the experience of participating in its development. Trying to make it work was like trying to run a marathon in somebody else's shoes. I don't think that experience was unique. I think that somebody else's program will always turn out to be a poor fit.

So our landfills are full of ill-fit programs that failed. Small wonder, though, that the pursuit of canned programs and models persists: It's good for business. When a program dies, all the so-called experts on the chicken and peas banquet circuit simply change their banners and start selling another brand of snake oil. Nice work if you can stand it.

Neil Postman makes a relevant observation in his 1995 book, *The End of Education*. He says, "There was a time when educators became famous for providing reasons for learning; now they become famous for inventing a method" (p. 26).

I think that the poor Programs and Models horse may have done itself in. Just couldn't bear the embarrassment any longer.

6. **Study Skills**. I know that the old proverb says it doesn't pay to beat a dead horse; but I like to beat this one just for the pure pleasure of it. Common sense has always told us—and the preponderance of available research is in agreement—that if you don't know what in hell is going on before you start to study, you won't know what in hell is going on after you've studied, no matter how snappy the acronym for your study skill may have been. Nev-

ertheless, study skills continue to be taught in content-free environments. And, worse, study skills continue to be taught with a kind of "one size fits all" assumption that displays a glib disregard for differences in individuals' background knowledge or for personal needs, aspirations, and style. I want to kick this dead horse because it continues to attract so many determined riders.

Mitchel Resnick makes a couple of points in *Turtles, Termites, and Traffic Jams* (1994) that I think we reading teachers ought to keep in mind when we think about ways to enhance our students' learning. He happens to be talking specifically about the teaching of geometry, but the points are valid across the curriculum. He says that we shouldn't be looking for the best way to do geometry; we should be looking for MORE ways of doing (and thinking about) geometry. Two reasons: First, "Different people find different approaches more accessible. . . . Too often, schools give special status to particular ways of thinking about mathematical and scientific ideas. By privileging certain types of thinking, they exclude certain types of thinkers" (p. 103). Second, "Everyone can benefit from learning multiple ways of thinking about things . . . . Understanding something in several different ways produces an overall understanding that is richer and of a different nature than any one way of understanding" (p. 103). Those statements are as relevant, I think, for teaching, say, history and literature as they are for teaching geometry.

Privileging certain types of thinking and limiting ways of understanding: That's what killed the Study Skills horse a long, long time ago. Time to get off and move upwind.

5. **Getting It Right**. Here's a dead horse that I might have missed if it hadn't been for the wisdom that Barry Sanders shares in a splendid book titled *A Is For Ox* (1994). This is what he says:

> Given the way that most schools currently teach reading and writing—the primary, traditional tools for knowing and reasoning—an observer might readily conclude that fiction has developed out of a spirit of determined seriousness, and that teachers have quite naturally committed themselves to continuing that somber tradition. But history actually reveals quite the contrary: the roots of storytelling lie buried deep in play and joking, a fact that the majority of teachers appears to have forgotten. . . . Schools draw on an opposite scenario. Young children give up the freedom and formlessness of play, and struggle to "get it right" in reading and writing. (pp. 79-80)

Small wonder, then, that so many people leave school not only unwilling ever to read again, but also perfectly willing to pay Hallmark three bucks a pop to express their innermost musings for them in writing. Sanders has lots more to say about the traditions of playfulness and the need for teachers to be playful in their approaches to reading and writing. He's happily offering us a horse of another color. Let's get on it and go!

4. **Reader Response**. It's a crying shame, but this once magnificent steed was ridden to death by riders who just never bothered to get to know their animal. Sadder still, it looks to me as if good intentions contributed heavily to its demise; I think lots of people who did manage to get off the dead *Getting It Right* horse and the dead *Study Skills* horse climbed onto the *Reader Response* horse and rode off at full gallop—in the wrong direction. Poor horse may have dropped dead of a broken heart.

It was a good thing to acknowledge that texts may have multiple meanings and that readers always bring very personal and sometimes quite idiosyncratic meanings to written words. It was good to see the privileged ways of thinking that follow from teacher-dominated interpretations of texts move away from center stage and to see multiple ways of understanding move a little closer to the limelight. It was a good thing to view students as active meaning makers rather than passive recipients of knowledge. But it was not a good thing to push the author far from the limelight, or, as some zealots would have it, off the stage entirely. To do this is, as Michael Smith (in press) so nicely puts it, to deny the intelligence that created the text in the first place.

When the Reader Response horse started pulling a bandwagon, too many people jumped onto one side and the wagon lost its balance. Maybe that's what killed the horse.

We educators have never been very good at striking balances. But we're real good at killing off promising horses.

3. **Teacher Training in Reading**. You say you're surprised to see a horse with so much life left in it on this Top Ten list? That's not what surprises me. What surprises me is that it's still got so much life left in it. And what irritates, agitates, and dismays me is that so many so called teacher education programs always have been, still are, and are likely to remain teacher *Training* programs—particularly in reading.

Now I'm not just quibbling over a trivial semantic point here. I mean to be saying that there is a vast difference between teacher training and teacher education; and the difference is exacerbated in the field of reading education because reading is generally approached as "method," not as "content"— or as anything else that has any inherent substance or value. Barry Sanders speaks to this point in *A Is For Ox* (1994). Sanders talks about

> . . . the critical difference between understanding literacy as inseparable from the cognitive development of the self and literacy as an externally measured set of skills—a commodity that can be quantified, packaged, and delivered by professionals. Reading and writing turn into literacy by measuring them through statistics—levels of reading skills,

rates of comprehension, and so on. Reading and writing are being lost as activities that transform a person into an entirely different creature, a person who has the capability of making continual discoveries about himself or herself. They are being lost as activities through which one finds constant surprises in sentences—both written and spoken—and in the self. (p. 200)

Personally, I'm convinced that another major reason why reading and writing are being lost as activities that transform, surprise and delight readers and writers is that prospective teachers of reading and writing continue to be *trained*. They are trained to be efficient users of so-called achievement measures and diagnostic tests and enthusiastic pushers of whatever instructional materials got the most visibility at the last IRA convention.

One fundamental problem, I think, is that we reading teachers have always given far too much attention to *how,* and far too little to *who, what, when, where, and why.* We could take a lesson from Anne Lamott. The subtitle of her bestselling book, *Bird by Bird* (1994), is "Some Instructions on Writing and Life." She's talking education, not training. And so is Sven Birkerts, in a book that's titled and sub-titled *The Gutenberg Elegies: The Fate of Reading in an Electronic Age* (1994). A reviewer for *The New York Times* says Birkerts' writing about reading "makes you want to go and do it." When's the last time you felt that way after reading a reading methods text?

Another fundamental problem, I think, is that we teachers of reading teachers have gotten carried away in our quest for self-importance. Richard Dawkins, the famed evolutionary biologist, sums up the problem quite nicely in a passage from a challenging book, *The Third Culture* (1995), edited by John Brockman:

> P. D. Medawar said that there are some fields that are genuinely difficult, where if you want to communicate you have to work really hard to make the language simple, and there are other fields that are fundamentally very easy, where if you want to impress people you have to make the language more difficult than it needs to be. And there are some fields in which—to use Medawar's lovely phrase—people suffer from 'physics envy.' They want their subject to be treated as profoundly difficult, even when it isn't. Physics genuinely is difficult, so there's a great industry for taking the difficult ideas of physics and making them simpler for people to undrstand; but, conversely, there's another industry for taking subjects that really have no substance at all and pretending they do—dressing them up in a language that's incomprehensible for the very sake of incomprehensibility, in order to make them seem profound. (p. 200)

Call me an unrelenting curmudgeon if you must; but, let's face it, we teachers of reading teachers are so smitten by physics envy that our affliction has reached the delusional stage. How else could we manage to stay on this long dead Teacher Training horse?

2. **Guess What I'm Thinking**. Michael Smith (in press) has another name for this horse; he calls it Keeping Secrets. By any other name, though, the horse is unmistakable: It's the one that has the answers to all kinds of questions, but seldom or never lets students in on how—or why—those particular answers were obtained.

Michael argues that teachers ought to be able to share their secrets, to tell their students how they, as experts, engage in reading and to explain how experts come up with all those answers. As it is, teachers are inclined to try to enlighten their students by giving them answers, but to leave them in the dark about finding answers on their own. What reading teachers need to do, Michael says, is to study their own behaviors to determine what their personal secrets are, because secrets that haven't been articulated can't be shared. The goal is not to encourage novices to copy experts, but to help novices understand what experts do.

Personally, I've long been troubled by how uncommunicative we ostensible "reading experts" are about how we ourselves tackle various reading tasks. Like Michael, I think the main reason is that most of us haven't done a very thorough job of articulating what goes on when we, ourselves, read. We reading teachers are much more inclined to look to strangers for descriptions of effective reading behaviors than to trust our own insights. So we tend always to be in the position of peddling second hand goods. Second-hand Roses, that's us.

We reading teachers need a better sense of where we are as readers and sufficient self assurance to talk openly about our own insights into the complexities and wonders of reading. There's a fresh horse waiting. We ought to ride it.

1. **Being Digital**. Okay, I admit it; I'm being defensive here, giving my Number One Dead Horse the same name that MIT's Media Lab founder Nicholas Negroponte gave his bestselling book, *Being Digital* (1995). I just don't want you to think that I'm an old fogy so ignorant of stuff like Negroponte's book that I simply knee-jerk reject anything and everything that smacks of high tech. In fact, it was Negroponte himself who convinced me that, insofar as the field of reading education is concerned, this horse is dead.

Of the three reasons he gives for choosing the old-fashioned book rather than a more exotic, multimedia format to describe the future, the third is the "more personal, slightly ascetic" (p. 8):

> Interactive multimedia leaves very little to the imagination. Like a Hollywood film, multimedia narrative includes such specific representa-

tions that less and less is left to the mind's eye. By contrast, the written word sparks images and evokes metaphors that get much of their meaning from the reader's imagination and experiences. When you read a novel, much of the color, sound, and motion come from you. I think the same kind of personal extension is needed to feel and understand what "being digital" might mean to your life. (p. 8)

And then Negroponte, a self-described dyslexic, adds, "You are expected to read yourself into this book. And I say this as somebody who does not like to read" (p. 8).

The media wizard, it seems to me, has a finer grasp of the essence of reading—and of what ought to be important to those of us who profess to teach reading—than far too many reading experts, whether they be certificated or self proclaimed.

I'm tempted, now, to shower you with quotations from the authors I've been mentioning—Sanders, Birkerts, Lamott, Resnick, Smith, Postman—to bolster my proclamation that the digital horse is dead. But then you could say I protest too much, particularly since I've already told you that I'm being defensive here. So I'll simply leave you in the company of these authors—including Negroponte—to contemplate the horse.

You may conclude that insofar as reading education is concerned, the Digital horse was stillborn, that it never got a chance to show how it might have run. You may even conclude that there is reason to hope that in the fullness of time there will be a resurrection.

And I wouldn't disagree.

## Some Spare Horses

When I finished my Top Ten list, I did what I always do when I finish writing something: I faxed it to Fats, who has his finger on the pulse of America. I knew he'd know if I'd managed to pick the biggest and the deadest of the horses that lie dead in the field of reading education.

The next day I called. "Hey, Fats," I said, "what do you think?"

"I think we ought to go fishing," Fats said. "I heard that the bluegills are biting in Partridge Lake." And then he told me about his new Winnebago—two bedrooms, four baths, and a walk-in cooler—and that we could park over by the river in Fremont and he'd pick me up in the morning. Finally, just as I was about to abandon hope, he said, "Oh yeah, about the horses. Those buggers look really dead to me . . . and big. But you might want to round up a couple of extras, just in case you don't manage to use up your whole hour."

And he was gone, no doubt to start stocking the walk-in cooler.

Which was okay with me, because with a few well chosen words he had, as usual, managed not only to put his finger on the pulse of a possible problem, but also to embolden me to do what I really wanted to do. Which was to have at least twelve horses on my Top Ten list.

So here's another one.

**Remedial Reading**. No question about this one: It's a real horse and it's really dead. The only reason it didn't make my Top Ten list is that I was too embarrassed to put it there after having taught the course for years and years. Because it is our bread and butter, we remedial reading teachers try to convince a gullible public that we possess magical potions and incantations that can transform late bloomers, listless dullards, the linguistically deprived, and the ineptly taught into successful and enthusiastic readers. Of course we've never been able to deliver on most of the promises we make, but never mind. We've come up with such good excuses that we've almost come to believe them ourselves.

It seems clear to me that it was never very sensible to get that poor old Remedial Reading nag up and running in the first place. If all the resources that have gone into remedial reading had been given over to sound instruction the first time around, we'd be riding a horse with a decent chance of finishing in the chips.

I don't think we ever really thought that Remedial Reading would win any races. But hey, we're human; we make mistakes. So let's admit that we made one. The horse is dead. We finished it off. Now let's *get off*.

Now here's the last one. I saved the best 'til last.

**Research.** My first impulse was to put Reading Research at the very top of my Top Ten list of dead horses. That's because after more than three decades in the business, I'd be hard pressed to say what positive effects have come out of all the so-called reading research that's gone on. Of course there have been some changes from time to time, but I'm inclined to argue that they haven't been very widespread and they haven't been really substantive. In any event, it seems to me that what changes there have been have come as a result of political and philosophical shifts, not research.

It was hard for me to see a horse for all the riders; but I figured if the Research horse wasn't going anywhere, it must be dead.

Still, I decided to take a closer look, and do you know what? I never did find a corpus delicti. I finally realized that I couldn't find a dead horse because there wasn't any horse. All those riders were just piled up on top of each other, so busy posturing and proclaiming that they didn't even notice that they weren't going anywhere. Worse yet, they were so happy strutting and showing off for each other that they couldn't care less about missing the horse.

So I'm pretty sure there's a perfectly sound Research horse out there someplace, fresh and waiting to be ridden. In this case, it isn't the horse that needs changing, it's the riders.

The underlying problem, I'm convinced, is that in reading research and in the larger enterprise of reading education, it isn't a search for truth that drives our efforts and defines our aspirations, it's a desire to be on the winning team. We reading educators have chosen to engage in a political struggle—to hell with truth and decency. Wendy Kaminer (1995), who happens to be one of my most treasured personal heroes, says that truth in a political struggle is dependent upon politics and is primarily ideological rather than factual in correctness.

Small wonder, then, that so many of us continue to ride dead horses. It isn't the horse that matters. It's the brand on its flank.

---

## References

Birkerts, S. (1994). *The Gutenberg elegies: The fate of reading in an electronic age.* New York: Fawcett Columbine.

Brockman, J. (1995). *The third culture.* New York: Touchstone Book/Simon & Schuster.

Friedman, K. (1993). *Elvis, Jesus, and Coca Cola.* New York: Simon and Schuster.

Friedman, K. (1994). *Armadillos and old lace.* New York: Simon and Schuster.

Hirsch, E. D., Jr. (1996). *The schools we need and why we don't have them.* New York: Doubleday.

Kaminer, W. (1995). *It's all the rage: Crime and culture.* Reading, PA: Addison Wesley.

Lamott, A. (1994). *Bird by bird: Some instructions on writing and life.* New York: Anchor Books/Doubleday.

Negroponte, N. (1995). *Being digital.* New York: Vintage Books/Random House.

Postman, N. (1995). *The end of education: Redefining the value of school.* New York: Knopf.

Rabinowitz, P., & Smith, M. W. (in press). *Resistance and respect in the reading of literature.* New York: Teachers College Press.

Resnick, M. (1994). *Turtles, termites, and traffic jams: Explorations in massively parallel microworlds.* Cambridge, MA: Bradford Book/MIT Press.

Sanders, B. (1994). *A is for ox: The collapse of literacy and the rise of violence in an electronic age.* New York: Vintage Books/Random House.

# Leaders
# in Literacy

At the 1996 College Reading Association Conference in Charleston, South Carolina, a special session entitled "Leaders in Literacy: Past, Present, and Future" was held. At this session, three long-standing CRA members, Lillian Putnam, D. Ray Reutzel, and William Henk presented their perspectives related to the past, the present and the future of literacy education. We are very pleased that all three were willing to share their comments with the wider CRA Yearbook readership through publication in this volume. In this section, the text of each speech is provided along with a photo of the speaker and brief biographical information.

The Editors

# Beginning Reading Methods: A Review of the Past

## Lillian R. Putnam

Professor Emerita
Kean College of New Jersey
An Address at the College Reading Association Conference
November, 1996

*Lillian Putnam is Professor Emerita at Kean College of New Jersey, where she taught graduate and undergraduate education courses and directed the Reading Clinic. Her background includes post-doctoral work at Harvard, Princeton, and Oxford University in England. Dr. Putnam has published over 90 articles in journals including* The Reading Teacher, The Journal of Reading, Language Arts, *and* Journal of Reading Instruction. *Her book publications include* Case Studies for Reading Teachers, Stories to Talk About: Helping Children Make Ethical Choices, *and* Readings in Language and Literacy, *a 1997 publication honoring Dr. Jeanne Chall. Dr. Putnam served on the editorial boards of* The Reading Instruction Journal of New Jersey *and* The Clinical Journal of College Reading Association, *as well as the Professional Standards Committees of the New Jersey Reading Association and the International Reading Association and the Exemplary Reading Program Committee of the New Jersey Reading Association. She has been honored for her service by professional associations including the New Jersey Reading Association and the College Reading Association, which named her its first "Laureate in Reading" in 1996. Dr. Putnam's professional interests include the diagnosis and remediation of severely disabled readers, clinical work, and teacher education.*

In ancient times, we know that cave dwellers painted pictures on the walls of caves. They were usually trees and things seen or animals chased and caught. Later the pictures embodied ideas and feelings, and were called ideograms. Hieroglyphics came later, representing symbols instead of pictures, and gradually symbols and words were broken down to separate sounds and letters.

Most of the reading methods used today are not innovations of the 20th century; they were used years ago. For example, if you think reading with phonics is new, it isn't. In 1612, Brinsley (Hoole, 1660, as cited in Smith, 1965) changed the method from learning the sounds of the whole alphabet at once to combining initial consonants with short vowels: ba, be, bi, bo, bu. This was evident in the New England Primer of 1727 and in Noah Webster's (1798) Blue Back Speller. Ward (1894) combined phonics with the sight word method in his books.

If you think teaching by the sight word method is new, it isn't. Comenius recommended it in 1500 (Smith, 1965). In the 1800's, Josiah Bumstead (1840) and John Russell Webb (1846) wrote primers using the sight word method.

If you think teaching by the sentence method is new, it isn't. In 1944, I observed a first grade teacher presenting long sentences on oak tag strips to children. The children would recite the whole sentence, but could not identify one single word.

If you think teaching by the paragraph method is new, it isn't. Albert Harris (1940) and Jeanette Veatch (1979) promoted the Language Experience Approach. In this method, the children had a common experience which they discussed. This promoted vocabulary and interest and maybe some new concepts. They dictated a story to the teacher, who wrote it on the board. The children played with the story, finding words and sentences they knew. In addition to learning sight words, the teacher could then pull out words with similar initial consonants and teach phonics (cat, come, can). The wise teacher could structure the experience around words which would teach the consonants she wanted.

If you think the tactile-kinesthetic method is new, it isn't. One of the oldest writings in existence is a table of stone, with deep grooves cut for children to move their fingers in or trace. This dates back to 4700 BC, and is in the Ashmolian Museum at Oxford University.

If you think making letters out of edible materials is new, it isn't. Horace recommended it in 427 BC (Smith, 1965). In 1700, Basedow, a German educator (Smith, 1965), recommended that every school should have a baker to make edible letters for children to learn and eat.

If you think teaching with a special phonetic alphabet is new, it isn't. In 1570, John Hart used a special phonetic alphabet in which vowels were marked as long or short, and silent letters were crossed out. This was a forerunner to the augmented Roman alphabet used by Sir Isaac Pitman and A. J. Ellis in teaching reading classes in Waltham, Massachusetts, in 1852 (Pitman, 1852; Smith, 1965). This method was the basis for the i.t.a. (Initial Teaching Alphabet) used by Sir James Pitman in England (Pitman, 1960) and brought to the USA by Mazurkiewicz and Tanyzer (1963). One year in March, I visited a first grade i. t. a. class in Bethlehem, Pennsylvania. The children were reading and writing four-page stories at that time. I have never experienced such prolific reading and writing in any other first grade class. One of the teachers said to me, "How do I turn it off?" This was remarkable. The difficulty came in the transition to traditional orthography. Although the transition was expected to occur at the end of grade 1, it often came much later, in grade 2 or 3.

If you think whole language is new, it isn't. I visited English schools in the 1970's, and one teacher said, "What is this new thing called whole language in the States?" I told her about it and she replied, "Well we have always been doing that. That's not new to us." There are many fine aspects of whole language. It reminded us that we should be integrating all the language arts with reading, something we had forgotten. It also brought us back to good literature, another thing we had forgotten, particularly in the early grades. Unfortunately, many teachers were not well trained to teach using the whole language method. They missed the scope and sequence provided in the basal readers. My own observations in classrooms showed that, although teachers said they taught decoding skills, actually this skill was frequently neglected or forgotten. Bill Honig, California State Superintendent of Schools, mandated whole language for the entire state. When the California NAEP scores fell to the lowest in the nation in 1994, he was removed from office. Decoding skills have now been mandated.

If you think that linguistic methods are new, they are not. Early linguists including Leonard Bloomfield, Henry Lee Smith, and Charles Carpenter Fries were recommending teaching by word patterns long ago (Bloomfield, 1942; Smith, 1965). They were interested not in phonics as such, but in word patterns. The Merrill Linguistic Readers (Fries, Fries, Wilson, & Rudolf., 1965) were based on word patterns or word families. The famous sentence, "The fat cat sat at a mat," was typical of the texts. Although teachers have criticized this as boring, I never heard children say that, because they were learning the code and could apply what they had learned directly to the text. Modern linguists like Noam Chomsky are interested in generative-transformational grammar. They remind us that language and grammar change over time (Smith, 1965). For example, during the Elizabethan period, the royals used double negatives in speech. When the commoners copied them, the royals stopped and declared that it was bad grammar.

Probably at no time was any one method used exclusively. Harris and Sipay (1985) maintain that we went from emphasis on visual perception, to auditory perception, to sensori-motor training, to cerebral dominance, to multi-sensory, to behavior modification. The variations in method certainly reflect this thinking.

Recently, I have become concerned about teacher education. Although we presently know more about various ways to teach reading, some of our undergraduates emerge from colleges with elementary certification, having had only one course in this field. This is certainly inadequate. In an informal survey (unpublished) of reading courses required by the various states, I found that some required only one course while others require as many as 12 semester hours in reading. Parents expect that, as a minimum, their children should learn to read, write, and spell. Minimum preparation fails to provide teachers who can teach regular reading adequately to the whole class. They are completely at a loss to aid the child with a reading disability, or anyone who cannot learn by the one method they know. This is a serious problem in teacher education and should be corrected. I believe our professional organizations should initiate political activity to increase minimal requirements in reading courses for certification.

Although pre-service teacher education is a major problem, there is a serious, concomitant concern in the professional field. Over a period of 300 years, many different reading methods have been proposed and tried. As each one was presented, teachers enthusiastically hopped on the proverbial bandwagon and became deeply engrossed, only to become disenchanted when the promised results failed to appear. This continues to happen because there has been and is a serious dearth in long term evaluation of results for each innovation. Our fanciful expectations should be replaced by:
1. Preparing teachers in advance to work with the new method.
2. Exploring the expected assets and limitations in pilot groups.
3. Conducting long term, carefully designed research on performance and achievement.
4. Exploring the variables of different children for whom the methods work best or least.

Data of this kind would yield practical information and remove the enthusiastic guess work. Such data would enable teachers to predict which specific methods would "probably" work best for specific groups of children. My human hunch says it would probably depend on a combination of factors—never on a single component.

*I wish to thank Estill Alexander for inviting me to speak on the history of beginning reading methods. It made me review volumes of material I had forgotten and also learn many new things.*

# References

Bateman, B. (1971). *Essentials of teaching: Dimensions in early learning series.* San Raphael, CA: Dimensions Publishing Co.

Bumstead, J. (1840). *My little primer.* Boston, MA: Perkins & Marwin.

Bloomfield, L. (1942). Linguistics and reading. *Elementary English Review, 19.*

Fries, C. , Fries, A. , Wilson, R., & Rudolf, M. (1965). *A basic reading series developed upon linguistic principles.* Columbus, OH: Charles E. Merrill.

Harris, A. (1940). *How to increase reading ability: A guide to diagnostic and remedial methods.* New York: Longmans, Green, & Co.

Harris A., & Sipay, E. (1985). *How to improve reading ability.* White Plains, NY: Longman.

Mazurkiewicz, A., & Tanyzer, H. (1963). *Early to read i/t/a program.* New York: Initial Teaching Alphabet Publishers, Inc.

Pitman, I. (1852). Phonotype method in Waltham, Massachusetts. *The Times Educational Supplement.* London: The London Times, July 21, 1961.

Pitman, J. (1960). *initial teaching alphabet.* London: i. t. a. Publications.

Smith, N. B. (1965). *American reading instruction.* Newark, DE: International Reading Association.

Veatch, J. (1979). *Key words for reading: The language experience approach.* Columbus, OH: Charles E. Merrill.

Ward, E. G. (1894). *Ward rational method in reading.* Boston, MA: Silver Burdett Co.

Webb, J. R. (1846). *The new word method.* New York: Sheldon, Lempart & Blakeman.

Webster, N. (1798). *The American spelling book.* Boston, MA: Isaiah Thomas & Ebenezer Andrews.

# CONTROVERSIAL PATHWAYS TO LITERACY: THE PRESENT

**D. Ray Reutzel**

Brigham Young University
An Address at the College Reading Association Conference
November, 1996

*D. Ray Reutzel is a Karl G. Maeser Distin-guished Research Professor and Associate Dean of Teacher Education in the David O. McKay School of Education at Brigham Young Univer-sity (BYU). Dr. Reutzel is the author of more than 90 articles, books, book chapters, and mono-graphs. He has published in* Reading Research Quarterly, Journal of Reading Behavior, Journal of Literacy Research, Journal of Educational Research, Reading Psychology, Reading Re-search and Instruction, Langauge Arts, Journal of Reading, Reading World, *and* The Reading Teacher, *among others. He is currently the Edi-tor of* Reading Research and Instruction *and a co-author of* Teaching Children to Read: From Basals to Books, *2nd Edition, published by Prentice-Hall/Merrill. He is a program author and consultant for Scholastic Incorporated's Literacy Place® school reading program.*

Since Dr. Estill Alexander called to ask if I would participate in this panel today, I have mulled over many controversial issues in literacy, ranging from the politics and power of literacy, to privilege and access, to literacy knowledge, skills, and strategies. The more I considered the possibilities, the greater became my anxiety. I have genuinely worried about which contro-versial issues to select as exemplars of the diverse voices and multiple per-spectives within our literacy community. After considerable inward turmoil, I selected two issues, not for the issues themselves, but for deeper, perhaps more troubling and vexing contradictions nested deep within these exemplar controversies. The two issues I have chosen are these: 1) the paradigm wars in reading research; and 2) the continuing chasm between the university literacy researcher and the classroom literacy practitioner. Please be reminded, I chose these two controversies primarily as exemplars of deeper, more problematic dilemmas, not necessarily for the controversies themselves.

## Continuing Paradigm Wars in Reading Research

The paradigm wars in literacy research are in themselves a lesson in paradox. Amid the admirable and persistent calls within the literacy community for greater cooperation, collaboration, and appreciation of a broader range of voices and methods in literacy research, there is also an increasing invidious incivility in our discourse that attacks the very heart of our community. Kamil (1995), in an article entitled "Some Alternatives to Paradigm Wars in Literacy Research," asks:

> What went wrong with [these] debates? When the idea for intellectual exchanges about literacy issues was conceived, it was thought they would promote productive dialogue about substantive issues. We have seen little of the sustained, productive dialogue that literacy researchers and practitioners would have desired. (p. 244)

Rather than making clear the benefits, possibilities, and opportunities new research paradigms offered us as a community, we have diffused much productive effort in polarizing the debate, pointing out the flaws and limitations of others' research paradigms, and sprinkling our debates with printed and verbal invectives.

John Ruskin (1976) once declared, "Education does not mean teaching people to know what they do not know; it means teaching them to behave as they do not behave" (p. 75). As the destructive diatribe of the research paradigm wars continues to descend upon our literacy community, the need for "education" as Ruskin describes it seems to be increasingly evident. Of all communities of intellect, those of us who love literacy and aspire to prepare classroom teachers of literacy should evidence refinement and civility in our conversations.

In an April 1996 article in the *U. S. News and World Report* (Marks) entitled, "The American [un]civil wars: How crude, rude, and obnoxious behavior has replaced good manners and why that hurts our politics and culture," the lack of civility was identified as a national phenomenon that is clearly denigrating our ability to effectively communicate and threatening our ability to maintain a sense of community. In fact, this recent article asserts a strong connection between incivility and increasing violence in our nation. Ninety percent of U.S. citizens polled believe that incivility contributes to the increase of violence in the country and 85% believe incivility divides the national community. As has recently been observed in the May/June, 1995 *Royal Bank Letter of Canada,*

> People might think of a civilized community as one in which there is a refined culture. Not necessarily; first and foremost it is one in which the mass of people subdue their selfish instincts in favor of a common good. (p. 2)

Kamil (1995) points out further that our arguments about research paradigms and methods have been made personal rather than professional. He notes that the goal of this controversy has been "winning," not the discovery of knowledge or insight.

When our intellectual discourse turns divisive and our dialogue becomes discourteous, this bespeaks a dim future for a community commonly united in a desire to privilege everyone—every individual, regardless of age, gender, race, creed, color, religion, etc.—with the dignity and self-esteem that flows from equal access to literacy and learning. In short, our debate over research paradigms bespeaks anything but civility and productivity. Rather, it speaks of crudeness, rudeness, and a total insensitivity to the feelings and rights of others. The controversy over research paradigms could be largely resolved by listening, respecting, and privileging diverse voices through cooperative and caring conversation. We can, will, and must have vigorous and rigorous disagreements, but must we be utterly disagreeable in so doing? I hope the College Reading Association will never lose the atmosphere of caring collegiality we have all enjoyed prior to this current divisive and ultimately destructive debate. There is enough room in CRA for all voices to be heard.

It is incumbent upon each of us to be intellectually honest about the limitations of our own preferred research paradigms and methods with others and ourselves. No one research method is sufficient to answer all research questions. We must openly admit the limitations of the research paradigms or methods we choose as well as defending their proper application, understanding, and benefits. If we do this, we will continue to experience the reasons we come each year to CRA, as they are so well described by Dinah Maria Mulock (1976).

> Oh, the comfort, the inexpressible comfort, of feeling safe with a person, having neither to weigh thoughts, nor measure words—but pouring them all right out—just as they are—chaff and grain together—certain that a faithful hand will take and sift them—keep what is worth keeping—and with the breath of kindness blow the rest away. (p. 165)

# A Continuing Chasm Between the University Literacy Researcher and the Classroom Literacy Practitioner

Now, the second controversial issue—the continuing chasm between university literacy researchers and classroom literacy practitioners. Several years ago, I was attending the National Reading Conference in New Orleans. As I rode the elevator to my room, which was near the top floor of the hotel, a family entered the elevator on the second floor. The father looked at my name tag which indicated the name of the conference. He inquired, "I see you along with many others are here for a reading conference. What do you do at a reading conference? Do you read?" Taken a bit by surprise, I replied, "Well, yes, but actually this is a group of university researchers interested in reading and literacy. We are here to learn about each other's research studies." He responded quickly to me, "Oh, I see. You guys study how to teach people to read and write better, huh?" I replied, "Yes, but that isn't all. We study how teachers feel about themselves as readers, how they feel about teaching reading, and how students feel about reading." He seemed perplexed and even a little put off: "Well, I suppose that's important, but as a parent I would want to know how I can help my children become avid and capable readers. They need to learn the skills and dispositions of good reading. Kids these days can feel good about knowing little or nothing. I've read about kids who graduate from high school today who can't tell you where Washington, D.C., is on a map. They don't know famous inventors like Eli Whitney. They don't seem to know much, but they feel good."

By his comments, the vocabulary, and the concerns of my elevator acquaintance, I knew this fellow was no rube. He had a command of the language and of thought that was obviously above average. I felt a bit rebuked by his candid observations. He was clearly pointing to a need for researchers and literacy research to be relevant to the needs of real children, teachers, families, and taxpayers.

Walter E. Williams (1996), an Associated Press writer for the *Washington Post*, wrote recently:

> American students rank No. 1 in the world in how good they feel about their math skills, but a 1992 international study by the Educational Testing Service (ETS) showed American students ranking last in math achievement (behind Slovenia). Research surveys show self-esteem levels at least as high among black students as white students, but a majority of either of them are unable to write a persuasive letter, date the Civil War, or calculate simple interest. (p. 13A)

For over a decade I have worked with classroom teachers in workshops, seminars, graduate classes, and research meetings. I frequently share with them published research articles. These classroom practitioners often groan when they read the titles, questions, and findings of these articles and remark something like this: "When are they going to study something real, relevant, and important to us? Why don't they ask us what the issues are that need to be researched?" These students are much like our university students, and seem to be suggesting that researchers are missing the significant issues associated with real students and real teachers, however they are defined in published research.

Kamil (1995) puts it this way:

> Although literacy researchers merrily engage in sophistry, nothing is done to help advance the plight of those for whom we profess to have concern. This profession should be about research in how to teach children to read. It should be about research in how best to equip workers to read informative manuals for their jobs. It should be about research in how individual speakers of one language learn to read in another . . . It should be about making certain that what we do is useful and applicable to real world contexts. (p. 244)

I admit Kamil may be slightly overstating his case, but I ask, do his observations deserve our careful attention as researchers and teacher educators?

Ken Zeichner, well known teacher education researcher, writes in a 1995 article entitled, "Beyond the Divide of Teacher Research and Academic Research":

> Despite the fact that many of my colleagues are known throughout the world for their research related to issues of equity, social justice, and schooling, these teachers [Zeichner's students] did not feel connected to this body of scholarship including his own and did not see it as offering them much guidance in dealing with their daily struggles to educate all students to high academic standards. (p. 159)

Richard and Joanne Vacca, longtime members of CRA, wrote a commentary years ago in the *Reading Research Quarterly* entitled "Two Less Than Fortunate Consequences of Reading Research in the 1970s" that may bear repeating today. They wrote, "Nevertheless, despite all that was good about reading research in the past decade, some of its broad social and political consequences may indeed have a deleterious effect on present and future inquiry in the field" (1983, pp. 382-383). Two of these consequences are interrelated and come to mind quickly:

> Consequence #1: The de-valuing of reading instruction research
> Consequence #2: The squeezing out of the reading educator

Vacca and Vacca continue:

> As reading researchers move squarely into the 1980's we hope that they do not work apart from one another; that the classroom teacher [and other stakeholders] play an integral role with researchers in deter-

mining what we should get smart about, that interdisciplinary teams continue to inquire into reading and its instructional implication and applications. (1983, pp. 382-383)

We cannot afford to exclude the voices of teachers, parents, and policy makers from our research. Failure to demonstrate relevance to these audiences may at some future time spell the diminution or outright dismantling of our literacy research community. Exclusivity in research paradigms, methods, or questions will no doubt lead most assuredly to the extinction of our community as it did to the dinosaurs of ancient date.

Consider the following poem concerning the need for relevant scholarship:

Today a professor in a garden relaxing
Like Plato of old in the academe shade
Spoke out in a manner I never had heard him
And this is one thing that he said:

Suppose that we state as a tenet of wisdom
That knowledge is not for delight of the mind,
Nor an end in itself, but a packet of treasure
To hold and employ for the good of mankind.

A torch or a candle is barren of meaning
Except it give light to men as they climb,
And thesis and tomes are but impotent jumble
Unless they are tools in the building of time.

We scholars toil on with the zeal of a miner
For nuggets and nuggets and one nugget more,
But scholars are needed to study the uses
Of all the great mass of data and lore.

And truly our tireless and endless researches
Need yoking with man's daily problems and strife,
For truth and beauty and virtue are
Confirmed by their uses in practical life.

[Anonymous]

As we consider these exemplars of controversy, I express a heartfelt plea that we, as CRA members, make a genuine effort to span the chasm between interested external stakeholders beyond the boundaries of our current literacy community and draw them into our circle of friends as colleagues in a caring conversation.

---

# References

The duty of civility. (1995, May/June). *Royal Bank Letter of Canada, 76* (3), 2.

Kamil, M. L. (1995). Critical issues: Some alternatives to paradigm wars in literacy research. *Journal of Reading Behavior, 27,* 243-261.

Marks, J. (1996). The American [un]civil wars. *U.S. News and World Report, 120 (16),* 66-73.

Mulock, D.M. (1976). In R. L. Evan (Ed.), *Richard L. Evan's quote book.* Salt Lake City, UT: Publishers Press.

Ruskin, J. (1976). In R. L. Evan (Ed.), *Richard L. Evan's quote book.* Salt Lake City, UT: Publishers Press.

Vacca, R. T., & Vacca, J. L. (1983). Guest editorial: Two less than fortunate consequences of reading research in the 1970s. *Reading Research Quarterly, 28,* 382-383.

Williams, W. E. (1996, September 13). U. S. students may feel good, but they still lack vital skills. *Deseret News,* p. 13A.

Zeichner, K. M. (1995). Beyond the divide of teacher research and academic research. *Teachers and Teaching: Theory and Practice, 1,* 153-172.

# FUTURE CONTROVERSIAL ISSUES IN LITERACY: THE SAME OLD STUFF OR A WHOLE NEW BALL GAME?

## William A. Henk

Pennsylvania State University, Harrisburg
An Address at the College Reading Association Conference
November, 1996

*William A. Henk currently serves as Director of the School of Behavioral Sciences and Education, and as Professor of Education and Reading at Pennsylvania State University, Harrisburg. Although his present duties are primarily administrative in nature, within the education programs he teaches courses in elementary level and diagnostic reading as well as in measurement and evaluation, reading psychology, curriculum integration, and current issues in education. He was the recipient of the College's Outstanding Teaching Award for 1991, the Distinguished Service Award of Phi Delta Kappa Harrisburg Chapter in 1996, and co-recipient of the Pennsylvania Educational Research Association's Outstanding Paper Award in 1997. Dr. Henk has written extensively in the areas of reading comprehension, instruction, and assessment as well as educational technology, having published in most major literacy journals.*

---

Generally speaking, predicting the future is risky business. Any individual foolhardy enough to propose a vision of the unknown runs the risk of being revealed as woefully shortsighted or laughably bold. In the field of literacy, the perils of prediction in this day and age are especially acute. That is, although literacy's traditional controversies tend to be longstanding, the advent of text-related computer technologies could completely revolutionize our current thinking about reading and writing. With these risks squarely in mind, I offer one tentative vision of six major future controversial issues in literacy, half of which relate directly to technology, while the remainder center on issues of the present that will almost certainly persist.

## The Impact of Technology

Text-related technologies have realized an unprecedented evolution in recent years. This emergence is not at all surprising. Advances in the capabilities of computer hardware occur so rapidly that newly purchased CPUs and peripherals no sooner arrive than they become relegated to yesterday's news. Likewise, new software emerges at an astounding rate as developers attempt to corner still another lucrative piece of the seemingly endless applications market.

### Reading as Writing

One major outcome of the avalanche of more powerful and sophisticated technologies is that *the distinction between reading and writing processes will become profoundly blurred.* In short, electronic texts will serve to make reading more constructivist in nature by providing readers with numerous presentation options. Most significantly, the expanded memory capabilities of personal computers will allow an even greater range of *hypertext* links to be embedded in otherwise traditional texts. Using hypertext, readers can go beyond the linear text material on the page to access additional textual, graphic, auditory, animated, or quick time movie information. This non-linear "writing" will be accomplished by uniquely accessing the multimedia links which define, describe, illustrate, demonstrate, and elaborate upon the meaning of unknown or interesting words, difficult concepts, and confusing text propositions. In effect, readers will literally be able to construct (or write, if you will) their own personalized texts in this digital post-typographic era (Reinking, 1995).

The continuing proliferation of computer-assisted *interactive fiction* will contribute further to making reading and writing processes more nearly alike. In interactive fiction, readers are given options at key points in a story which allow the plot to proceed in several possible directions. Readers can traverse a story repeatedly, taking a different pathway of events nearly each time. As with hypertext, the reading is non-linear and dynamic so that, in effect, readers construct the equivalent of custom texts which conform to their various episodic preferences.

A related, constructivist text-reading opportunity made possible by technology is the notion of *multiple perspectives* (Bolter, 1991). These texts can be read from the respective viewpoints of different characters in the story. Readers may elect to read a narrative told exclusively by one character through the entire text, or they could choose to switch among the full range of varying characters' perspectives that have been provided by the author. Imagine, for instance, being able to experience scenes through the sensory, perceptual, cognitive, and emotional lenses of any major character. Obviously, the original writing of such a text would be enormously time consuming; however, I suspect that, in the future, authors will invite readers to construct novel character perspectives that could become part of a virtual living text.

One final way that reading and writing processes are becoming ever more similar is through the use of *multimedia* courseware. This powerful combination of visual, auditory, kinetic, and mixed modes of delivery demands a deeply thoughtful presentation of concepts in which authors anticipate the whole spectrum of necessary textual aids that diverse readers will require, expect, or desire. Multimedia texts represent an extremely formal approach to delivery that should clearly abide by the principles of effective instructional design. As such, multimedia authors must configure their software with the greatest care and effort.

For that matter, the branching capabilities made possible by the other technologies discussed thus far (hypertext, interactive fiction, and multiple perspectives) also make extensive demands on the author. Trying to anticipate the possible preferences for plot options and character perspectives, not to mention the specialized learning needs of a universe of readers, represents a daunting task for writers, even with very user-friendly development software.

Another intriguing issue related to the technologies discussed thus far revolves around how reading comprehension can be validly assessed. On one hand, tracking the routes of readers through these malleable texts will be relatively easy for the computer. Still, one wonders how the tensions between reading efficiency, depth of understanding, and reading appreciation will ultimately be reconciled.

These technologically-delivered texts truly stretch the limits of constructivist learning and, as such, present reading educators and researchers with a wealth of altogether new possibilities and challenges. Some authorities have gone so far as to suggest that the interactive capability of electronic texts signals the eventual demise of books as the primary written communication medium (Reinking, 1995).

### *The Diminishing Importance of Reading?*

A second major controversial literacy issue of the future is that *reading could become less of a priority*. On the surface, this assertion would seem to run counter to repeated warnings about the increased literacy demands of an advanced technological society. Surely, the demands will be different. Locating and managing information (using electronic dictionaries, encyclopedias, the World Wide Web, databases, spreadsheets) and an ability to decipher procedural texts that facilitate the use of the technologies will almost surely gain in importance and promote greater amounts of specialized reading. However, the demands need not necessarily overwhelm the reader. Although hardware configuration remains a mystery to most of us, many software applications are sufficiently user friendly that reading the documentation becomes an option rather than a necessity. This increased ease is made possible largely by the ascendancy of non-verbal elements (e.g., icons, drawings, photos, animation) in cutting edge microcomputer software.

Advanced technologies might also have the dual effects of (1) making the reading process less challenging and/or (2) subverting reading in favor of visual literacy. With regard to reducing the challenges of reading, technologies such as *reading machines* and *voice recognition-activated word processors* have already exerted an impact on the importance of reading. For example, the Kurzweil Reading Machine, originally developed for use with blind individuals, can accurately pronounce the overwhelming majority of words that appear on nearly any page of English text (Rickelman & Henk, 1990). Put another way, the Xerox-like machine or its hand-held equivalent can convert practically any text from a reading to a listening exercise, even for sighted users. Given the popularity of books on tape with commuters, one wonders how the potential general availability of reading machine technology might affect the priority status reading currently enjoys.

The voice-activated word processors could also devalue the reading process, but in a different way. Using this software, writers will tend to focus on the auditory component of the message rather than its visual characteristics because the latter will be provided for them automatically. Admittedly, if the writer must reread the text for the purposes of revision, the re-inspection demands would promote literacy acquisition. However, the newer software will have a "reverse" capability, like the reading machine, to read the text back to the author orally. The point here is that the reading growth that would naturally occur as individuals, especially children, engage in conventional writing activities might be circumvented almost altogether if they opt to use voice recognition word processing technology. In short, both the reading machine and the voice-recognition writing programs beg the question, "Will children engage in the act of reading if it can just as easily be avoided?"

Two other threats to the significance of reading stem from society's increasing fascination with *visual literacy* and the emergence of *virtual reality* technologies. Each day it seems that we are bombarded with increasingly seductive visual messages through the media which, in turn, may render print contexts boring, particularly in the eyes of our youth. Television broadcasting, including high tech advertising and music videos, is ever-present; movie theaters sell out with the release of each new blockbuster; and video games and movie rentals have become a pervasive leisure option in our society. Collectively, great effort is devoted to shaping viewing contexts that garner and maintain the public's attention because the potential commercial rewards are staggering. In turn, this new visual literacy possesses the potential to undermine the appreciation of literature in the minds of our most impressionable factions of society.

Virtual reality, although in its infancy, could become another major competitor for the relatively high status that reading has held over the years. At present, virtual reality creates the impression in users of being immersed in a fairly authentic, albeit imaginary, context. Through the use of various viewing and kinetic devices that are networked interactively with an executive control computer, this technology permits users to experience a powerful set of sensations and perceptions in response to their actions in the virtual world. These simulations have the potential to compete with and ultimately surpass the vicarious experiences readers enjoy when engaged with even the most riveting of texts. This multifaceted technology will ultimately allow users to experience simulations of reality across the entire sensory spectrum. Taken to its extreme, virtual reality augmented by the holographic technologies of the future (similar to those portrayed on the Holodeck of *Star Trek's* Starship Enterprise) will permit "readers" to forego the written word altogether. Virtual reality "readers" could experience text worlds so directly and completely that they will move from the role of interested lexical bystanders to that of nearly full participants.

### Technology and Ethical Dilemmas

A third set of future controversial issues derives from the notion that *technology could create additional ethical problems in literacy*. The majority of my concerns here focus on the capacity of technology to manage information in an unjust manner. Technologies such as e-mail will invariably become susceptible to *tampering* and violations of confidentiality. Electronic messages can be altered or attributed in a fraudulent but convincing manner, and the consequences for the victim could be severe. There is also a distinct possibility that technology will encourage and facilitate plagiarism and other forms of *academic dishonesty*. I fear that the now infamous web site "School Sucks" which provides users with already written term papers is just the tip of the iceberg. It's true that the papers at that site are substandard, but I doubt such resources will always be low in quality. Moreover, I presume that competitors for this ignoble trade will proliferate once services are made to be more profitable and essentially untraceable. To make matters worse, the *integrity of copyrights* and the concept of *ownership of ideas* are clearly in jeopardy in a dynamic electronic literacy environment.

Perhaps the most dangerous dimension of technology's impact on literacy is *privileged access*. Our society is decidedly culpable for already having created a literacy chasm between dominant and subordinate social and economic classes, races, and cultures. Unfortunately, technology may serve to exacerbate the situation. Here the potential for another kind of Matthew Effect is ripe; that is, those rich in literacy stand to get richer by virtue of technology access, while those poor in literacy will be left even further behind. It is imperative, therefore, that every conceivable effort be made to ensure equal access to technology for all citizens. Anything less is unconscionable, albeit likely.

## Chronic Literacy Controversies

In speculating about future controversial literacy issues, one experiences a curious irony. On one hand, the probability that technology will exert an extraordinary impact stands in sharp contrast to the equally distinct possibility that many of today's most divisive literacy issues will continue to be debated indefinitely. This latter prospect looms large because the history of education as a discipline has been marked by a remarkable resistance to true change; unfortunately, its concomitant controversies tend to be equally resilient.

### *Innovative Instructional Literacy Practices Under Siege*

The formidable resistance to holistic forms of literacy instruction lead me to believe that *political pressures for instructional conservatism will persist*. In particular, whole language has been, and will continue to be, under relentless attack from the conservative right. To some extent, the opposition seems warranted. Numerous educational communities bought into whole language without a solid understanding either of its tenets or its eventual implementation obstacles (Walmsley & Adams, 1993). Even in the absence of an agreed-upon operational definition of whole language (Bergeron, 1990), many educators accepted the philosophy on the basis of intuition rather than on scientific evidence. From a pragmatic standpoint, most would-be whole language school districts hastily mandated implementation without providing the types of professional development opportunities that teachers needed to be successful. It is not surprising, then, that the reviews on whole language are mixed (Stahl, McKenna, & Pagnucco, 1994), causing many avid supporters to consider the more moderate literacy instruction associated with transitional, balanced, literature-based, or eclectic approaches (McIntyre & Pressley, 1996; Routman, 1996).

Despite these criticisms, there are a host of extremely commendable features of holistic literacy instruction that warrant continuance (e.g., authentic texts, relevant tasks, self-evaluation, cooperative learning, thematic curricula). Unfortunately, these elements may fall prey to a general political siege on whole language that has been masterfully orchestrated by its right-wing opponents. The most radical adversaries (Blumenfeld, 1996) suggest that society will be thrown into utter chaos if progressive whole language advocates (i.e., elitist reading professors) have their way. In effect, they charge that whole language endeavors to impose a socialistic agenda on the country by purposely limiting the literacy acquisition of children. The reasoning follows that these illiterate children will be far more susceptible to the pagan, Marxist political agendas of the left. While this logic is so absurd as to be laughable on one hand, it is downright offensive to the countless educators who have committed their very lives to the betterment of children. To suggest that teaching professionals at any level would intentionally prevent children from realizing their full intellectual potential is patently outrageous. Sadly, the propagandistic properties of the attack on holistic literacy instruction are sufficiently well disguised that an uninformed lay public might just embrace this rhetorical drivel.

### *The Assessment Debate Wages On*

A second chronic literacy controversy for the future is that *the debate over the use of standardized tests versus authentic assessments will almost certainly endure*. For years, advocates of more innovative types of literacy instruction have claimed that standardized measures are wrong minded (Valencia, Hiebert, & Afflerbach, 1994). These authors suggest that the norm-referenced approach simply fails to resonate with the progressive nature of the instruction and therefore cannot hope to assess its impact. Moreover, they argue that standardized assessments provide little useful instructional information, lack a sensitivity to small yet important changes in performance, and ultimately mislead parents, teachers, and administrators alike (Goodman, Goodman, & Hood, 1989). Traditionalists, on the other hand, tend to dismiss the value of authentic assessment on the grounds that it is unscientific (i.e., subjective and soft). They contend that global indicators of reading and writing achievement in the form of standardized tests are absolutely necessary for determining how children, their teachers, and their schools are performing. In this sense, they claim that, in the absence of norms, there is no reliable way to evaluate the general effectiveness of literacy instruction on an inclusive basis. To their way of thinking, all of the school's constituencies (parents, school boards, communities, legislators) deserve the quality control that standardized testing allows.

Regrettably, little hope for timely compromises appears to exist. The competing philosophies that undergird this assessment conflict are held with the firmest of resolves by their respective camps. Holistic educators resent having their orientations being held to an inappropriate benchmark of accountability, and they rail loudly about nearly any type of normative assessment. They believe that comparisons between groups of children do nothing to advance the literacy attainment of an individual child. Conversely, the more conservative educational element maintains that school districts must be held up to a set of verifiable standards, and that it is their duty to share the results with their constituencies. Their belief is that accountability will be a strong incentive for school systems to perform at the highest levels, and in turn, children will be the beneficiaries of the increased public vigilance.

In my opinion, education as a whole would be better served if we viewed both authentic and standardized assessments in their proper perspectives. Let's face facts. There will always be a need for schools to demonstrate their competency to the societies they serve. The key here is that this evidence can take disparate forms. Personally, I adhere to the philosophy that standardized tests represent merely one indicator of a child's literacy achievement. These normative results should be viewed in concert with the multiple measures that emerge naturally from the literacy instruction itself. This approach, while hardly original, strikes me as being concomitantly reasonable, realistic, and responsible. Yet, resistance to this kind of compromise is formidable in some literacy circles, which leads me to believe that the controversy will probably endure for years to come.

I am hopeful, though, that new assessment instruments can be developed which might appease both camps in the future. These instruments would revolve around literacy tasks that are essentially authentic, yet allow for the construction of norms. Some noteworthy headway has been made in this regard. In particular, newer commercial reading inventories like the *Qualitative Reading Inventory-II* (Leslie & Caldwell, 1995) and the *Basic Reading Inventory* (Johns, 1996) emphasize versatile usage and include more authentic texts, retelling rubrics, think aloud provisions, and prior knowledge and strategy assessments, while offering some degree of comparative possibilities.

In addition, some affective dimensions of literacy like reading attitude and literacy self-perceptions, which are important considerations in holistic instruction, have been shown to be amenable to standardized assessment. In particular, instruments like the *Elementary Reading Attitude Survey* (McKenna & Kear, 1990), the *Reader Self-Perception Scale* (Henk & Melnick, 1995), and the *Writer Self-Perception Scale* (Henk, Bottomley, & Melnick, 1996) have shown promise in the affective domain. Perhaps over time, these instruments and others yet to come can help to bridge the current enormous assessment void.

### *The Persistence of the Paradigm Wars*
A final literacy controversy of the future is that *the unfortunate paradigm wars in literacy research of the present are unlikely to abate any time soon.* As others have noted (Kamil, 1995), the rift between experimental and ethnographic researchers runs very deep and seems to be growing ever larger.

This philosophical polarization over what represents truth in research has festered for a number of years, but has proliferated of late (see Edelsky, 1990; Grundin, 1994; McKenna, Robinson, & Miller, 1990a, 1990b; Stanovich, 1993; Taylor, 1994; West, Stanovich, & Mitchell, 1993) despite calls for a cessation of hostilities (Stanovich, 1990). And as Ray Reutzel argues so eloquently (this volume), the accompanying discord threatens the integrity of the field as a whole. Sadly, the struggles go well beyond mere disagreement. The dialogues between quantitative and qualitative researchers often degenerate into disrespectful, personal attacks that intentionally or otherwise belittle the belief systems of other literacy professionals. Such combative language has been termed by some as a "discourse of derision." Frankly, the purpose of these mean-spirited missives eludes me.

Besides a general preference for civility, why should we be bothered by this research chasm? Among other things, I don't believe that literacy educators can afford to air their dirty laundry publicly. Education is under fire generally. Providing our critics with additional ammunition diminishes us all and reduces our chances of acquiring and maintaining necessary resources. Moreover, the profession has reached the point where the individuals we prepare in higher education don't know what to believe any more. In some contexts, I am fearful that the pressure to be indoctrinated into one perspective or the other will prevent both preservice and inservice teachers from taking a broader, more inclusive view of literacy research and pedagogy.

In large measure, my fear of indoctrination stems from the fact that literacy represents a truly multifaceted construct. Viewed in this way, it seems extremely peculiar to me that any single research perspective could be viewed as ultimately and exclusively valid. I believe that literacy researchers would do well to examine phenomena using as many different appropriate lenses of inquiry as possible, to aggregate and synthesize the data, and to draw maximally informed interpretations. In my opinion, the usefulness of many quantitative studies would be enhanced if subsequent qualitative inquiry was done with outlier subjects. Likewise, numerous qualitative studies lend themselves to quantitative follow-ups that would yield a more complete picture of the phenomena under study and lend credence to proposed category trends. Surely a middle ground exists in which quantitative and qualitative research paradigms can share a complementary coexistence. At the same time, as Kamil (1995) points out, this middle ground needs to extend well beyond mere detente. The warring factions cannot simply go about their business, co-existing by essentially ignoring each other or adhering to the concept of incommensurability. All parties must participate actively in the debate or we will not move forward as a field. However, I share Kamil's belief that by failing to enter into a productive, courteous dialogue, researchers will fall short of remedying the plight of those whom we profess to serve.

## A Final Word

Only time will tell if any of the predictions made in this paper will ring true. Perhaps technology will fail to exert as dramatic an impact on literacy as proposed here. By the same token, innovative literacy instruction might withstand the intense political pressure it labors under; authentic and standardized assessment indicators could be utilized in a complementary fashion; and the factions favoring disparate research paradigms could seek a mutually beneficial collaboration. At the risk of being naive, I believe literacy educators and researchers can resolve their differences with good faith dialogues within a climate of respectfulness. I also feel that we have the expertise and wherewithal to harness the power of technology for the common good. At any rate, literacy professionals need to anticipate several possible futures to prepare for the numerous challenges and opportunities that lie ahead. The very quality of our children's lives hangs in the balance.

---

# References

Bergeron, B. (1990). What does the term whole language mean? *Journal of Reading Behavior, 22,* 301-329.

Blumenfeld, S. (1996 ). *The whole language/OBE fraud.* Boise, Idaho: The Paradigm Company.

Bolter, J. (1991). *Writing space: The computer, hypertext, and the history of writing.* Hillsdale, NJ: Erlbaum.

Edelsky, C. (1990). Whose agenda is this anyway? A response to McKenna, Robinson, and Miller. *Educational Researcher, 19,* 7-11.

Goodman, K., Goodman, Y., & Hood, W. (Eds.). (1989). *The whole language evaluation book.*Toronto, Ontario: Irwin.

Grundin, H. (1994). Who's romanticizing reality? A response to Keith Stanovich. *Reading Teacher, 48,* 8-9.

Henk, W., Bottomley, D., & Melnick, S. (1996). Preliminary validation of the *Writer Self-Perception Scale.* In E. Sturtevant & W. Linek (Eds.), *Growing literacy, Eighteenth yearbook of the College Reading Association,* (pp. 188-199). Harrisonburg, VA: College Reading Association.

Henk, W., & Melnick, S. (1995). *The Reader Self-Perception Scale (RSPS):* A new tool for measuring how children feel about themselves as readers. *The Reading Teacher, 48,* 470-482.

Johns, J. (1996). *Basic reading inventory* (6th ed.). Dubuque, IA: Kendall-Hunt.

Kamil, M. (1995). Some alternatives to paradigm wars in literacy research. *Journal of Reading Behavior, 27,* 243-261.

Leslie, L., & Caldwell, J. (1995). *The qualitative reading inventory-II.* Glenview, IL: Scott, Foresman.

McIntyre, E., & Pressley, M. (Eds.). (1996). *Balanced instruction: Strategies and skills in whole language.* Norwood, MA: Christopher-Gordon.

McKenna, M., & Kear, D. (1990). Measuring attitude toward reading: A new tool for teachers. *The Reading Teacher, 44,* 626-639.

McKenna, M., Robinson, R., & Miller, J. (1990a). Whole language: A research agenda for the nineties. *Educational Researcher, 19,* 3-6.

McKenna, M., Robinson, R., & Miller, J. (1990b). Whole language and the need for open inquiry: A rejoinder to Edelsky. *Educational Researcher, 19*, 12-13.

McKenna, M. C., Stahl, S. A., & Reinking, D. (1994). A critical commentary on research, politics, and whole language. *Journal of Reading Behavior, 26*, 211-233.

Reinking, D. (1995). Reading and writing with computers: Literacy research in a post-typographic world. In K. Hinchman, D. Leu, & C. Kinzer (Eds.), *Perspectives on literacy research and practice, Forty-fourth yearbook of the National Reading Conference*. Chicago, IL: National Reading Conference.

Rickelman, R., & Henk, W. (1990). A machine that "reads." *The Reading Teacher, 44*, 512-513.

Routman, R. (1996). *Literacy at the crossroads: Crucial talk about reading, writing, and other teaching dilemmas*. Heinemann: Portsmouth, NH.

Stahl, S. A., McKenna, M. C., & Pagnucco, J. R. (1994). The effects of whole- language instruction: An update and a reappraisal. *Educational Psychologist, 29*, 175-185.

Stanovich, K. (1990). A call for the end of the paradigm wars in reading research. *Journal of Reading Behavior, 22*, 221-231.

Stanovich, K. (1993). Romance and reality. *Reading Teacher, 47*, 280-291.

Taylor, D. (1994). The trivial pursuit of reading psychology in the "real world", A response to West, Stanovich, and Mitchell. *Reading Research Quarterly, 29*, 276-289.

Valencia, S., Hiebert, E., & Afflerbach, P. (Eds.). (1994). *Authentic reading assessment: Practices and possibilities*. Newark, DE: International Reading Association.

Walmsley, S. A., & Adams, E. L. (1993). Realities of whole language. *Language Arts, 70*, 272-280.

West, R., Stanovich, K., & Mitchell, H. (1993). Reading in the real world and its correlates. *Reading Research Quarterly, 28*, 34-50.

# EXPLORING LEARNER DEVELOPMENT

# Recreational Reading Choices: How Do Children Select Books?

**Charlene E. Fleener**
**Susan Morrison**
**Wayne M. Linek**
Texas A&M University-Commerce

**Timothy V. Rasinski**
Kent State University

## Abstract

*Providing access to a rich variety of reading materials is an important step for motivating students to read recreationally, but it doesn't ensure that students possess selection strategies. This study, conducted in two states, focused on how intermediate students make choices for pleasure reading. Quantitative and qualitative analyses of data provide a profile of intermediate students' book selection behaviors, the teacher's role in the process, and possible classroom implications.*

If students are to become life-long readers, it is critical that they learn strategies to successfully self-select appropriate books for recreational reading. Although much recent attention has been devoted to the teaching of a strategies-oriented approach to reading instruction (Tierney, Readence & Dishner, 1995), there is a dearth of information on strategies that students use to select books for voluntary reading (Hiebert, Mervar, & Person, 1990). Teachers need to be aware of the strategies students actively employ during the process in order to promote a lifetime love of books and reading.

Many individuals read for pleasure, but a large number do not. What factors determine whether a child will become a recreational reader? Is it possible that non-recreational readers simply have never learned how to find appropriate and enjoyable books? What actually separates recreational readers from non-recreational readers? Reading ability may have little to do with the choice to read for pleasure or not. Gambrell (1995) found that motivation to read is not dependent upon proficiency, but rather upon other factors including access to plenty of books, opportunities to share and discuss readings with peers, and the freedom and encouragement to self-select books for recreational reading. Morrow and Weinstein (1986) found that even poor readers can be drawn into the love of reading by providing a supportive literacy environment. Given these findings it is important to investigate how students actually select books for recreational reading in order to be certain that the process is a positive one that will enable them to find that "perfect" book time and time again.

When students select books for leisure reading, what do they commonly consider important? Past studies (Au, Kunitake, & Blake, 1992; Hoffman, Roser, & Battle, 1993) have found that students generally rely on surface structure features (cover, thickness of book, number of pages, illustrations) in selecting books for recreational reading. In addition, Au et al. found that students typically do not have a broad repertoire of strategies from which to draw when choosing books. By studying the behaviors of students as they make book choices for pleasure reading, perhaps educators can learn more about what makes them successful or what appears problematic for finding the "right" book. The current study investigates the strategies used by different levels of readers when making recreational book selection choices.

## Method
### Subjects
This study included 32 children in grades five and six in two elementary schools, one in Oklahoma and the other in Texas (see Table 1). Both schools were in rural communities. All classes were heterogeneously grouped and involved students from families of varying socioeconomic levels. Students selected for the study were those whose parents granted consent for their participation. Students were identified by their teachers as highly proficient

**Table 1. Characteristics of the Subjects Included in the Study**

| State | Gender | | Ability Level | | | | | | Grade | | | |
| | M | F | High | | Medium | | Low | | 5th | | 6th | |
| | | | M | F | M | F | M | F | M | F | M | F |
|---|---|---|---|---|---|---|---|---|---|---|---|---|
| Texas | 9 | 12 | 4 | 7 | 2 | 3 | 3 | 2 | 6 | 5 | 3 | 7 |
| Oklahoma | 4 | 7 | 1 | 3 | 2 | 1 | 1 | 3 | 4 | 7 | 0 | 0 |
| Totals | 13 | 19 | 5 | 10 | 4 | 4 | 4 | 5 | 10 | 12 | 3 | 7 |

readers, average readers, or below average readers. For the purpose of this study reading proficiency was defined as low, average, and high based on teacher judgment as reflected by students' reading grades, class performance, and comparisons with peers. Grade level, gender, and reading proficiency were the three variables used for analysis.

## *Procedures*

Students were interviewed individually by the researchers concerning their book selection habits (see Appendix ). During the interviews students were asked to assign degrees of importance to various aspects of book selection for recreational reading ranging from 1 (very important) to 4 (not at all important). In addition to the interviews students were asked to keep logs of the titles of the books selected and read. Researchers, acting as participant observers, also shadowed student participants twice during their library periods to glean information concerning book selection behaviors. Qualitative analysis of data using the constant comparative method (Strauss & Corbin, 1990) was employed to analyze the findings from the triangulated data.

# Findings

Findings indicated that several specific points related to surface features, recommendation and location sources, and authors and genres were deemed as "very important" or "somewhat important." Upon close examination of the data, there appeared to be little difference between the criteria valued for book selections by students from each state. The more interesting differences were instead found between gender, ability level, and grade level of the students involved.

## *Surface Features*

Consistent with prior findings (Au et al., 1992), data from this study revealed that students relied heavily on the surface features of books. Features which children viewed as very important or somewhat important included book covers, length, illustrations, and descriptions.

Students of all abilities frequently used the cover of the book to gain information about a book. When considering gender, ability level, and grade, the cover was viewed as more important by the girls, the low proficiency students, and the fifth graders (see Table 2). Some students explained that interesting-looking covers attract their attention and are frequently a good indicator of what the story or book may be about, or at least give the reader a glimpse of something they can expect to find in the book. Perhaps one reason for some recreational readers' non-reliance on the cover of the book was summed up during a student interview when one male student replied, "My mom says not to judge a book by its cover."

**Table 2. Surface Feature Criteria Students Use for Choosing Books**

| Criteria | Gender | | Ability Level | | | | | | Grade | | | |
|---|---|---|---|---|---|---|---|---|---|---|---|---|
| | M | F | High | | Medium | | Low | | 5th | | 6th | |
| | | | M | F | M | F | M | F | M | F | M | F |
| Length | 54 | 32 | 40 | 20 | 75 | 50 | 75 | 40 | 70 | 33 | 33 | 29 |
| Illustrations | 54 | 48 | 20 | 40 | 75 | 50 | 75 | 60 | 70 | 42 | 00 | 57 |
| Type Size | 33 | 16 | 40 | 10 | 25 | 25 | 25 | 20 | 20 | 17 | 67 | 14 |
| Cover | 47 | 69 | 20 | 50 | 50 | 75 | 75 | 100 | 60 | 75 | 00 | 57 |
| Description | 54 | 95 | 60 | 90 | 50 | 100 | 50 | 100 | 60 | 100 | 33 | 86 |
| Difficulty | 8 | 11 | 00 | 10 | 00 | 25 | 25 | 00 | 10 | 08 | 00 | 14 |

*Note: The values represent mean percentages of students in each category indicating these criteria as being very important or somewhat important.*

Length of a book was more a matter of importance for boys than girls, for average and low proficiency students than high proficiency students, and for fifth rather than sixth grade students. It is possible that maturity may be a contributing factor (see Table 2). It was also found through student interviews that some of the high proficiency students considered the length question somewhat differently. For some of these students, length was deemed important not for finding a book short enough, but rather for finding a book long enough to last the weekend.

About half of all students considered illustrations important, but that number rose to over 65 percent for the responses of low to average proficiency students.

Book descriptions found on the jackets or inside the books were deemed very important or somewhat important by 78 percent of all students and 90 percent of the girls. Factors considered of negligible importance by all groups included television recommendations, type size, and difficulty of material.

## Recommendation and Location Sources

Of the students studied, most reported that the school and public libraries were either very important or somewhat important locations they used for selecting a book to read for fun (see Table 3). Students seemed to use the school libraries much more than any other location, with 82 percent of all students identifying them as important places for choosing recreational reading material. Fewer low proficiency than average or high proficiency students found their books in public libraries. The low proficiency students appeared instead to prefer classroom, home, or school libraries for making their selections. The sixth graders indicated a preference for public libraries more than the fifth graders. In addition, girls considered home libraries, book stores, and classroom libraries as important locations much more than boys.

Interviews and observations conducted for this study indicated that social interactions and recommendations were a valued source of book selection (see Table 3). However, the value assigned the recommendation depended on the source of that recommendation. Ratings of "very important" and "somewhat important" were given less frequently to recommendations from mothers and fathers than to those from teachers, peers, and other family members. High proficiency readers seemed to rely much more heavily on recommendations from peers than did the low or medium proficiency readers. Interestingly, low proficiency readers rated recommendations from their teachers considerably higher than did medium or high proficiency readers.

One unexpected finding of the current study was that 82 percent of the students in the Oklahoma school said they relied on the recommendations

**Table 3. Recommendation and Location Sources Students Use for Choosing Books**

| Criteria | Gender | | Ability Level | | | | | | Grade | | | |
|---|---|---|---|---|---|---|---|---|---|---|---|---|
| | M | F | High | | Medium | | Low | | 5th | | 6th | |
| | | | M | F | M | F | M | F | M | F | M | F |
| School Lib. | 75 | 85 | 80 | 90 | 75 | 75 | 75 | 80 | 80 | 92 | 67 | 71 |
| Public Lib. | 67 | 50 | 60 | 60 | 75 | 50 | 50 | 40 | 60 | 42 | 67 | 71 |
| Book Clubs | 47 | 32 | 40 | 20 | 50 | 00 | 75 | 60 | 60 | 42 | 33 | 00 |
| Classroom | 54 | 74 | 60 | 50 | 25 | 75 | 50 | 100 | 40 | 75 | 67 | 57 |
| Home | 31 | 74 | 20 | 80 | 50 | 75 | 75 | 80 | 50 | 75 | 33 | 86 |
| Book Stores | 31 | 74 | 20 | 80 | 75 | 100 | 00 | 40 | 40 | 67 | 00 | 86 |
| Mother | 24 | 43 | 00 | 70 | 25 | 25 | 50 | 00 | 30 | 42 | 00 | 86 |
| Father | 16 | 37 | 00 | 50 | 50 | 50 | 00 | 00 | 20 | 17 | 00 | 71 |
| Other Family | 47 | 74 | 40 | 80 | 50 | 100 | 50 | 40 | 50 | 75 | 33 | 71 |
| Teacher | 62 | 69 | 60 | 60 | 50 | 50 | 75 | 100 | 60 | 83 | 67 | 43 |
| Friends | 62 | 58 | 80 | 80 | 50 | 25 | 50 | 20 | 60 | 58 | 67 | 57 |
| Librarian | 24 | 48 | 20 | 30 | 50 | 75 | 25 | 60 | 40 | 58 | 00 | 29 |

*Note: The values represent percentages of students in each category indicating these criteria as being very important or somewhat important.*

of the school librarian, while only 19 percent of the students in the Texas school listed the school librarian as being an important source of recommendations. One possible explanation for this might be the fact that the Texas school library was staffed by an aide rather than a state-certified librarian.

## Authors and Genres

Authors and genres were most notably recognized as criteria for book selection among high proficiency readers (see Table 4). Eighty percent of the high proficiency students considered genres as either very or somewhat important when selecting books, as compared to only 23 percent from the low proficiency group. Additionally, 74 percent of the high proficiency group deemed looking for books by a particular author in the top two levels of importance. Only 34 percent of the low proficiency students reported that a favorite author had such an impact on book selection strategies.

Of the favorite authors discussed by the students, Laura Ingalls Wilder, R.L. Stein, C.S. Lewis, Madeline L'Engle, Bill Wallace, Carolyn Keene, and Betsy Byers were the most frequently cited. Favorite series of books included Baby-Sitters' Club, Little House, Goosebumps, American Girl, Nancy Drew, and Sweet Valley Twins.

Topping the list of favorite genres were fantasy and fiction. Also popular among fifth and sixth graders were historical event books, science fiction, mysteries, and adventure selections. Topics of interest varied with gender. Girls were interested in animal books, especially horse stories. Boys were interested in sports, dinosaurs, animals, and various other content areas ranging from Ancient Egypt to weather.

In sum, as prior studies have indicated (Au et al., 1992, Hoffman, et al., 1993), data from this study revealed that students tended to rely heavily on the surface features of books. Recommendations and locations of book sources were quite influential in their decision making. Students in general often depended on social interactions with friends and family and ease of accessi-

**Table 4. Authors and Genres as Criteria for Choosing Books**

| Criteria | Gender | | Ability Level | | | | | | Grade | | | |
| | M | F | High | | Medium | | Low | | 5th | | 6th | |
| | | | M | F | M | F | M | F | M | F | M | F |
| Authors | 47 | 68 | 60 | 80 | 25 | 75 | 50 | 20 | 50 | 50 | 33 | 86 |
| Genres | 54 | 53 | 100 | 70 | 50 | 75 | 25 | 20 | 50 | 42 | 100 | 86 |

*Note: The values represent percentages of students in each category indicating these criteria as being very important or somewhat important.*

bility when making book selections. Finally, authors and genres played a key role in sixth grade students' book choices.

## Limitations

This study is a pilot and a part of a larger, national study. It therefore involved a limited number of students, which precludes generalizing the findings beyond the scope of this study. Another limitation is the fact that two times more fifth graders were studied than sixth graders and none of the sixth graders were identified as being low proficiency readers. Thus, the pool of information on sixth graders is small. Although content validity of the survey instrument has been established (Rasinski, Mohr, Linek, Marcy, & Peterson, 1994), the survey continues to undergo refinement. Finally, the survey questions concerning recommendations of parents do not distinguish between parents who have and parents who have not made recommendations.

## Discussion and Conclusions

Students seem to recognize that surface features of books can be an important tool in the book selection process. However, such selection strategies alone are not sufficient for successful decision making. Students need to understand how and why such features can be used in tandem with other strategies to enhance the likelihood of appropriate selection. Students may make more satisfying and encouraging choices if they can be shown how to critically examine covers; read book jackets, tables of contents, first pages and author information; and frame questions concerning books relevant to their particular interests and needs. In addition, if they can learn to use several of these in combination instead of just one or two, the probability for making successful choices may be much greater.

In some ways, children are no different than many adults when selecting books to read for leisure. Frequently, adult readers like to discuss books and share recommendations with family and friends. Findings from the current study indicated that children often rely on the advice of friends and family members for suggestions for finding the right book to read. Morrow (1987) pointed out in her study that children prefer and need time for interaction with their peers concerning books because peer influences serve as strong motivators to read particular books. Students need opportunities and time to read and share what they have read with others "just-for-the-fun-of-it" during the school day so that they may realize the value of such experiences and learn from one another.

What made the difference in the two schools regarding the role of the school librarian? This is an area which needs further study. School librarians, media specialists, and library aides may vary in their levels of expertise and credentials. Some schools employ only certified, degreed librarians, whereas others may have library aides or noncertified, nondegreed staff filling library positions. Some librarians perceive their role as that of one who provides lessons on library and media utilization, story hour experiences, and guidance in locating needed information and references. Others assume a more managerial and custodial role. Investigating ways in which library personnel influence student recreational reading choices may provide further insight.

Fostering a love of reading and building recreational reading habits should not be taken for granted, or reserved or expected only of "good" readers. The practice of reading itself enhances and develops the performance and skill of the reader. If students of all abilities can develop and utilize tools and strategies for making recreational reading selections, the possibilities for positive reading experiences improve and everyone gains.

---

# References

Au, K. H., Kunitake, M. M., & Blake, K. M. (1992, December). Students' perceptions of how they became interested in reading. In *Exploring children's disposition to learn: The role of motivation and interest in reading.* Symposium conducted at the annual meeting of the National Reading Conference, San Antonio, TX.

Gambrell, L. B. (1995). Motivation matters. In W. M. Linek & E. G. Sturtevant (Eds.), *Generations of literacy* (pp. 2-24). East Texas State University: The College Reading Association.

Hiebert, E. H., Mervar, K. B., & Person, J. (1990). Research directions: Children's selections of trade books in libraries and classrooms. *Language Arts, 67,* 758-763.

Hoffman, J. A., Roser, N. L., & Battle, J. (1993). Reading aloud in classrooms: From the modal toward a "model." *The Reading Teacher, 46,* 496-503.

Morrow, L. M. (1987). Promoting inner-city children's recreational reading. *The Reading Teacher, 41,* 266-273.

Morrow, L. M., & Weinstein, C. S. (1986). Encouraging voluntary reading: The impact of a literature program on children's use of library centers. *Reading Research Quarterly, 21,* 330-345.

Rasinski, T. V., Mohr, K. A. J., Linek, W. M., Marcy, E., & Peterson, C. S. C. (1994, November). Voluntary reading choices: The strategies employed by intermediate students. Paper presented at the annual meeting of the College Reading Association, New Orleans, LA.

Strauss, A., & Corbin, J. (1990). *Basics of qualitative research: Grounded theory procedures and techniques.* Newbury Park, CA: Sage Publications.

Tierney, R. J., Readence, J. E., & Dishner, E. K. (1995). *Reading strategies and practices: A compendium* (3rd ed.). Boston: Allyn and Bacon.

## Appendix: How Students Choose Their Books

Interviewer Name _____

Student's First Name _____

Grade Level (limit to 4th grade or above) _____

School _____

Description of School:    \_\_\_\_Low SES    \_\_\_\_Middle SES    \_\_\_\_High SES
    \_\_\_\_Urban    \_\_\_\_Suburban    \_\_\_\_Rural

Reading Level:  H  M  L     Gender:  M  F

*Ask students the following questions. Transcribe their responses as accurately as possible.*

1. Think about when you go to the library to choose a book to read for fun (not as a school assignment). How do you go about choosing your book? How do you decide what you will choose to read? What steps do you go through to find a book to read?

    _____
    _____
    _____

*Have the student rate the relative importance of each in helping him or her choose books to read recreationally. (Say: How important is this in helping you choose books to read recreationally or for fun?) Use this scale for importance: 1=Very important; 2=Somewhat important; 3=Slightly important; 4=Not at all important.*

            *Importance*

2. (a) My mother recommends books to me.       _____
   (b) My father recommends books to me.      _____

3. Other family members recommend books to me.  _____
   Who? _____

4. My teacher recommends books to me.     _____

5. My friends recommend books to me.     _____

6. (a) The school librarian recommends books to me.  _____
   (b) The public library librarian recommends books to me.  _____

7. I look at how long or short the book is.    _____

8. I try books that are recommended on TV programs.  _____
   Name the TV program(s) _____
   Are you able to find the recommended books? _____

9. I look for books that have interesting pictures and illustrations.  _____

10. I look for books that have large letters or type.  _____

11. I look at the cover of the book.    _____
   *(Probe for what is important about the cover.)*

12. I read the description of the book on the inside or back cover.  _____

13. I look for books by a particular author.  _____
   *(If important, ask student to name some favorite authors.)*
   Who are your favorite authors? _____

14. I look for a particular type of book such as science fiction, historical, fantasy, etc.
    Which type do you prefer? _____    _____

15. I look for books on particular topics of interest to me.
    *(If important, ask student to name some topics of interest.)*
    What topics do you prefer? _____

16. I check the card catalog to find books of interest to me.    _____
    *(Probe for how the catalog is used. Probe for knowledge:*
    *"Do you know how to use catalog?")*

17. I look for books that have won awards such as the
    Caldecott or Newbery.    _____

18. I look for books that are easy to read.    _____
    *(Ask "What makes a book easy for you?")*

19. I look for books in a series.    _____
    (ex. American Girl, Baby-Sitter's Club, Goosebumps)

20. What else do you use to help you pick out books that
    you would like to read?    _____

21. Where do you normally find your books to read for fun?
    ____school library          ____classroom book collection
    ____public library          ____home library/collection
    ____book clubs              ____book stores
    (Troll, Scholastic)

22. When you find a book you like, do you tell anyone about it?    _____
    Who (parent, teacher, friend)?

23. How often do you go to the public library?    _____

24. How often do you go to the school library?    _____

25. How often do you get books as gifts?    _____
    Who gives them to you?_____
    Do you read them? _____

26. How often do you get books from school book clubs
    such as Troll or Scholastic?    _____
    What types of books have you ordered? _____

27. How many books do you normally read in a week?    _____

28. About how many books have you read in the last year?    _____

29. How does your teacher help you choose books?    _____

30. How does the librarian help you choose books?    _____

31. Describe the kinds of books you *don't* like to read.    _____

# THE ROLE OF TEXTBOOKS AND READING IN CONTENT AREA CLASSROOMS: WHAT ARE TEACHERS AND STUDENTS SAYING?

**Teresa Murden**
**Cindy S. Gillespie**
Bowling Green State University

## Abstract

*This study explores the role of reading in 36 content area classrooms. Teachers' uses of textbooks, and both teacher and student perceptions of content reading are examined. Data include observations and teacher and student interviews.*

Hands-on science. Manipulative mathematics. Books on tape. All of the aforementioned "improvements" in teaching methodology may be leading to criticisms of text-based instruction as a second-rate approach to other instructional approaches such as hands-on, discovery, or other more direct encounters with content (Schallert & Roser, 1989). The textbook and reading in content area classrooms could become extinct, in favor of more pictorial, aural, and verbal presentations of content material. With the advancements in technology, as well as changing beliefs about how best to teach content in the middle and secondary schools, it may be time to awaken William S. Gray's cry that every teacher should be a teacher of reading.

Researchers in the past decade (Alvermann, 1982,1983; Alvermann, Dillon, O'Brien & Smith, 1985; Alvermann, O'Brien & Dillon, 1990; Davey, 1988 ; Gillespie & Rasinski, 1989; Hinchman, 1987; Memory, 1983; O'Brien & Stewart, 1990; Schallert & Roser, 1989; Smith & Feathers, 1983a, 1983b; Stewart & O'Brien, 1989; Sturtevant, 1995) have sought to evaluate the role that textbooks and reading play in content area classrooms. Many of these authors concluded that: (1) textbook assignments which require students to read and write answers to questions appeared to "drive" the lesson making the reading assignment the context for the rest of the lesson rather than vice versa; (2) because some texts are inconsiderate, teachers may choose to work around the subject area textbook rather than to work with it; (3) students may depend upon the teacher's lecture, not the text, as their primary source of information; (4) teachers, like students, may tend to minimize the text's role as a primary source of information, thereby making the text seem an unimportant and unnecessary part of subject area learning; and (5) text-based instruction may be perceived as a second-rate approach to teaching content.

Stewart and O'Brien (1989) speculated that content reading instruction has not been universally embraced by secondary preservice and practicing teachers even though they have completed coursework which focused on content reading. Additionally, they suggested that preservice teachers still harbor many misconceptions about content area reading instruction: teachers reported feelings of inadequacy or lack confidence in their effectiveness to incorporate reading instruction into their content lessons; they doubted whether reading instruction should fall within their domain; and some teachers still believed there was no need for content reading coursework.

Moje (1993, p.3) claimed that previous research has concentrated on assessing teachers' practice in relation to their beliefs. She adds that other studies have examined teacher's beliefs about content literacy by examining teachers' attitudes toward "literacy or reading per se." Few investigations, however, have focused on what students and teachers are actually saying about how textbooks and reading are being used in content classrooms (Davey, 1988; Smith & Feathers, 1983a,1983b). Therefore, the purpose of this investigation was to examine the role of textbooks and reading in content area classrooms by interviewing teachers and students regarding practices. Observational data, triangulated with teacher and student interviews were also included.

## Design of Study

The design of this study was patterned after two investigations by Smith and Feathers (1983a, 1983b) and one by Davey (1988). All three of these investigations focused on inquires into the area of content reading as they related specifically to textbook use, teacher/student assumptions, perceptions regarding the learning goals and objectives in specific content areas, and the role of reading in associated classrooms.

Smith's and Feathers' first study (1983a) examined the realities of the classroom by focusing on both teacher stated goals and learning objectives and student perceptions of these. The researchers also examined relationships between stated goals and objectives and the students' perceptions of these to the role of reading in the classroom and beyond. The second study

(Smith & Feathers, 1983b) examined the role of reading in the content area classroom by considering how teachers' assumptions about content area reading manifest themselves in a real way in the classroom. Davey (1988) later expanded the aforementioned investigations by specifically targeting her investigation toward how teachers use textbooks.

This study expands these previous studies. The study of teacher and student perspectives by Smith and Feathers (1983a, 1983b) is expanded by both teacher observation and interview, along with student interview data, thus providing a more complete view of the relationship between the teacher and student perceptions and actual classroom practice. Davey's (1988) study is expanded through the examination of teacher use of other sources in place of, or in addition to, textbooks in order to explore how other sources are actually being used in the classroom. Specifically, the purpose of this investigation was to examine what teachers and students said about how textbooks were used in their classrooms.

Eighteen middle school and eighteen high school classes representing a variety of subject areas (math, social studies, history, government, science, English literature, language arts, physics, psychology, photography, music theory, choir, computer programming), all having a core of content specific to a designated subject to be learned as a common goal, participated in this study. The 36 classrooms were selected from those of 40 teachers who had agreed to participate in the investigation. Each class was visited by a team of 3 observers who were enrolled in a content area reading class. The observations and interviews were conducted toward the end of the semester in which the students were enrolled. The specific day and time of the interviews and observations were not announced in advance to avoid the teacher "teaching to the observers." Each team collected the following data: 1) one content area teacher interview, 2) one content area teacher observation, and 3) two content area student interviews. The data included a total of 36 teacher interviews, 36 observations, and 72 student interviews.

Each interview form (teacher and student) and observation form consisted of open-ended questions designed to solicit information regarding: (1) the role of reading in the content area classroom, (2) how the classroom teachers used textbooks, and (3) teacher and student perceptions of content reading. Parallel questions were asked of the teacher and the students (see Table 1). Each team worked collaboratively to submit one set of data per classroom.

## Table 1. Interview Questions

| *Teacher* | *Student* | *Observer* |
|---|---|---|
| What do you expect your students to learn? | What do you think the teacher is trying to teach you? | Briefly summarize the topic of today's lesson. |
| How much reading do you expect your students to do per week? | How much reading does the teacher expect you to do per week? | |
| What percent do you believe actually read the material? | Do you always complete the assigned reading? | |
| Are your assignments from the textbook or from other sources? | Are your assignments mostly from the textbook or from other sources? | What materials were used in today's lesson? |
| Do your students read orally in class? How often? | Do you read aloud in class? How often? | |
| Do you spend time helping your students with reading problems? | When you have difficulty reading your assignments, what steps do you take to help you learn the material? | What reading skills were evident in class? |
| What percent of your tests is based on text knowledge? | What percent of the tests is based on material from the text? | |
| Do you teach vocabulary? | Does your teacher introduce new vocublary? | Was any new vocublary introduced? |
| Do you use study guides? | Does your teacher give study guides to be filled out while reading? | |
| If students attended class, but didn't read the text, they would probably earn a letter grade of _____ | If you attended class, but did not read the text, you would probably expect a letter grade of _____ | |
| When you lecture in class, what percent of the material is taken directly from the text? | What percent of your teacher's lecture is taken directly from from the text? | What was the teaching style used in the class (lecture, discussion, assigned reading, etc.)? |

## Data Analysis

The organization of this study relied heavily on the methodology of Davey (1988) for quantifying sections of the teacher and student interviews. In the case of responses to open-ended questions, when two or more respondents provided more than one response to a question, each received proportional weight in a category (e.g. with 3 responses, each counted as 1/3 of a response under its category) (Davey 1988).

Teacher observations were less easy to categorize largely because the questions required a more in-depth evaluative and often interpretive answer than the interviews. Few of these observations could easily be categorized or quantified. Consequently, an open coding methodology (Corbin & Strauss, 1990) was adopted. Through a process by which concepts were identified and developed in terms of their properties and dimensions, questions were asked about the data. Comparisons were made for similarities and differences between each incident, event and other instances of phenomena; similar events and incidents were labeled and grouped to form categories. Both methods for categorizing, quantifying, and labeling data were used both to corroborate findings with prior research and to discuss new findings from this investigation.

## Findings

For reporting purposes, the findings will be referred to as belonging to one of three categories: (1) the role of reading in the content area classroom, (2) how classroom teachers use textbooks, and (3) teachers' and students' perceptions of content reading.

### *The Role of Reading in the Content Area Classroom*

With respect to the question regarding the amount of reading expected of students, teachers' responses in this study indicated that teachers estimated they assigned middle-schoolers to read an average of 15.28 pages per week while high school teachers estimated they expected their students to read an average of 26.67 pages per week. Student interviews revealed different results, indicating that students estimated they were expected to read 12.13 pages per week at the middle school level while 15.11 pages per week were estimated at the high school level (see Table 2).

The second question asked whether or not teachers helped students with reading problems and what students did when they had difficulty reading. When students in both middle school and secondary school encountered reading problems, the teacher was listed as the number one solution by 90% of the middle school students and 85% of the high school students. Middle school and high school teachers responded similarly to the question, "Do

**Table 2. Quantifiable Data From Interviews**

|  | *MSS* | *MST* | *HSS* | *HST* |
|---|---|---|---|---|
| Length of assignment (estimated number of pages per week) | 12.13 | 15.28 | 15.11 | 26.67 |
| Teacher is solution to problems with reading | 90% | 63% | 85% | 80% |
| Vocabulary is taught | 90% | 100% | 90% | 100% |
| Use of study guides | 22% | 22% | 33% | 60% |
| Use of 1 text selected by teacher | 72% | 72% | 67% | 67% |
| Oral reading | 61% | 67% | 17% | 44% |
| Silent reading | 72% | 61% | 17% | 67% |
| Lecture material comes from text | 76% | 60% | 57% | 71% |
| Exam comes from text | 67% | 88% | 76% | 87% |
| Learning is about goals involving decision making, application of knowledge to real-world situations, citizenship, thinking skills, and acquisition of general knowledge. | NA | 78% | NA | 67% |
| Teacher is expecting us to learn "test material" or "what the teacher wants us to learn." | 89% | NA | 90% | NA |
| Students who complete assignments | 44% | 68% | 22% | 33% |
| Grade "C" or better without reading any assignments | 78% | 76% | 82% | 78% |

*MSS=Middle School Student Responses, MST= Middle School Teacher Responses*
*HSS=High School Student Responses, HST= High School Teacher Responses*

you spend time helping students with reading problems? Why or Why not?" Each group (63.6% of middle school teachers and 80% of high school teachers) said they did help whenever possible. Most of the affirmative answers to this question were qualified with some sort of limitation as to the kinds of help the teachers were prepared to give. For example, 11 of 18 middle school and 10 of 18 high school teachers indicated that the school either employed a reading specialist or had remedial courses to help students beyond the occasional classroom intervention such as helping students pronounce a new vocabulary word or helping students with confusion over content comprehension. Teachers who said they did not help students with reading problems (36.4% in middle school and 20% in high school classes) cited limited time with students and/or the presence of a reading specialist on staff as reasons for not devoting class time to student reading difficulties. However, observations of both middle school classes and high school classes included notations indicating that not much reading, and consequently not much assistance, were apparent in the classes observed (see Table 2).

The teaching of, or attention to, vocabulary in the classrooms was reported as standard practice by students in both middle school and high school classes indicating that the teachers introduced new vocabulary with varying degrees of emphasis from time to time in their classes. According to student interviews, 33 of 36 students in both middle school and high school reported vocabulary work in their classes. Teacher interviews also indicated an emphasis on vocabulary instruction in their classes with both middle school and high school teachers reporting at 100% in this area. Observers noted that one-third of the teachers in the middle school explained vocabulary specific to the content they were discussing while in 10 of the 18 high school classes observed, the teachers introduced vocabulary in conjunction with the content they were teaching (see Table 2).

When questioned about study guides, 8 of 36 middle school students reported that study guides were used on a regular basis and 12 of the 36 high school students reported that study guides were used. Middle school teachers corroborated the estimates indicated by their students (4 of the 18 indicated they used study guides). High school teachers estimated a greater use of study guides than was acknowledged by their students with 60% of the high school teachers reporting the use of study guides in their classrooms. (see Table 2).

### How Classroom Teachers Use Textbooks

Most teachers reported that they relied predominantly on textbooks rather than on readings from other sources to provide content information to students in their classes. Both teacher and student interviews among middle school and high schoolers corroborated these findings: 72% of middle school and 67% of high school teachers reported using the text most often for reading assignments (see Table 2).

With respect to oral and silent reading in class, teachers and students alike indicated that reading as a regular classroom activity occurred more often than was observed. Twelve of 18 middle school teachers indicated that they incorporated oral reading into their classroom practice on a regular basis and 11 of 18 middle school teachers maintained they used silent reading as a part of the daily classroom routine. Eight high school teachers reported using oral reading in the classroom, while 12 of 18 high school teachers indicated they gave students time to read silently at almost every class meeting (see Table 2). Both middle school and high school classes indicated they were allowed class time for reading in over 51% of the classes studied. Of the 36 middle school students interviewed, 22 reported oral reading as a class activity at least once a week and 26 reported silent reading as a regular occurrence (often 4 to 5 times a week) in their classes. High school students offered the opposite results with 6 students reporting oral reading and 6 reporting silent reading as regular classroom activities.

Regarding the percent of lecture taken directly from the text, 56.92% of all high school and 75.67% of all middle school students believed that lecture material came directly from the text. Teachers agreed that a majority of lecture material came from the text with middle school teachers reporting a 59.72% reliance on the text for lecture material and high school teachers reporting usage of the text material in their lectures 70.83% of the time. Observers noted that teaching style and lesson topic were often combined but focused primarily on content delivery; observers used terms such as, "lecture—toxic waste" and "lecture—civil war" to describe what was occurring in the classrooms (see Table 2).

Teachers and students were asked about the relationship between textbooks and exams. Teachers reported that approximately 80% (87.67% middle school and 86.39% high school) of test questions on exams were text based, while students revealed slightly lower perceptions. Middle school students perceived that an average of 67.19% of tests were derived from the text. High school students perceived a slightly higher relationship with 75.82% of tests drawn from the text book materials (see Table 2).

### Teachers' and Students' Perceptions of Content Reading

When the classroom teachers were asked: "What do you expect students to learn?", a majority of teachers (14 of 18 middle school and 12 of 18 high school) emphasized goals involving decision making, application of knowledge to real-world situations, citizenship, thinking skills, and acquisition of general knowledge. They gave these goals and objectives a higher priority than content or course information. Observers reported that of the 18 middle school teachers, 12 demonstrated an emphasis on delivery rather than efforts to meet the identified goals and objectives in classroom practice. Observers noted a similar pattern in the classrooms of high school teachers in that of the 18 classes observed, 17 teachers focused on content delivery identified by topic summaries such as: "lecture—geography" and "lecture—remedial math topics." Observers indicated that 10 of the 18 teachers included discussion or some type of group activity in their delivery of content. When students were asked "What is the teacher trying to teach you?", 89% of middle school and 90% of high school students responded that the teacher was trying to teach them what was going to be on the test (see Table 2).

Whether or not students actually read the assignment was another issue considered. Forty-four percent of middle school students claimed they read the assigned reading while their teachers indicated that they expected nearly 68% of students had read the assigned material before class. Among high school students, only 22% claimed to have read the assigned material while their teachers estimated 32.5% of students had read the material before class (see Table 2).

When students and teachers were asked to predict possible letter grades for the course based on never having read the text material, both groups speculated that, on average, 75% of students could receive a grade ranking somewhere from A to C. Overall, both middle and high school students rated themselves slightly higher than their teachers in terms of grade potential in this context without text reading. Middle school students speculated they could receive a C or better without reading the text 78% of the time. The high school students speculated they could receive a grade of C or better without reading the material 82% of the time. Teachers speculated that 76% of middle school students and 78% of high school students who did not read the assigned text could pass with a grade of C or better (see Table 2).

## Discussion

The results of this study are in agreement with past research, particularly Smith and Feathers (1983a, 1983b) and Davey (1988), who suggested that: (1) textbook assignments appeared to "drive" the lesson making the reading assignment the context for the rest of the lesson; (2) teachers appeared to choose to work around the subject area textbook rather than to work with it; (3) reading materials were selected by the teachers who relied predominately on a single textbook; (4) students depended upon the teacher's lecture, not on the text, as their primary source of information; (5) teachers tended to minimize the text's role as a primary source of information; (6) little reading instruction occurred in content area reading classrooms with vocabulary instruction being the most prevalent form of reading instruction in content classrooms.

There are limitations to this study which must be acknowledged. First, observers were in the classrooms for one period on one day. This significantly affects what the observers saw. Additionally, the observers, while enrolled in a content area reading class and working in teams, may have missed instances of reading, references to reading, or other occurrences within the classroom which may have yielded different results. Students and teachers were randomly selected for interviews. Purposeful selection of students and teachers to interview may have yielded different results. Some of the interview questions called for speculation on the parts of students and teachers. For example, students and teachers were asked to predict grades they might receive if they did not read the assigned material and to estimate the number of pages read per week. These predictions cannot be verified.

## Implications

In sum, textbooks were not perceived as important to student learning by the students or the teachers in this investigation. Textbooks were not viewed as a major source of information for students. Smith and Feathers (1983a) identified two assumptions often made about the role of reading in content classrooms: (a) that it is necessary for students to read their textbooks and (b) that students actually do so. Based on this investigation, it was clear that the two assumptions may be, in reality, more the exception in today's content classroom, rather than the norm. Reading was not viewed as an integral part of classroom activities.

Davey (1988) expressed a concern that "the way teachers use their textbooks can signal their relative importance for content learning and as a consequence, some content teachers may unwittingly communicate that textbooks play an unimportant role in class requirements (p. 340)." Smith and Feathers (1983a) ultimately defined the role of reading in the content area classroom as narrow to nonexistent based on the limited time and attention placed on reading activities that could be directly linked to content learning.

The results of this investigation also validate what other researchers (Alvermann, 1982,1983; Alvermann, Dillon, O'Brien & Smith, 1985; Alvermann, O'Brien & Dillon, 1990; Davey 1988; Gillespie & Rasinski, 1989; Hinchman, 1987; Memory, 1983; O'Brien & Stewart, 1990; Schallert & Roser, 1989; Smith & Feathers, 1983a, 1983b; Stewart & O'Brien, 1989; Sturtevant, 1993) have concluded: that secondary content area classroom teachers may not be transferring what is learned in the college classroom to their practices as preservice and inservice teachers. This suggests that it may be time to reevaluate what is taught in content area reading classes.

Content area reading course instructors may need to dispel misconceptions that preservice and inservice teachers have about incorporating reading into their instruction. Perhaps the misconceptions could be eliminated if instructors began their content area reading classes like Stewart and O'Brien (1989) by asking students why they believe such a course is required and what they expect to learn that will help them become better teachers. Memory (1983) recommended adding a practicum to the content area reading course. O'Brien, Stewart and Moje (1995), recognizing the personal pedagogical conceptions that preservice bring with them from their past experiences in their own schooling, suggested that reflecting on and analyzing personal theories, beliefs, and values by using autobiographies, dialogue, writing and field work might also facilitate the transition from the "ivory tower" to "real life."

Another foci of content area reading classes should be on effective decision making regarding the use of literacy strategies. Preservice and inservice teachers will not be able to use content area reading strategies effectively (if they use them at all) if they do not receive instruction as to how, when, and why literacy strategies should be used and modified to fit their students' needs. The ultimate goal of strategy instruction should be to enable preservice and inservice teachers to adapt strategies to the needs of their students, taking into consideration the contextual constraints of each classroom (Moje, 1992, 1996; O'Brien, Stewart & Moje, 1995).

Alvermann, Dillon, O'Brien and Smith (1985) suggested that preservice and inservice teachers may need to be instructed in the ways in which textbooks can be used effectively during discussion. They suggested: (1) the textbook may be used to verify points made during lecture-discussion; (2) indirect references may be made to previously read portions of the text without actually rereading the text; (3) discussions may be refocused by turning students' attention to the text; and (4) students may use the text to paraphrase responses to questions.

Content area reading instructors continue to face the challenge of helping preservice and inservice teachers understand the importance of textbooks and reading in subject area classrooms. According to Schallert and Roser (1989), a new challenge has been added to the mix: the criticism that text-based instruction is a second-rate approach to other instructional approaches such as hands-on, discovery, or other more direct encounters with content. Continued research on the use of textbooks and reading in the content classroom, combined with research utilizing the "newer" instructional strategies, is essential if preservice and inservice teachers are to make effective, informed decisions about literacy instruction in their classrooms.

## References

Alvermann, D. (1982). *Textbook reading assignments at the secondary level: Relating teacher behaviors to student performance and attitude.* Paper presented at the Annual Meeting of the National Reading Conference. ERIC Document Reproduction Service (ED 230 924).

Alvermann, D. (1983). Putting the textbook in its place-Your student's hands. *Academic Therapy, 18,* 345-351.

Alvermann, D., Dillon, D., O'Brien, D., & Smith, L. (1985). The role of the textbook in discussion. *Journal of Reading, 29,* 50-57.

Alvermann, D., O'Brien, D., & Dillon, D. (1990). What teachers do when they say they're having discussions of content area reading assignments: A qualitative analysis. *Reading Research Quarterly, 25,* 296-322.

Corbin, J., & Strauss, A. (1990). *Basics of qualitative research: Grounded theory procedures and techniques.* Newbury Park, Ca.: Sage Publications.

Davey, B. (1988). How do classroom teachers use their textbooks? *Journal of Reading, 31,* 340-345.

Gillespie, C., & Rasinski, T. (1989). Content area teachers' attitudes and practices toward reading in the content areas: A review. *Reading Research and Instruction, 28,* 45-67.

Hinchman, K. (1987). The textbook and three content-area teachers. *Reading Research and Instruction, 26,* 247-263.

Memory, D. (1983). Implementing a practicum in a required content area reading course. *Reading World, 23,* 116-123.

Moje, E. (1996). I teach students, not subjects: Teacher-student relationships as contexts for secondary literacy. *Reading Research Quarterly, 31,* 172-195.

Moje, E. (1993). *Life experiences and teacher knowledge: How a content teacher decides to use literacy strategies.* Paper presented at the Annual Meeting of the National Reading Conference. ERIC Document Reproduction Service (ED 364 838).

Moje, E. (1992). *Literacy in the chemistry classroom: An ethnographic study of effective teaching.* Paper presented at the Annual Meeting of the National Reading Conference. ERIC Document Reproduction Service (ED 352 624).

O'Brien, D., Stewart, R., & Moje, E. (1995). Why content literacy is difficult to infuse into the secondary school: Complexities of curriculum, pedagogy, and school culture. *Reading Research Quarterly, 30,* 442-463.

Schallert, D., & Roser, N. (1989). The role of reading in content area instruction. In D. Lapp, J. Flood & N. Farnan (Eds.), *Content area reading and learning: Instructional strategies* (pp. 25-33). Englewood Cliffs, NJ: Prentice-Hall.

Smith, F., & Feathers, K. (1983a). Teacher and student perceptions of content area reading. *Journal of Reading, 26,* 348-354.

Smith, F., & Feathers, K. (1983b). The role of reading in content classrooms: Assumption vs. Reality. *Journal of Reading, 27,* 262-267.

Stewart, R., & O'Brien, D. (1989). Resistance to content area reading: A focus on preservice teachers. *Journal of Reading, 32,* 396-401.

Sturtevant, E. (1995). *Beliefs about content literacy meet "reality" in secondary school mathematics: Nontraditional student teachers share their experiences.* Paper presented at the Annual Meeting of the National Reading Conference. ERIC Document Reproduction Service (ED 379 607).

# GRADUATE STUDENTS' EXPLORATIONS: THEIR OWN WORDS ON RESEARCH AND WRITING

## J. YeVette McWhorter

Texas Woman's University

## Abstract

*This study chronicled graduate students' research and writing as they participated in a Research Exploration Project. This description provides glimpses of students' procedures as they selected and narrowed topics, searched databases, read and charted research articles, and participated in weekly writing groups. Responses to open-ended questionnaires throughout an eleven week period are utilized to help identify potential problem areas for students engaged in writing syntheses. Instructional implications are addressed.*

College students are often engaged in incorporating facts and concepts from a multitude of sources into their own prose (Bridgeman & Carlson, 1985). Reasons for the proliferation of research papers, literature reviews, and other forms of synthesizing and summarizing on the college level include the idea that writing improves thinking (Angeletti, 1991; Tierney, Soter, O'Flahavan, & McGinley, 1989), aids in retention (Speaker & Grubaugh, 1992), and improves metacognitive skills (Murnane, 1990). These traits are especially important for graduate students as they prepare to produce research papers, literature reviews, and theses. Although the reasons for requiring such products are fairly straightforward, there is still much to learn about how college students, especially those on the graduate level, work their way through thinking, reading, and writing as they examine a specific topic (Tierney et al., 1989) and produce an original written product based on multiple sources.

Research investigating students' writing from sources has given some insights to students' processing. For example, Spivey and King (1989) concluded writers use repetition in content of the original sources to aid in their construction of a new meaning. Students may also rely heavily on original source material for their own organization (Nash, Schumacher, & Carlson, 1993). Consequently, similarities among source materials influence the quality of the final written product.

Other influences on students' writing from sources are task perceptions, difficulty of source texts, students' willingness to consider multiple perspectives, and students' prior knowledge (Many, Fyfe, Lewis, & Mitchell, 1996). In addition, students need complex strategies because the ability to produce text is a learned skill that encompasses a great many restrictions (Flower & Hayes, 1984).

It also appears that when students are writing from sources, they do not proceed in a sequential order through prereading, reading, postreading, prewriting, and writing. Although all students tend to refer to sources during their composing, they do so at different points (Kennedy, 1985). Students also display wide differences in strategies they use for locating and gathering information (Nelson & Hayes, 1988).

Furthermore, Flower and Hayes (1984) suggested experts tend to represent knowledge differently than novices. Thus, graduate students are trying to use semantics and technical vocabulary like experts, as well as reporting important actions and details and making appropriate inferences for other professionals (Flower & Hayes, 1984). As a result, graduate students find they need new skills to help them successfully engage in reading and writing academic texts.

The overall purpose of this endeavor was to describe graduate students' research and writing processes as they participated in an authentic writing task. A major objective of the study followed students' processes as they selected and narrowed topics, searched databases, read and charted research articles, and participated in a writing workshop involving composing, sharing, and revising drafts. Students focused on the research designs and general findings of the studies they reviewed.

## The Research Exploration Project

The Research Exploration project was conceived as a way to encourage graduate students to become critical consumers of research and to aid in their technical writing. Students investigated topics across several research studies and theoretical pieces looking for similarities, differences, strengths, and weaknesses and then composed a synthesis. The project was based on concepts Nelson and Hayes (1988) detailed to encourage students to use high investment strategies such as taking a personal interest in a topic, starting work well in advance, making multiple searches for information, using an issue-driven approach to research, using notes to stimulate thoughts, writing exploratory drafts, and using conceptually global revisions as they produce research papers.

The Research Exploration Project was also based on ideas posed by Stotsky (1991) in her work on research processes. According to Stotsky, the focus of writing from sources may depend on how much information is gathered in an initial search and how students evaluate and organized their final notes. Moreover, awareness may take place during the search process rather than during the composing stage when students are engaged in academic reading and writing. Revisions and refining then occur during drafting.

The Research Exploration Project served as a tool to encourage students to use high investment strategies to guide their research and writing processes and to aid in organizing and synthesizing complex data on research design from research articles. The project involved several steps. First, students selected, and more importantly, narrowed a topic. Second, they used databases to locate at least seven research articles appropriate for their topic. Due to the limited number of articles used, students were repeatedly reminded of the dangers of making incomplete conclusions about their topic of interest. Third, they charted information from the articles, including research questions, definitions, subjects, methodologies, analyses, findings, and areas for future research. Fourth, charts were examined for patterns of similarities, discrepancies, strengths, and weaknesses in the body of research examined. Fifth, students' used their charts to write syntheses based on the aspects of design which they examined. Students were then encouraged to look across studies at key words and concepts, identify patterns, and write a paper that synthesized subject selection processes in their research articles. Sixth, students shared their writing by bringing rough drafts to class, talking through their writing and revising, and making comments on other students' written drafts. This occurred in small groups that met weekly for 30-45 minutes during the last portion of class. Finally, students prepared a formal presentations highlighting their findings.

## Context and Design

Ten students enrolled in a masters' level reading research course participated in the project. Most of the students were veteran classroom teachers, and all had some experience teaching. Students were at various stages in their coursework. Nine students were working on their Masters of Education degree and one student was working on her elementary teaching certification. One student had taken a required Research in Education course which emphasized design and methodology, and one student had taken an advanced statistics course. The majority of students' coursework in reading had been taught from a practitioner's point of view. For many, this was the first opportunity to get a real picture of the quantity and quality of research available on various topics of interest.

The students were generally uncomfortable with the idea of working with research articles as the course began. Consequently, participants were also uneasy with the task of writing a synthesis based on several research articles. Most students had more practice writing summaries of individual articles than synthesizing groups of articles. In addition, they were more familiar with "how to" articles that dealt with ideas for classroom instruction than with research articles.

One of the goals of the Reading Research course was to help students become critical consumers of research. The Research Exploration project was the tool for inviting students to delve into the pool of research studies on a topic of their choice and write a synthesis. General information covered in the course involved how to read a journal article, differences between qualitative and quantitative research, terms associated with design and methodology for each paradigm, possible confounds or problem areas for empirical research studies, internal and external validity issues, and the differences between writing a summary and a synthesis. Additionally, literacy-related topics such as whole language instruction, phonemic awareness, assessment, content reading instruction, literacy and special populations were interwoven throughout the semester. Course readings were reflective of these topics. The general text was *What Research Has to Say About Reading Instruction* (2nd ed.) (Samuels and Farstrup, 1992). Readings from refereed journals in the fields of reading, educational psychology, and education were also included.

In addition to assigned readings and subsequent class discussion, students participated in the Research Exploration Project. Students shared topic choices, database experiences, and finally their charts and drafts. At assigned points in the semester, students brought their charts and drafts to class. As students talked about their charts, they pointed out key words, ambiguities, similarities, and differences they saw among studies, as well as interesting findings. As a result, problem areas that were unclear or ill-defined were tackled by the group. Clarification from the instructor was given when necessary. As drafts were composed, students talked through their syntheses, while their group members helped with clarity, coherence, word choice, and conventions such as punctuation, sentence structure, and usage.

As the semester progressed, students also responded to open-ended questionnaires (see Appendix) at three points. In order to encourage students to be forthcoming, comments were submitted without students' names and transcribed by a paid transcriber.

# Discussion

Based on questionnaire responses it appears students were able to reflect on their actions during planning, selecting sources, charting pertinent information, and writing/revising drafts. Students also shared insights into the world of databases and web sites. Students were open to discussing their progress within a small group setting and appreciated the opportunity to troubleshoot and refine their products.

The following discussion is based on students' responses to various aspects of their project. A brief overview is given based on student responses to the three questionnaires. Then illustrative tables are provided with samples of students' actual comments.

## Selecting and Narrowing Topics and Using Databases

For the most part, students depended on initial database searches to help narrow topics. Abstracts or descriptors following the abstract were used as first screening devices. Based on participants' comments, the use of databases was particularly frustrating. Students' initial and subsequent attempts to use databases sometimes led to topic changes (see Table 1).

## Table 1. Students' Comments on Selecting and Narrowing Topics

*Advice for students who need to narrow their topics:*
1. Try to answer just one specific question about the topic of interest.
2. Look at the descriptors that are being used for references coming up on the screen.
3. Use the ERIC thesaurus and descriptors for new ideas. Look at references cited in back of other resources for ideas.

Problem areas for students as they utilized databases included knowing what database to use, finding the right combination of descriptors, finding time to peruse entries, and in some cases, learning how to use computer databases efficiently and effectively. One student discussed the need to "develop a 'sense' of playing with descriptors" until an appropriate source was identified. Although a session with a reference librarian was conducted during one class period, students felt they needed more assistance during the actual search process.

## Reading and Charting Articles

After students located their articles, they proceeded with the task of charting the information. Students identified the following problem areas: (a) sifting out statistical information, (b) knowing how much or how little to write, (c) finding time to read and chart, and (d) determining what type of format to use. Students had the most difficulty creating charts about data collection and general findings (see Table 2).

**Table 2. Students' Comments and Advice Given About Using Databases**

*Experience of searching databases:*

1. To be as current as possible with my first topic, I attempted to use First Search. When I didn't have any luck with that, I tried ERIC. I still wasn't getting much. On another occasion, I tried many different combinations on ERIC and still wasn't getting much. I did notice that what I was getting was somewhat related to what I wanted to explore, so I revised my topic.

2. ERIC wasn't too bad. My topic was rather limited for articles. After this class, I used the thesaurus key, this opened more doors for me—I found more articles. Locating wasn't difficult. Knowing what to use was difficult (appropriate or not)

3. At first it was frustrating because I didn't know that much about it. The librarians were very helpful. Had I been familiar with how to use ERIC and helpful things like using Thesaurus on ERIC to narrow and fine tune my search, I could have saved a lot of time. I am now familiar with ERIC and feel comfortable using it. Got sidetracked in the stacks and ended up pulling a big stack of articles not on my topic—kind of fun.

4. Using the databases was no problem as I have quite a bit of experience with this. However, finding the actual journals was sometimes frustrating.

*Advice for students trying to negotiate databases:*

1. Be realistic. You may spend hours finding an appropriate article. When one good article is found, check the references to find more articles. While using ERIC, do not be afraid to ask questions.

2. Be patient.

3. Give yourself plenty of time to explore.

4. Practice. Ask for help. Practice. Narrow your topic. Practice. Don't give up.

5. Plan on spending time learning how to retrieve the information. I believe many people, or at least some, used articles because they were expedient.

---

Only one student made reference to looking up information in a text on research design, and she was disappointed because it was not particularly helpful. However, students asked few questions about statistics or qualitative procedures in class discussions. This may be because they were asked to write about data collection and not data analyses. In addition, once a format for charting was chosen (i.e. type or write, color code, horizontal/vertical) few students modified their method. Only one student voiced her difficulty with charting and opted to use notecards throughout the course. Her insight into her own processing was illuminating:

I think the reason for charting is to get information into workable blocks so it is not so intimidating. My procedure of using notecards (back to Stone Age research) is simplest because they can be manipulated into patterns. AHA—that's been the problem—when I tried to chart on a folder, couldn't rearrange in meaningful way.

Others may have experienced difficulty with charting but used the procedure either because they had seen photos of other students' charts or because their assignment was presented as a chart.

After students had the majority of their articles charted, they were questioned about the process (see Table 3). All participants who had charted felt they were better organized and were getting more adept at extracting important information. In addition, they perceived charting as a way to help them understand the research articles. Although they found charting useful, students were concerned about the time involved and apprehensive about how it would all fit together when they wrote their synthesis. For example, one student was already looking ahead to the final product required for the master's degree: "The charts are a good way to complete this assignment since I already know the divisions in the paper that are required. Still, doing a paper and manipulating 75 sources will be very involved."

### *Writing Process and Research Groups*

The second set of questions asked students to explain how they wrote a paper. Not surprisingly, each detailed a recursive process approach to writing. Although students had charted their information, once they were ready to write, they usually imposed more structure on their initial charts.

The majority of students reported writing two drafts; however, lines between drafts may not be clear because of the ability to constantly revise at the computer. Students reported in the questionnaire that they revised their hard copies once after sharing in their small groups. However, most made references to revising while they composed. Students' revisions after meeting with their groups were often surface level (i.e. usage issues such as when to use affect and effect), to resolve ambiguities, or to add information.

Students appeared to like the structure imposed by the requirement of writing drafts in weekly increments, although it was an intrusion into some students' style of writing. At the conclusion of this project, most participants felt they were able to read more critically, to look for "common threads," and to better understand the design elements of research articles (see Table 4). Informal comments during class discussions echoed their new found skills—students were able to articulate the strengths and weaknesses of articles. They became irritated with writers who did not give enough or clear information.

## Table 3. Students' Comments about Charting Articles

*Difficult aspects:*
1. Finding the time to adequately do it was the most difficult aspect; especially sifting out statistical information in ways that I could comprehend.
2. Knowing how much or little to write. What is relevant data and what is extra.

*Easy aspects:*
1. Having specific categories to concentrate on helped keep the tasks manageable.
2. I felt organized.

*Advice to others:*
1. Do two readings of the article before you begin charting so that you can be as brief as possible, but complete.
2. Organize it in a way that is meaningful to them making retrieval easy and efficient.
3. Analyze how you already do research and what has been suggested and see how to fit two together. Become familiar with article first—Don't just look for topics—mark article and make notes in margin or will not be able to find info. again—It gets easier.

*Feelings about process:*
1. I feel that it is going to be so much easier to write and understand the paper.
2. Relief . . . It is very time consuming, but I think I was able to extract the necessary information at a quicker rate after I had done a few. As I was charting, though, I kept thinking about whether or not I had the right articles . . . hoping I was on the right track.
3. The process takes time, however, charting helped me to better understand the readings.

*Explanation of process:*
1. Don't be intimidated. It's a valuable organizational tool. I'd show her several examples and tell her to choose a format she's comfortable with. Read the article through once, then start charting.
2. It's time consuming. The organizational procedure will be helpful in writing longer papers. Basically, the topic is limited through notes.

*Advice to others:*
1. Think about how you organize your thoughts. Color coded, pictures, key words, vertically design your chart for you.
2. Better to record more, I found I had to go back to my articles more often.
3. Look at what other people do, but know your own style of thinking.

**Table 4. Students' Comments about Being Research Consumers**

*View of self:*

1. Better prepared. The charting really gives me a way to "see" things clearly.
2. As more knowledgeable, more critical when reading articles, more aware of always looking for "common threads" on the topic when reading articles. Probably more organized, too, feeling more "research friendly".
3. I feel as though I am reading the info. in research articles more critically. I am more attuned to looking for patterns. I think I have a better understanding, overall, of what a research article should look like and some things to look for.

## Instructional Implications

Although this project is limited by the small number of participants and the use of self-report data, it does reveal some interesting insights into this group's efforts to produce a piece of writing based on multiple sources. Graduate students' attempts at writing about research are often frustrating because they may still be unfamiliar with the format and formality of research articles. In addition, they are still honing their own academic writing and research skills. Instructors may also assume students have all the necessary tools for academic writing and not provide an adequate instructional framework to help students with the process.

In an effort to demystify research and to help graduate students become critical consumers, the Research Exploration Project was constructed. Time was allotted for students to share and receive feedback from an audience during their information gathering and drafting. For many, this was a new approach to research and writing. Participants' willingness to share their problem solving as they encountered topics, databases, and research articles, as well as their efforts at drafting, revising, and polishing give insights to those who teach this population.

Students' comments should give pause to those who work with graduate students as they prepare written products. It is definitely worthwhile to use class time for students to discuss procedures and share drafts. Although a rather large portion of class time was set aside in this particular setting, smaller time increments may also aid graduate students as they work through the process of academic writing. A balance between process and procedures (Many et al., 1996) is needed in these advanced instructional settings. In addition, it is imperative that the entire process from idea to database to drafting to polishing, receive some attention through modeling and sharing examples. In this particular project, students were shown sample charts but were not allowed to read sample papers. In hindsight, sample paragraphs on the overhead would have been helpful. Several students voiced the need for more guidance, and while sharing entire papers would not be appropriate, sample passages would demonstrate how to put everything together as well as how to cite sources.

Encouraging students to brush up on their library and information retrieval skills is also important. Avenues for accessing information are constantly changing. Students need to be aware of full text options, how to obtain information on the World Wide Web, and updates on campus library computer systems.

Although the Research Exploration Project was a successful experience for students, it is only one way to organize information. One interesting drawback to using the system was that some students were so caught up in creating their charts that they almost forgot their sole purpose: to view several studies at one time in order to help them more easily construct a synthesis.

It is not possible to give students a formula for academic writing and the research that must accompany the task. However, the process can be supported by the Research Exploration Project or any method that helps students see how to organize information across several studies to establish key terminology, patterns, and inconsistencies.

## References

Angeletti, S. R. (1991). Encouraging students to think about what they have read. *The Reading Teacher, 45,* 288-296.

Bridgeman, B., & Carlson, S. B. (1984). Survey of academic writing tasks. *Written Communication, 1*(2), 247-280.

Carson, J. G. (1993). *A model of faculty collaboration: Focus on academic literacy.* Washington, DC: Fund for the Improvement of Postsecondary Education, Washington, DC, (ERIC Document Reproduction Service No. ED 366 261.)

Flower, L., & Hayes, J. R. (1984). Images, plans, and prose: The representation of meaning in writing. *Written Communication, 1,* 120-160.

Kennedy, M. L. (1985). The composing processes of college students writing from sources. *Written Communication 2,* 434-456.

Many, J. E., Fyfe, R., Lewis, G., & Mitchell, G. (1996). Traversing the topical landscape: Exploring students' self-directed reading-writing-research processes. *Reading Research Quarterly, 31,* 12-35.

Murnane, Y. (1990). Writing as a thinking tool: How writing can foster metacognition. In B. Anderson (Ed.), *Teacher education for literacy around the world* (pp. 61-64). St. Cloud, MN: Organization of Teacher Education in Reading.

Nash, J. G., Schumacher, G. M., & Carlson, B. W. (1993). Writing from sources: A structure-mapping model. *Journal of Educational Psychology, 85,* 159-70.

Nelson, J., & Hayes, J.R. (1988). *How the writing context shapes college students' strategies for writing from sources* (Technical Report No. 16). Berkeley, CA: Center for the Study of Writing.

Samuels, S. J., & Farstrup, A. E. (Eds.) (1992). *What research has to say about reading instruction* (2nd ed.). Newark, DE: International Reading Association.

Speaker, R. B., Jr., & Grubaugh, S. J. (1992). The development of memory for writing: Examining cloze performance and meaning changes at four grade levels. *Reading Research and Instruction, 31*(3), 64-73.

Spivey, N.N., & King, J.R. (1989). Readers as writers composing from sources. *Reading Research Quarterly, 24*(1), 7-26.

Stotsky, S. (1991). On developing independent critical thinking: What can we learn from studies of research process. *Written Communication 8,* 193-212.

Tierney, R. J., Soter, A., O'Flahavan, J. F., & McGinley, W. (1989). The effects of reading and writing upon thinking critically. *Reading Research Quarterly, 24*(2), 134-173.

## Appendix: Questionnaires
*First Set of Questions (after charing majority of articles)*
1. What was the most difficult aspect of charting your first article?
2. What was the easiest aspect of charting your first article?
3. How did you decide which article to tackle first?
4. How did you proceed as you charted? In other words, what did you do first, second?
5. If you were going to tell someone how to chart an article, what advice would you give?
6. Now that you have had an opportunity to see someone else's chart, what will you do differently (if anything)?
7. Try to describe your experience as you searched databases for articles to use.
8. How did you determine if an article was appropriate?
9. Describe your procedure for writing a research paper.

*Second Set of Questions (after first draft of paper)*
1. Now that you have the majority of your articles charted, how do you feel about the process?
2. If you were explaining your procedure for charting to a classmate, what would you say?
3. Have you noticed any patterns in your articles?
4. Have you started thinking about what you will be writing on the basis of your chart? If so, what?
5. Are you still searching for articles at this time? If you are, how do you plan on proceeding at this point?
6. At this stage, how do you see yourself as a "consumer of research"?

*Third Set of Questions (end of project)*
1. After meeting with your classmates about subjects, what revisions did you make and why?
2. When you began to write your second section, was it more difficult or easy? Why?
3. How do you feel about your progress? Why?
4. Are your charts working for you? Why?
5. When you are writing a section, how do you begin?
6. How many drafts did you write for this last section?
7. How do you know when you are finished with a section of your paper?
8. What advice do you have for students who are trying to negotiate databases?
9. What advice do you have for students who need to narrow their topics?
10. What are some other ways students could organize their information besides charting?
11. What advice do you have for students who are trying to write similar products?

# STORYBOOK READING IN EVEN START FAMILIES

Nancy D. Padak
Timothy V. Rasinski
Jennifer A. Fike

Kent State University

## Abstract

*Because parent-child read-aloud sessions have long been recommended as an effective means of introducing children to literacy, family literacy participants are typically encouraged to read frequently at home, both parent reading to child and child reading to parent. Yet research suggests that how parents and children interact while reading may be as important as if they read together. This study describes storybook reading sessions among parents and children in Even Start family literacy programs. Data were gathered by trained observers using instruments that focused on apparent interest, reading behaviors, and the nature of parent-child interactions, including parents' responses to children's reading errors. Results provide a fairly detailed description of parents' and children's behaviors during these storybook sessions, a description that has curricular implications for family literacy programs.*

Parent-child read aloud has long been recommended as effective means of introducing children to literacy. Research from the 1970s, 1980s, and 1990s (e.g., Chomsky, 1976; Dickinson, 1994; Snow, 1983; Teale & Sulzby, 1986) consistently identified strong relationships between parent-child reading in the home and children's later literacy achievement. Indeed, a recent meta-analysis of studies related to parent-preschool child reading (Bus, van IJzendoorn, & Pelligrini, 1995) supports the hypothesis that parent-child book reading positively affects acquisition of the written language register, which in turn enables learning to read.

Given this longstanding emphasis on the benefits of parent-child storybook reading, it is not surprising that family literacy programs to support low-literate parents and their children typically encourage reading aloud. In commenting on the value of helping parents learn how to interact with children while reading and making books available for families, Darling and Paull (1994) conclude that "[i]t is good to know, that in a world characterized by complexity and ambiguity, this simple, direct approach can be effective in encouraging and enabling parents to share the gift of literacy with their children" (p. 277).

Several family literacy researchers contend, however, that this "simple, direct approach" may not be so simple. Edwards (1989, 1994), for example, found many parents eager to support children by reading aloud but unsure of how to do so. Likewise, Krol-Sinclair (1996) showed how parent participants in family literacy programs benefited from learning how to interact while reading to their children.

Moreover, the nature of what transpires during parent-child reading appears to matter a great deal, perhaps more than the mere fact that parents and children read together (Mikulecky, 1995). Among the storybook reading activities found to influence young children's literacy achievement are rereading favorite books and stories (Harlin, 1984), discussions about books and stories (Harlin, 1984; Lancey & Bergin, 1992), asking questions about and encouraging connections to children's experiences (Beals, De Temple, & Dickinson, 1994), and keeping the reading atmosphere light and "fun" (Lancey & Bergin, 1992). Merely advocating that parents read to their children, then, is not sufficient. Family literacy educators need to show parents how to read to their children and support their efforts at doing so.

Such activity will be most successful if it is based on parents' typical behaviors. Unfortunately, little descriptive research documents how low-literate parents and their children interact during storybook reading sessions. The study reported here is a first attempt at providing these baseline data. As part of a larger evaluation of several Even Start (ES) programs, we conducted observational studies of ES parents and children reading to one another in order to determine typical parent and child behaviors during reading.

## Method

Even Start (ES) programs are intended to "improve educational opportunities of the Nation's children and adults by integrating early childhood education and adult education for parents into a unified program" (PL 100-297, Sec. 1051). Parents and children participate in ES as family units. In general, families qualify when a) parent(s) are eligible for adult basic education (i.e., they lack a high school diploma or equivalent academic skills) or are in high school and b) children are younger than age eight. The goals of ES are to a) help parents become full partners in the education of their children, b) assist children in reaching their full potential as learners, and c) provide basic education and literacy training for parents.

## Sites and Participants

All data for this study were gathered from families participating in ES programs in Northeast Ohio. One program, in existence for four years, is in a first-ring suburb of a large metropolitan city. Another, a second-year program, is located in a medium-sized city. The other two, one a third-year program and the other a first-year program, are situated in small city/ rural areas. Thus, the participant pool for the study reflects considerable geographical diversity.

Because of the large turnover rate in ES programs and because of the exploratory nature of the study, we made no attempt to conduct separate analyses for the four programs or to locate and follow families from one year of ES participation to the next. Instead data from all family storybook reading sessions in all four programs over all years of program operation were pooled. All together, the data set for the study includes 288 storybook reading sessions when parents read and children listened and 269 storybook reading sessions when children read (or pretended to read) and parents listened. Nearly all of the children were preschoolers; a few were enrolled in grades K-2.

## Data Collection and Analysis

As part of the evaluation protocols for these ES programs, parents and children read to each other at least annually in the presence of trained observers. These storybook reading sessions typically took place in families' homes; parents and children were free to select any book to read.

Two adaptations of an instrument developed by Lancey and Bergin (1992) were used to record storybook reading behaviors (see Figures 1 and 2). During the storybook reading session, the observer tallied the number and nature of parent-child interactions. When children read (see Figure 2), the observer also tallied parents' responses to children's errors. After the storybook reading sessions, the observer holistically rated several other aspects of the sessions, such as interest and reading ability, by marking points on continua.

Observers were employees of the ES programs who were well known to both parents and children. Families' familiarity with observers and free choice of books to read enhance the validity of findings, as does the location of the storybook reading sessions in families' homes.

Observer training consisted of explaining and defining the constructs represented on the instruments and providing guided practice. In addition, we answered questions and offered informal support when asked.

Despite the use of common instruments and the training offered observers, some error in the data is likely. Raters' understandings of the constructs might have differed, for example; two raters might have drawn different holistic

**Figure 1. Parent-Child Reading Observation (Parent Reads).**

Family _____ Date _____

Book Read _____

Observed by _____

| *Parent:* | always | sometimes | never |
|---|---|---|---|
| reads fluently w/expression | ├————————————————┤ | | |
| encourages child's involvement | ├————————————————┤ | | |
| | high | average | low |
| parent's interest | ├————————————————┤ | | |
| child's interest | ├————————————————┤ | | |

*Parent-child interactions focus on (tally):*

| | |
|---|---|
| words | _____ |
| story (literal) | _____ |
| story (nonliteral) | _____ |
| child's experiences | _____ |
| emotions | _____ |

Adapted from Lancy, D., & Bergen, C. (April, 1992). *The role of parents in supporting beginning reading.* Paper presented at the meeting of the American Educational Research Association, San Francisco.

conclusions about aspects of a storybook reading session. A conservative choice for data analysis is one way to diminish the impact of error. Consequently only percentages were calculated to analyze data resulting from the storybook observations, as opposed to statistical tests. We used visual inspection of marks on continua to assign responses to categories (e.g., "always," "sometimes," "never").

## Results

A summary of observations recorded while parents read storybooks is provided in Table 1. As can be seen, low-literate parents typically chose books to read to their children that they could read fluently. More than half of the storybook sessions were "always" characterized by the observer as fluent reading; another third were "sometimes" fluent. Moreover, low-literate parents and their children maintained a very high degree of interest in storybook reading sessions (80%- parents; 78%- children).

More than half (58%) of the observed parents "always" encouraged their

## Figure 2. Parent-Child Reading Observation (Child Reads).

Family _____ Child _____

Date _____ Book Read _____

Observed by _____

| *Child:* | always | sometimes | never |
|---|---|---|---|
| reads fluently w/expression | ├───────────────────┤ | | |
| handles book properly | ├───────────────────┤ | | |
| "reads" pictures | ├───────────────────┤ | | |
| reads print | ├───────────────────┤ | | |

*Parent-child interactions focus on (tally):*

words _____

story (literal) _____

story (nonliteral) _____

child's experiences _____

emotions _____

*Parent error correction (tally):*

says "no;" asks child to repeat _____

asks child to sound out _____

helps child to sound out _____

asks child to focus on meaning _____

tells child word _____

Adapted from Lancy, D., & Bergen, C. (April, 1992). *The role of parents in supporting beginning reading.* Paper presented at the meeting of the American Educational Research Association, San Francisco.

children to respond to the storybook reading. The nature of these parent-child interactions was primarily at a literal level: 33% of the interactions focused on single words and another 21% on literal information from the stories.

A summary of observations recorded while children read storybooks is provided in Table 2. An assessment of children's reading behaviors, such as whether they "read" pictures or read print, reveals that as a group, children were still developing into readers. Only 8% of the children "always" read print. The children's book handling abilities were well developed.

Parent-child interactions while children read were balanced among a focus on words, literal information, the child's experiences, and the child's

**Table 1. Parents Read to Children**

|  | Always | Sometimes | Never |
|---|---|---|---|
| Parent reads fluently with expression (N=282) | 175 (62%) | 91 (32%) | 16 (6%) |
| Parent encourages child's response (N=288) | 168 (58%) | 83 (29%) | 37 (13%) |
|  | High | Average | Low |
| Parent's interest (N=137) | 109 (80%) | 22 (16%) | 6 (4%) |
| Child's interest (N=145) | 113 (78%) | 27 (19%) | 5 (3%) |

**Focus of Parent-Child interactions (N=288)**

| words | 33% | child's experiences | 15% |
|---|---|---|---|
| story (literal) | 21% | emotions | 20% |
| story (nonliteral) | 14% | | |

**Table 2. Children Read to Parents**

| Children | Always | Sometimes | Never/NA |
|---|---|---|---|
| Reads fluently with expression (N=197) | 28 (14%) | 60 (30%) | 109 (55%) |
| Handles book properly (N=276) | 199 (72%) | 50 (18%) | 27 (10%) |
| "Reads" pictures (N=184) | 126 (68%) | 38 (21%) | 20 (11%) |
| Reads print (N=259) | 22 (8%) | 44 (17%) | 193 (75%) |

**Focus of parent-child interactions (N=269)**

| words | 24% | child's experiences | 19% |
|---|---|---|---|
| story (literal) | 20% | emotions | 20% |
| story (non-literal) | 16% | | |

**Parent error correction**

| Says "no;" asks child to repeat | 13% |
|---|---|
| Asks child to sound out | 11% |
| Helps child to sound out | 27% |
| Asks child to focus on meaning | 17% |
| Tells child word | 32% |

emotions. When compared to interactions while parents read, there was less focus on words (33% vs. 24%) and slightly more focus on children's experiences (15% vs. 19%).

Low-literate parents employed several correction strategies while their children read. Most often, they prompted some kind of phonic analysis, either by helping the child to sound a word out (27%) or asking the child to sound a word out (11%). Another frequent response to a child's error was simply to provide the word (32%).

## Discussion

The results of this study offer a portrait of how low-literate parents and their children behave during storybook reading sessions. Most aspects of the portrait are quite positive. Parent-child storybook interactions can be characterized as informal, informative, interactive, and enjoyable. All this provides a firm foundation upon which to continue fostering children's developing knowledge about reading and parents' expertise in scaffolding their children's literacy learning.

Results of the study also point to at least two areas, types of interactions and error correction strategies, where parents' choices during interactions with their children might need further development. Fortunately, both these areas could easily become topics for study in family literacy programs. Results of this study suggest that they should be.

Parents frequently interacted with their children while reading, which most literacy educators would view as desirable. However, these interactions tended to focus on surface-level information (individual words or literal information) from stories, especially when parents read to their children. Thus, low-literate parents may benefit from exploring the value of inferential or predictive responses to reading and from learning ways to encourage nonliteral response among their children.

Literature circles or "book clubs" could be established in family literacy programs as a way to achieve both aims. Several family literacy programs have documented success with this model. For example, one component of the Beginning with Books project in Pittsburgh (Segel, 1994) is a parent Read-Aloud Club, in which parents read and discuss children's literature, share ways to read aloud effectively, and brainstorm ideas for encouraging children's response to the literature.

Handel and Goldsmith's (1988, 1994) Family Reading Workshop has similar emphases:

> The family reading workshop series uses children's literature to promote reading development and integrates practice of all reading strategies into demonstrations and discussions of the books. . . . The informal sessions

not only provide familiarity with a wealth of good children's books, but are often the first occasion for participants to share and discuss books in a nonjudgmental setting. Throughout the workshop experience participants are invited to construct meaning and to encourage their children to do the same. (Handel & Goldsmith, 1994, p. 153)

As part of their workshop experiences, parents in this program also keep track of questions they might ask their children during and after storybook reading sessions.

In a project to help parents learn to read aloud in children's school classrooms, Krol-Sinclair (1996) detected a great deal of transfer to home reading situations. That is, parents used what they had learned about school reading situations in the home setting as well and consequently demonstrated more sophisticated interactions with their children at the end of the study. Thus, parental learning about reading to and with their children in one context is likely to generalize to other contexts.

All three of these models feature common aspects. Each involves reading and discussing children's literature. Each also includes attention to sharing or modeling response possibilities. And as part of each model, parents have opportunities to explore the nature of the reading process, for example, to learn why it's good to invite nonliteral/inferential response to literature. As such, instruction based on models like these may help low-literate parents learn the value of nonliteral/inferential response and ways to interact with their children around nonliteral/inferential issues.

Parents' error correction strategies are the second aspect of their interactions with children that may need further support from literacy professionals. Although the children in this study were, as a group, not independent readers, their parents most often encouraged phonic resolutions to problems children encountered. This suggests that low-literate parents may benefit from learning about the nature of emergent literacy and, perhaps, about options for helping young readers solve problems. With regard to the latter, the best advice for parents listening to young children read is probably to tell them the words they need, and, if they so choose, return to unknown words at the end of the session.

This advice, of course, is based on understandings about young children's development into reading, which itself could be a curricular focus in family literacy programs. Through reading, observation, and discussion, parents can learn that becoming literate is a natural and developmental process. They can also learn about ways to support their children's early attempts at reading.

Early childhood educators recommend parent-child reading as a way to foster children's literacy development. Adult educators also see potential for growth for low-literate parents in storybook reading sessions (e.g., Dickinson,

1994). For these benefits to be realized, however, parents need more than just admonitions to read to their children. They need knowledge of the reading process and early literacy development. They also need to understand their options when reading to and with their children. Parents can learn about the value of different types of interactions and discussions during storybook reading, for example. Addressing these issues can and perhaps should become curricular goals in family literacy programs.

In this study we attempted to describe the nature of parent-child read alouds in Even Start families. We found that the low-literate parents we observed responded positively to the information they received in their programs regarding reading with their children. Moreover, we found that the level and type of parent-child interaction during reading should lead to children's further development in literacy. These findings are encouraging and should be viewed as a call for further research, especially research that addresses the impact of parent education, and for more family literacy initiatives.

---

# References

Beals, D., De Temple, J., & Dickinson, D. (1994). Talking and listening that support early literacy development of children from low-income families. In D. Dickinson (Ed.), *Bridges to literacy: Children, families, and schools* (pp. 19-40). Cambridge, MA: Blackwell.

Bus, A., van IJzendoorn, M., & Pelligrini, A. (1995). Joint book reading makes for success in learning: A meta-analysis of intergenerational transmission of literacy. *Review of Educational Research, 65,* 1-21.

Chomsky, C. (1976). Creativity and innovation in child language. *Journal of Education, 158,* 21-24.

Darling, S., & Paull, S. (1994). Implications for family literacy programs. In D. Dickinson (Ed.), *Bridges to literacy: Children, families, and schools* (pp. 273-284). Cambridge, MA: Blackwell.

Dickinson, D. (Ed.). (1994). *Bridges to literacy: Children, families, and schools.* Cambridge, MA: Blackwell.

Edwards, P. (1989). Supporting lower SES mothers' attempts to provide scaffolding for book reading. In J. Allen & J. Mason (Eds.), *Risk makers, risk takers, risk breakers: Reducing the risks for young literacy learners* (pp. 222-250). Portsmouth, NH: Heinemann.

Edwards, P. (1994).Responses of teachers and African- American mothers to a book-reading intervention program. In D. Dickinson (Ed.), *Bridges to literacy: Children, families, and schools* (pp. 175-208). Cambridge, MA: Blackwell.

Handel, R., & Goldsmith, E. (1988). Intergenerational literacy: A community college project. *Journal of Reading, 32,* 250-256.

Handel, R., & Goldsmith, E. (1994). Family reading—still got it: Adults as learners, literacy resources, and actors in the world. In D. Dickinson (Ed.), *Bridges to literacy: Children, families, and schools* (pp. 150-174). Cambridge, MA: Blackwell.

Harlin, R. (1984). *Prereaders' story processing strategies.* ERIC Document Reproduction Service No. ED 254 834.

Krol-Sinclair, B. (1996). Connecting home and school literacies: Immigrant parents with limited formal education as classroom storybook readers. In D. Leu, C. Kinzer, & K. Hinchman (Eds.), *Literacies for the 21st century: Research and practice* (pp. 270-283). Chicago: National Reading Conference.

Lancey, D., & Bergin, C. (1992, April). *The role of parents in supporting beginning reading*. Paper presented at the meeting of the American Educational Research Association, San Francisco.

Mikulecky, L. (1995). Family literacy: Parent and child interactions. In *Family literacy: Directions in research and implications for practice* (pp. 55-56). Washington, DC: US Department of Education, Office of Educational Research and Improvement.

Segel, E. (1994). "I got to get him started out right": Promoting literacy by Beginning with Books. In D. Dickinson (Ed.), *Bridges to literacy: Children, families, and schools* (pp. 66-79). Cambridge, MA: Blackwell.

Snow, C. (1983). Literacy and language. Relationships during the preschool years. *Harvard Educational Review, 53*, 165-189.

Teale, W., & Sulzby, E. (Eds.). (1986). *Emergent literacy: Writing and reading.* Norwood, NJ: Ablex.

# Parents in a Family Literacy Program: Their Attitudes, Beliefs, and Behaviors Regarding Literacy Learning

## Patricia E. Linder

Texas A&M University-Commerce

## Abstract

*Perceptions of reading and writing affect the literacy learning of adults who attend literacy classes. This article reports part of a study of eleven low-income parents of varying reading levels who were enrolled in a family literacy program. By writing responses to structured prompts given in daily dialogue journals, these parents described their literacy attitudes, beliefs, and behaviors. Seventy-two percent of the parents enjoyed reading for information on topics of their interest. While eight of the parents engaged in writing activites only as necessary, both high-level and low-level readers enjoyed reflective writing. In general, these parents recognized that effective readers and writers use strategies and attach meaning to the act of reading and writing. Regardless of reading levels, preference and attitude toward reading and writing tended to influence the variety of materials participants read.*

Adult and family literacy programs strive to meet the learning needs of participants. However, understanding adult literacy learners may be impeded by long-standing perceptions, or misperceptions, of low-income adults who attend literacy classes. These include that program participants may not value literacy in the same ways as adults who are gainfully employed and/or not dependent on welfare; that literacy behaviors of welfare-dependent adults may be limited to simple functional reading and writing such as reading the mail and filling out forms; and that reading and writing to learn or for simple enjoyment may be rare or nonexistent literacy behaviors. This article describes one aspect of a larger study (Linder, 1996) of low-income parents in a family literacy program who wrote daily in dialogue journals with their adult education teacher. Analysis of the journal entries revealed how these parents felt about reading and writing, their perceptions of effective reading and writing behaviors, and their descriptions of their own literacy behaviors. The article concludes with a comparison of the parents' literacy attitudes, beliefs, and behaviors with those of adults in general. Further, it details some implications for planning effective adult and family literacy programs.

## Theoretical Framework

Adult and family literacy programs often are initiated with the hope of helping families rise out of poverty through raising literacy levels of economically dependent families (Brizius & Foster, 1993). Studies of low-income families indicate a variety of literacy levels, perceptions about literacy learning, and literacy behaviors that may be similar or dissimilar to families who are economically independent (Heath, 1983; Purcell-Gates, L'Allier, & Smith, 1995; Taylor & Dorsey-Gaines, 1988). However, assumptions that low-literacy levels account for economic dependence may not be addressing what families who depend on welfare need to rise out of poverty (Auerbach, 1995). Exploring how literacy perceptions of parents dependent on welfare are the same or different than economically independent adults may provide clues into how these families may be better served in effective literacy programs.

Attitudes toward reading and writing vary widely among adults. Adults may use literacy for functioning in the work place, in daily life, and in recreational activity. Smith (1990) found that most adults who like to read will read often and from a variety of materials such as books, newspapers, and magazines. However, adults who do not like to read tend to find other sources of information such as radio, television, friends, and co-workers (Smith, 1996). Adults with low literacy levels have been found to have misperceptions of reading and writing processes that affect how they approach literacy learning (Fagan, 1988).

## Purposes of the Study/Research Questions

The purpose of this study, therefore, was to explore the literacy attitudes and beliefs of parents in a family literacy program. Dialogue journals were used as a data source because dialoguing by writing informally in journals with a teacher/ expert has been found to be an effective way to promote literacy learning for students of all ages (Gambrell, 1985; Staton, 1987). Several studies document the effectiveness of dialogue journal writing in elementary, secondary, ESL, and college classrooms (Bean & Zulich, 1992; Bode, 1989; Hennings, 1992; Jones, 1988; Kreeft, Shuy, Staton, Reed & Morroy, 1984; Lee & Zuercher, 1993; Peyton & Staton, 1993). However, little has been documented regarding the use of dialogue journals with low-income and/or low-level reading adults in literacy classes (Linder, 1996). Research questions included:

1. What attitudes about reading and writing did these parents describe?
2. What did these parents perceive as good reading and writing?
3. What did they believe they needed to improve their own reading and writing?
4. How did they describe the nature of their daily literacy behaviors?

## The Study

A community outreach center in a small suburb in northeast Ohio served as the site for the family literacy program. Participants in the study were ten mothers and one grandmother of pre-school and school-aged children. The parents, who all received government assistance, enrolled voluntarily in the family literacy program and in the study. The ages of the participants ranged from 21 to 55 years. Most mothers were in their middle to late thirties. Six were African-American and five were Caucasian.

Classes in the family literacy program met four days per week through-out the school year. The program itself followed the Kenan Trust model program (National Center for Family Literacy, 1994) and had four compo-nents: Adult Education class; Early Childhood Education class; Parent & Child Interaction Time (PACT); and a Parent Education/Support class.

Dialogue journal writing was a daily activity in the adult education class. For the first 15 minutes of every class, the participants wrote in their jour-nals. They initiated their own freely chosen topics or responded to ques-tions or comments the teacher had written. Each day the teacher responded in writing to participants' entries. Confidentiality was strictly maintained and an informal letter writing format was used.

For the purposes of this study, approximate reading levels were derived from year-end *Tests of Adult Basic Education* (TABE) (CTB/McGraw-Hill, 1987) and *Comprehensive Adult Student Assessment System* (CASAS) (Life Skills/CASAS, 1989) scores. These tests were administered periodically and were required by the agency sponsoring the family literacy program. In this pro-gram, TABE scores were interpreted as academic grade equivalent scores while CASAS scores referred to levels of functional reading competence below approximately 6th grade equivalency. Table 1 shows the participants' read-ing levels. All names are pseudonyms.

Tina, Lisa, Maxine, and Molly had earned high school diplomas. For a variety of personal reasons, they entered the program in order to review their skills as their first step toward improving their lives for themselves and their children. In spite of having earned a high school diploma, Molly scored at the lowest reading level. All of the other participants expected to eventually earn a G.E.D. so they could apply for jobs and become independent of gov-ernment assistance.

**Table 1. Approximate Reading Levels of Parents**

| Level | Parent | TABE/GE Score[a] | CASAS/Level Score[b] |
|-------|--------|------------------|----------------------|
| High | Tina | 12.9 | |
| High | Lisa | 12.9 | |
| High | Maxine | 12.9 | |
| Mid | Judy | 10.6 | |
| Mid | Becky | 10.4 | |
| Mid | Janet | 9.0 | |
| Mid | Patsy | 8.2 | |
| Low | Holly | | Level D |
| Low | Sharon | | Level C |
| Low | Roxanne | | Level C |
| Low | Molly | | Level C |

[a]*grade equivalencies*   [b]*reading levels*

To elicit responses that would answer the questions regarding their own literacy perceptions and descriptions of their literacy behaviors, eight prompts were designed. On each of eight days, the parents responded to one of the prompts during their journal writing time. These responses were analyzed according to the constant comparative method (Glaser & Strauss, 1967; Strauss & Corbin, 1990).

## Results/Findings: Categories of Responses

Analysis of the journal entries provided a picture of how these parents viewed reading and writing. Quotations taken from written responses are recorded exactly as written to preserve the flavor of the parents' writing.

### How the Parents Felt About Reading and Writing

Several categories or reasons for reading and writing emerged from analysis of responses to Prompts 1 and 2, which addressed the parents' attitudes toward reading and writing:

Prompt 1: Why do you read? Do you like reading? Why or why not?

Prompt 2: Why do you write? Do you like writing? Why or why not?

One common reason given for both was to improve their skills as readers and writers. Roxanne, a low-level reader, wrote that she read to "be a better reader." She also reported that writing helped her become better at spelling. Tina, a high-level reader, on the other hand, said she read in order to "expand my mind."

Several participants wrote that reading and writing were activities they used for escape, for relaxation, and to relieve the tensions of daily life. Tina found reading as a way to "divert my mind from my problems." Judy, a mid-level reader, claimed she used writing "to let off steam." Sharon, a low-level reader, and Janet, a mid-level reader, found writing to be "something to do" to pass the time.

Two high-level readers claimed they read because reading had been modeled to them in their childhood. Tina wrote she had "been reading since I was a child." Lisa claimed, "There was always reading in my home."

Many parents wrote that they used reading and writing because of the utility of literacy. For example, 45% of the parents reported reading to get information. Roxanne wrote about reading "to keep up with what's going on in the world" and "to understand what other people have been going through." Lisa, who already had achieved a high literacy level, read "for learning" while Molly, a low-level reader, read "to find out things [you] can only get from reading."

Twenty-seven percent of the parents recognized the utility of communicating through writing. Judy used writing "to get my point across." In class Judy verbally reacted to issues and situations and used the opportunity of writing in the journal to explain her positions on several topics.

The parents had mixed responses to whether or not they liked reading and writing. Eighty-two percent, regardless of reading level, claimed they liked to read. Becky, a midlevel reader, wrote that she "live[d] to read." Indeed, she read several books and their sequels on her own after they had been read aloud in class. On class trips to the public library, she selected children's literature to read and did research on expository topics of her own interest. Perhaps assuming others liked reading as much as she did, Becky sat around the lunch table chatting about the latest book she had read.

Seventy-five percent of the mid-level and low-level readers said they liked writing occasionally or wrote only when they had a need. Roxanne wrote, "I wright [sic] when I have something to say." Becky, who "lived to read," said she would write "only if the subject is good."

Patsy, a mid-level reader, wrote some interesting responses regarding reading and writing: " I don't like to read" because "it takes a lot of time. I'm a slow reader." In addition, she liked to write "only when I have to" and explained that she wrote "short things like cards to bring happiness to people."

Maxine, a high-level reader who claimed to read voraciously, wrote twice that she did not like to write. "I can get my point across better in person," she wrote. Maxine attended only 11 of the 24 scheduled classes during the six-week study. Yet she wrote 11 journal responses during that period.

Three participants claimed they liked to write very much. Sharon, a low-level reader, wrote "I do it every chance I get at home." In another entry, she wrote, "I would rather write than talk." Sharon rarely volunteered oral responses to whole-group discussions during class. However she occupied much of her time writing in her journal and writing self-selected workbook assignments. She seemed comfortable working one-on-one with the teacher or with a peer. Two high level readers, Lisa and Tina, consistently read and wrote throughout all their classwork. Their journal entries were lengthy and detailed. Tina wrote that she used the "daily journal writing for material for my book." This book was discussed on at least five occasions in her journal. Lisa wrote she "craved reading when I was young and found writing activities." Lisa's journal entries showed that she appeared to use reading and writing for personal problem-solving as well as exploring new academic learning.

### What Good Readers and Writers Do

The participants revealed several beliefs about reading and writing when they responded to Prompts 3 and 4 which asked about their perceptions of good reading and writing:

Prompt 3: What do you think good readers do when they read?

Prompt 4: What do you think good writers do when they write?

Sixty-four percent recognized that good readers and writers use strategies. Holly, a low-level reader, thought good readers "look over the book before they start; pick out the words they don't know; ask lots of questions." Roxanne, another low-level reader, believed good readers "pick out the good points; read the back; get an idea what the book is about." Several parents believed good readers predict what will happen. A good reader "wonders, thinks a lot" Sharon wrote. Patsy believed a good reader would "put self in place of the story."

Three parents recognized that good readers have different purposes for reading. Maxine wrote good readers "read different things for different reasons," while Holly wrote that good readers "study lots of different things."

Fifty-five percent of the participants believed good readers read for enjoyment. Lisa wrote they "LOVE to read." Janet claimed good readers "enjoy it" and Tina acknowledged good readers "read with interest." Two low-level readers observed what the good readers in the class did. "They read lots of books," Holly reported. Sharon wrote, "They laugh alot *[sic]* when reading."

When asked about writing, 36% of the participants said they believed good writers use some pre-writing strategies. Sharon wrote that good writers "really think alot *[sic]* about what there *[sic]* going to write." Tina believed good writers "write their thoughts and organize them." Holly suggested good writers "gather good information from different things." Roxanne thought good writers "do a lot of research; read a lot of books; maybe make clusters."

In addition to strategy use, three parents believed good writers use the mechanical conventions of writing. Tina wrote they "work on spelling and grammar." Maxine believed good writing "should have an opening introduction for interest." Patsy thought good story writing should "always have a beginning, middle, and end."

Four participants recognized that good writers write for meaning. "You got *[sic]* to have a feeling for writing," Becky wrote. Janet believed that good writers "write things that make sense and are understandable." Good writers "get enough detail to make the writing clear," Maxine wrote. Perhaps the most sophisticated response was Lisa's: good writers "understand the reader."

### Becoming Better Readers and Writers

Prompts 7 and 8 were designed to elicit responses regarding what the participants believed would help them improve their own reading and writing.

Prompt 7: What do you think you will need to be a better reader?

Prompt 8: What do you think you will need to be a better writer?

The participants reported several needs. In order to be better readers, four participants said they needed help with decoding skills. Holly and Becky wrote about needing "help with spelling." Becky added that spelling might help her "pronounce words." To be better readers, Sharon and Patsy reported they needed to "know alot *[sic]* of different words."

Like decoding skills for better reading, four participants wrote about needing mechanical skills for better writing. "Spelling" topped the list of Becky's, Sharon's, and Patsy's needs. While Becky and Patsy wrote that they could use "more English," Janet wrote she needed "better vocabulary and punctuation" in order to improve her writing. Patsy recognized a need for editing when she wrote, "I need someone to check my writing."

Two participants believed they needed comprehension skills for better reading while four reported needing process skills for better writing. Becky thought she would be a better reader if "I understand what I'm reading." Lisa felt her reading would improve with more "memory." Becky needed the process skills of "sequencing ideas, main characters, and know[ing] the genre" to improve her writing. Lisa believed having "a burning desire of an idea" would help her write. Roxanne wrote of the connection between reading and writing when she suggested she needed to "read more and understand what to wright *[sic]* about; know what to wright *[sic]* and what to wright *[sic]* about."

Practice played a role in improving both reading and writing. Sharon wrote, "I need to read a lot of things, some very nice books." About improving her writing, Sharon added, "I need to write more." Roxanne wrote that she needed to "read more, need time to read at home."

Two parents thought they needed special materials in order to be better readers. Molly wrote that "lots of good stories, good books" would be needed.

Janet, one of the older participants, wrote she would be a better reader if she had "new glasses."

Three low-level readers perceived a relationship between good writing and good handwriting. In order to be better writers, Molly and Sharon both wrote they needed "good handwriting." Holly wrote she needed "lots of practice with writing in cursive."

### Reading and Writing Behaviors

Lastly, Prompts 5 and 6 asked the parents to describe their daily reading and writing behaviors.

Prompt 5: What kinds of things do you read? Why?

Prompt 6: What kinds of things do you write? Why?

Seven parents responded that they read useful informative materials. Maxine, a high-level reader, reported her reading consisted of "informative things." Similarly, Roxanne, a low-level reader, reported she read "things that tell real things." Janet and Sharon wrote about reading newspapers and magazines. Patsy specified she read "the *Newsleader,* flyers, cards, Bible stories, etc." When asked why they read such things, a typical response was "because short things don't take much time." In her journal, Tina reported reading *The Wall Street Journal.* She explained that, although she didn't have the money to invest at this time, she still liked keeping up on financial matters.

Short things appeared to dominate the types of writing that 45% of participants attempted. This functional writing consisted of notes, lists, and letters. Roxanne wrote, " I wright *[sic]* notes to people," while Judy shared that she wrote "grocery lists and notes to teachers." Patsy's functional writing consisted of "this journal, notes for my kids, cards, and things to give answers." Janet and Sharon listed some functional and entertaining writing such as "letters, questionnaires, and search words." The participants' most common response to why they wrote was "because I have to."

Seventy-two percent of the participants reported reading materials that were interesting to them and 64% wrote pieces that required reflective thinking. Roxanne wrote that she liked reading "things that get down to the good stuff" while Judy concurred she liked reading "things that are steamy." Judy said she read "steamy" fiction books and magazines because "they're interesting to me." Sharon wrote about reading "mysteries and funny things" and she was observed reading those materials during her free time in class. Janet said she liked reading "children's books." On several occasions when the teacher shared children's literature with the group, Janet said, "I read that." Holly, who collected weekly newspaper renditions of fairy tales into a little book for her son, wrote that she liked reading "fairy tales, fiction, action stories, love stories, and stories for my son." She read all these things to "build my own reading skill so my son will be able to read, write, and tell stories."

Two high-level readers named authors they liked to read. Lisa read Stephen King's novels because they "make you think about the world around you." Tina read V. C. Andrews novels because "you cannot predict what will happen." She also read several novels by Kathryn Friedman. Tina found Friedman's works "interesting" but added, "I'm getting tired of her themes."

Seven participants reported reflective writing in and out of class. Referring to what she wrote in her journal, Roxanne enjoyed writing "things that happen to me in my life." On her own time, Judy said she wrote many "love letters to [her] husband." Either through classroom discussions or through independent reading, Becky became intrigued by topics such as the Titanic disaster, cardiovascular health, and Elizabeth Taylor. On her own volition, she researched the topics and wrote essays. In her journal she wrote she would rather read than write and saved writing for "only subjects of interest."

A prolific writer, Lisa responded she had "a wish to write everything I think about." She did this because of a "need to control my stream-of-consciousness thinking." Lisa's journal entries were generally lengthy and highly reflective. She admitted staying up nights to write in her personal journal as a way of expressing herself and working through her problems. Tina, another prolific writer, wrote lengthy classroom dialogue journal entries and kept a personal journal as well. She, too, used journal writing for working through her problems but also planned to use the daily records as "material for a novel."

Holly, one of the low-level readers, also used her dialogue journal for self-expression. In an early journal entry she wrote about her life in Barbados and her immigration to the United States. Nearly every entry included detailed information about her toddler son. In response to the prompt about what she wrote and why, Holly reported she liked to write "about my home, family, and son. It is so amazing watching him grow from a tiny thing."

## Limitations

This study had several limitations. The findings of this descriptive study of 11 participants cannot be generalized to all adult and family literacy programs. Furthermore, this group of parents included three high-level readers and did not include the very lowest-level readers who typify many adult literacy classes. Yet this composition of readers yielded some interesting contrasts regarding adult literacy attitudes, perceptions, and behaviors.

After a year of being immersed in literacy learning, the participant's journal entries demonstrated many literacy attitudes, beliefs, and behaviors that could be expected from students who had been instructed in the elements of the reading and writing processes. For instance, Roxanne thought good writers "probably make clusters." Pre-writing organizational skills had been discussed and practiced in whole-group activities. Becky could research topics of interest to her because the opportunity to do so was available in the context of the family literacy program. In addition, the audience for the parents' writing was their teacher, which may have encouraged them to respond to the prompts as if they were being tested on their instruction. If the study had been conducted at the beginning of the school year, the responses may have been quite different.

## Conclusions

A previous study of low-level adult readers (Fagan, 1988) suggested these readers may not connect strategy use and meaning to the act of reading and writing. Low-level readers in Fagan's study thought good reading was sounding out the words and good writing was good spelling and good handwriting. By contrast, in the current study, even low-level readers believed good readers and writers use strategies and read for meaning. However, while readers at all levels recognized the need for spelling and decoding skills, the three low-level readers mentioned needing good handwriting to be better writers. Readers at all levels listed several reading and writing strategies that they used and/or believed good readers and writers used. They displayed both their knowledge of reading and writing strategies and their metacognitive awareness of using these strategies. Finally, low-level readers in this study clearly attached meaning and purpose to the act of reading and writing. Holly believed good readers "study lots of different things." Roxanne wrote about good readers "asking lots of questions." Janet wrote that good writers "write things that make sense and are understandable."

Smith (1990) found that less proficient readers tended to limit their reading to functional use rather than enjoyment. However, choosing to read for enjoyment and enrichment was not limited to the proficient readers in this study. Holly, a low-level reader, chose to read several different types of fiction and non-fiction materials. This appeared to be part of her quest to understand the culture of the United States and provide rich learning experiences for her young son. Roxanne reported she liked to read so that she could "keep up with what's going on in the world and understand what other people have been going through." Becky wrote that she "live[d] to read." She even discussed her latest readings informally with her peers during several lunch periods. As in the Smith (1996) study, the classroom morning newspaper was regularly perused by several parents regardless of their reading levels.

Like many adult readers and writers, the majority of this group wrote only when they "had to." However, two high-level readers were prolific writers and two lower-level readers chose writing as a form of entertainment. On the other hand, one high-level reader rejected writing as a form of communication or entertainment.

Thus, the attitudes, beliefs, and behaviors of these adults regarding reading and writing varied widely and did not necessarily reflect their proficiency levels. It seems their perceptions of good reading and writing grew partly out of their experience in the family literacy classroom. Their behaviors were more in line with their preferences than their proficiencies; these behaviors were consistent with their attitudes. In essence those who liked reading and writing read and wrote often and read from a variety of materials regardless of their proficiency levels. Those who reported they didn't care to read or write, also reported they read or wrote only when necessary.

By having the opportunity to write on a frequent basis and in the non-threatening format of the dialogue journal, these participants were able to express their learning needs in their own voices. The voice of the participants responding through dialogue journaling was also used to inform instructional design throughout the year, which facilitated a participatory curriculum (Auerbach, 1992). In other words, the journal entries told and showed what this group of learners needed on a daily basis. This picture and knowledge of their needs enabled the teacher to plan instruction that had immediate relevance.

## Implications

When serving the needs of parents in a family literacy program, it may be important to consider how literacy attitudes and preferences affect performance. Understanding adults' motivation for reading and writing and meeting their affective learning needs may play an important role. For instance, in this study Holly saw everything she learned and did in class as something that would help her create a better life for her son. She wanted to "build my own reading skill so my son will be able to read, write, and tell stories." Roxanne struggled with reading and writing as a way to improve herself and enter the camaraderie of this community of learners. She reported needing to improve her skills so that she could "know what's going on in the world."

In order to serve the needs of adult learners, it also would be helpful to know why learners enter literacy programs and what becomes and/or remains important as they continue their literacy studies. Using literacy for relevancy to practical and affective needs appeared to be important to this group of learners. A productive area for future study or investigation might be motivation and attribution as related to adult literacy learning environments.

These learners attached meaning to reading and writing, recognized the use of strategies, and specifically suggested they needed help with spelling, decoding, and process skills in order to improve their literacy learning. They also displayed well-developed perceptions of reading and writing processes. This may have enabled them to articulate their literacy learning needs. Analysis of dialogue journals in other adult literacy populations might reveal different needs and provide further clues to effective instruction.

When planning instruction for effective adult and family literacy programs, agencies should consider the practical and affective learning needs of the parents and children rather than focusing solely on school-based literacy learning. To be effective for adults, in particular, learning must have some immediate relevance to daily life requirements (Auerbach, 1989, 1995; Linder & Elish-Piper, 1995). In this small group of adult learners, a positive attitude toward reading and writing was associated with literacy engagement. Literacy programs that meet the practical, affective, and immediate needs of adults for themselves and their children may help create positive attitudes necessary to sustain continued engagement in reading and writing. This continued engagement could contribute to enabling parents to become lifelong learners who would be better prepared to pass the legacy of literacy on to their children.

---

# References

Auerbach, E. R. (1989). Toward a social-contextual approach to family literacy. *Harvard Educational Review, 59,* 165-181.

Auerbach, E. R. (1992). *Making meaning, making change: Participatory curriculum development for adult ESL literacy.* Washington, DC, and McHenry, IL: Center for Applied Linguistics and Delta Systems.

Auerbach, E. R. (1995). Deconstructing the discourse of strengths in family literacy. *Journal of Reading Behavior, 27,* 643-661.

Bean, T. W., & Zulich, J. L. (1992, December). *The other half: A case study of asymmetrical communication in content area reading student-professor dialogue journals.* Paper presented at the meeting of the National Reading Conference, San Antonio, TX. (ERIC Document Reproduction Service No. ED 352 621)

Bode, B. A. (1989). Dialogue journal writing. *The Reading Teacher. 42,* 568-571.

Brizius, J. A., & Foster, S. A. (1993). *Generation to generation: Realizing the promise of family literacy.* Ypsilanti, MI: High/Scope Press.

CTB/McGraw-Hill. (1987). *Tests of adult basic education.* Monterey, CA: Author.

Fagan, W. T. (1988). Concepts of reading and writing among low-literate adults. *Reading Research and Instruction, 27,* 47-60.

Gambrell, L. B. (1985). Dialogue journals: Reading-writing interaction. *The Reading Teacher, 38,* 512-515.

Glaser, B. G., & Strauss, A. L. (1967). *The discovery of grounded theory: Strategies for qualitative research.* Chicago: Aldine.

Heath, S. B. (1983). *Ways with words: Langague, life, and work in communities and classrooms.* Cambridge, England: Cambridge University Press.

Hennings, D. G. (1992). Students' perceptions of dialogue journals used in college methods courses in language arts and reading. *Reading Research and Instruction, 31,* 15-31.

Jones, P. M. (1988). *Knowing opportunities: Some possible benefits and limitations of dialogue journals in adult second language instruction.* Unpublished master's thesis, School for International Training, Vermont.

Kreeft, J., Shuy, R., Staton, J., Reed, L., & Morroy, R. (1984). *Dialogue writing: Analysis of student-teacher interactive writing in the learning of English as a second language.* Final Report to the National Institute of Education, NIE-G-83-0030. Washington, DC: Center for Applied Linguistics.

Lee, S., & Zuercher, N. (1993). Promoting reflection through dialogue journals. In L. Patterson, C. M. Santa, K. G. Short, & K. Smith (Eds.), *Teachers are researchers: Reflection and action* (pp. 183-196). Newark, DE: International Reading Association.

Life Skills/CASAS. (1989). *Comprehensive adult student assessment system.* San Diego, CA: Author.

Linder, P. E. (1996). *A qualitative analysis of dialogue journal responses of parents in a family literacy program.* Unpublished doctoral dissertation: The University of Akron.

Linder, P. E., & Elish-Piper, L. A. (1995). Listening to learners: Dialogue journals in a family literacy program. In W. M. Linek & B. Sturtevant (Eds.) *Generations of Literacy,* (pp. 313-325). Pittsburg, KS: College Reading Association.

National Center for Family Literacy. (1994). *Knight family education program implementation training.* Louisville, KY: Author.

Peyton, J. K., & Staton, J. (1993). *Dialogue journals in the multilingual classroom: Building language fluency and writing skills through written interaction.* Norwood, NJ: Ablex.

Purcell-Gates, V., L'Allier, S., & Smith, D. (1995). Literacy at the Harts' and the Larsons' : Diversity among poor, innercity families. *The Reading Teacher, 48,* 572-578.

Smith, M. C. (1990). The relationship of adults' reading attitude to actual reading behavior. *Reading Improvement, 27,* 116-121.

Smith, M. C. (1996). Differences in adults' reading practices and literacy proficiencies. *Reading Research Quarterly, 31,* 196-219.

Staton, J. (1987). The power of responding in dialogue journals. In T. Fulwiler (Ed.), *The journal book* (pp. 47-63). Portsmouth, NH: Boynton/Cook Heinemann.

Strauss, A., & Corbin, J. (1990). *Basics of qualitative research: Grounded theory procedures and techniques.* Newbury Park, CA: Sage.

Taylor, D., & Dorsey-Gaines, C. (1988). *Growing up literate: Learning from inner city families.* Portsmouth, NH: Heinemann.

# COHERENCE: ONE ASPECT EXAMINED OF THE TEXTUAL FEATURES OF ELECTRONIC MESSAGES

## Liqing Tao

Western Kentucky University

The phenomenal growth of personal computers and networks has made electronic mail (e-mail) communication a part of the daily lives of millions of users around the world. Noticing the potential benefits e-mail communication will bring into schools and colleges, educators and educational researchers have been making efforts to bring e-mail into educational settings (D'Souza, 1991; Fey, 1994; Hawisher & Moran, 1993). E-mail has been used to teach writing, broaden students' perspectives by connecting them with people beyond their classrooms, facilitate collaboration, and understand pre-service teachers' reflective processes. Despite the wide-spread use of e-mail communication in education, quality research of e-mail and its effects on education is much needed yet still to come (Herring, 1996a; Tao, 1995), particularly on the textual nature of e-mail messages.

Textual nature of e-mail refers to the fact that e-mail messages are composed of words rather than graphics. It has been listed as one of the characteristics of e-mail communication (Garton & Wellman, 1995). However, researchers in education have focused more on the social aspects of e-mail in educational settings than on its textual nature, which is mentioned, if at all, in a more or less after-thought manner. For example, Hawisher and Moran (1993) remarked from their own observations that e-mail messages are fragmentary, lacking coherence, and distractive. Romiszowski and de Haas (1989) made similar observations concerning students' use of e-mail. Wilkins (1991) examined students' language use on e-mail communication using social-linguistic perspective, identified some informal language features. Yates and Orlikowski (1992) suggested that e-mail messages should be studied from a genre perspective by classifying them according to their different characteristics such as memo, letters, and so forth.

Recently there have been some initial attempts at a systematic study of e-mail's textual features (Collot & Belmore, 1996; Herring, 1996b; Yates, 1996). Collot and Belmore (1996) examined six dimensions of electronic language in a large corpus of electronic messages using an established written language and spoken language model. Yates (1996) used a Hallidayan model in examining another large corpus of electronic messages. Both of these studies found wide variation in electronic language along the written and spoken continuum. Herring (1996b) used electronic messages from two mailing lists to look for any basic e-mail message structures and for gender differences as reflected through variants of the basic structures. Yet up to now, e-mail studies have not closely examined one of the most important textual features of communication: coherence. Herring's study (1996b) touched on the concept of coherence, but her focus was more on discovering the basic e-mail message structures as a whole. The present study investigates the coherence of a group of e-mail messages taken from an academic list serve under one topic.

## Theoretical Framework

Coherence is an important contributor to the comprehension of a text. Different communication models may demonstrate different techniques in realizing coherence. For example, traditional written texts cannot depend upon immediate feedback such as facial expressions for comprehending discourse as oral conversations can. Therefore, knowledge of the degree of coherence in e-mail texts would contribute to successful communication via e-mail.

A word of clarification regarding the terms coherence and cohesion is in order here. Coherence and cohesion are sometimes used loosely in describing the connectedness of a discourse. Here we are adopting Campbell's (1995) discussion concerning the nature of coherence and cohesion because it is clear and practical. In Campbell's classification, cohesion is co-textual, referring to linguistic elements within a discourse. While coherence is contextual and points to the mental representation these elements create in a reader or receiver.

Conventional discourse analyses of cohesion and coherence have been performed with some success (Halliday & Hasan, 1976; Kintsch & van Dijk, 1978). For example, the typology of cohesive types identified by Halliday and Hasan (1976) have been consistently applied to text analysis (see Campbell, 1995). Kintsch and van Dijk's macro and micro structures depend upon propositions in a text for coherence and have been used extensively in text research. However, as some researchers (Campbell, 1995; Stoddard, 1991) have pointed out, Halliday and Hasan's cohesion theory and other theories of similar nature have very limited applicability to naturally occurring text. For instance, Campbell (1995) has observed that Halliday and Hasan's extensive cohesive ties in discourse analysis are only applicable in analyzing a short text and would be severely restricted in application to any longer text. Likewise, the propositional approach of Kintsch and van Dijk (1978) is only practical when the text is short.

Based on his understanding of the limitations of Halliday and Hasan's (1976) original schema, Campbell (1995) has suggested that continuity be consdiered as an aspect of coherence. Two of the most salient and interesting elements he points out in discourse analysis are based upon Gestalt's perception of continuity: similarity and proximity. Within a discourse, according to Campbell, similarity refers to the semantic, syntactic, and even visual parallels while proximity refers to the spatial perceptions of the elements similarity. It is mainly the function of similarity and proximity that establishes the continuity of a discourse and the reader's perception of continuity. A high level of similarity within a discourse makes the discourse more coherent than a low level of similarity. Likewise, the proximity also provides an indication of coherence. The present study adopts Campbell's perception of continuity with appropriate modifications in discussing the coherence issue in e-mail messages.

Before we proceed, it is necessary to look at the physical and conceptual similarities and differences between conventional written discourse and e-mail messages taken from a list serve discussion group (see Table 1).

First both conventional and e-mail discourse are written, and therefore share the same visual symbols (here they are the 26 English letters), which are presented on a surface, whether the surface be a piece of paper or a computer screen. Second, the grouping of these symbols involves the same grammatical rules (such as punctuation and capitalization) in either form of written discourse. Third, like conventional written discourse, e-mail messages can be reread and preserved for future reference or use. This latter feature helps the text overcome the barrier of time and space.

**Table 1. Features of Three Discourse Types**

|                            | Written | E-mail | Spoken |
|----------------------------|---------|--------|--------|
| Visual presentation        | +       | +      |        |
| Uses punctuation           | +       | +      |        |
| Timelessness               | +       | +      |        |
| Single author              | +       | *      |        |
| Smileys                    |         | +      |        |
| Multiple participants      |         | +      | +      |
| Interactiveness            |         | *      | +      |
| Synchrony                  |         | *      | +      |
| Use of tone                |         |        | +      |
| Uses nonverbal expressions |         | +      |        |
| Uses sound                 |         |        | +      |

+ *Feature of this discourse type.*
* *Sometimes a feature of this discourse type.*

The differences between e-mail messages and conventional written discourse stem from the interactive or semi-interactive nature of e-mail. E-mail messages are usually written with a clearer audience in "sight": the participants in the discussion group. Participants can always "drop in" for the discussion. Thus, e-mail messages usually represent multiple voices, and consequently multiple styles, rather than a single voice and style as in conventional discourse forms, such as a paper. People join in e-mail discussions from different places and at their own convenience. Due to this participation pattern, e-mail messages are usually written in a more casual way than a formal written text. Less attention is allocated to spellings in e-mail situation than in conventional writings.

A closer look at the differences between e-mail messages and written discourses reveals that these differences move e-mail messages more toward conversation or spoken discourse. When multiple voices are represented in a group of e-mail messages, they are similar to a conversation carried on by multiple interlocutors. The casual styles of e-mail messages also resemble those of conversation. However, e-mail messages have characteristics which differ from conversations. First, e-mail is not as interactive as a face-to-face or phone conversation. Because most of the e-mail messages in a discussion group are sent at the sender's convenience, e-mail discussions do not engage participants at the same time. Second, unlike a conversation, e-mail messages are not as evanescent as usual conversation and can be kept beyond the time when they were produced.

Considering the nature of their text-based representations, e-mail messages should be subject to discourse analysis using traditional methods in regard to the message coherence. However, the textual nature of e-mail messages is such that multiple styles are represented in a lengthy body of texts. Traditional discourse analysis methods of either cohesive types or the propositional approach do not provide an appropriate analysis of this special discourse form because traditional methods are limited in their application to lengthy text and multiple styles.

But with the concepts of similarity and proximity introduced by Campbell (1995), it is possible to analyze for coherence the e-mail messages from a discussion group. Because e-mail messages from a discussion group, though with multiple styles, are all concerned with a similar topic, we can recognize common recurring themes using the similarity principle. The proximity principle is another useful measurement for multiple messages, which might be on a similar theme but composed at a different time and with other messages set in between them.

The present study investigated coherence in e-mail messages by employing Campbell's (1995) similarity and proximity principles. Specifically, the research questions guiding this study were:

1) Were e-mail messages from a discussion group under a similar topic coherent?

2) How were the e-mail messages measured in terms of coherence using similarity and proximity principles?

### Method and Procedures

Discussions on an instructional technology list-serve were monitored for one month. The instructional technology list-serve is an open forum with several hundred subscribers across the world. Participants are mostly academic professionals and other professionals associated with the list's focus on instructional technology.

E-mail discussion messages on several topics were collected during the monitoring. Although this study focused on one topic, the others were collected for the sake of making meaningful comparisons in terms of the length and duration of the discussions on these topics. The discussions around a topic were defined as all the messages that bear the same title or slightly altered title in the title line of the e-mail messages. The group of e-mail messages examined was under the title "No Jokes" and contained 24 messages ranging from 11 words to 887 words. This group was comparable to messages contained in the other topical discussions monitored. The other two groups collected at the same time were "Mastery Learning" (28 messages, ranging from 14 to 1438 words) and "Learner-Center Education" (30 messages, ranging from 45 to 1420 words).

The targeted body of e-mail messages was scrutinized for themes by employing a qualitative content analysis procedure. In this study, the data were not exhausted to the point of saturation as the grounded analysis (Strauss & Corbin, 1990) would dictate. However, repeated readings were done over a period of 4 weeks to identify possible themes. A definition for the themes was established. A simple count of frequency of the themes was used after the themes were identified. A theme was defined as the idea that was distinctly the central subject of a discourse or discussion. The following example illustrated the theme of "lack of humor in instructional design":

> One of the problems I've always had with Instructional Design is its total lack of humour. It's not simply because ID textbooks don't contain any jokes (in fact no text seems to be complete without a cliched reprint from Peanuts or Calvin & Hobbes), but it's because all the instructional designers I know totally neglect the value of humour as a teaching tool. I once went to an instructional design conference and the best joke was an OHP of a recursive loop.

Sometimes a discourse had more than one theme. Usually a new theme was realized through another message focusing on a subordinate idea in a previous message. For example, the above paragraph was quoted in message number six but was given a new twist for a different theme, "Complaint about high cost of reprint":

> That's a great idea, who wants to pay for the rights to use the cartoon? Anything that is reprinted in a book usually is done so at a hefty price. For example, we wanted to reprint a sample word problem from a math book (about 1/2 page in length) and the publisher wanted $500+. We ended up creating our own example problem to illustrate the concept. Other publishers are more reasonable (like $50 to reproduce a well known algorithm).

When all the themes were identified, the similarity principle was used to measure the occurrences of different themes. Likewise, the proximity principle was then applied to the identified themes to gauge the temporal and spatial (inter-message) distance of the same and different themes.

## Results

During the monitoring period a total of 24 messages were sent from participants around the world. Two of these messages were personal messages, apparently sent in error, which did not relate to discussion topics. The other 22 messages contained themes:

> lack of humor in instructional design, value of humor in instruction, cross-culture difference of humor, an IBM story, grounds of being offended, complaint about high cost of reprint, humor appreciation on individual basis, complaint about the tone of discussion, technology-instruction debate.

A graphic presentation of the results is provided in Table 2.

### Similarity

In the 24 messages, there were 9 themes. One theme, "value of humor in instruction," was picked up in 14 messages, although 4 of these only touched on the theme in discussion. That is, they mentioned it and then digressed into their own anecdotal experiences which had little to do with the central theme. Seven of these 14 cited various portions of the targeted messages to allow readers to connect with the messages to which they were responding.

Four of the themes were mentioned in 3 messages, while the others were only mentioned once or twice.

### Proximity

The humor theme was interspersed with other themes in the 14 messages referring to it. These other themes were discussed 20 times in 16 messages. The messages were sent during a period of 10 days. However, the main body of the message group concentrated on a two-day period with 19

## Table 2. Description of messages within the discussion group

| Msg No. | 1 | 2* | 3 | 4 | 5 | 6 | 7 | 8 | 9 | 10 | 11 | 12 | 13 | 14 | 15 | 16 | 17 | 18 | 19 | 20 | 21 | 22 | 23 | 24 |
|---|---|---|---|---|---|---|---|---|---|---|---|---|---|---|---|---|---|---|---|---|---|---|---|---|
| Country of origin | HK | US | JP | SE | ZA | US | UK | US | US | US | US | UK | HK | UK | US | US | US | US | US | US | US | US | US | US |
| Day sent | 1 | 1 | 2 | 2 | 2 | 2 | 2 | 2 | 2 | 2 | 2 | 3 | 3 | 3 | 3 | 3 | 3 | 3 | 3 | 3 | 3 | 5 | 5 | 10 |
| Sender | 1 | 2 | 3 | 4 | 5 | 6 | 7 | 8 | 9 | 10 | 6 | 7 | 1 | 11 | 12 | 13 | 10 | 9 | 14 | 15 | 15 | 16 | 14 | 17 |
| Lack Humor * | T | | | | M | | | | | | | | | | | | | | | | | | | |
| Value Humor | T | | T | | | T | T | M | T | | T | | M | T | M | | T | T | | | T | | | M |
| Culture Humor | T | | T | | | | | | | | | | | | | | | | | | | | | |
| IBM Story | T | | | | | | | | | | | | T | | | | | T | | | | | | |
| Offend | | | T | T | T | | | | | | | | | | | | | | | | | | | |
| Complaint Cost | | | | | | T | | | | | | | | | | | | | | | | | | |
| Appreciate Humor | | | | | | | | | T | | | | | | | | | | | | | | | |
| Complaint tone | | | | | | | | | | | | | T | | | | | T | | | | | | T |
| Debate | | | | | | | | | | | | | T | T | | | T | | | | | | | |
| Quote Msg | | W 1 | | | | P 1 | P 1 | P 4 | W 1 | P 7 | | P 10 | W 12 | | | P 12 | | P 12 | P 12 | | | | W 22 | |

*Note.*  T=*theme being picked up.*  M=*marginally touched theme.*
W=*whole message quoted.*  P=*portion(s) of a message quoted.*
*Agrees with message 1; no further comments or elaboration
*Country of Origin:*  HK=*Hong Kong*  JP=*Japan*
SE=*Sweden*  UK=*United Kingdom*
US=*United States*  ZA=*South Africa*

messages sent in this period. Eleven messages out of 14 related to the humor theme were sent within these two days. Twelve people from the United States, the United Kingdom, South Africa, Hong Kong, Sweden, and Japan contributed to these 14 messages.

## Discussion

In the present study, themes are used as the indicator for similarity, and space and temporal distance as the indicator for proximity. This is an initial attempt to study e-mail's textual coherence through discussion group messages. In using the theme as the indicator for establishing coherence, the researcher may have overlooked details that might be better represented by cohesive ties. In the current study the dynamic nature of e-mail communication may have been overlooked to some extent. In addition, because e-mail discussion groups are different from individual e-mail communications, no conclusions can be directly drawn from the present study concerning one-to-one e-mail communications.

The analysis indicates that the similarity level of the present e-mail message group under one common topic is fairly low. Fourteen out of 24 messages relate to the humor theme that is in the title line of this group of e-mail messages. This is close to what Herring (1996b) discovered about notional coherence. The dissimilarity due to the variety of themes is fairly high and is detected in two aspects. First, nine themes are embedded in 24 messages. Second, there are 20 times when the 8 themes other than the humor one are discussed or mentioned in the 24 messages. The high frequency of the occurrence of dissimilarity makes the message group multiply focused rather than centrally focused. If we factor in the occasional jargons and mentioning of events discussed in some previous message groups, the dissimilarity level further increases. Besides, not all participants seemed to take advantage of the easy quotations of any previous message in an e-mail situation, which may have exacerbated the dissimilarity level. Only 12 out of 24 messages contain quotations from previous messages. Given the easy message quoting functions of e-mail, this is an interesting phenomenon.

Most of the messages related to the humor theme were sent within a period of two days. According to the proximity principle, this creates a sense of being in the same group on the part of the participants. The fact that many senders are from different countries should not have affected the space distance between messages because e-mail is usually sent and received within a matter of minutes despite the physical distance between the sender and the receiver. But when the discussions of the central theme or the topic are interspersed about 20 times with the other 8 themes, the inter-message proximity level might have suffered.

## Conclusions

The following conclusions are offered based on the analysis.

1. The e-mail message group examined seems to lack similarity in themes. The high dissimilarity level makes the group discussion less centered than the topic indicates. In other words, the present e-mail messages around a same topic are about many different themes and appear to be fragmented in nature. This may be an evidence of less coherence in list-serve e-mail messages. This coincides with the intuitive feelings some researchers have in regard to e-mail communication (Hawisher & Moran, 1993).

2. Due to the differences in styles and lengths, among the varied contributors to the discussion of the humor theme, the temporal proximity might be less important. In other words, dissimilarity might overshadow proximity of time. This, if confirmed, might mean less coherence when being read by readers. Further, the inter-message prox-

imity is also low with the other 8 themes interspersed across 24 messages 20 times.

3. Based on the measures of similarity and proximity, this group of e-mail messages seems to be lacking in coherence. The dissimilarity created by multiple themes in this group of e-mail messages may have strongly contributed to this lack of coherence.

4. While the 24 messages ranged from scholarly citations of literature to witty jokes, they look more like a mosaic than a solid whole. Consequently, the themes are seldom developed in any depth. This appears to resemble a conversation in which every party talks more to generate more interaction than content depth. This finding is consistent with Romiszowski & de Haas's (1989) reflection on their experience with e-mail in their class.

## Implications

Some implications for future research on e-mail in education are offered here.

First, the nature of the e-mail discussion groups can be further explored by using more detailed textual analyses in addition to the similarity and proximity measures used in this study. Researchers could deal with large e-mail databases by investing in computer programs that help parse the data.

Second, the present study suggests that this less coherent feature of e-mail discussion groups deserves our special attention, especially when we want to involve our children in e-mail discussions. The cognitive characteristics of children at different developmental stages should be fully considered before e-mail communication can be used effectively in educational settings. For example, children in elementary schools may need more guidance and direction in using e-mail discussions than children at the middle grades.

Finally, readers' actual responses to the lack of coherence should be investigated in future studies in order to understand better the nature of e-mail discussion groups and e-mail communication. For example, studies concerning the reading strategies of students in reading e-mail discussion groups can provide useful information about the coherence nature of e-mail discussion groups.

---

## References

Campbell, K.S. (1995). *Coherence, continuity, and cohesion: Theoretical foundations for document design.* Hillsdale, NJ: Lawrence Erlbaum Associates.

Collot, M., & Belmore, N. (1996). Electronic language: A new variety of English. In S.C. Herring (Ed.), *Computer-mediated communication: Linguistic, social and cross-cultural perspectives.* Philadelphia, PA: John Benjamins North America.

D'Souza, P. V. (1991). The use of electronic mail as an instructional aid: An exploratory study. *Journal of Computer-Based Instruction, 18,* 106-110.

Fey, M.H. (1994). Finding voice through computer-communication: A new venue for collaboration. *Journal of Advanced Composition, 14,* 221-238.

Garton, L., & Wellman, B. (1995). Social impacts of electronic mail in organizations: A review of the research literature. In B.R. Burleson (Ed.), *Communication Yearbook, 18,* 434-453.

Halliday, M. A. K., & Hasan, R. (1976). *Cohesion in English.* London: Longman.

Hawisher, G. E., & Moran, C. (1993). Electronic mail and the writing instructor. *College English, 55,* 627-643.

Herring, S. C. (1996a). Introduction. In S.C. Herring (Ed.), *Computer-mediated communication: Linguistic, social and cross-cultural perspectives.* Philadelphia, PA: John Benjamins North America.

Herring, S. C. (1996b). Two variants of an electronic message schema. In S.C. Herring (Ed.), *Computer-mediated communication: Linguistic, social and cross-cultural perspectives.* Philadelphia, PA: John Benjamins North America.

Kintsch, W., & van Dijk, T. A. (1978). Toward a model of text comprehension and production. *Psychological Review, 85,* 363-394.

Romiszowski, A. J., & de Haas, J. A. (1989). Computer mediated communication for instruction: Using e-mail as a seminar. *Educational Technology, 29,* 7-14.

Strauss, A., & Corbin, J. (1990). *Basics of qualitative research: Grounded theory procedures and techniques.* Newbury Park, CA: Sage.

Stoddard, S. (1991). *Text and texture: Patterns of cohesion.* Norwood, NJ: Ablex Publishing Corporation.

Tao, L. (1995). *What do we know about e-mail—An existing and emerging literacy vehicle?* Paper presented at the annual meeting of the National Reading Conference, New Orleans, LA.

Wilkins, H. (1991). Computer talk: Long-distance conversations by computer. *Writing Communication, 8,* 56-78.

Yates, J., & Orlikowski, W.J. (1992). Genres of organizational communication: A structural approach to studying communication and media. *Academy of Management Review, 17,* 299-326.

Yates, S. J. (1996). Oral and written linguistic aspects of computer conferencing. In S.C. Herring (Ed.), *Computer-mediated communication: Linguistic, social and cross-cultural perspectives.* Philadelphia, PA: John Benjamins North America.

# Exploring Professional Development

# A Prototype Tool for Assessing Instructional Discourse in Literacy Teaching

**Kathleen Roskos**

John Carroll University

**Barbara Walker**

Montana State University-Billings

## Abstract

*Based on an analysis of teacher-student verbal exchanges in reading tutorials, a prototype assessment tool for practitioners' use in analyzing instructional discourse in professional education and classroom contexts is proposed. Analytic categories and the design of the tool were derived from an evaluation of the functional efficacy of existing discourse schemes and observations in the reading clinic setting. Preliminary trials indicate the tool's potential for revealing instructional discourse patterns and supporting teachers' learning. Exploratory at this stage, the research highlights the importance of well-designed tools for informing and improving teachers' practices.*

In this paper we provide analytic categories that may aid practitioners' assessment of instructional discourse in their own literacy teaching. Our approach to instructional talk draws on sociolinguistic research, which focuses on the examination of linguistic processes in school settings (National Institute of Education, 1974). A central theme in this tradition emphasizes understanding the cognitive and social functions of language in classroom contexts. How teachers talk during instruction has a bearing on how students learn, and sociolinguistic research has helped to reveal important subtleties of this truism. But teaching teachers how to talk so as to facilitate and advance students' learning is far less obvious. Our research interest is in designing tools that help teachers "see" how they talk during instruction. By observing and analyzing their talk, teachers can adapt and improve their own instructional discourse in everyday literacy teaching situations.

# Background

## Observations of Classroom Talk

Considerable research work has examined classroom speech events such as reading lessons and, as a result, produced powerful analytic tools for observing classroom discourse. One practical example is the three-part *IRE discourse structure* of teacher initiation (I), student response (R), and teacher evaluation (E), which serves as a template for close scrutiny of teacher and student talk in a lesson sequence (e.g., Mehan, 1979).

The *participation structure* is another helpful analytic tool which has illuminated variations in teachers' verbal strategies and students' verbal repertoires. Using this tool, Philips (1972) uncovered significant differences in Warm Spring Indian children's communicative competence between home/community and school. Learning activities outside of school stressed observation, apprenticeship, and private, self-initiated testing of skill, while those in school demanded nearly the opposite: verbal recitation, passive involvement, and public assessment of competence. As a result of this communication mismatch, Indian children appeared incompetent in school learning activities—not because they could not speak English, but because they did not know all the sociolinguistic rules underlying communication in classroom learning events. In making these observations, the *participation structure* as an analytic frame helped to unravel the complexities of discourse in context and showed the demands made on children's communicative competence in different situations.

## Observations of Classroom Interactions

Teacher and peer interactions that assist conceptual learning have also received substantial attention in recent years, viewed in particular through the theoretical lenses of Vygotsky and Leont'ev (e.g., Newman, Griffin & Cole, 1989). Much has been said in educational work, for example, about the benefits of small group discussion (Gambrell, 1996), guided participation in tasks (Rogoff, 1990), instructional conversations between teacher and students (Goldenburg, 1992-93; Tharp & Gallimore, 1988), and collaborative work among peers (Roth & Bowen, 1995) in the classroom setting.

Fine-grained analyses of adult-child and child-child interactions in instructional contexts indicate several means of assisting the learner's performance: modeling, contingency managing, feeding back, instructing, questioning, and cognitive structuring (Tharp & Gallimore, 1988). These are the communication tools of teaching — verbal and nonverbal actions applied in infinite variety by individual teachers to create more or less accomodating conditions for individual learners. Done well, the give-and-take between teacher and students and among students around substantive matters, it is argued, creates richly layered opportunities for advancing conceptual and linguistic development of diverse learners (Collins, Brown, & Newman, 1989).

### From Observations to Teaching Practice

Thus, over the past two decades, sociolinguistic research contributed by linguists, anthropologists, sociologists, and education scholars has yielded powerful ideas and analytic tools related to the nature and functions of classroom discourse. Many have led to methodological innovation and change. Some ideas, such as "developing communities of learners" (Brown, 1994), are now part of the current ideology and influential in educational reform. But few, very few, have been investigated or applied in studies of teacher learning and development. How do teachers, for example, become aware of their discourse patterns? How do they know when they have skillfully used instructional talk and when their efforts have faltered? How do they become more adept at managing teacher-student exchanges so as to enhance the potential for learning? We need to learn a great deal more about these practicalities of teaching performance if the insights gleaned from sociolinguistic research are to flow in the everyday talk of the classroom.

As discussed above, a number of critical concepts and related analytic procedures have been mined from the study of classroom discourse. These hold potential as resources of practice for classroom teachers in terms of knowledge and teaching strategies. For example, we know that teacher discourse which seeks to develop student understanding during instructional lessons includes certain features (Goldenburg, 1992-93; Walker, 1996a). Teachers often shift their role from interrogator of students to co-conversationalist *with* students during discussion. They listen carefully and actively to what students say and respond flexibly, much like in everyday conversation when people actually have something to say to each other. They value and extend what others say, overlapping and connecting ideas among participants and with shared experiences. And they elaborate others' thinking by adding ideas, restating, and probing for more information. Yet, while we may recognize that these features can enhance the cognitive and social qualities of an instructional episode, we still don't know enough about how to help teachers develop the interactional skills such "instructional conversations" require or how to nurture the personal qualities they demand.

## Designing Tools for Practice

Interested in developing teachers' skill in instructional conversation in their teaching practice, we initiated research work to design practical observation and assessment tools that might support teachers' self-critique, adaptation, and improvement of their instructional discourse. The essence of this work is to find ways to teach current and future teachers how to observe and analyze instructional discourse as if they were researchers, thus engaging them in inquiry processes that promote constructed knowing. As Dewey

(1929) argued, teachers must develop scientific habits of thinking if they are to escape "trial and error" habits of practice (McAninch, 1993).

However, the traditional read-and-recite script is deeply ingrained in classroom discourse, often unnoticed by teachers as they go about their instructional work. If teachers had an analytical tool to analyze their interactions with students, they might more easily discern how their talk influences students' responses. For instance, noting that they primarily asked questions without acknowledging what the student said, teachers might become more sensitive to the quality of their talk and might begin to shift toward discussing ideas collaboratively with their students. Relatedly, teacher educators could use discourse analysis tools in field experiences. Observing or videotaping their students, they could assess and discuss students' instructional interactions, offering concrete feedback about the qualities of their instructional talk. As Sykes (1997) observed, teacher educators are quite proficient at teaching the knowledge of practice, but have few methodologies for teaching practice per se. An analytical tool such as the one proposed may provide a means for teacher educators to teach practice as well as knowledge about the practice.

To begin the detailed work of designing tools for everyday practice, this study focuses on several excerpts of teacher-student exchanges in literacy tutorials as a data source for generating analytic categories. We first explore several ways of analyzing teachers' discourse for conversational qualities, employing existing analytic schemes developed for research purposes and applying them to the excerpts. Next we compare and contrast the results with the intent of extracting a number of differentiating features in the schemes and of examining how these features reflect different ways of learning about language use in instruction. Using these features as a "working" set of analytic categories, we then construct and apply a prototype tool for practitioners' use in assessing qualities of instructional talk in contexts of professional education and classroom teaching.

## Method
### *Participants and Setting*

Five students, randomly selected from a larger pool of graduate students enrolled in a reading practicum course, were invited to participate. All were females in their mid to late thirties who had taught elementary school for ten years or more. Seeking master's degrees in education and reading specialist certification, the women were in the final stages of their advanced studies. They were enrolled in graduate programs at two different university sites which were comparable in size, student composition, and general professional education curriculum.

## Description of the Reading Practicum

The content and procedures of the practicum course offered at the two university locations were developed collaboratively by the researchers and reflected a constructivist perspective on children's literacy learning (Dixon-Kraus, 1996) and an inquiry approach to professional education (Cochran-Smith, 1989; Feiman-Nemser & Buchanan, 1987; Schön, 1987).

Content focused on the application of reading pedagogy concepts (e.g., strategy instruction) and diagnostic skills (e.g., miscue analysis) within an instructional framework derived from literacy research (Clay, 1993; Walker, 1996b). The framework served as the architecture of daily tutorials and included five recurring activities across a five to six week period: (1) warm-ups to ease into literacy instruction, (2) familiar text time for sharing what children know well and can already do, (3) new text time where readers apply strategies and skills in unfamiliar text situations, (4) strategy and skills lessons wherein teachers explictly model new strategies and skills for students to try out in familiar reading selections, and (5) personalized reading and writing activities that offer students literacy choices.

Teaching procedures were tied to three primary activities that fostered the intersection of practical and personal experience with theoretical understandings: (1) the formation and development of teaching teams, which encouraged collaboration among peers; (2) on-the-spot assistance from instructors during tutorial sessions that forged connections between practical experience and theoretical knowledge; and (3) ample opportunity for reflection on instructional actions through shared text experiences such as journal articles, daily recording of observations, assessing selected teaching episodes, and periodic conferences with instructors, colleagues, and parents.

While our day-to-day instruction necessarily adapted to local conditions at each site, we maintained fidelity to the instructional framework and central procedures through weekly communication, joint problem solving, and sharing of student work.

## Procedures

All practicum participants were required to videotape at least one of their lessons over a 5-week period and to select a 5 minute segment from the lesson which they viewed as especially productive. They were asked to transcribe the segment verbatim, study it, and provide a rationale as to why they thought it represented effective instruction. Each transcription was about 4-5 pages in length and provided a detailed account of verbal and nonverbal interactions that occurred between teacher and student during instruction. No analytic scheme was prescribed; thus teachers were left to apply their own interpretive means in providing a rationale.

From this total set, five samples were randomly drawn for in-depth analysis. We then followed a four-step procedure for deriving and developing analytic categories for practical use. First, we each read and reread the samples and individually applied three existing discourse coding schemes: (1) an elicitation/response model (adapted from Schachter, 1979) for observing adult-child interactions; (2) Goldenburg's (1992-93) rating scale for examining reading lessons and elements of instructional conversation (adapted from Tharp & Gallimore, 1988); and (3) a rubric devised by Newman and Wehlage (1995) to analyze instruction for instances of substantive conversation. After each application, we compared our results and resolved differences through discussion.

Second we developed a checklist matrix (Miles & Huberman, 1984) to assess the general usability of the categories as well as their relative strength in describing the participatory and instructional qualities of teachers' language use. We were especially attentive to the sociocultural and conceptual functions of instructional discourse. According to Barnes (1976), the sociocultural function serves to negotiate social relationships in the situation, conveying information about roles, routines, and how to participate in what is going on. The conceptual function organizes the content of the lesson, that is, the learning to be done. It builds a framework or "scaffold" for children to fill in, thus encouraging them to construct meaning while simultaneously providing a model for verbal reasoning. We are keenly interested in this latter language function, since such talk may add intellectual precision that enhances student learning (Mercer, 1993). Skillfully applied, it forces learners to grapple with alternative ways of thinking that help them make new concepts and ideas their own.

We next adjusted, clarified, and collapsed categories to develop a "working" set of analytic categories which formed the basis for a prototype assessment tool. We then individually applied the tool to test its utility, once again using the five samples.

### Data Analysis

The primary goal of our analysis was to derive and develop a set of analytic categories for use in practical contexts, such as practica, classrooms, literacy programs, and professional development activities. To analyze the efficacy and flexibility of existing coding schemes, we employed a checklist matrix—a qualitative technique that aids systematic organization and evaluation of several components of a variable (Miles & Huberman, 1984, pp. 95-99). Considering our research goals, the matrix was developed to compare and contrast the relative adequacy of existing schemes across a number of features clustered into four domains: (1) sociocultural function of language, (2) conceptual function of language, (3) usability, and (4) instructive power. Criterial domains and related features were derived from sociolinguistic research into language functions and investigations of situated learning into usability and instructive power (Suchman, 1987). An analytic scheme that performed well with respect to the conceptual function of language, for example, would show to what extent discourse maintained a thematic focus and encouraged higher order thinking, features that indicate an emphasis on knowledge to be learned.

For category development and selection, we used analytic induction (Goetz & LeCompte, 1986), since it permitted us to propose new categories and modify existing ones through an iterative process of searching the data set, studying the checklist matrix results, and negotiating to resolve differences. It allowed us to shuttle back and forth between the data at hand and existing categories, which sharpened our interpretations of the discourse and helped to unbundle the complex variables the coding categories represented.

To construct a prototype tool, we employed a clustering analysis that aided identification and early verification of categories which ultimately shaped the format of a prototype assessment tool (Miles & Huberman, 1984). This required a good deal of joint summarizing and reworking to clarify and collapse categories into a workable set that was practical yet sufficently rich to be instructive. We then cross-checked the categories by individually applying them to our samples, comparing our results, and resolving differences. Finally, we formatted them into a "working" prototype for further research.

## Results

### *Functional Efficacy of Existing Analytic Schemes*

To frame the matrix analysis, we first briefly describe the three discourse coding schemes in relation to our samples, then discuss their adequacy vis a vis the evaluative criteria we established.

Schachter's elicitation/response scheme (1979) rates individual utterances as *elicitations* if the teacher directs the child, provides an explanation, or reports information. Comments are coded as *responsives* if the teacher replies with clarifying information, confirms a child's response, or elaborates on a child's response. Applied to the samples, the scheme indicated that our experienced teachers used more elicitations than responsives. Given the tutorial context, this is not surprising, since the teacher must somehow engage the student and the student must respond in some way to her requests.

The *instructional conversation* scheme (Goldenburg, 1992-93; Tharp & Gallimore, 1988) considers lesson discourse as a whole and rates it on a 0-1-2 scale along ten distinct categories of instructional interactions: thematic focus, use of background knowledge, direct teaching, promoting more complex expression, promoting a basis for thinking, fewer known-answer questions, responsivity, connected discourse, non-threatening environment, and degree of participation. For example, after reading and rereading a transcript we would rate the thematic focus as 0 (no clear theme), 1 (theme identified but not consistently the focus or connected to the textual theme), or 2 (textual theme was a focus throughout). Next we considered each of the other categories until we had evaluated all 10 categories. Using this approach, we observed that the five teachers maintained a thematic focus, seldom engaged in direct teaching, and tended to use more open-ended than closed questions in their instructional interactions.

Newman and Wehlage's (1995) rubric for identifying substantive conversation in instruction also is applied to the discourse of an entire lesson. The rubric uses a 0-1-2-3 scale which rates the discourse in a holistic way. To obtain a score of 3, the highest rating, instructional discourse needs to include four features: (1) focus on *content* and higher order thinking, (2) *shared dialogue,* (3) development of *shared understandings,* and (4) at least *3 consecutive interchanges* between teacher and student or between students. (An interchange is a statement by one person and a response from another.) Our samples averaged a score of 2 based on the rubric, showing an emphasis on literacy content and instances of shared dialogue with at least 2 interchanges. However, although development of shared understandings was attempted, it was not consistently achieved to a high level across the five participants.

The samples, of course, are inadequate for drawing any inferences about the teachers' instructional discourse as reading teachers. But they can serve to evaluate the utility of the different analytic schemes as learning tools for teacher educators and practitioners seeking to develop more interactive instructional discourse skills. For this purpose, we used a checklist matrix described in Table 1 to evaluate the functional efficacy of the schemes.

Our evaluation proved insightful along several indices of adequacy. First, none of the schemes met all four criteria, lacking important features across one or more of the domains. Interestingly, none fully met the criterion of instructive power, which seriously limits their potential as "tools of the trade." All lacked explanatory qualities that would allow general users to interact instructively with them in ways that might inform their own subsequent actions. Although they have been successfully employed by researchers with expertise in communicative interactions, the schemes were nevertheless too complex and inscrutable for informing teachers of their designers' intentions or for responding to teachers' varying circumstances and needs.

Second, in comparing and contrasting the schemes further, we observed their different strengths and weaknesses in terms of design. The elicitation/response model (Schachter, 1979), for example, was simply too broad to have any instructive power. In fact, it revealed very little of the conceptual function of instructional interactions. It did, however, convey some sense of shared meaning construction between teacher and student as indicated by the fre-

**Table 1. Evaluation of Research-Based Instructional Discourse Schemes as Tools for Assessing and Developing Teaching Practices**

| Evaluation Criteria | Analytic Scheme | | |
|---|---|---|---|
| Domain and Related Features | Elicitation/Response (Schacter, 1979) | Instructional Conversation (Tharp & Gallimore, 1988; Goldenburg, 1992-93) | Substantive Conversation (Newman & Wehlage, 1995) |
| Sociocultural function evidenced by: | | | |
| • connected dialogue | — | + | + |
| • shared meaning construction between speakers | — | + | — |
| Conceptual function evidenced by: | | | |
| • maintenance of a thematic focus | — | + | + |
| • presence of a model for thinking | — | + | — |
| Usability indicated by: | | | |
| • teachability to nonexperts | + | — | + |
| • manageability in situations of practice | + | — | — |
| Instructive power indicated by: | | | |
| • precision | — | — | — |
| • ability to explain or inform | — | + | — |

quency of responsives. Organized around two utterance categories (elicitations and responsives), its simplicity was also a strength in that it could be rather easily explained to non-experts and was quite manageable in terms of coding. The Tharp-Gallimore/Goldenburg scheme (Goldenburg, 1992-93; Tharp & Gallimore, 1988), on the other hand, was too cumbersome to be of real use in the practical situations of professional education or daily practice. To remember and manipulate 10 categories while reading and rereading instructional exchanges would be time-consuming and inevitably frustrating. Yet the 10 categories yielded excellent information about the sociocultural and conceptual functions of discourse during a lesson, making the scheme especially strong sociolinguistically. Lastly, the Newman/Wehlage (1995) rubric appeared too global to function as a precision tool for assessing of instructional discourse. While it afforded information about connectedness in discourse and maintenance of a thematic focus, the rubric failed to supply sufficient discreteness in terms of categories to reveal a personal pattern of communicative interactions.

### Category Development

To identify and select categories in the design of our tool, we initially relied on information derived from the application and evaluation of the three models in relation to our samples. From this information, we distilled two design principles. First, instructional discourse should not be parsed too finely, (by single utterance) or too broadly, (by the whole lesson), a principle which is heeded in related research (Barnes & Todd, 1977). Second, the unit of analysis or coding category must be sufficiently precise to "explain" itself so that teachers learn—the mark of a well-designed tool (Suchman, 1987).

Guided by these principles, we adopted the concept of an interchange from the Newman/Wehlage (1995) rubric, since it appeared to "chunk" interactions into manageable segments, yet to preserve essential meaning of ongoing communication. We defined an interchange as an instance of verbal interaction between teacher and student that may include one or more comments, as in:

> Teacher: Ryan, what story did we read earlier with Lisa?
> What was the name of the story?
> Student: *The Very Hungry Caterpillar.*

Examining the teacher's language in the interchange, we reasoned, would show how it functioned to set up and maintain instruction.

We then analyzed our data to identify categories in two ways. Some of the categories were derived from our evaluation of the three coding schemes and underlying related research, while others emerged from repeated reading of the five samples. From our analysis, we induced six categories that reflected conceptual and sociocultural functions of instructional discourse (see Table 2). The focusing, naming, and elaborating categories included features indicative of a conceptual function while the categories of overlapping, directing and discussing suggested the sociocultural function of instructional talk.

### Category Refinement and Trial

Our final analysis resulted in the construction of a prototype that evolved from trials, using our discourse samples to assess the functional efficacy of the categories as well as tool design.

**Table 2. Analytic Categories For Assessing Conceptual and Sociocultural Functions of Instructional Discourse.**

| Category | Definition | Example |
|---|---|---|
| Focusing | The teacher scaffolds the student's thinking by drawing attention to lesson focus through questioning, modeling, and eliciting background knowledge. | T: Think of all the things that we have been learning in these last two weeks about dogs. What are some of the things we have found out? And maybe we could find out these things about a keeshond. |
| Naming | The teacher names the strategies or content that the student is using. | T: I like the way you pick up the book to help you out. What's the solution? S: How dare you stare. T: OK, that is the start of the solution. |
| Elaborating | The teacher supports the student's thinking with comments and questions, with the intent of eliciting more complex verbal responses, or guides analytic reasoning. | T: Do you know anything else about them (keeshonds)? S: They have lots of hair. T: Anything else about them? S: Their tail is like a shih tzu. T: How do you know that? S: (elaborates with explanation) |
| Overlapping | The teacher connects the student's comments, using restatements, probes, and feedback that respond to what the student says. | T: You said something spooky was going to happen. Do you still think that is going to happen? Do you want to add anything to that? |
| Directing | The teacher uses commands or direct questions to focus the student's attention. | T: OK, now, were there people in this book? S: No. T: What's in the book? S: Animals. |
| Discussing | The teacher uses open-ended questions or comments that indicate no "right way" to respond, thus creating a more risk-free atmosphere. | S: (reads book title) T: What do you think it's about? S: Ummm . . . Spooky . . .She Umm. I forgot what she does, but I remember what she is—a teeny, tiny woman. T: Oh-h-h! Great, anything else? S: A tiny woman. She does funny things. |

After trying several designs, we observed that some of the dynamics of instructional interchanges were lost by coding each interchange into only one category. As a case in point, the first example in Table 2 reflects talk aimed not only at focusing the student, but also at overlapping previously learned information with the task at hand. Thus the tool was restructured to accomodate the possibility of multiple coding of interchanges, while remaining relatively easy to manage. Still, we found that categories lacked specificity, thus limiting their instructive power. We attributed this partially to our sample, which was seriously limited both in terms of number and source, i.e., the tutorial context. Further refinement of categories, we decided, would need to be addressed in subsequent trials with a larger, more diverse sample.

The prototype we finally selected as most viable at this point, which we refer to as the Instructional Talk Assessment Tool, is illustrated in Table 3 (see Table 3). Basic procedures for using the tool include: (1) numbering each interchange in the transcript of a lesson, (2) recording the number of the interchange in the appropriate column, (3) analyzing the instructional features of each interchange, and (4) computing the percentage for each feature. The analysis reveals the characteristics of instructional talk in a teaching episode and its general function.

Table 3, for example, shows an analysis of interchanges related to a story retelling in the tutorial context. We have included the entire set of interchanges

**Table 3.  The Instructional Talk Assessment Tool: A Protoype Tool for Assessment of Instructional Discourse in Practice**

| Interchange No. | Conceptual Function | | | Sociocultural Function | | |
|---|---|---|---|---|---|---|
| | Focusing | Naming | Elaborating | Overlapping | Directing | Discussing |
| 01 | | | | | | + |
| 02 | | | | | | + |
| 03 | | | | | | + |
| 04 | | | | + | | |
| 05 | | | | + | | + |
| 06 | | | | | | + |
| 07 | + | | | | + | |
| 08 | + | | | + | + | |
| 09 | | | | + | | + |
| 10 | | | | + | + | |
| 11 | | | + | | | + |
| 12 | | | + | | | + |
| Total | 2 | 0 | 2 | 6 | 4 | 7 |
| Per Cent | 17 | 0 | 17 | 50 | 33 | 58 |

in the appendix. While we cannot go into a detailed explanation of our thinking, we can, however, convey the tool's purpose with a few brief observations. First, the teacher's talk in this situation is used primarily to "keep the conversation going" as indicated by the number of interchanges devoted to sociocultural functions. Achieving the retelling appears uppermost as the teacher creates a comfort zone for doing so, using open-ended questions or comments, overlapping on the reteller's account, and periodically directing to assure continuity. Much less talk is used to purposefully focus the retelling around the goals of the lesson (e.g., developing comprehension) or to challenge meaning construction around narrative concepts (e.g., story grammar). In brief, the instructional talk in this situation appeared to enable the student's retelling attempt, but not necessarily to advance it to higher levels of performance.

Preliminary application of the tool indicates that it holds promise for revealing patterns of instructional talk that inform practitioners about their discourse and offers opportunties for fruitful critique. Further category refinement and trials across a much broader range of samples are needed, however, to verify the effectiveness and practicality of the tool.

## Discussion

Much has been gleaned from sociolinguistic research about what teachers could say and what could happen in instructional interchanges to improve the chance that all children will learn to write and read well in classroom settings. Yet we have not moved very far in ensuring literacy for all who enter the school doors (Graves, 1996). What's missing, some argue, is an emphasis on the teacher, who in the end sets up the social relationships and the communication system of the classroom (Sykes, 1996). As learners themselves, teachers need resources—knowledge, strategies, tools, and time—if they are to change their practice to achieve the more ambitious teaching goals envisioned by sociolinguistic insights.

Certainly exploratory at this stage, our study attempted to begin the mundane work of developing a practical tool that supports practitioners, including teacher educators, in infoming and improving discourse practices. Our aim was to identify a set of analytic categories, derived from research work, and to design a prototype assessment tool for general use. We recognize the difficulty of this task. For tools to serve as valuable resources of practice, they must not only be functional and easy-to-use, but also "smart" in that they afford teachers ample opportunity to learn in the process of using them.

The design of tools that encourage teachers as learners and problem solvers in their own professional development and practices, however, suffers from lack of attention and systematic research. There is a tendency to assume that tools designed for research can slip easily into practice with little modification or direction. But we argue that the path to action is not necessarily straight; adaptations need to be made that preserve a tool's purpose, yet enhance its functional capacity to inform and respond to the actions of its users. This requires, we think, "engineering" coupled with well-grounded analyses that ultimately produce well-designed tools for practice.

In this work, our analytic effort yielded six categories which represented an amalgamation from different research-based schemes and our own observations in the reading clinic setting. The categories met four criteria that we viewed as critical to the design of an instructional discourse analysis tool for everyday use: indicators of sociocultural and conceptual functions, usability, and instructive power. Initial trials in applying the tool suggest its potential for informing and bettering teachers' discourse practices, particularly in the clinic setting. Further applications of the tool in broader clinic and classroom contexts are now necessary to assess its adequacy, precision, and value as a resource for practitioners—a course of action we plan to pursue.

---

## References

Barnes, D. (1976). *From communication to curriculum.* Middlesex, England: Penguin Books.

Barnes, D., & Todd, F. (1977). *Communication and learning in small groups.* Boston, MA: Routledge & Kegan Paul.

Brown, A. (1994). The advancement of learning. *Educational Researcher, 23*(8), 4-12.

Clay, M. (1993). *Reading recovery: A guidebook for teachers in training.* Portsmouth, NH: Heinemann Educational Books.

Cochran-Smith, M. (1989). *Of questions, not answers: The discourse of student teachers and their school and university mentors.* Paper presented at the Annual Meeting of the American Educational Research Association, San Francisco.

Collins, A., Brown, J.S., & Newman, S.E. (1989). Cognitive apprenticeship: Teaching the craft of reading, writing, and mathematics. In L.B. Resnick (Ed.), *Knowing, learning and instruction: Essays in the honor of Robert Glaser* (pp. 453-494). Hillsdale, NJ: Lawrence Erlbaum Associates.

Dewey, J. (1929). *The sources of a science of education.* NY: Teachers College Press.

Dixon-Kraus, L. (1996). *Vygotsky in the classroom.* NY: Longman Publishers.

Feiman-Nemser, S., & Buchanan, M. (1987). When is student teaching teacher education? *Teaching and Teacher Education, 3,* 255-273.

Gambrell, L. (1996). What research reveals about discussion. In L. Gambrell & J. Almasi (Eds.), *Lively discussions: Fostering engaged reading.* Newark, DE: International Reading Association.

Goetz, J., & LeCompte, M. (1986). *Ethnography and qualitative design in educational research.* NY: Academic Press.

Goldenburg, C. (1992-93). Instructional conversations: Promoting comprehension through discussion. *The Reading Teacher, 46,* 316-326.

Graves, M. (1996). The continuing quest toward literacy for all children. In M. Graves, P. van den Broek, B. Taylor (Eds.), *The first R: Every child's right to read.* NY: Teachers College Press & International Reading Association.

McAninch, A.R. (1993). *Teacher thinking and the case method.* NY: Teachers College Press.

Mehan, H. (1979). *Learning lessons.* Cambridge, MA: Harvard University Press.

Mercer, N. (1993). Culture, context and the construction of knowledge in the classroom. In P. Light & G. Butterworth (Eds.), *Context and cognition: Ways of learning and knowing* (pp.28-46). Hillsdale, NJ: Lawrence Erlbaum Associates.

Miles, M.B., & Huberman, A.M. (1984). *Qualitative data analysis: A sourcebook of new methods.* Thousand Oaks, CA: Sage Publications.

National Institute of Education (1974). Conference on studies in teaching. *Report of Panel 5: Teaching as a linguistic process in a cultural setting.*Washington, D.C.: National Institute of Education (DHEW). (Eric Document Reproduction Service No. ED 111 806).

Newman, D., Griffin, P., & Cole, M. (1989). *The construction zone: Working for cognitive change in school.* NY: Cambridge University Press.

Newmann, F., & Wehlage, G. (1995). *Successful school restructuring.* Alexandria, VA: Association for Supervision and Curriculum Development.

Philips, S. (1972). Participant structures and communicative competence: Warm Springs children in community and classroom. In C. Cazden, V. John, & D. Hymes (Eds.), *Functions of language in the classroom* (pp. 370-394). NY: Teachers College Press.

Rogoff, B. (1990). *Apprenticeship in thinking: Cognitive development in social context.* NY: Oxford University Press.

Roth, W., & Bowen, G.M. (1995). Knowing and interacting: A study of culture, practices and resources in grade 8 open inquiry science classrooms guided by a cognitive apprenticeship metaphor. *Cognition and Instruction, 13,* 73-128.

Schachter, F.F. (1979). *Everyday mother talk to toddlers: Early intervention.* NY: Academic Press.

Schön, D. (1987). *Educating the reflective practitioner.* San Francisco, CA: Jossey-Bass.

Suchman, L. (1987). *Plans and situated actions: The problem of human-machine communication.* NY: Cambridge University Press.

Sykes, G. (1996). Reform of and as professional development. *Phi Delta Kappan, 77,* 464-467.

Sykes, G. (1997). *The ivory tower under seige: The university as anachronism in teacher education?* Paper presented at the American Educational Research Association Meeting, Chicago, IL.

Tharp, R., & Gallimore, R. (1988). *Rousing minds to life.* NY: Cambridge University Press.

Walker, B. (1996a). Discussions that focus on strategies and self-assessment. In L. Gambrell & J. Almasi (Eds.), *Lively discussions: Fostering engaged reading* (pp.286-296). Newark, DE: International Reading Association.

Walker, B. (1996b). *Diagnostic teaching of reading.* Columbus, OH: Merrill Publishing Co.

## Appendix: Instructional Segment

This five minute segment between a second grade student and her teacher includes a story introduction, an oral reading of the story, and a retelling. Each interchange is indicated by an I and is numbered, as in I-1, I-2, I-3, and so on. Some of the detail of the transcript has been omitted (e.g., gestures).

I-1

S1—(reads) Teeny, Tiny Where . . .
T1—Woman.What do you think it's about?
S1—Umm. Spooky. She . . . umm . . . I forgot what she does, but I remember what she is. A teeny, tiny woman.

I-2

T1—What's it about?
S1—A tiny woman. Ummm. She does funny things.
T1—And she does funny things.
(Student reads two sentences slowly with 2 self-corrections, 3 repetitions.)

I-3

T1—OK. So what just happened?
S1—She went for a walk. And I know what happens on her walk.

I-4

T1—You said something spooky was going to happen? Do you still think that was going to happen? Do you want to add anything to that?
S1— Not until I get to it.

I-5

T1—Can you think of what else might happen?
S1—She meets a monster.
S1—(Reads the story)

I-6

T1—Tell me about the story.
S1—It was about a skeleton that was trying to get his bone back from the dead.

I-7

T1—Ohhh and who was the main person who took the bone?
S1—The teeny, tiny woman.

I-8

T1—The teeny, tiny woman.Where did she find the bone?
S1—Um. In the graveyard.

I-9

> T1—Oh. She found it in the graveyard. What was your favorite part of the story?
> S1—The skeleton.

I-10

> T1—Did they ever say it was skeleton in the story?
> S1—'Cause he had a bone.

I-11

> T1—Oh, you thought. It didn't really say it was skeleton, but you know it was cause it had a bone. Is that what skeletons are made of?
> S1—Bones. We are bones.

I-12

> T1—Where are our bones?
> S1—Way deep inside us. Right here (squeezes her ribs).
> T1—Can you feel them? Your ribs?

# Instructional Teams
# in a University Clinic

**Linda L. Hughes**
Northern State University

**Catherine K. Zeek**
Texas Woman's University

## Abstract

*This paper describes a university reading clinic in which undergraduate and graduate students formed collaborative teams to plan and implement instruction for children in grades kindergarten through six. The focus here is on the individualistic ways the teams functioned to develop lessons, solve problems, and direct their own learning. Implications for teacher education and clinic structure are included.*

Throughout this century, university reading clinic structures have followed patterns based on a positivist medical model (Johns, 1992). The traditional reading resource teacher worked with individuals or small groups of children outside the integrated or self-contained classrooms. Clinics prepared reading or special education majors to function in these pull-out settings. Local children were referred to the university reading clinic with diagnosed or undiagnosed reading deficiencies, batteries of tests were administered in a clinical setting, results were compiled and interpreted, and a program of remediation to address identified deficiencies was outlined. Within the university setting, reading and special education majors often administered standardized diagnostic instruments, provided one-on-one remedial instruction, and administered posttests to measure the success of the remediation.

Trends in current research and practice support transition from skills-based deficiency models found in traditional clinic settings (Cothern, 1994; Johns, 1992). Teacher education programs are increasingly designed around field-based experiences with heterogeneously grouped students. Field-based experiences provide teacher candidates with intensive extended instructional practice supported by mentoring, reflection, and feedback (Goodlad, 1994).

In addition, roles of reading specialists have changed to require more collaboration. The trend toward inclusion often means that students receive special services in the regular classroom (Texas Education Agency, 1983).

The reading resource teacher in an inclusion model may work primarily within the classroom setting in collaboration with the classroom teacher. The team of classroom teacher and reading resource teacher addresses the needs of all students in the context of the heterogeneously grouped classroom.

Changing roles of teachers require changes in the experiences provided in undergraduate and graduate preparation programs. This study describes the efforts of one university to restructure its clinical practicum experience. As part of this program change, undergraduate and graduate students formed instructional teams to plan and implement literacy learning activities. This paper describes the following:

1. How instructional teams were formed and how they functioned.
2. How team functioning seemed to affect planning and implementation of instruction.
3. How growth was facilitated and evidenced among instructional team members.

## Procedures

This study took place on the campus of a small southwestern university located in a rural community. Prior to their student teaching, those preservice teachers who were undergraduate reading majors were enrolled in a summer clinical reading practicum. Students in master's degree programs in reading were enrolled in a graduate-level section of the practicum.

### *Participants*

During the summer of 1995, 18 graduate students and 25 undergraduate students enrolled in separate sections of the reading practicum. These groups combined to collaboratively provide instruction to children enrolled in the clinic. Prior to the practicum, the undergraduates had completed university general studies, an Introduction to Teaching course with 30 hours of field experience, and two literacy methods courses. The literacy methods courses included experiences and theory focused on the importance of providing meaningful learning experiences in a literacy rich environment. Undergraduates consisted of one male (who withdrew from the course before completion) and 24 females.

The graduate students were working toward master's degrees in education. All were certified female teachers whose public school teaching experience ranged from 2 to 12 years, primarily in elementary, self-contained classrooms. All said they had never had a student teacher and had not worked with teachers in training previously.

### Structure of the Clinic

The clinic was patterned after the university's field-based teacher education model (see Sampson et al., this volume). Undergraduates and graduates formed instructional leadership teams (ILT's), with each team having at least one graduate student in the role of mentor, with undergraduates as interns. Teams were determined by the grade-level interests of mentors and interns. A total of six ILTs were formed: two for kindergarten, one for each grade level 1-3, and one multiage combined 4-6 team. Participant observers included one instructor, a doctoral student working in the clinic as an instructional intern and a doctoral student enrolled in the graduate practicum.

Teams composed of interns and mentors planned and taught lessons to groups of children. Teams with more than one mentor developed a means for both to have opportunities to lead in planning and instruction. Mentors taught model lessons after which interns taught the majority of the summer clinic lessons. Mentors guided interns in lesson planning, with each literacy lesson including shared reading, shared writing, comprehension, and language development or vocabulary strategies.

Seminars were planned at the request of mentors and interns on topics which addressed needs, including lesson planning, reading strategies, assessment, and professional development. Some seminars were separate for mentors and interns, while others included both groups.

### Data Collection and Analysis

Data sources included observational notes on lessons, planning sessions, and seminars; syllabi of both undergraduate and graduate practicum; and artifacts from final team portfolios including all lesson plans, self-assessments, peer-assessments, and copies of the children's work. The three participant observers created a schedule of observations so that each could observe each team during a 4-day week. Teams left lesson plans available to assist observations. Participant observers met each day to discuss and reflect on observations, raise issues, and suggest areas of focus for additional observations.

Participant observer notes and course artifacts were transcribed and analyzed according to the constant comparative method (Strauss & Corbin, 1990). All notes and artifacts were read by all researchers, who separately constructed categories. Participant observers then met to share and negotiate categories and meanings collaboratively.

## Results

Five categories were constructed through the data analysis. Within each category, participant observers analyzed how the dynamics of each category affected team functioning. The five categories were roles, initiative, responsibility, teaming, and assessment. The reporting of results will define each category and the range of behaviors that characterized it.

## Roles

Team functioning was characterized by social negotiation and definition of roles. Early in the practicum, teams brainstormed expectations for team members, with the listed qualities used as an evaluation tool. Within the guidelines of the course, ILTs were free to further define their roles. As teams formed and began to plan and deliver instruction to clinic children, observers noted and agreed that the flexibility of roles varied from team to team. Some teams negotiated their various activities through flexible exchange and interchange of roles with members participating in a variety of roles. Some teams functioned with no obvious separation or differentiation of roles, while other teams sharply defined roles between expert, experienced mentors and inexperienced interns.

On teams with greater role flexibility, members often moved from leadership roles to supportive roles fluidly. Members anticipated the need to take on a variety of roles, moved into roles as needed, and shed roles as quickly. Interns and mentors seemed to maintain "withitness," the ability to maintain focus on the children and each other. Members were constantly aware of changing dynamics of social interactions. Both verbal and nonverbal communication allowed for role flexibility to address needs of children and team members.

Teams with little role flexibility maintained clearly defined roles. Members did not easily move from leadership to supportive roles, but maintained identifiable separation between interns and mentors, and from each other. Mentors conveyed information while interns received it. Roles were rigidly defined and divided, "withitness" was reduced, and activity was traded for passivity. Team members became uncomfortable with these closely structured roles. On one team, interns who were not provided teaching time by the mentor confronted the mentor to express anger and negotiate for more teaching time. The mentor indicated that she was modeling and planned to provide interns with teaching time following an extended period of modeling. Clear role delineation appeared to be associated with a concept of teaching as conveying.

## Initiative

Initiative was defined as willingness on the part of both interns and mentors to offer ideas, generate leadership, and take risks. Initiative included promptness in offering ideas, stating suggestions, sharing resources, and donating time to a creative endeavor or activity, as well as a willingness to try the new and different, to offer and accept responsibility for a specific aspect of a plan.

On some teams, initiative occurred frequently, constantly, and without hesitation. Members supported each other when ideas were offered. Little or no hesitation was observed in generating of suggestions, taking risks, and supporting the process of generation and initiation. The dynamics of the planning meetings allowed mentors and interns to function in various collaborative roles.

On other teams, hesitations were observed and became more frequent in number. Members who initiated were left to carry out ideas and take risks with little or no support. Mentors became leaders, initiating and handing out roles. Members seemed to practice a behaviorist philosophy of instruction with the designated leader giving information and directions on how instruction was to be implemented. One such team, whose mentor modeled a very structured reading program, asked the course instructors to negotiate with the mentor to allow more intern-generated planning and instruction.

### *Teaming*

Teaming was defined as the level of collegiality and cohesiveness observed within groups, the spirit that identified a group as an entity with a sense of "we-ness." Teaming was characterized by high levels of acceptance of all members and activities demonstrating inclusiveness and oneness. Teaming included open sharing that facilitated a climate of comfort among members.

Some teams delivered lessons characterized by spontaneity, unity, and mutual good feelings among ILT members. Comfort was demonstrated during team planning and instructional activities in which members showed consideration for one another in a climate of acceptance.

Other ILTs were characterized by more structure-bound planning and instructional sessions. On one team, members grew to resent the dominance of the mentor, who at first taught all the lessons, then withdrew from the teaching. At this point she allowed the interns to do all the teaching while she directed, concerned that they instructed "correctly." The mentor would not give up control, with the result that the team did not develop a spirit of cooperation, but first followed instructions and later resented the lack of choice. The interns asked the course instructor to intervene with the mentor. Teaming characteristics varied as individuals negotiated roles.

### *Responsibility*

Teaming required that members have a sense of shared responsibility, a feeling that the success of one was a reason for all members to celebrate. Team successes belonged to members and concerns were the shared concerns of each individual. The extent to which shared responsibility was observed varied from team to team.

Some teams were characterized by members demonstrating mutual support. Responsibilities were shared, with each member willing to assist other members, openly expressing collegial support and offering back-up should the unexpected occur. Concerns were addressed through team reflection and group-negotiated solutions and resolutions.

On other teams, responsibilities were parceled out and divided among members. One member's inadequacy was not viewed as the inadequacy of the team or the support system, but as that individual's lacking or "fault." Frequent use of the pronouns *I* and *you* characterized conversations in these teams. Successes and failures fell on individual shoulders rather than being shared by the team as part of its problem-solving activity.

### Assessment

Assessment was defined as the ability of the members to reflectively self and team-assess the effectiveness of lesson planning and implementation. Assessment also included the extent to which self assessments and peer assessments were perceived by members as positive and constructive.

Assessment on some teams was on-going, continuous, growth-producing, and shared. Assessment was facilitated through guided reflection, as team members shared their self assessments in the form of mutual learning experiences. Individuals initiated self assessment within the ILT, soliciting suggestions and recommendations, and the team affirmed and added recommendations. The collegial atmosphere created support for positive self assessment.

On some teams, assessment originated with a mentor or other team member rather than with individuals. Assessment occurred more as "telling" than as reflective activity, with the intern receiving information. The intern's role was characterized by listening and agreeing, with the facilitator taking the role of "expert," information giver, and evaluator.

### Results Across Categories

The categories described above were overlapping, dynamic, and interactive. Team functioning in each category affected both the inner workings of the team and the implementation of team agendas. The interaction of the individuals on each team and the roles they negotiated contributed to the situated planning and instructional implementation. Thus, the same dynamics were important in both planning and implementation activities.

## Discussion and Conclusions

In the alternative clinic model described in this study, teams were formed based on the number of children enrolled in the university clinic, the age and level of achievement of the children, and the number of graduates and undergraduates enrolled. Team membership was determined by university students' areas of interest. Guidelines for group functioning were based on consensus of group members and the overall requirements of the practicum. Thus, groups functioned through self-determination, with the skills, abilities, and beliefs of individuals serving as team resources.

This alternative clinic model provided experiences in collaborative planning to undergraduate and graduate students. The model facilitated professional growth for both undergraduates and graduates and provided support for reflection on practice. For the most part, undergraduates felt they were supported in the learning process by being able to work closely with experienced professional teachers. Graduates appreciated the opportunity to try a mentoring role, with some wanting additional opportunities to support teacher candidate growth.

Limitations of the study that may have contributed to differences in team functioning were the brief (5 week) summer term and lack of training for students in collaborative decision-making. Teams had a limited time to become acquainted and plan for the children they would teach. Collaborative group function assumes group members will monitor and facilitate self and team growth through shared goals, but this did not always occur. While some teams demonstrated growth in all categories, more time for growth in team facilitation could have resulted in greater growth for teams with role flexibility issues. Additional sessions on collaborative models and personality types may also have facilitated team functioning.

Follow-up studies are needed to explore relationships between team characteristics, student achievement, and students' perceptions of learning and teaching. Clinic children frequently spoke of having many teachers and identified both interns and mentors as teachers, indicating they perceived participation from both graduate and undergraduate students. Further research could determine the significance of multiple teachers on children's short and long-term perceptions of learning and teaching.

Participant observers noted a possible relationship between characteristics of team planning and instructional implementation. This observation supports research on collegial planning, team teaching, and cooperative teaching that suggests that strong collaborative abilities and the ability to reflect with peers are complementary.

This study raises questions about the types of reading practicum experiences offered to undergraduate and graduate students as they prepare to function within the changing dynamics of the classroom. Current philosophies in literacy instruction no longer support the medical model of linear learning. A social constructivist perspective requires teacher educators to introduce undergraduate and graduate reading majors to the dynamics of integrated instruction in the clinical reading setting. Constructivist reading practica can provide experiences in holistic instruction and assessment. These supported experiences prepare students to function in educational settings, with the dynamics of change as a constant.

---

# References

Cothern, N. B. (1994). *Whole language theory and practice: Teachers and children learning together.* The Delta Kappa Gamma Bulletin, 38-43.

Goodlad, J. I. (1994).*Educational renewal: Better teachers, better schools.* San Francisco: Jossey-Bass.

Johns, J. I. (1992). *From traditional reading clinics to wellness centers.* Literacy Research Report Number 16. Dekalb, IL: Northern Illinois University.

Strauss, A. L., & Corbin, J. (1990). *Basics of qualitative research : Grounded theory procedures and techniques.* Newbury Park, CA: Sage Publications.

Texas Education Agency (1983). *State board of education rules for handicapped students.* Austin, Tx: Author.

# Preparing Preservice Elementary Teachers for Professional Collaboration with Special Education Literacy Teachers

### A. Lee Williams

Slippery Rock University

## Abstract

*In order to prepare preservice elementary education teachers for collaboration with another professional, as is the case when children with literacy difficulties are in an inclusion classroom, the preservice children were paired with a student in a special education class and asked to collaborate on an assignment. They were given the task of choosing one of three inclusion "students" from instructor-prepared cases and designing appropriate adaptations of regular instruction. Using an action research model to study benefits to students from this assignment, successful collaboration happened between students who had less or equal knowledge than did their partners (in both classes) and whose partners took the project as seriously as they did. Philosophical differences between the university elementary education and special education departments concerning literacy acquisition influenced the nature of the task given to the students and negatively impacted some as they completed the collaboration assignment.*

Elementary classroom teachers today are likely to have a very different role in meeting the needs of students identified as having special learning needs or protected disabilities, especially in reading, than teachers of only a few years ago, given the rapidly growing popularity of classroom inclusion models for meeting student needs (Thousand & Villa, 1990). In recent years there has been a growing dissatisfaction with pulling students out of the regular classroom in order to meet special instructional needs. Johnson, Allington and Afflerbach (1985) described the lack of congruence of curriculum and teaching between remedial reading and Chapter 1 classrooms and the regular reading classroom. Haynes and Jenkins (1986) noted students placed in resource rooms for reading instruction spent 52% of their time doing seatwork and only 25% of their time reading. Other difficulties inherent in pullout programs, including wasted time as children moved from room to room, could be ameliorated by having the specialist come to the classroom, rather than by having the child leave the classroom to go to the specialist. Pull-in or inclusion classrooms, with specialists working in the classroom alongside the regular education teacher rather than having children leave the classroom to attend pull-out programs, attempt to overcome the identified lack of student success when students follow the traditional remedial curriculum (Knapp, Turnbull and Shields, 1990).

Today's inclusion classrooms serve not only children experiencing reading difficulties, but also children identified as having other disabilities that may have previously been addressed in a special education resource room. When the regular classroom teacher and the reading teacher or the special education teacher taught separate curriculums in separate places, issues of congruence and collaboration could be ignored, whether such ignorance was or wasn't truly bliss. However, with two or more professionals sharing the same workspace and the same students, issues of collaboration among teachers become crucial. Such differences may be about roles and power relationships or they may be about goals and purposes (philosophy). Either way, these issues often make true collaboration difficult and schools do not usually offer adequate support for this type of change process (Thomas, Correa & Morsink, 1995).

## Inclusion, Collaboration, and Beliefs About Teaching and Learning

Students in the elementary education program at the medium-sized university where this study took place are likely to have a double major or a minor in special education, although such courses are taught by another department in another building on campus. Students begin taking special education courses their freshman year if they follow that department's prescribed sequence; they begin taking elementary education courses their junior year, only after special admittance to the program. Therefore, by the time students are enrolled in elementary methods courses dealing with teaching reading and language arts, they often have already had special education courses that have covered similar topics.

One issue of concern expressed informally by both students and faculty in our institution is the lack of congruence between the understanding of language acquisition and the role of teachers of literacy for children with special needs between the special education and the elementary education departments and how that difference affects preservice teachers' developing belief systems. The beliefs a teacher brings to instruction may be powerful contributors to practice (Vacca, Vacca, & Gove, 1995). The reading textbook used in the special education department for example, describes a typical beginner's reading lesson thus:

> Students must learn the most common sound associated with each letter first. . . . Letters are usually introduced one at a time after a review of previously learned letters. Students can be grouped easily for letter-sound knowledge, because there are only a certain number of letters to be learned...Teachers need to determine the rate (fluency) at which students can identify letters as well as their level of accuracy. At any given time during the instructional process, students should be able to read a list of letters previously taught at a rate of 100 or more per minute. Such automaticity is necessary so that students can concentrate on other reading skills at a later date. (Mastropieri & Scruggs, 1994, p.130-131)

This contrasts with beginning reading as described in the most commonly used reading textbook in the elementary education department:

> If beginners are going to make a smooth transition from emergent to fluent literacy, they must feel at the onset that they belong to a class-room community of readers and writers. The challenge of working with beginners lies in scaffolding learning and weaving together experiences that build on children's knowledge of language and their previous interactions with text. (Vacca, Vacca, & Gove, 1995, pp. 108)

These two textbooks describe very different belief structures concerning teaching reading and reading instruction. Special education professors at this institution tend to offer a behaviorist explanation for learning and elementary education tends to offer a social cognitive explanation of learning. Particularly in reading and language arts methods classes where the difference between bottom up, behaviorist understandings and top-down, constructivist understandings seem most pronounced, students challenge what they perceive as discrepant information in a course or a textbook, asking, "Who is telling the truth? What version of teaching are we to believe?"

Students at this university often choose a double elementary/special education major because they believe they will be more marketable in an extremely competitive local job market. Students want to be attractive hires for principals and superintendents, but they are unprepared for the differences in roles that special education and regular elementary education teachers will be required to play in the actual classroom. They are equally unprepared for the differences in philosophical grounding between the two departments. Thus, two problems surfaced in preparation of preservice teachers: the problem of philosophical congruence between special and elementary education instruction as well as the lack of preparation for working with another professional to plan and deliver instruction in an inclusion classroom.

I wanted to help my regular elementary education students understand the complexity of teacher beliefs in relationship to practice and of identifying evidence for best practice. I also wanted them to work closely with the special education teacher in an inclusion classroom. In addition, I wanted to learn more about what my colleagues in special education were teaching the students who sat in my classroom on alternate days. Did we have more or less in common that the students could perceive? Were there ways our elementary education majors could practice the skills of collaboration needed to successfully work with another literacy professional, even if he or she did not fundamentally agree on how language was learned and how classrooms should look to foster growth in literacy?

## Interdepartmental Collaboration Between Elementary and Special Education

I suggested to a colleague in the special education department that we work on fostering collaboration among students in special education and in elementary education. We decided eventually that the best way to do this was to pair students to work collaboratively on a project. We agreed that collaboration skills were of primary importance in inclusion settings; by having students work collaboratively in a preservice setting we hoped to model interdepartmental collaboration because we ourselves were willing to work together and give students the opportunity to experience the process of shared decision making themselves.

In order to investigate student's experiences with the collaboration assignment I designed an action-research study to collect and analyze data from the assignment. My colleague also collected and shared data from her classes. As action research, I wanted to use the results to refine my instruction and the collaboration project in future semesters to make it more meaningful and useful for students.

## Research Questions

The following general questions framed the inquiry: (1) What are the perceptions of the elementary education students concerning their role in an inclusion classroom, especially in regard to collaborating with the special education teacher, and how are these perceptions influenced by the implicit and explicit differences in prevailing instructional philosophy concerning reading and language arts in the two departments? If preservice teachers do perceive differences in philosophy of instruction, will this influence their willingness to engage in collaboration? (2) Can instructors overcome real and perceived obstacles to collaboration in the preservice setting so that students are more prepared for the important role collaboration will occupy in their professional lives, especially given the preponderance of full and partial inclusion of children with special learning needs in today's regular elementary classrooms?

## Course Assignments to Foster Collaboration Among Students

Students from three sections of ELED 352 Methods and Materials for Teaching Elementary Language Arts and two sections of SPED 200 Classroom Management were randomly paired and given an assignment that would require they work together. Before beginning work with their cross-class partners, the language arts students were asked to design an inquiry-based, thematic framework for instruction that used reading and writing to learn across the curriculum. Some worked in teams of two while others completed the assignment alone. The students in Classroom Management were given case studies of three special needs students who might be in an inclusion classroom. The assignment given to the language arts classes was to collaborate with the special education student to choose one of the three case studies, and to modify the classroom setting or planned instruction in their thematic framework in some way to meet the special needs of the student described in the case study. They also were to reflect and report on the process of collaboration. The special education students taking Classroom Management were assigned to share and explain the case studies, to collaborate with their language arts partner in choosing one, and to design an adjunct instructional intervention from among those studied in their class that reflected a basis in the language arts.

In order to support collaboration among students who might otherwise find it difficult to meet or telephone in real time, students were required to make at least one contact through electronic mail (e-mail). All students automatically have a campus e-mail address and access to their account at any computer lab on campus. They could also use home e-mail addresses if they wished. Since the classes met on different days, access to and encouragement of other than real time collaboration was encouraged so that scheduling conflicts were minimized as a barrier to collaboration.

## Investigating the Assignment's Benefits to Students: Data Collection and Analysis

Students in the elementary education sections were given a short answer pre-project anonymous survey about their class status, major, courses taken in each department and perceptions about collaboration and of how literacy is taught in each department. They were asked to note places where the departments might to be sending differing messages about appropriate instruction. Students were also asked to envision their ideal teaching job (see Appendix A). Students in the elementary education sections ranged from second semester sophomores to first semester seniors and post-baccalaureate students working only toward certification. All had been admitted to the College of Education. The students in the special education sections ranged from freshmen to post-baccalaureate and may or may not have been admitted to the College of Education.

Student reflections on the actual process of collaboration were included as part of the language arts assignment (Appendix B). These reflections were copied and analyzed. Additionally, students in both elementary and special education sections filled in anonymous response forms concerning the assignment at the end of the semester (Appendix C), and three students from the special education sections and three students from the elementary education section were asked to form a focus interview group to reflect on and explain their experience with the collaboration assignment. Since the students in the language arts class had written reflections on the project, one who identified a failed collaboration was asked to be interviewed, and two students who worked together on the thematic framework and reported a successful collaboration with their special education partner were asked to be interviewed. Special education students to be interviewed were identified by the instructor of that course. This group interview (Appendix D) with students and both instructors was audio tape recorded, and students were given the questions beforehand and asked to write preliminary responses.

The data from the surveys and interviews were coded into emergent categories and analyzed for frequency and content using the constant comparison method (Strauss & Corbin, 1990) and frequency analysis. Additionally, two tapes of instructor planning sessions of the collaboration assignment were transcribed and coded. After the semester ended, the instructors used these transcripts to discuss their own perceptions of the project and to develop categories related to both their concerns and the successes of this assignment.

## Limitations of This Study

Designed primarily as teacher-action research, this study investigates my own students and my own teaching. While results of this type of project may be beneficial to other teacher educators, results are generalizable only in a heuristic sense given the situatedness of the investigation. Also, the students' beliefs and practices concerning collaboration in methods classes may not reflect their actual practices once they begin teaching in schools.

## Results

### *Before the Collaboration Assignment:*
### *Beliefs Concerning Special Education And Inclusion*

Seventy-five students were enrolled in the elementary education language arts classes; sixty-eight returned pre-collaboration project survey responses. None of the juniors (n=32; 53% of total respondents) perceived a philosophical conflict between departments, although 85% of the senior and post-baccalaureate students perceived a difference or conflict between what they learned in special education classes and what they learned in elementary education classes. Among those students who noted a difference between departments, 19% students attributed the difference to the learning theory espoused departmentally:

> In the SPED classes they stress teacher directed instruction instead of the constructivist theory that many methods courses stress. This seems confusing.

> I am the parent of a learning-disabled student and I disagree with the bottom up approach used in SPED literacy program. . . . Many of the strategies SPED presents are doubting the child's ability to learn. A top-down approach is more effective . . .

> SPED concentrates on task analysis and behavior modification, ELED on whole language.

When students who did not perceive a conflict between departments expressed concerns, they wrote about conflicts in their own understanding— between what they wanted to learn but did not seem to be "getting" or what they thought they should learn. Eight percent of students wrote comments about lack of knowledge or practice.

> I don't know how I will make special ed. students fit into my classroom. We learned the methods but not how to incorporate them.

> Both departments talk about inclusion, but both departments do not teach inclusively.

## Student Assessment and Reflection
## on the Collaboration Assignment

Out of a total of 126 students in both sections, only four students (3%) reported that they could not reach their assigned partner by either e-mail or telephone. In this case, students were reassigned to other partners or given the opportunity to construct the project without collaboration, reflecting on how and why the collaboration failed. Students who made no effort to collaborate and whose partners submitted e-mail copies of unanswered requests to share information were given no credit for this assignment.

Students had mixed reactions to the project as they worked with their partners. As I categorized concerns, I recognized the responses of the students as concerns teachers themselves express. Students were concerned with having to collaborate in the first place in terms of ownership and time:

> I planned my lesson carefully and then another person wanted to critique and change it. Their ideas might be okay, but I'm not sure I like them telling me what to do.

> I got the inquiry question set, had my concepts organized with good discovery activities, had stuff from science methods and math, and I wanted to be done with it. It takes too much time to try to agree on what to do with another person.

> I know about language arts and what this assignment should be like and this person is just a freshman and is clueless.

Others were disturbed if a collaborative spirit didn't emerge and the assigned collaborators worked at seeming cross purposes:

> My partner didn't take my inquiry question seriously. She just wanted to make some game she could turn in for points. How does a . . . game fit an inquiry classroom?

> I got the feeling I took this way more seriously.

Several of the upper-class elementary education students who were also special education majors or minors believed they did not learn much from the collaboration project. Of the 53 elementary students who filled out the end of semester feedback form 51% (all double majors or minors) believed that they did not learn anything from the collaboration assignment about students with disabilities. Twenty-two percent of these students, however, did mention their ability to help their special education partner: "I didn't learn much, but I think my partner learned a lot." Some students in the elementary education sections (11%) also explained they learned about the collaboration process itself (time involved or sharing of insights) rather than about students with disabilities. On the other hand, of the 49 special education students who responded to the end of semester feedback form, 86% replied that they learned something from working on the project about at least one aspect of teaching the language arts. Only 10% of these students had taken the elementary methods course focusing on language arts previously.

The responses of the special education students ranged from clearly related to the elementary education course, "Language overlaps so many areas. A child struggling with reading will have a hard time with science and history for reasons that have nothing to do with science and history," to a response that seemed unrelated to the thematic reading and writing-to-learn project required of the elementary students, "I learned specifics about phonics and word attack." Again, upper division students who were double majors reported learning little about content from the project (although they said they learned about collaboration). Ten percent of the special education students reported that they had already had the elementary methods course and did not learn about teaching any of the language arts from completing the project.

Some students, however, found that discovering ideas about teaching through talk and shared decision-making was a positive and productive experience. Nearly all students (97%) mentioned the importance of patience or compromise at least once in their language arts reflections. Students also reported learning the most from the project when two factors were present: (1) they were equally or less knowledgeable than their partner, and (2) their partner took the assignment as seriously as they did and ideas offered were discussed respectfully.

> It was really fun to talk to someone and explain to them my ideas. I could tell by their reaction what made sense and what was just an idea in my head no one else got. It was like writing workshop for teaching.

> Sometimes it's hard to know what to do with kids who might have trouble. The two of us talking about it gave me some ways to really think about what I'll do.

> In the long run, two teachers can work together if they put the needs of the student first.

> [By talking with my partner] . . . I realized I need to think carefully about *all* the students in my classroom.

Two categories for the success of collaboration emerged from the group interviews at the end of the collaboration assignment. First, these students recognized that collaboration took time, but felt it was worth the time when new ideas were created in discussion and sharing. All six students, even the one who had unsuccessfully tried to connect with the special education partner, valued collaboration and wanted to be able to share ideas with the good of a child in mind. A second factor interviewed students identified as important for successful collaboration was that both parties needed to have "open minds." Students in the group interview had a pragmatic "whatever works when you try it out" approach to instruction that appeared different from the philosophical grounding of either course.

## Student Reports on Using E-Mail to Collaborate

Given general student interest in technology and especially the Internet, I envisioned they would also find e-mail a beneficial method of communication and collaboration. However, students found e-mail less satisfying than face-to-face planning. The work of collaboration was done during meetings. Although a face-to-face encounter was not a requirement of the project, all of the student teams that made any kind of collaborative contact had at least one face to face meeting. For 98% of students, e-mail was a neutral experience, a way to share schedules and set up meetings where the real work was done. Only one student in the elementary sections and one in the special education sections (both non-traditional students living more than an hour's drive from campus) specifically mentioned e-mail as an important benefit of this project for saving time and facilitating collaboration. For another student (also a non-traditional student living over an hour's drive from campus), e-mail was a "horrible experience." She reported that between the inadvertent closing of her e-mail account and spending "days" on the phone and running from office to office to get her account re-opened (only to have lost all her on-line data) she would "never use e-mail again." Such a strong negative reaction was unmatched by any other students, however.

## The Impact of the Collaboration Assignment of Student's Beliefs

Several structural complications arose in this assignment. The instructors did not have similar on-campus schedules, and both were responsible to students in field settings off campus, making instructor on-going collaboration difficult. Differences between the class level and experience of students in the two courses made pairing the two classes difficult—first year students were paired with upper-class students and were expected to collaborate as equals. Left unexamined were the fundamental differences in departmental philosophy in designing the assignment. The design of a thematic, across the curriculum inquiry based-framework for the language arts students reflects my own language learning beliefs. When I envisioned that students would construct adaptations in collaboration with their assigned partner, I assumed the special education students would know how. Yet the special education students were not familiar with the issue of adaptation or modification of curriculum in terms of inquiry-based teaching. On the other hand, my colleague in special education required that her students design an adjunct product (a game, a classroom design, a specific adaptive worksheet or assignment) related to language arts and I had not given my students any instruction in this area. Although the project requirement for my students and for my colleague's students was different, we both envisioned an assignment that created a real need for discussion and sharing among the pairs of students. This was our shared value. The students who reported a positive learning experience were not troubled by the difference in their assignment outcomes and they too valued the sharing itself. However, this difference in assignment outcomes was noted by 23% of the students in either final reflections in the language arts assignment or the final survey given to all students.

> There has to be some agreement between the collaborating individuals about what the final goal is. Without a common goal this is a difficult process. My collaborating individual did not need to collaborate with me because she had a totally different project than I did.

We did not anticipate the resistance some students gave to collaboration and sharing knowledge with another student based on two different project outcomes. Yet differing ideas about what instruction will entail and differing responsibilities of the regular education and special education teacher is an occurrence both my colleague and I had experienced in our work as public school teachers. What we envisioned as an invitation to discussion was not perceived that way by all students.

An assignment of this nature has the potential to positively affect students' abilities to work collaboratively with colleagues, and such professional collaboration seems inevitable as current trends for inclusion of special needs students into regular education classrooms grows in practice (Shaw, Biklin, Conlon, Dunn, Kramer & DeRoma-Wagner, 1990). However, in order to do so, students must be helped to appreciate collaboration's messier features. Students found lack of time and lack of cooperation as detriments to the process; they were troubled if they thought they "knew" more than their partner did. They saw lack of congruence between assignment products as instructor-based rather than as discipline or situationally based. For some, this perceived difference in assignments (which I attribute to a difference in instructor philosophy) negatively impacted their feelings of successful collaboration. For others, the assignment created an opportunity to discuss and share strategies for ensuring student learning success. Sharing ideas with a knowledgeable and caring colleague was the primary motivation for appreciating collaboration.

Using e-mail, for the most part, did not ameliorate a further concern, that of time to meet in order to collaborate. Face-to-face discussion and sharing were considered far more important to successful collaboration than the access outside of real time and space that e-mail provides.

As my colleague and I continue this collaboration assignment, I want to help students realize from the start that the special education and elementary education students are not working at cross-purposes even when project outcomes for the two courses are different. The philosophical differences between departments is perceived by some students as a difference in assignment outcome (the add-on game or worksheet versus the modification of existing assignments); their focus on a preservice teacher outcome rather than an imagined special need student outcome created an atmosphere that discouraged collaboration. This philosophical difference is real, but must not be allowed to interfere with necessary collaboration. My aim is that students eventually understand what several students wrote in their reflection about the project, that "it is putting the needs of the student first that makes collaboration work." It also seems important to make clear to students that learning to negotiate issues of successful collaboration are as important as learning specific content or strategies for literacy or special education instruction. Teaching students how to recognize potential areas of disruption and interpersonal relationship strategies will help to keep the collaboration process productive.

While I did not get followup feedback from students specifically focused on the concerns they earlier expressed about departments' different learning theories, many students who successfully collaborated seemed less interested in understanding beliefs or learning theory and more interested in strategies for ensuring student success. Given their novice status as teachers, helping students gain the confidence to deal with inclusion and collaboration by providing a broad repertoire of teaching and collaboration strategies may be as important as making beliefs explicit. However, the requirement that students reflect on the process of collaboration seemed to function as a mechanism for students to examine what works and what doesn't work, judgments that are ultimately belief-based.

Collaboration is an essential skill for teachers who will work with other professionals to plan and implement instruction. Working with a colleague in another department gave me the impetus to assess and learn about my own teaching in terms of student perceptions of success, and it provided for sharing and discussion that helped me turn ideas into practice. This assignment gave students avenues for attitude adjustment and reflection about what they can do and still need to practice in order for collaboration to be a success when working to assure that all students learn. As one student wrote,

It is easier to discuss what I want for my future students with someone in another class than in [my own] class because I think about what I can do in my own classroom someday. I am learning how to talk about what *I* think is important. If I collaborate with someone, I feel less alone and overwhelmed.

# References

Donoahue, Z. (1996). Collaboration, community and communication: Modes of discourse for teacher research. In Z. Donoahue, M. A. Van Tassell, & L. Patterson (Eds.), *Research in the classroom: Talk, texts and inquiry* (pp. 91-107). Newark, DE: International Reading Association.

Haynes, M. & Jenkins, J. (1986). Reading instruction in special education resource rooms. *American Educational Resource Journal, 23,* 161-190.

Johnson, P. H., Allington, R. L. & Afflerbach, P. (1985). The congruence of classroom and remedial reading instruction. *Elementary School Journal, 85,* 465-477.

Knapp, M., Turnbull, B., & and Shields, P. (1990). New directions for educating the children of poverty. *Educational Leadership, 48* (2), 4-8.

Mastropieri, M. A. & Scruggs, T. E. (1994). *Effective instruction for special education* (2nd ed.). Austin, TX: ProEd.

Shaw, S., Biklin, D., Conlon, R., Dunn, J., Kramer, J. & DeRoma-Wagner, V. (1990). Special education and school reform. In L. M. Bullock and R. L. Simpson (Eds.) *Critical issues in special education: Implications for personnel preparation.* Denton, TX: North Texas University.

Strauss, A., & Corbin, J. (1990). *Basis of qualitative research: Grounded theory procedures and techniques.* Newbury Park, CA: Sage Publications.

Thomas, C.C., Correa, V. I., & Morsink, C. V. (1995). *Interactive teaming: Consultation and collaboration in special programs.* Englewood Cliffs, NJ: Prentice-Hall.

Thousand, J., & Villa, R. (1990). Sharing expertise and responsibilities through teaching teams. In W. Stainback & S. Stainback (Eds.). *Support networks for inclusive schooling: Integrated interdependent education,* pp. 151-166. Baltimore, MD: Paul H. Brookes.

Vacca, R. T., Vacca, J. & Gove, M.. (1995). *Reading and learning to read* (3rd ed.). New York, NY: HarperCollins.

# Appendix A
# Early Semester Survey Given to Language Arts Classes

1. What is your class rank? (circle one)
   junior 1   junior 2   senior 1   senior 2   post bacc   other

2. What is your major(s)? Minor(s)

3. If you could have any teaching job, what would your dream position be?

4. What elementary or early childhood methods classes are you taking now?

5. What special education classes are you taking now?

6. What ELEC classes have you taken previously?

7. What SPED classes have you taken previously?

8. What do you know about a regular elementary literacy teacher's role in inclusion classrooms? What would you like to know?

*If you have taken classes in SPED, please respond to the following:*

9. Compare what you have learned about literacy in your ELEC classes with what you have learned in SPED. How is the information alike? How is it different? Explain anything you find confusing or contradictory.

If you are willing to be interviewed about this survey, please write your name and phone number here:

## Appendix B
## Language Arts Assignment

Log of Collaborative Conferences:
Name of Language Arts teacher(s):
Name of Special Education Professional:

Case Study Chosen:

Modifications/Adaptations to curriculum agreed upon for this child:

How will you ensure that your instruction remains focused on meaningful, authentic literacy activities and inquiry as you adapt your instruction for this child's special needs?

List date, type, and content of conferences. Note in your reflection what happened and how that seemed to help or hinder your goals for planning your thematic framework.

Conference Record

| Date | Type: phone e-mail, in person | Content: What was discussed? What decisions were made? | Reflection: How did it work? How did it feel? |
|------|------|------|------|
|  |  |  |  |
|  |  |  |  |
|  |  |  |  |
|  |  |  |  |

Write a one or two page reflective summary of the process and product of your collaborative efforts.

# Appendix C
# Final Survey Given to All Sections of Language Arts and Classroom Management Classes

Special Education Teachers' [Language Arts Teachers']
Collaboration Project Feedback

Directions: Please comment on the following issues related to the collaboration project you completed recently.

1. What is the most important aspect of collaboration you learned following the completion of your project?

2. What is the most important aspect of your skills and knowledge in language arts you learned following the completion of your project?

3. What is the most important aspect of your skills and knowledge working with students with disabilities you learned following the completion of your project?


# Appendix D
# Focus Group Interview Guide Questions

1. What preparation for collaboration had you received in the College of Education prior to this project?

2. What made you decide to choose the particular case study, area of language arts, and assessment of instructional strategy with your peer?

3. Did you have any difficulties or concerns about collaboration as you worked with your peer?

4. Has the completion of the project affected your collaboration views?

5. Do you have a better sense of the benefits and pitfalls of collaboration as a result of this project?

6. What do you think is the ideal collaborative arrangement for preservice teachers preparing to work in general education/special education classrooms?

7. What types of preparation do new teachers need in collaboration to meet the range of student diversity in inclusion classrooms?

# The Evolution of a Professional Development Center: Collaboration, Reflective Assessment and Refinement

**Mary B. Sampson**
**Wayne M. Linek**
**I. LaVerne Raine**

Texas A&M University-Commerce

**Pat Westergaard**

Greenville Independent School District

## Abstract

*Professional development centers involving the collaborative efforts of public schools and universities have been cited as a viable method of facilitating change in teacher education programs. However, collaborative efforts between universities and public schools have a history of unequal partnerships. The teacher education program described has evolved and experienced growth as a result of implementing refinements based on the collaborative reflective assessment of all partners. This article examines the impact of reflective assessment upon the Northeast Texas Center for Professional Development and Technology (NETCPDT) teacher education program—and the resulting integration of literacy-related strategies throughout the public school and university curriculum.*

Change has been called for in teacher-education programs (Commeyras, Reinking, Heubach, & Pangucco, 1993; Dixon & Ishler, 1992; Holmes Group, 1986). This call for reform of teacher education programs is not a new phenomenon. A century ago, the Committee of Ten was formed to explore ways to improve elementary and secondary schools. The participants reached the consensus that universities should collaborate with public schools in order to improve instruction and learning in schools (Clark, 1988). However, studies in the United States have found little change in instruction since the beginning of the common school (Cuban, 1984; Goodlad, 1984; Jackson, 1986).

A recent focus of school reform has been on restructuring public school education by empowering teachers to become interactive, dynamic decision makers (David, 1989). These teacher decision makers collaborate with other educators in order to refine and extend their own roles and, consequently, improve teaching and learning (Holmes Group, 1986; Lieberman & Miller, 1986; McCarthy & Peterson, 1989; Murphy, 1990). As a method of facilitating the opportunity for collaboration, attention has been focused on the possibility of public schools and universities forming partnerships (Holmes Group, 1990) in order to "bring practicing teachers and administrators together with university faculty in partnerships that improve teaching and learning on the part of their respective students" (Holmes Group, 1986, p. 56). Goodlad (1991) identified the use of clinical or "teaching" schools which incorporated university and public school collaboration to enhance the learning of school children and pre-service teachers as a critical component for the redesign of teacher education in the nineties.

The collaboration of public schools and universities has a history intertwined with challenges (Roemer, 1991; Sarason, 1982; Tye & Tye, 1985). A pervasive view that theory is the exclusive domain of the university and practice the responsibility of the public school (Zeichner, 1992) has often counteracted the growth of common interests and bonds of trust (Booth, Furlong, & Wilkin, 1990; Goodlad, 1991). Therefore, collaboration does not always provide equal voice and responsibility for all participants.

Whitford, Schlechty, and Shelor (1987) describe three types of collaboration: cooperative, symbiotic, and organic. Traditionally, many universities enter into cooperative or symbiotic collaborations with public schools. While cooperative collaborations are characterized by one entity providing a service or doing a short-term project with little reciprocation from the other participant, symbiotic collaborations usually involve some type of reciprocation such as, "We'll provide a workshop for your teachers if you let us place student teachers in your school." In both symbiotic and cooperative collaborations, the primary responsibility for decision making and leadership rests with one of the institutions, typically the university. In contrast, organic collaboration involves a redefinition of roles, responsibilities, and the decision making procedure so that all partners are on level ground. While the Holmes Group (1986) supports organic collaboration between universities and public schools as a method of instigating change in education, the literature on school reform primarily documents school change that does not include university and public school collaboration on teacher education (Scharer, Freeman, Lehman, & Allen, 1993; Shapiro, 1994). Goodlad (1984) summarized this dilemma by stating: "In short, the joining of school (and school district) and universities in commonly purposive and mutually beneficial linkages is a virtually untried and therefore, unstudied phenomenon" (p. 12).

This article focuses on the evolutionary process in which Texas A&M University-Commerce and public school partners engaged while creating a field-based program (Northeast Center for Professional Development and Technology—NETCPDT). Our program is based on the concept of all partners having equal voice and choice. Our organic collaboration, or "level ground" process is ongoing and promotes collaborative reflection and discussion concerning "what is working?" and "what should we do differently?"

## The Quest Begins

In 1991, the Texas Legislature responded to the call for teacher education reform by designating grant funds for the formation of partnerships involving universities and public schools. In order to receive funds, universities and public schools had the opportunity to collaborate and submit grant proposals describing how their partnerships would reform and positively impact preservice teacher education, in-service teacher education and, ultimately, the achievement of the public school student. When the *Requests for Proposals* were sent out by the Texas Education Agency, Texas A&M University-Commerce (TAMU-C) was placing student teachers in numerous school districts. Therefore, TAMU-C issued an open invitation to school districts who were currently working with our student teachers to form a collaborative partnership and submit a proposal for grant funds. Three school districts accepted the invitation and agreed to be partners in the grant writing.

The grant writing occurred during the spring of 1991, with two university grant writers collaborating with representatives from each of the three districts. The NETCPDT partnership was informed in August of 1991 that a planning grant had been awarded. The process had begun.

Since organic or "level ground" collaboration was a stated goal, representatives from each entity of the newly formed partnership began meeting in the fall of 1991 to brainstorm goals and develop a program that would meet the needs of both university and public school students. A goal in the grant proposal was that all partners, including public school and university faculty, would have equal "voice and choice" in the development and implementation of the program. The program could not be developed and mandated by partners who were not teaching in the public school and university classrooms. Therefore, the majority of the program developers were public school and university teaching faculty. The initial meeting included the one or two university faculty members who would be working with the first group of field-based students in each of the districts (a total of 5-6 university faculty), principals from interested buildings in each of the three districts (usually two to three per district), two to three public school faculty members from each building, the dean of the college of education, the elementary education department head, a business representative, a central office administrative representative from each district (superintendent or assistant superintendent) and educational consultants from the Regional Service Center. As a result of the meeting, the following vision was developed for the professional development center:

> . . . one that is designed, implemented, delivered, monitored, evaluated, and modified by a collaboration of partners with representation from all constituents of the program, i. e., teacher educators, university students, public school classroom teachers and administrators (Governing Board of NETCPDT, 1994, p. 1).

The guiding principles behind the mission statement are collaboration and shared decision making—in effect a true partnership. The fall of 1991 and spring of 1992 were spent in collaborative planning with the addition of university students, the secondary education department head and faculty members, and representatives from departments on campus that delivered coursework for teacher education majors. However, the collaborative decision was made that the majority of representation must continue to be public school and university teachers. This group was named the NETCPDT Governing Board and initially met formally one to three times per semester. It became the vehicle for formalizing the basic framework of the program.

One of the first changes in teacher education effected by the partnership involved the basic character of the program. Both public school and university faculty had often commented that the framework and timetable of the traditional program were "set in stone." Traditionally, student teachers spent ten weeks with one cooperating teacher. In those instances, district placements were made by the university and student teachers were assigned to teachers by public school administrators. Cooperating teachers were required to follow a timetable of phasing the student teacher into instructional responsibilities following a university mandated schedule. The university supervisor conducted four formal evaluations and assigned the grade for student teaching. This model of student teaching had been implemented in each district, building, and grade level in the same manner year after year.

In contrast, the NETCPDT professional development program was to be evolutionary, "changing and refining, often requiring evaluation and modification," in which "the roles of professors and teachers may change from time to time" (NETCPDT, 1992). The new emphasis was on continually meeting the needs of the students in the public school. Consequently, partners decided that the time pre-service teachers spent in public school classrooms should be extended from ten weeks to include the final two semesters of a pre-service teacher's university experience. The first-semester students are called *interns* and spend two full days per week in the public schools and one day at a university seminar. During their second semester, or *residency*, students only return to the university campus for instructional seminars once every two weeks; the remainder of the time is spent in public schools. Pre-service teachers are eligible to graduate from the university and receive certification to teach at the conclusion of a successful residency. Since elementary education majors would be certified to teach grades 1-8, partners believed pre-service teachers should have exposure to more than one teacher and grade level. As a result of this shared planning, a program began to evolve for interns/residents which provided intensive exposure to the "real-world" of the public schools by membership in a support system of an Instructional Leadership Team (ILT). The ILT consisted of an intern and/or resident, a minimum of two public school teachers at different grade levels who would be called mentor teachers, and a university faculty member who would be referred to as a liaison.

Collaborative planning and implementing of a new framework requires communication, time, trust, and flexibility. Communication and planning at the public school district and building level and within the university education department were ongoing processes during the fall of 1991 and spring of 1992 while continuing with the traditional teacher preparation program. Interested faculty on the seven public school campuses involved in piloting the new program began planning based on the needs and schedules of the public schools. University faculty who expressed interest in being liaisons met with administrators and prospective mentors in formal and informal meetings after school on each public school campus to discuss the initial framework, suggestions, concerns, and refinements. District level meetings were held to pull university and public school partners together for planning and refinement. Grant funds were used to provide substitutes for teachers who were planning to be mentors to meet with university liaisons during the school day. A three-day planning retreat was held for each district during the summer of 1992, involving building principals, mentors, liaisons, and central office administrative representatives.

Communication among all partners was essential for the evolutionary process to continue. Therefore, partners designed a flexible needs-based communication framework. The communication framework did not drive the program—the needs of public school and university students remained central. If a critical issue surfaced that needed discussion, the appropriate partners met quickly and their concerns were communicated and addressed. The goal of the communication framework was to ensure that communication occurred, even if concerns were not evident. However, it was not designed to set a chain of command in place, but to facilitate level ground communication among all partners.

It quickly became apparent that the "heart and soul" of the program was the ILT; therefore, partners believed informal ILT meetings should occur weekly. Mentor teachers continually verbalized the importance of sharing ideas and concerns with other mentors on their campuses; therefore, partners decided campus meetings after school involving the mentors, interns, liaisons, and building administrators should be scheduled monthly. Since several buildings in each district were involved in the program, communication among campuses was important. Therefore, each building selected one to two mentors and interns to go with their principal and university liaison to a district steering committee. District steering committees met at least once per semester and included mentors, liaisons, interns, residents, a district administrative representative (assistant superintendent or superintendent), and a college of education administrator. Partners continually explored the existing student teaching program and the proposed framework of the new program. Adjustments were made based on the needs of the children in the individual districts. The feedback and suggestions were then taken back to the Governing Board where program directions were explored until consensus was reached by all partners. It was agreed that since each district and building had unique needs, program decisions which impacted the entire collaborative had to be flexible enough to allow varied implementation at the building level.

One concern that surfaced in district steering committee meetings was quickly brought to the NETCPDT Governing Board. This was the realization that implementation of a program which placed an adult learner in a public school classroom for an entire year in a teaming situation could be negative if the mentor was not comfortable with the placement. Therefore, an early decision involved creating a collaborative procedure to place interns in schools. Public school and university faculty felt that public school input into the placement process should be increased. Therefore, it was agreed that interns would participate in an interview process involving mentor teachers, university faculty, and public school administrators. Each district had the flexibility to organize the interviews in a way which best met its needs, and the process provided the public schools with the opportunity to identify interns whose strengths, needs, and qualifications were the "best fit" for their campuses.

Collaboration continued through sharing and discussing views concerning what knowledge and qualities a good teacher possessed and what experiences facilitated acquiring these traits. State requirements were examined and ways to enable pre-service teachers to become proficient in these areas were brainstormed. Nine proficiencies were identified as critical for teaching. Public school and university faculty resolved to provide opportunities for pre-service teachers' growth in each of these nine proficiencies.

Initial implementation of the program focused on these proficiencies; however, evolution occurred as partners continually collaborated to refine the program to enhance the growth of the interns and residents. During this evolution, it became evident that the collaborative process promoted growth in the nine proficiencies for *all* pre-service and in-service educators—interns, residents, mentors, liaisons, and administrators. Therefore, an examination of the evolutionary process will provide anecdotal references to the growth all partners experienced.

## Examining the Evolutionary Process

Partners decided fall 1992 was the target for initial implementation of the NETCPDT program. Since the program was developing while implementation occurred, or as one partner stated "flying this airplane as we are building it," consensus was reached to implement the program in one district per semester. In the fall of 1992, 11 interns and one liaison began on two public school campuses with 22 mentor teachers in the first district. Implementation continued at the site in the spring of 1993 as those 11 became residents and were joined by 10 more interns and another liaison. The same spring, new implementation began with 12 interns, 2 liaisons and 24 mentors on three campuses in the second district. In the fall of 1993, implementation began in the third district with 10 interns and one liaison on two campuses. At the same time, 12 interns, 14 residents, and a liaison affiliated with four campuses in the second district, and 14 interns and one liaison joined the ten residents in the first district. At this point a total of 60 interns and residents, 121 mentors, 6 liaisons, and 7 public school campuses were actively involved in the program. Throughout this implementation period, all partners continued to plan, refine, and extend based on shared experiences. This evolutionary process is examined here through a discussion of the rationale, implementation, and evolution of the nine proficiencies. Quoted material has been gleaned from field notes and anecdotal records of the authors, minutes of campus meetings, artifacts from joint planning meetings, and response/reaction journals of interns/residents.

### Proficiency #1: Demonstrates an Understanding of and Sensitivity to Students, Professional Peers, and Parents.

**Rationale/Implementation.** Since the university students were to be in the school for an entire school year in a team situation, sensitivity to others was considered a critical attribute. This had not been a major concern in the traditional program, since the university students entered the public school after school had been in session, only remained ten weeks, and had limited interaction with people other than their cooperating public school teacher. The situation for the interns was very different. Public school teachers felt that the first two weeks of the school year were a critical time period for establishing relationships among teachers, students, parents, and professional peers. Consequently, a consensus was reached that the intern should begin the school year with the public school team on the very first day of in-service and remain with that team for two full weeks before returning to the university for seminar. University and public school faculty felt that, prior to the first day of in-service, university liaisons should conduct an orientation session for interns to provide a broad overview of the semester and give a framework for observation of classroom management and organization during the first two weeks. The public school faculty felt that these two weeks were an important time for the intern to identify with the school and "bond" with his/her team; therefore, they asked that university faculty "stay away" during this time. In addition, a joint decision was made that interns would be treated as faculty members. They would attend functions in which teachers had the opportunity to interact with others, including faculty meetings, planning meetings, inservice presentations, and parent conferences. Interns would interact with students on the first day of class, be introduced as a part of the instructional team, and be involved in interactions with the students as the new school year began.

**Evolution.** As the first semester progressed, several areas of concern emerged. While the interns felt welcome on the campus during the first two weeks, they also were overwhelmed. The intensity of being on the public school campus every day during the first two weeks of school without university support caused many of the interns to feel abandoned and wonder "What have I gotten myself into?" As a result, the public school and university faculty decided that the university liaison should "touch base" with the interns during the end of the first week and/or the beginning of the second week.

While it had been acknowledged that this experience was new and unknown for interns, it also soon became evident that mentor teachers and university liaisons were exploring new territory. Mentor teachers voiced a need for assistance in demonstrating sensitivity as they learned how to work with an adult learner. Planning for and with an intern required new interaction skills as mentor teachers found they needed to team with an intern and share their class. Although many mentors had supervised student teachers in the traditional program, they had never experienced having an adult learner in their class from the beginning of school. As noted by one intern in her response journal during the first week of instruction, children quickly learned to test the communication and sensitivity skills of the adults in the classroom:

It's amazing how quickly children learn to play one adult against the other. For example if one teacher won't let them do something, then he/she asks the other one. Once we (intern and mentor) got these trivial things worked out with the students we were well on our way to a wonderful year together.

University liaisons also raised issues, especially a concern about "treading on the territory" of the public school teachers. The program required extensive interaction among interns, teachers, and university liaisons. Therefore, it was critical that the university liaisons be viewed and view themselves as part of the team rather than being the person in charge. Mentor teachers voiced concerns that their teaching might be evaluated or judged by university liaisons and/or interns and discussed in seminars. Consequently, interns, mentor teachers, and university liaisons quickly identified communication and trust as critical components for all involved, and brainstorming sessions were held to determine ways to facilitate open communication and trust.

Other means of communication also were developed. Instructional leadership teams decided to schedule short weekly meetings for perception checking. Monthly after-school meetings brought all of the interns, mentor teachers, administrators, and university liaisons together to discuss general items such as successes, concerns, and requirements. A "Seminar News" was created which gave the mentors an overview of what occurred in seminar and what assignments the interns were to be working on. Grant funds were available for substitutes, and an open invitation was given to mentors and administrators to attend seminars at any time.

Sharing of seminar activities was to occur while interns collaborated with their mentors and completed an Instructional Teacher Education Plan (ITEP) (Appendix A). The ITEP gave interns the opportunity and the responsibility to collaborate with mentor teachers and determine a plan for fulfilling the assignments from seminar. During the collaboration, the intern filled in the proposed activities. After the planned event was completed, the intern filled in the date. At the conclusion of the week, the intern was responsible for evaluating the progress made toward completing the plan and making recommendations for the next week's plan. Mentor teachers were then asked to sign the ITEP to signify that the intern had collaborated and communicated with them.

During this time period, mentor teachers and university liaisons also requested assistance in enhancing their communication skills, particularly in the areas of communicating with adult learners and problem solving. As a result, staff development sessions conducted by consultants addressed these areas with the understanding that participating mentor teachers and university liaisons would assume staff development leadership on these issues as new mentors and liaisons entered the program.

## Proficiency #2: Demonstrates Effective Observation Skills.

**Rationale/Implementation.** Observation was recognized as a valuable learning tool by both public school mentors and university liaisons; therefore, they designated two methods to record observations. In order to plan for and document time spent in observational roles the ITEPs were utilized. In addition, interns were required to complete daily reaction/reflection logs. When in an observation role they were required to follow a clinical model by giving a minute-by-minute account of what they saw. They then wrote what they learned from the experience and how the information would impact their future instruction. It was assumed at this point that observation roles would precede opportunities for the intern to interact with students in instructional roles and would occur primarily during the first few weeks of the intern semester.

**Evolution.** It soon became evident that "observing does not necessarily equal seeing." Interns often did not know what to look for; therefore, it was difficult for them to identify the components of an instructional activity which facilitated success. As a result, many interns were not able to discuss how observing the lesson would have an effect upon their plans for future instruction. The majority of mentor teachers decided that they typically designed their lessons around a lesson cycle which included the following components: a focus or introduction, relating new material to prior knowledge, an interactive presentation of the material, opportunities for guided practice, opportunities for independent practice, and a closure activity. Evaluation continued throughout the lesson in order to monitor students' understanding and adjust instruction as necessary. Mentor teachers voiced the belief that these lesson cycle elements were also the components they considered necessary for an intern to incorporate in a lesson. Therefore, a lesson observation form was collaboratively designed by interns, residents, mentors, and liaisons which focused attention on the areas which mentor teachers had designated as important.

As interns completed the observation phase of their semester and moved into more instructional responsibilities with individuals, small groups, and/or whole groups, they were only beginning to understand the lesson cycle. They voiced a desire to have more opportunities to observe experienced teachers. The experience of teaching had the effect of making observation a more valuable learning experience. Therefore, Instructional Leadership Teams began scheduling observation opportunities within and across campuses for interns based on the individual intern's needs.

## Proficiency #3: Demonstrates Effective Classroom Management Skills.

**Rationale/Implementation.** Ways to enhance interns' growth in effective classroom management were brainstormed and discussed by classroom mentors and university liaisons. The importance of interns "being there" from the first class day, so that they could observe and participate in students becoming familiar with the management and instructional practices and procedures of the classroom was cited as a critical experience in order for interns to be able to appreciate how the students act in November and know what it took to get them to that point. Mentor teachers and university liaisons expressed hope that a full year of experience in the classroom would enhance the classroom management skills of the intern.

**Evolution.** Interns quickly expressed concern and fear about their competence in classroom management. They asked for more opportunities to observe the classroom management strategies of teachers other than those in their own ILT. Interns wrote and discussed accounts of their experiences in classroom management and the resulting successes, failures, and fears such as this excerpt from an intern's written summary of her growth in classroom management skills at mid-term:

> After observing several classrooms, I have come to the conclusion that classroom management is the most important element to the success of the child and the classroom as a whole group. It is vital to everyone involved that the class as a whole respect (one another and their property). I think if you gain this respect between teacher and student at the beginning of the year a teacher has a better chance of maintaining control the remainder of the year (what a dream!). I hope it is a possible goal. I have seen it incorporated; the class as a whole is a much happier group of children.
>
> My goal is to try to maintain this respect among my students during my intern semester . . . I only hope I can be as consistent as my mentor. She has set a good example for me to follow. . . . She has incorporated an effective management plan in the classroom. She is consistent and efficient in classroom management. She has shown me the importance of attaining high expectations for the children. This helps to reinforce the need for appropriate behavior so that learning can take place.

A group of interns on one campus decided to keep a log of successful management strategies which they had observed. This method of documentation was adopted by the majority of the interns and included in their portfolios. In addition, interns requested that university seminars include time devoted solely to classroom management. University faculty and liaisons, mentors, teachers, and school district administrators presented management strategies and systems throughout the semester. However, the consensus from mentors, liaisons, and interns was that one acquires and refines only with "experience, experience, experience."

## Proficiency #4: Demonstrates Professional Behavior

**Rationale/Implementation.** Professionalism was viewed as a some-what abstract concept that mentors and liaisons expected interns to demonstrate, but was often difficult to define. During the initial orientation session conducted by the university liaisons professionalism was addressed. Interns brainstormed what they considered professional behavior, and their ideas were elaborated and refined by group discussion and liaison input. In addition, an administrator from the public school discussed what professionalism meant in her particular district. Issues which received emphasis included confidentiality, dress, speech, punctuality, attendance, preparedness, demonstrating initiative, and being responsible.

**Evolution.** Once again, exposure to concepts did not ensure consistent comprehension. When the students began attending public schools, it was apparent that differing definitions of items such as professional dress, punctuality, and preparedness sometimes existed between mentor and interns. In some instances, standards varied from mentor to mentor on the same campus and differences were evident between campuses. Therefore, it became critical that mentors and liaisons collaborate to provide a clear definition of professionalism for the interns. Principals and mentors were asked to verbalize their definitions of professionalism and specifically state what they expected in certain areas. For instance, an intern might view being punctual as walking in the room when the children did. If a mentor felt this was not acceptable, he or she should tell the intern what was acceptable, such as being in the room 15 minutes before class started.

In order to facilitate discussion, university liaisons listened to the concerns of mentor teachers and they collaboratively designed a *Preliminary Evaluation of Professionalism.* During the first semester both mentors and interns completed separate forms based on their perceptions of the intern's professionalism. They then compared and contrasted the forms, and interns wrote a reflection related to the experience. Mentors felt the experience was valuable for the intern, but completing the form was too time consuming for mentors. In addition, mentors felt uncomfortable being placed in an evaluative role so soon after the intern had arrived in their classroom. Consequently, the process was changed to place the intern in a self-evaluative role and the mentor in a discussant position. The form was renamed *NETCPDT Self-Evaluation of Professionalism* (Appendix B). The interns completed this during their first two weeks in the public school and then shared it with their mentors, recorded mentors' reactions and suggestions, and had the mentors sign the completed evaluation. The process provided an impetus for reflective assessment and discussion.

## *Proficiency # 5: Demonstrates Ability to Plan Instruction*

**Rationale/Implementation.** Students had planned literacy lessons and had written thematic units in two reading methods courses before entering the field-based program; however, they lacked experience in planning lessons for actual implementation with public school children. Thus, mentors and liaisons decided that one of the initial assignments for the interns should be to plan a literacy lesson which would fit into the "ebb and flow" of their mentor's classroom. Interns were to: 1) meet with their ILT 2) have ideas and instructional strategies brainstormed, 3) collaborate with ILT and decide when and what ideas to implement, 4) complete a literacy lesson plan following the lesson cycle, 5) share the plan with the mentor in whose class the literacy lesson was going to be implemented at least two days before implementation, 6) receive feedback and suggestions from team members, 7) "play" the literacy lesson in their minds before implementation and imagine challenges and/or surprises that might arise and plan ways of addressing these situations such as ways to reteach, alternate activities, or extension activities, 8) engage in final preparation and collection of all resources/materials for the lesson.

**Evolution.** Some mentors expressed concern that the interns did not grasp the lesson cycle as they planned their literacy lessons. Therefore, university liaisons and mentors developed a format describing each part of the lesson cycle and provided a framework for interns to address each component in their planning for literacy instruction. In addition, university liaisons devoted seminar time to demonstrating a literacy lesson which contained identifiable components of the lesson cycle, engaged interns in reflection on the cycle, and then collaborated with the interns to complete the lesson plan framework.

Interns began to realize the depth and breadth of planning necessary for all children to achieve success. Planning literacy lessons in university courses had previously involved meeting objectives and addressing curriculum requirements. In the field-based program, interns began to realize that planning in the "real world" involved more than covering the curriculum because they were responsible for meeting the needs of the children. In addition, interns quickly became aware that literacy strategies were an integral component of any lesson—regardless of subject matter. One intern voiced concern in the following journal entry:

> I have found in all of my planning that I sometimes doubt where the child might fit. I have a fear that I will plan beyond his comprehension and frustrate the child. I hope at the end of my residency I will feel a little more secure in my ability to assess and meet the needs of the child.

## *Proficiency #6: Demonstrates Ability to Teach*

**Rationale/implementation.** During the joint planning sessions, mentors and university liaisons discussed that interns would not have taken the methodology courses that traditional student teachers had completed before entering the public school classroom. As a result, more observation time was planned for interns, as well as a slower progression of assuming instructional responsibilities. Both mentors and university liaisons agreed that it would be difficult to pre-determine a timetable for assumption of instructional duties due to the differences in interns and the varied needs of the public school classrooms. Mentor teachers voiced fears about being required to turn over their classes to interns who might not be ready to assume the responsibility, particularly as time grew near for state mandated tests. Commitments were made by public school and university faculty that the needs of the public school students must be the first priority, and the intern's schedule would depend upon his/her competency and the needs of the classroom. After an examination of the courses for which the interns would be receiving credit (math methods, science methods, and reading comprehension) it was determined that a minimum of two lessons with formal evaluations in each subject area would be required.

**Evolution.** As with all areas of the program, communication became an essential component. When the first assignment was given, interns were asked to plan and implement a literacy lesson, complete a self evaluation, have the mentor complete an evaluation, and bring both evaluations for discussion to seminar the next week. As liaisons arrived at the schools for their visits, they were immediately greeted with the feedback that one week was not enough time to plan a literacy lesson, implement it into the natural flow of a mentor's classroom, and evaluate the lesson. This was a valid observation, and immediate adjustments were made. Two to three week periods then were given for implementation of formal lessons.

After completion of the first literacy lesson, it also became evident that trying to plan formal lessons based on course requirements was counterproductive. Interns quickly realized that instruction in any content area involved reading comprehension. Consequently, the utilization of reading strategies and literature extensions in each subject area became goals. The original requirement of two formal evaluations in math, two in science, and two in reading became more flexible, and instruction became more integrated and student centered.

Other shifts occurred. Interns commented that while the self evaluation was extremely valuable, having the mentor fill out an evaluation form on their first lesson was extremely stressful. Mentors and liaisons listened and acknowledged that formal evaluation, even if the purpose was for growth, can be viewed as stressful and a detriment to risk taking. Therefore, mentors, liaisons, and interns agreed that, during the intern's first two lessons an evaluation by the mentor would be optional. The intern was required to complete a written self evaluation, but had the option of soliciting oral comments from the mentor, identifying them as mentor feedback and adding them to the self evaluation, or requesting the mentor to complete an evaluation form. Interestingly, after receiving voice and choice, most interns requested that the mentor complete a written evaluation.

### *Proficiency #7: Demonstrates Effective Evaluation Skills (Students/Self)*

**Rationale/implementation.** A shared goal of mentors and university liaisons was to help interns realize the dual nature of evaluation. It was discussed that each time an instructor was interacting with students, self evaluation was also necessary. A major component of this self evaluation required the intern or resident to assess their performance based on the success of the students.

Interns were asked to engage in numerous self evaluations, including self evaluations of professionalism, lessons, and instructional or classroom management situations. Some self-evaluations were made in response/reaction journals. At midterm and final portfolio conferences, interns also were asked to self evaluate their growth by assigning themselves a rating in each of the nine proficiencies using a five-point scale.

In addition, interns wrote summaries of their growth and goals for each proficiency and provided documentation in their portfolios which supported their ratings. Interns' self evaluations were contrasted with the mentors' evaluations at the mid-term and end of semester portfolio conferences.

Interns and residents continually struggled with this expanded concept of evaluation. Self evaluation was one of the requirements they considered most difficult. Some continually ranked themselves much lower than their mentors due to lack of confidence or a sense of modesty. Others, who had a traditional view of evaluation, consistently ranked themselves higher because they equated ratings with grades (5=A, 1=F). The evaluation process was therefore perceived as very stressful and the concept that the purpose of evaluation was to establish a framework for growth required constant reinforcement.

A situation which consistently signaled a potential "at-risk" intern or resident was when the self evaluations were consistently much higher than those of the mentors. In conferences, these interns or residents would continually focus on what they had done without acknowledging the needs or successes of their students. Those who became successful seemed more able to shift their focus to their students. Thus, a critical component of the ability of an intern or resident to move into a growth cycle seemed to be the ability to engage in realistic self evaluation based on the performance of their students.

As interns and residents coped with self evaluation, mentors and liaisons struggled with meeting the challenges of evaluating adult learners in an evolving program. Mentors were uncomfortable rating interns or residents because they did not want to be viewed as "judges" or "adversaries" while trying to establish a "teaming" relationship with them. University liaisons were committed to the concept that hands-on experience in the classroom was a valuable learning experience that required a high degree of risk taking. They believed it was critical for interns to know they would not be penalized for trying out new strategies nor feel they could only teach lessons they were certain would be successful. On the other hand, the university required that the interns receive grades of A, B, C, D, or F for the coursework they were receiving credit for during internship. This required university liaisons and mentors to develop processes for equating hands-on experience with the assignment of traditional grades.

Collaboration accelerated as the semester progressed. Mentors and liaisons requested training in evaluative procedures, and workshops were presented by outside personnel addressing supportive evaluation. Interns were continually given responsibility in the evaluative process by completing self evaluations, responses, and documenting growth in their portfolios. Comprehensive perception checks were conducted at midterm conferences where self evaluations, evaluation by mentors and liaisons, responses and reactions from interns, and the portfolio were shared and discussed. Goals were written for the remainder of the semester utilizing input from the intern, mentors, and liaison.

If an intern was determined to be significantly lacking in growth at midterm, the ILT designed an individual growth plan. The end-of-semester conference was similar in framework, in that both intern and mentors rated the intern's growth in nine proficiencies, wrote summary statements, and formulated goals; however, interns, mentors, and assigned liaisons each suggested grades for each course. During the end-of-semester portfolio conference, the evaluations, ratings, and documentation from the portfolios were shared and turned in to the building liaison. The entire team of liaisons from the center then met to examine portfolios and other evaluative pieces. If there was a discrepancy between what the intern, liaison, and mentors suggested for grades, the entire team of university liaisons reviewed the portfolio, made comments, and a conference was scheduled with the ILT to reach a final decision.

## Proficiency #8: Demonstrates Knowledge of Content in Language Arts, Math, Science, and Social Studies

**Rationale/Implementation.** Interns and residents each enrolled for 15 hours of credit in a variety of courses, including content methods, technology, psychology, classroom management, and field experience/student teaching. During the first semester of the program, interns received a separate syllabus for each course, and a seminar sequence was attempted for addressing course content. Initially, classroom organization and management were emphasized, followed by literacy theory and strategies, science concepts, and mathematics. There was an attempt to weave the classroom management and cultural diversity content throughout the semester by requiring students to compile a case study of a student from a culture different than their own. As each content area was emphasized in campus seminars, students were required to observe public school teaching of that particular area, then plan a lesson in that content area, and implement the lesson with an individual, small group, or whole class in the public school. Interns were to complete a self evaluation form and ask their mentors to evaluate the lesson. The lesson plan, lesson implementation, evaluation records, and samples of children's work (if appropriate) were included in the intern's portfolio.

**Evolution.** If the original intent of the partnership was to allow the intern to learn by merging into the "ebb and flow" of the instructional environment of the public school classroom, then it was evident that a predetermined sequence with specific assignments with deadlines matching seminar instruction was not a feasible plan. While some students were in classrooms where all subject areas were interwoven into a unifying theme, others were in departmentalized situations where they shifted to different subject areas every two to three weeks. By the time the seminar shifted to a science emphasis, interns might be spending time in a language arts classroom. Therefore, observation and lesson assignments would disrupt the plan the Instructional Leadership Team had devised. Consequently, students were told the number of observations and lessons they would be responsible for by mid term and by the end of the semester, but the sequence of implementation of the lessons became the responsibility of the ILT.

The university and public school partners decided that seminar instruction and assignments must become more integrated. As a result, the content of math, science, social studies, and literacy was addressed throughout the semester though seminar instruction and assigned readings. Interns were initially exposed to elements that were common to all public school classrooms, such as classroom organization and management strategies and awareness of cultural diversity, but then seminar instruction moved to integration of the content areas rather than sequential instruction. Liaisons and mentor teachers collaboratively planned and taught seminar sessions which demonstrated content lessons. Liaisons also began teaching model lessons in public school classrooms when invited.

## Proficiency # 9: Demonstrates Knowledge of Teaching/Learning Strategies

**Rationale/Implementation.** Initially, the partners decided that university faculty would model teaching/learning strategies in seminars that would then be applied in the field. At this initial stage, university faculty were perceived as the teaching experts who knew the most about teaching/learning strategies. Thus, university instructors decided upon which strategies to present and demonstrate in seminars, demonstrated them, assigned implementation of a specific strategy in the public school classroom, required interns to complete self evaluations, and asked mentors to evaluate the lesson by the next seminar. In addition, interns and residents were assigned readings explaining various strategies and were asked to keep logs of strategies observed in seminars and public school classrooms.

**Evolution.** During ILT meetings and other interactions, it became evident that assigning a specific literacy strategy based on a demonstration in a seminar did not always meet the needs of public school classrooms. The partners began to notice that students were exposed to a variety of literacy strategies in both seminars and public school classrooms. A turning point in the perception that university faculty were the only experts occurred during the first semester of implementation when one mentor said, "We are modeling strategies on a daily basis. Why do the interns have to teach only what you have demonstrated in seminars. Don't you trust us?" This comment was shared with the entire partnership and became an impetus for liaisons and mentors to value the classroom experience as a viable source of knowledge of strategies. As a result, partners decided that instead of assigning a specific literacy strategy such as a DR-TA (Stauffer, 1976), a general assignment, such as implementing a literacy strategy would be given. Then the intern would plan with the ILT and decide which literacy strategies could mesh with the current area of study. As a result, an intern in one classroom could be implementing a content reading strategy; another intern could be engaged in process writing in a different classroom; and yet another intern could be conducting a shared reading lesson. Implementation of the strategy would then be documented by the intern's plans, self evaluation, mentor's comments, and student artifacts (if appropriate). During seminar, interns were given opportunities to describe their implementation of strategies and discuss how they implemented and/or modified a literacy strategy to meet the needs of their students. As a result, strategy knowledge expanded and diversified.

At the beginning of the semester, both mentors and liaisons observed that many interns seemed to lack the confidence to plan a lesson utilizing literacy strategies they had not observed in classrooms or experienced in seminars. Through the encouragement and insistence of both mentors and liaisons, the students gained experience and confidence and began to think like teachers and scavenge for ideas rather than wait for someone to "show them what to do." Now, when interns shift to residency, the expectation is that they will select and implement literacy strategies appropriate to the public school curriculum and which meet the needs of the public school students. The strategy implementation policy has been facilitated by individual public schools emphasizing that mentor participation must be voluntary and mentors must be willing to allow interns/residents the opportunity to implement strategies that they as mentors may not be utilizing in their classrooms. This understanding has aided in bridging the gap between mentors who have instructional methods and/or styles which are different from scenarios which have been presented in previous university literacy courses and/or seminars. Many public school teachers have stated they volunteered to be mentors in order to have access to new literacy strategies and expand their repertoire.

## The Ongoing Evolution

As we move into the fifth year of this evolving program, ongoing assessment, reflection, refinement, extension, and elaboration continue. Growth has been rapid. Fall 1996 began with 386 interns and residents on 62 campuses in 11 public school districts. Thirty-six university liaisons and over 800 mentor teachers were involved. The first four years have produced induction year teachers who, according to district administrators, look and act like experienced teachers. In addition, the districts who have employed graduates of the program have found that these new teachers are staying in the profession and assuming leadership roles. Therefore, NETCPDT partners are realizing that risk taking has many rewards, including successful first year teachers who remain in the district, national recognition, and partnership relationships among mentors, liaisons, interns, residents, and public school and university administrators.

However, the collaborative/reflective assessment process can be a double-edged sword. The joy involves celebrating successes and strengths; the struggle encompasses identifying areas which require restructuring and growth. There has been a need for constant redefinition of program goals, participant roles, and the concept of level-ground collaboration. Throughout the past five years, identifying areas requiring refinement has been viewed as a sign of ongoing growth and an opportunity for collaboration rather than a negative indicator.

While this experiment was initially designed to improve preservice teacher education, the process of ongoing collaborative reflection and assessment has empowered educators and created a synergy that has led to a cycle of growth for all partners. Perhaps this impetus for growth is the most beneficial component of the collaborative process. As stated by Dewey:

A progressive school is primarily concerned with growth . . . with transforming existing capacities and experiences; what already exists by way of native endowment and past achievement is subordinate to what it may become. Possibilities are more important than what already exists, and knowledge of the latter counts only in its bearing upon possibilities. (Dewey, 1959, p. 119)

At NETCPDT, we have found that reflective assessment is an integral component of the growth process of a professional development center. School reform becomes a possibility when public schools and universities have opportunities to reflect upon and assess past activities and achievements without fear or blame and collaboratively make decisions for the future.

---

# References

Booth, M., Furlong, J., & Wilkin, M.( Eds.). (1990). *Partnership in initial teacher training*. London: Cassell.

Clark, R. W. (1988). School-university relationships: An interpretive review. In K. A. Sirotnik & J. I. Goodlad (Eds.), *School-university partnerships in action* (pp. 32-65). New York: Teachers College Press.

Commeyras, M., Reinking, D., Heubach, K. M., & Pagnucco, J. (1993). Looking within: A study of an undergraduate reading methods course. In D. J. Leu & C. K. Kinzer (Eds.), *Examining central issues in literacy research, theory, and practice* (pp. 297-304). Chicago: National Reading Conference.

Cuban, L. (1984). *How teachers taught: Constancy and change in American classrooms, 1890-1980*. New York: Longman.

David, G. (1989). *Restructuring in progress: Lessons from pioneering districts*. Washington, DC: National Governors' Association.

Dewey. J. (1959). Progressive education and the science of education. In M. S. Dworkin (Ed.), *Dewey on education*. New York: Teachers College.

Dixon, P.N., & Ishler, R. E. (1992). Professional development schools: Stages in collaboration. *Journal of Teacher Education, 43*, 28-34.

Goodlad, J. I. (1984). *A place called school*. New York: McGraw Hill.

Goodlad, J. I. (1991). Why we need a complete redesign of teacher education. *Educational Leadership, 48*(4), 4-10.

Governing Board of the Northeast Texas Center for Professional Development and Technology. (1994, April). *Northeast Texas Center for Professional Development and Technology field-based teacher education programs: Criteria for participation*. Paper presented at the Northeast Texas Center for Professional Development and Technology Teacher Education Planning Retreat, Sulphur Springs, TX.

Holmes Group. (1986). *Tomorrow's teachers*. East Lansing, MI: Author.

Holmes Group (1990). *Tomorrow's schools: Principles for the design of professional development schools*. East Lansing, MI: Author.

Jackson, P. (1986). *The practice of teaching*. New York: Teachers College Press.

Lieberman, A., & Miller, L. (1986). School improvement: Themes and variations. In A. Lieberman (Ed.), *Rethinking school improvement: Research, craft and concept*. (pp. 96-111). New York: Teachers College Press.

McCarthy, S. J., & Peterson, P. L. (1989, March). *Teacher roles: Weaving new patterns in classroom practice and school organization.* Paper presented at the meeting of the American Education Research Association, San Francisco.

Murphy, J. (1990). Helping teachers prepare to work in restructured schools. *Journal of Teacher Education, 41*(4), 50-56.

Northeast Texas Center for Professional Development and Technology. (Fall, 1992). *Intern commitment contract.* (Available from Northeast Center for Professional Development & Technology, Texas A&M University-Commerce, Commerce, TX 75429).

Northeast Texas Center for Professional Development and Technology. (Spring, 1993). *Fall 1993 syllabus for intern semester.* (Available from Northeast Center for Professional Development & Technology, Texas A&M University-Commerce, Commerce, TX 75429).

Northeast Texas Center for Professional Development and Technology. (1996). *Preparing tomorrow's teachers today: Field-based teacher education program handbook. Commerce, TX: Texas A&M University-Commerce.*

Roemer, M. (1991). What we talk about when we talk about school reform. *Harvard Educational Review, 61,* 434-448.

Sarason, S. (1982). *The culture of the school and the problem of change* (2nd ed.). Boston: Allyn & Bacon.

Scharer, P. L., Freeman, E. B., Lehman, B. A., & Allen, V. G. (1993). Literacy and literature in elementary classrooms: Teachers' beliefs and practices. In D. J. Leu & C. K. Kinzer (Eds.) *Examining central issues in literacy research, theory, and practice* (pp. 359-366). Chicago: National Reading Conference.

Shapiro, J. (1994). Moving toward change: One school's experience. In E. G. Sturtevant & W. M. Linek (Eds.), *Pathways for literacy: Learners teach and teachers learn* (pp. 85-96). Pittsburg, KS: College Reading Association.

Stauffer, R. G. (1976). *Teaching reading as a thinking process.* New York: Harper & Row.

Whitford, B. L., Schlechty, P. C., & Shelor, L. G. (1987). Sustaining action research through collaboration: Inquiries for intervention. *Peabody Journal of Education, 64,* 151-169.

Zeichner, K. (1992). Rethinking the practicum in the professional development school partnership. *Journal of Teacher Education, 43*(4), 296-307.

## Appendix A
## NETCPDT Individual Teacher Education Plan (ITEP)

Intern/Resident _____ District and Building Assignment _____

I. List of Activities and/or Experiences to be Accomplished
   During This Period

| Activities for the Week of _____ | With Whom | Date |
|---|---|---|
| | | |
| | | |
| | | |
| | | |
| | | |

II. Evaluation of Individual Education Plan

III. Recommendations for Next ITEP

| | |
|---|---|
| Mentor Signature            Date | Intern/Resident Signature     Date |

(Northeast Texas Center for Professional Development and Technology, 1996, p. 38)

## Appendix B
## NETCPDT Self-Evaluation of Professionalism

This preliminary evaluation form is designed so that the interns become aware of all aspects of professional behavior early in the program. Interns will rate each item on the left using the following criteria and make comments on the right. Then they will share and discuss their self-evaluations with their mentors.

4=Professional
3=Somewhat professional, but needs refinement
2=Minimally professional, needs improvement
1=Questionable, needs major improvement
0=Remove from program
N=Not known

Rating of Professionalism for _____ Date _____

Rating     Comments
_____     Is enthusiastic and positive about teaching
_____     Works cooperatively and enthusiastically with team
_____     Works cooperatively with administrators
_____     Demonstrates an interest in the community
_____     Follows the policies and procedures of the district
_____     Maintains confidentiality
_____     Is punctual and regular in attendance
_____     Enthusiastically accepts responsibility
_____     Completes duties assigned outside of instruction and/or the classroom
            with quality
_____     Presents a professional appearance and demeanor
_____     Demonstrates professional behavior and integrity in interactions with
            others
_____     Demonstrates the ability to override problems that defy immediate reso-
            lution
_____     Has a sense of humor
_____     Uses good judgement
_____     Exercises emotional control
_____     Is flexible when circumstances require it
_____     Participates in staff development activities
_____     Accepts criticism gracefully
_____     Responds to suggestions for change or improvement
_____     Is enthusiastic and positive about the intern and resident program

Signatures: Mentor/s _____

TAMU-C Liaison: _____     Intern: _____

(Northeast Texas Center for Professional Development and Technology, 1996, p. 39)

# Learning to Teach in the "Real World": Reflections on Field-Based Reading Instruction

## Evangeline V. Newton

The University of Akron

## Abstract

*Historically, the primary objective of teacher preparation programs was to equip prospective educators with an assortment of teaching skills through direct instruction in university classrooms. In recent years, however, research in several fields has deepened our awareness of the complex nature of learning, compelling university teacher educators to re-examine what and how they teach. This article describes experiences with an undergraduate reading diagnosis course that moved from the university to a local elementary school in order to provide a "real world" learning opportunity for preservice teachers. It suggests that university classes taught in school contexts present both challenges and opportunities for teacher preparation programs.*

## Introduction

Historically, the primary objective of teacher preparation programs was to equip prospective educators with an assortment of "generic teaching skills" commonly perceived as "equally effective across all subjects and/or grades" (Myers, 1991, p. 395). These requisite skills, moreover, were usually dispensed to preservice teachers through direct instruction in university classrooms.

In recent years, however, research in several fields has deepened our awareness of the complex nature of learning (Piaget, 1964; Strickland & Feeley, 1991; Vygotsky, 1978). Knowledge acquisition is no longer seen as a linear transmission of information or insight from expert to novice. Rather, it is viewed as a social construction, a synergistic evolution to which expert, novice and sociocultural context all contribute (Fosnot, 1996; Vygotsky, 1978). This epistemological shift has compelled university teacher educators to re-examine what and how they teach (Brown, 1993; Holmes Group, 1986; Myers, 1991; Schon, 1987).

Similarly, new understandings about reading and writing have had deep implications for teacher preparation in literacy education. Once regarded as simple decoding or encoding of sound and symbol, reading and writing are now viewed as symbiotic and developmental meaning-making processes (Flower & Hays, 1981; Galda, 1984; Goodman, 1969, 1976; Graves, 1983; Rosenblatt, 1978; Smith, 1994). These processes, moreover, have cognitive, affective, social, cultural, and contextual dimensions (Bloome & Green, 1984; Cazden, 1985; Cramer & Castle, 1994; Heath, 1983). Consequently, childrens' reading and writing fluency depend not only on their knowledge of isolated skills, but also on how well they can negotiate those skills with specific texts and in specific contexts (Bloome, 1985; Heath, 1983).

While new perceptions of reading and writing are compatible with the epistemological paradigm shift in teacher education, they have highlighted an incongruity in teacher education praxis: How can the organic nature of meaning-making be understood in a decontextualized college classroom where transmission through lecture is the dominant instructional mode?

Many recent articles document efforts by teacher educators to close this gap between their own theory and practice. Efforts include use of innovative teaching methods that recognize the importance of authentic contexts and provide opportunities for collaborative reflection. Some universities have developed partnerships with school districts to provide preservice teachers with "hands-on" field experiences designed to supplement college classroom learning (Herrmann & Sarracino, 1993; Mosenthal, 1996; Risko, Peter & McAllister, 1996; Roskos & Walker, 1994a).

This article will describe some of my experiences with one undergraduate reading diagnosis course that moved from the university to a local elementary school in order to provide a "real world" learning opportunity for preservice teachers. A brief description of the course history will precede discussion of its design, based on tenets of situated learning theory (Lave & Wegner, 1991). Finally, I will share observations from an instructional perspective about how field-based practice has affected course curriculum and students' efforts to construct knowledge. While based solely on the experience of one course, these observations suggest that university classes taught in school contexts present both challenges and opportunities for teacher preparation.

## Background

At this university, most undergraduates majoring in elementary education come to "Classroom Diagnosis and Intervention of Reading Problems" after an introductory reading course in which they are acquainted with different instructional models of the reading process. By the end of this first course, students are most knowledgable about the sociopsycholingustic model (Smith, 1994). They have also engaged in some field experience, primarily through observation of reading instruction in elementary classrooms.

Some students have also taken a second literacy course, "Teaching Reading and Writing Across the Curriculum." Instructional emphasis here is on text-based strategies that structure content area reading events for a variety of curricular purposes. By the end of this course, students have a greater understanding of how to use fiction, non-fiction, and textbooks in classroom instruction. During their field experience, preservice teachers practice interactive strategies with small groups of upper elementary or middle school students.

## Course Design

According to the undergraduate catalogue, the goal of "diagnosis and intervention" is to understand "difficulties experienced by children in reading with emphasis on diagnostic and intervention techniques for the classroom teacher." Originally, this goal was met through a "presentation-practice" approach. The university instructor presented important concepts through lecture and then invited further exploration through practice in small group activities. After several weeks of lecture and simulated tasks, students added two one-hour tutorial sessions with at-risk readers who came to our campus for a reading clinic. (For a detailed discussion of how this course developed over time, see Roskos and Walker, 1994a.)

In course evaluations, preservice teachers commonly cited the tutorials as their most effective learning experiences. But integrating these tutorials with lecture and small group activities was difficult. First, there was often a gap between the intervention strategy or assessment tool presented in lecture and the needs of individual children on concurrent days. Second, it was difficult to provide students with meaningful feedback. Once the tutorial sessions had ended, preservice teachers had no opportunity to share insights or concerns with each other. Third, because the children came to our campus from different institutions, they themselves did not share a sense of school community. University classrooms were not a natural or familiar learning environment for them. While tutorials were superficially authentic teaching situations, the atmosphere was sterile, impersonal, and artificial.

In redesigning the course, faculty sought to bridge the gap between abstract learning theory and concrete classroom practice in light of current beliefs that knowledge is socially constructed. Specifically, students needed ongoing and intensive opportunities to 1) interact with children in true school environments; 2) experience course content in meaningful ways; and 3) reflect, synthesize, and construct new understandings through interaction with faculty and with peers.

Situated learning theory provided a broad theoretical framework that addressed each of these perceived needs (Lave & Wegner, 1991). Claiming that novices become experts by moving from simple to complex learning tasks, situated learning theory also underscores the critical role in that process of a social environment with multiple opportunities to observe and share.

From this perspective, Roskos and Walker (1994a) developed four principles as central to the reading diagnosis course: 1) expertise comes through participation that gradually grows more complex; 2) "communities of practice" invite exploration, examination, and application of knowledge; 3) social interaction is critical to the exchange and extension of knowledge; and 4) opportunities for reflection help people consolidate and again extend what they have learned.

Currently, we operationalize these principles through three main activities: 1) simulations, 2) teaching tutorials, and 3) collaborative reflection. Simulations demonstrate specific assessment and intervention strategies, often through fictional case studies. They invite preservice teachers to analyze an identical problem in a comparatively risk-free environment. During simulations, students often work in cooperative learning groups.

After three weeks on campus, teaching tutorials begin as the course moves to a local school. Each preservice teacher is paired with an at-risk reader for a fifty-minute tutorial. While instructional activities are planned to fit the needs of each learner, all sessions follow a similar routine based on the diagnostic and intervention principles in *Interactive Activities in Reading Diagnosis and Teaching* (Roskos & Walker, 1994b) (see Appendix A).

When the children have gone, preservice teachers meet to review what occurred in their tutorial and to plan the next lesson. Talking through their experience immediately afterward gives them an opportunity to reflect, focus on issues of concern, discuss potential strategies, and evaluate success and failure. In addition, preservice teachers meet with me once a week for thirty minutes in permanent groups of four. During this time, I use anecdotal notes to raise issues from my observations. Sometimes I review or introduce new material through mini-lessons. Students may also raise questions for group members to consider.

Ultimately, this three-step process enables preservice teachers to construct knowledge through engagement with a real child and in an authentic teaching situation. Emergent understandings are then refined through written reflection and verbal collaboration. Feedback from preservice teachers, from school personnel, and from my own observations indicates that this format has resulted in learning gains for both preservice teachers and at-risk readers (Roskos & Walker, 1994a).

## Negotiating School and University Goals

Five years ago the principal and reading specialist of the public elementary school hosting this course responded enthusiastically to our suggestion that preservice teachers work with their at-risk readers each semester. We met a few times to discuss how our course purposes might dovetail with the needs of their students in ways that would result in growth for both preservice teachers and at-risk readers.

During these meetings, we shared our respective objectives. I wanted preservice teachers to interact with at-risk readers across grade levels to enable comparisons in age and development. The reading specialist insisted that we work only with children from primary classrooms where, she believed, intervention would be most effective. Consequently I adapted my course content to accommodate younger learners. Simulations, for example, emphasized issues of emergent literacy.

Far more serious to resolve, however, were the differences between the university's view of reading as a sociopsycholinguistic process and the school's reading program of systematic and intensive instruction in phonic rules. These two views of reading often employ antithetical procedural and content knowledge. I wondered how the school and university could forge a working partnership when they held such disparate beliefs about reading instruction. What kind of relationship could preservice and classroom teachers develop, particularly if our students had to embrace a reading program that I was unwilling to reinforce in my own instruction? Likewise, what impact would the school curriculum have on my students' understanding of the concepts and strategies I would present?

After much discussion, we resolved our dilemma about instructional approach by carefully developing an independent purpose for the field experience that still satisfied both our goals. Rather than focusing on skills or tasks identified by classroom teachers, our tutorials became a twice-weekly after school enrichment program. Classroom teachers selected children to participate; I supervised all tutorials. This enabled me to scaffold novice teachers' comprehension and implementation of both content and procedural knowledge. School officials endorsed the notion of enrichment and knew their students would be closely supervised.

After-school "enrichment" was an honest and apt compromise. The format has, in fact, changed little in five years. On their first building visit, preservice teachers are oriented to the school and meet their readers' classroom teachers. Classroom teachers profile students' strengths and weaknesses. Periodically, preservice teachers may informally discuss progress, raise questions or share learning actvities with the classroom teacher. At the end of the semester, preservice teachers write an in-depth profile of each child as a reader, which is made available to the classroom teacher.

Parents are involved as well. When children join the program, each parent receives a letter explaining the kinds of activities in which their children will be engaged and the literacy principles that support them (Appendix B). In this way parents understand that while reading improvement will be the goal, our activities will not duplicate or extend classroom tasks. They are invited to meet preservice teachers in our first week and to celebrate childrens' accomplishments at a pizza party during our last week.

Surprisingly, the after-school enrichment structure fostered an instant and unexpected sense of community among our at-risk readers. Twice a week 20 students bound into a spacious and sunny library, dragging their book bags with them. Preservice teachers greet them, share a snack, and briefly inquire about the day's events. Tutorials include a variety of reading and writing activities, some in collaboration with other students. Every few weeks, we gather together for a Reading Party during which our young learners read texts they have written or discuss favorite projects with the entire group. Their work is on permanent display in the library. Each spring we publish a volume of "Our Favorite Books" to share with others. Three copies are presented to the library in an elaborate end-of-year ceremony where young readers receive books, certificates, and kudos from preservice teachers, classroom teachers, parents, and friends.

## Monitoring Students' Knowledge Construction

A situated learning environment decenters instructional authority (Mosenthal, 1996). Students' knowledge construction is, therefore, influenced not only by the university instructor but also by students' continuous interaction with all members of the school community. Because knowledge construction is in part a context-sensitive integration of prior beliefs with new information, scaffolding student learning can be more complicated than it is in a university classroom.

The elementary school in which this course is taught, for example, stands a few blocks from our university. But in some ways it is worlds apart. A public school in a well-integrated neighborhood, the student body is largely African-American. Most of our preservice teachers, however, have attended suburban, largely white, parochial schools. For them, the home and school culture of these children is often enigmatic.

This has significant implications for preservice teachers in two ways. First, their efforts to assess reading behaviors and identify appropriate instructional strategies are sometimes impeded by lack of familiarity with the sociocultural backgrounds of these children. While this is a well-documented problem for all teachers who work in cultures different from their own, it is an added challenge for preservice teachers with rudimentary conceptual and procedural knowledge.

A second consideration is the sometimes mercurial influence of context on preservice teachers' evolving and fragile self-image as professionals. In a review of 40 "learning-to-teach" studies, Kagan (1992) found that preservice teachers have memories of themselves as students and personal beliefs about good teachers that must be "modified and reconstructed" for growth to occur. Similarly, an initial focus on the self appears to be necessary in the early stages of teacher development. To grow from this ego-centered disposition, novice teachers need "extended opportunities to interact with and study pupils in systematic ways" (p. 142).

Certainly situated learning provides opportunity for systematic study. Furthermore, Lave and Wegner (1991) believe an "interplay of conflict and synergy is central to all aspects of learning in practice" (p. 103). For our preservice teachers, however, this task is complicated: they must comprehend a new school ethos while also developing their conceptual and procedural knowledge about at-risk readers. Moreover, because of disparate home and school cultures, their memories of school experiences often obstruct attempts to make informed judgements about the learners with whom they work.

Each semester, preservice teachers develop a portfolio which includes lesson plans and reflections, assessments, an in-depth diagnostic profile, and a final reflection synthesizing their greatest insights. In these final reflections, preservice teachers often refer to their altered understanding of the teacher-student role. Recollections of early tutorial sessions chronicle frustrated efforts to replicate personal literacy experiences or to assuage their battered self-confidence. Marjorie's comment is typical:

> I came into the tutoring with expectations about what I would do. For example, I went through my children's books and picked out many favorites of mine. . . . I was somewhat devastated by the reality. Wayne was not the least bit interested in any of the books or topics that I had planned . . .

Kagan (1992) found that novices, through continual interaction with children, "may begin to stand back from their personal beliefs and images, acknowledging where they are incorrect or inappropriate" (p. 155). Gradually, as "the image of self as teacher is resolved, attention shifts to the design of instruction and finally to what pupils are learning from academic tasks" (p. 155). Excerpts from Amy's final reflection support Kagan's finding:

> When I began tutoring, I felt that if I came up with an incredible lesson that was so creative and thought-provoking it would knock my student's socks off, that was all I needed . . . However, after much frustration, failure and thought, I discovered that my particular student was not ready for the mind boggling lessons that I was preparing. I learned a big lesson in scaffolding . . . I was taking all of these successes and failures to heart

and having them really affect me. I learned to step away from the emotion and look at myself and my student more objectively . . .

Preservice teachers who are necessarily focused on their own effectiveness and whose field experience is not well-integrated with their prior beliefs may respond by rejecting the important form of knowledge provided by an unfamiliar context. Consequently, the initial dissonance novices feel when making instructional decisions must again be scaffolded carefully. Occasionally preservice teachers will make instructional choices that belie superficial or stereotypic beliefs about their reader's home culture. Such assumptions must be carefully monitored and explored through discussion. If not "unpacked," the field experience could tacitly confirm preconceptions that would limit, rather than promote, professional development.

## Conclusion: Opportunities and Challenges

As a university educator, teaching in the field has been a powerful experience on several levels. Each semester, I come to know both preservice teachers and the young readers with whom they work quite well. I read lesson plans and listen to tutors "talk through" success and failure. When observing tutorials, I sometimes model a pertinent strategy or share a favorite book. This opportunity for ongoing interaction with real children in a real school environment has helped me understand the many diverse influences on childrens' literacy development. It has also helped me understand the dilemma of teachers who daily face the complex task of uniting theory and practice.

In its blueprint for school reform, the Holmes Group (1986) called for university faculty to enter schools but noted that "there are few precedents for managing the complex jobs that swim in the limbo between agencies" (p. 19). For me, the "complex jobs" were quickly apparent because this neighborhood school was distinctly different from our university in its culture and in the theoretical framework of its reading curriculum. But I believe my experience with field-based teaching raises a critical issue for all teacher educators in situated learning environments: What is the proper role of university faculty in a school setting?

As a literacy educator, I feel a responsibility to demonstrate the efficacy of assessment and intervention strategies from a research-supported sociopyscholinguistic perspective. In a university classroom these efforts are not constrained by opposing beliefs from a host school. Likewise, in a university-sponsored clinic the reading program of participants would be significant only in terms of identifying individual strengths and weakenesses. When a course is taught on site, however, such philosophical and procedural disparities must be resolved. In this example, school and university agreed on a *modus operandi* acceptable to both. Ours is a popular program and well-supported by school faculty who frequently praise our efforts with their students. In fact, two years ago the principal wrote to our university, noting that, "The one-on-one language arts experience . . . has proven to be a huge success for both groups." But while we have successfully worked together for the benefit of at-risk readers, the university presence has had no impact on classroom reading instruction at this school. If one role of higher education is to model innovative practice for all teachers, then this partnership has not taken advantage of our expertise. And while I believe I have grown in my understanding of learners and learning contexts, my own practice has been unaffected by my school-based colleagues.

How, then, do university and school—both educational institutions but often with profound differences in mission and beliefs—form true partnerships so that together we can improve the quality of instruction for all? There has long been a perception, perhaps justified, that preservice teachers learn little of practical value from their college instructors (Kagan, 1992; Myers, 1991). Kagan's (1992) study indicates, in fact, that "information presented in courses is rarely connected to candidates' experiences in classrooms" (p. 154). For the university, situated learning offers an opportunity to make such connections.

Schon (1987) has called upon teacher preparation programs to place a "reflective practicum" at the center of their programs "as a bridge between the worlds of university and practice" (p. 309). This practicum might begin with "tasks where they [teachers] can explore their own learning" (p. 322). It would include ongoing work with children and encourage students to regard teaching "as a process of reflective experimentation in which they try to make sense of the sometimes puzzling things chidren say and do" (p. 323). Furthermore, students would be "encouraged to think of adapting to or coping with the life of the school as a component of their practice equal in importance to their work with children" (p. 323). In short, the practicum would create opportunities for both "reflection-in-action" and "reflection on reflection-in-action" (p. 309).

Despite its limitations, our after-school program approximates Schon's (1987) reflective practicum by creating a classroom community in which preservice teachers can regularly experience and reflect on a social constructivist perspective of literacy learning in a school context. And since most children in this program quickly become enthusiastic participants in a range of literacy events, we have many concrete pedagogical experiences to evaluate together.

The issue of motivation is one example. Traditionally, educators viewed motivation as "something we 'do' to children rather than something that comes out of their natural inclinations as curious, exploring, social, and self-determining human beings" (Oldfather & Dahl, 1994, p. 140). Through the structure of this field-based course, however, preservice teachers can witness how participation in literacy activities helps children construct understandings about language. As a byproduct, they also see how socially-embedded practice motivates by stimulating the natural curiosity of children.

This experience could never be duplicated in an impersonal and decontextualized university setting. Even in classrooms where literacy events are socially constructed, preservice teachers in individual placements do not have the advantage of a shared experience to evaluate or a university instructor to scaffold their observations.

Ultimately, then, field-based teaching creates a community of adult learners within a community of young learners. In the process, it offers boundless opportunities to connect theory and practice. Perhaps the last paragraph of Matt's final reflection describes how:

> Despite all of the confusion and stress . . . I always looked forward to my sessions with Jon. Jon taught me that you don't have to be the best at something to enjoy it. His enthusiasm and personality were delightful. I was amazed at how far a positive attitude can take you. I relished every step that Jon took as a reader. I learned that reading is a human endeavor. As with all human endeavors, you must not overlook the human element.

---

# References

Bloome, D. (1985). Reading as a social process. *Language Arts, 62*(2), 134-142.

Bloome, D., & Green, J. (1984). Directions in the sociolinguistic study of reading. In P.D. Pearson (Ed.), *Handbook of reading research* (pp. 395-421). New York: Longman.

Brown, R.G. (1993). *Schools of thought*. San Fransisco: Jossey-Bass.

Cazden, B. C. (1985). Social context of learning to read. In H. Singer and R. B. Ruddell (Eds.), *Theoretical models and processes of reading* (3rd Ed. pp. 722-750). Newark, DE: International Reading Association.

Cramer, E.H., & Castle, M. (1994). *Fostering the love of reading: The affective domain in reading education*. Newark, DE: International Reading Association.

Fosnot, C.T. (1996). *Constructivism: Theory, perspectives, and practice*. New York, NY: Teachers College Press.

Galda, L. (1984). The relations between reading and writing in young children. In R. Beach & L. Bridwell (Eds.), *New directions in composition research* (pp. 191-204). New York: Guilford Press.

Goodman, K. S. (1969). Analysis of oral reading miscues: Applied psycholinguistics. *Reading Research Quarterly, 5*, 9-30.

Goodman, K. S. (1976). Behind the eye: What happens in reading. In H. Singer & R. B. Ruddell (Eds.), *Theoretical models and processes of reading* (2nd Ed. pp. 470-496). Newark, DE: International Reading Association.

Graves, D. (1983). *Writing: Teachers and children at work.* Portsmouth, NH: Heinemann.

Heath, S.B. (1983). *Ways with words: Language, life, and work in communities and classrooms.* Cambridge: Cambridge University Press.

Herrmann, B.A., & Sarracino, J. (1993). Restructuring a preservice literacy methods course: Dilemmas and lessons learned. *Journal of Teacher Education, 44,* 96-106.

Holmes Group (1986). *Tomorrow's teachers: A report of the Holmes group.* East Lansing, MI: Author.

Kagan, D.M. (1992). Professional growth among preservice and beginning teachers. *Review of Educational Research, 62,* 129-169.

Lave, J., & Wegner, E. (1991). *Situated learning: Legitimate peripheral participation.* New York: Cambridge University Press.

Mosenthal, J. (1996). Situated learning and methods coursework in the teaching of literacy. *Journal of Literacy Research, 28,* 379-403.

Myers, M. (1991). Issues in the restructuring of teacher preparation. In J. Flood, J. Jensen, D. Lapp, & J.R. Squire (Eds.), *Handbook of research on teaching the English language arts* (pp. 394-404). New York: Macmillan Publishing Co.

Oldfather, P., & Dahl, K. (1994). Toward a social constructivist reconceptualization of intrinsic motivation for literacy learning. *Journal of Reading Behavior, 26,* 139-158.

Piaget, J. (1964). Development and learning. In R.E. Ripple & V.N. Rockcastle (Eds.), *Piaget rediscovered: Conference on cognitive studies and curriculum development.* Ithaca, NY: Cornell.

Risko, V.J., Peter, J.A., & McAllister, D. (1996). Conceptual changes: Preservice teachers' pathways to providing literacy instruction. In E.G. Sturtevant & W.M. Linek (Eds.), *Growing literacy: Eighteenth yearbook of the College Reading Association* (pp. 104-119). Commerce, TX: College Reading Association.

Rosenblatt, L. (1978). *The reader, the text, the poem: The transactional theory of the literary work.* Carbondale, IL: Southern Illinois University Press.

Roskos, K., & Walker, B.J. (1994a). Learning to teach problem readers: Instructional influences on preservice teachers' practical knowledge. *Journal of Teacher Education, 45,* 279-288.

Roskos, K., & Walker, B. (1994b). *Interactive activities in reading diagnosis and teaching.* New York: Macmillan.

Schon, D.A. (1987). *Educating the reflective practitioner.* San Fransisco, CA: Jossey-Bass.

Smith, F. (1994). *Understanding reading: A psycholinguistic analysis of reading and learning to read* (5th ed.). Hillsdale, NJ: Lawrence Erlbaum Associates.

Strickland, D.S., & Feeley, J.T. (1991). Development in the elementary school years. In J. Flood, J. Jensen, D. Lapp, & J.R. Squire (Eds.), *Handbook of research on teaching the English language arts* (pp. 286-302). New York: Macmillan Publishing Co.

Vygotksy, L.S. (1978). *Mind in society: The development of higher psychological processes.* Cambridge, MA: Harvard University Press.

## Appendix A: ED328—Daily Lesson Plan

Name: _____

Date: _____

Student: _____

Reading behaviors observed from last session: _____

_____

Area(s) of focus for this session: _____

_____

Procedure

    warm-up:

    familiar text:

    new text (explain choice):

    strategy and skill:

    instruction/assessment tool:

    personalized reading/writing activitiy:

## Appendix B: Letter to Parents

Dear Parents:

Welcome to the _____ Reading Enrichment Program! We are happy to have this opportunity to work with your child this semester.

Every Monday and Wednesday your child will be reading and writing with a student who is studying to become a teacher. Most sessions will follow a similar pattern. First, children will read a book or poem that they have read before. Next, they will be introduced to a new book or poem. Tutors will also work with your child on reinforcing skills that are being introduced in their regular classrooms. Each session will end with a writing activity. Reading and writing activities will vary.

Our reading enrichment program is based upon the following principles about how children learn to read and write:

1) The more children are exposed to the world of print the more they come to understand how language works.

2) The more success children experience as readers and writers, the more confident they become. Self-esteem grows as achievement grows.

3) Children who are read to and/or who share their reading experiences with others become more confident and better readers and writers.

4) The reading and writing processes support each other. When children write, they practice reading and they learn about the world of print.

Young learners need many opportunities to read and write, to share what they have learned, and to make mistakes in a supportive environment. We hope that participation in our program will help your child's literacy growth. Please join us on _____ for a final party celebrating the children's accomplishments.

Sincerely,




Your child's tutor is _____

He/she can be reached at _____ (Department of Education).

# Promoting Diversity:
# A Learning Community Project for College Reading Programs and Teacher Education Programs

**Mary Sheehy Costello**
**Norman A. Stahl**

Northern Illinois University

## Abstract

*The need for greater diversity in our nation's teaching workforce continues to increase as the number of teachers of color graduating from colleges of education remains low. This paper describes the current need for more minority teachers, as well as the theoretical framework and design of a learning community project. The project incorporates developmental reading, writing, freshman experience, and teacher education to increase the number of students of color recruited and retained in teacher education.*

Among the critical issues faced by American educators is the recruitment and preparation of a more diverse teaching force to meet the demands and challenges of the 21st century. Social, economic, and cultural diversity is woven into the fabric of our national community to a degree unparalleled in the nation's history. Of particular importance for educators interested in the future of the nation is meeting the needs of the expanding number of children of color in our preschools, elementary schools, middle schools, and secondary schools.

Reviews of student and teacher demographics (Delpit, 1995; King, 1993; Yopp, Yopp, & Taylor, 1991) show that the proportion of minority teachers in the nation's teaching force is diminishing. Presently, 10% of our teachers are either African Americans, Asian Americans, Latinos, or indigenous peoples, and it is estimated that only 5% of the nation's teachers will be people of color in the year 2000.

This downward trend is due in part to the decline in the number of ethnically and linguistically diverse people enrolling in and graduating from teacher preparation programs. Equally troubling is the parallel decline in the number choosing to enter and stay in the teaching profession. Delpit (1995) has offered several powerful reasons why people of color leave teacher education programs or the teaching profession including the lack of culturally relevant pedagogical practices, the marginalization or invalidation of minority students' experiences and voices, and racial discrimination in teacher education programs and beyond. In addition to these explanations, other factors which mitigate against greater diversity in the teaching force include "the increased prevalence of competency examinations, the lack of prestige for teaching as a profession, low salaries, and less than optimal working conditions" (Delpit, 1995, p. 106). The review by Yopp et al. (1991) argues that the factors that most critically influence the shortage of minority teachers include fewer minorities going to college, lower college retention rates of minorities, and increased opportunities for minorities in previously closed fields.

Conversely, while the representation of minority teachers dwindles, the enrollment of children of color has grown to over 30% of the total population of elementary, middle, and secondary schools (Gay, 1993). Hence, there has been a trend in the teaching field since the 1960's where fewer and fewer children of color are being taught by teachers of color (King, 1993). Even more dramatic are estimates that by the year 2020, children of color will comprise nearly half of all children in public elementary, middle, and secondary schools (King). How many of these children will be taught by teachers of color? Consequently, it is apparent that there exists an urgent need for greater diversity in our nation's teaching force.

Many experts suggest that all children, regardless of their ethnic or cultural backgrounds, need connections with minority teachers to enrich their learning experiences and better prepare them to live and work in an increasingly multicultural society. Beyond the need for representative minority teacher and leader role models is the concern that the absence of such individuals works to limit children's worldview, as well as their place in the world. It is important to consider that "many teachers simply do not have the frames of reference and points of view similar to their ethnically and culturally different students because they live in different existential worlds" (Gay, 1993, p. 287). Teachers of color "bring different kinds of understandings about the world than do those whose home lives are more similar to the worldview underlying Western schooling" (Delpit, 1995, p. 102). They can also provide diverse perspectives and instruction that reflect culturally relevant pedagogical practices (Ladson-Billings, 1992).

Over recent years, numerous projects have attempted to address the concern over limited minority representation in education, by involving postsecondary institutions in meeting the challenges of promoting diversity and retention in preservice teacher training programs, and in the teaching profession. Yet, Jones and Clemson (1996) have pointed out that commonly recommended projects such as future teachers' groups, monetary incentives, grow-your-own programs, postbaccalaureate programs, alternative certification programs, advertising/public relations campaigns, mentor programs, and public-oriented dissemination projects have been less than successful.

On the other hand, college developmental reading, writing and learning, and writing programs successfully serve a full range of nontraditional students (Boylan, Bliss, & Bonham, 1997) during their first year in college. It is puzzling why these programs have not worked more closely with colleges of education to promote greater opportunity for nontraditional students—often of color—to gain entry to teacher education programs. This article describes the critical theory and practice behind a project that draws upon the power of a professional learning community (Tinto & Goodsell, 1993, Tinto, Goodsell-Love, & Russo, 1994; Tussman, 1969; Wilcox, delMas, Stewart, Johnson, & Ghere, 1997) to target potential educators enrolled in a university special admissions program.

## Theoretical Framework

Educators need to question dominant educational and societal structures if we are to grapple with the low percentage of minority students in teacher education programs and with recruiting and retaining more people of color. These demographics illuminate the need to examine critically the classroom instruction and professional preparation of future teachers. Teacher educators concerned with such imbalance would best focus on a discourse of student experience and emancipatory pedagogical practices drawn from the critical theory of schooling advocated by Giroux (1989). He notes that such an examination requires an analysis of social practices and categories, such as class, race, gender, and ethnicity. A "theory of schooling as a form of cultural politics" acknowledges these "specific configurations of power and politics" (p. 147). Hence, Giroux would argue that teacher educators must emphasize the diverse lived experiences of future teachers. A learning community with its integrated classes, flexible scheduling, and expanded curriculum is a viable mechanism for undertaking such a critical examination.

Curriculum theory as a form of cultural politics (Aronowitz & Giroux, 1993) is inextricably linked to the language of critique and possibility. Critique involves engaging future educators in dialogue about how the dominant school culture maintains the interests and values of the dominant culture while dismissing and marginalizing the forms of knowledge, language, and experience valued by subordinate groups.

Underlying the notion of a language of possibility and the discourse of experience is the commitment to hope, emancipation, and self- and social empowerment. Empowering education is an "active, cooperative, and social practice" for social change, and invites students to be "change agents and social critics" (Shor, 1992, pp. 15-16). The process of empowerment for self- and social change consists of students bringing together their understandings, language, and experiences while extending their perspectives. In a democratic community, such as a learning community, a dialogue of understanding evolves from recognizing, respecting, and valuing the alternative perspectives and realities of others. When students openly share their readings of the text and the world, they collide with the readings or understandings of others and begin to see beyond their original perspectives or boundaries. Through this social learning process, students extend their understandings by listening to each other and considering alternate perspectives (Pradl, 1996). Thus, dialogic relationships grow in an atmosphere of trust, creating pedagogical practices that seek not to marginalize people, but to validate their stories and their histories.

Culturally relevant instruction apprentices students into a learning community and develops the curriculum not from the canon of the dominant culture, but from the lived experiences of the students (Ladson-Billings, 1992). Teachers and students view themselves as political beings and engage in a collaborative struggle against the status quo. Through reading, writing, and discussion, this community of learners examines the "current socioeconomic and political conditions [that] are inequitable and unjust" and constructs ". . . the understanding that teachers must understand and participate in the world outside the classroom . . ." (p. 388) in order to facilitate social change.

## The Collaborative Project

The impetus for this collaborative partnership comes from a variety of efforts in university settings which promote diversity in preservice preparation programs. The possibilities are generated by developmental reading and writing programs, special admissions programs, freshman experience projects, and colleges of education. Students of color may be recruited by identifying entering special admissions or developmental education students who are interested in the teaching profession. Programs may provide culturally relevant instruction and thematically linked developmental courses directly related to their teaching pursuits, as well as support systems that offer academic guidance, tutoring, and mentoring.

### Project Goals

The Professional Preparatory Program includes three basic goals:
1. Increasing the retention and graduation rate of minority students within all teacher preparation programs.

2. Involving special admissions pre-education majors in a learning community. Their multiterm courses are built upon thematically linked, integrated, preprofessional and developmental experiences focused on the critique and possibilities of education in the 21st century. These reading, writing, and reflective dialogue experiences are rooted in critical pedagogy, and empowering educational practices.

3. Preparing cohort members through course work, workshops, and tutoring, if necessary, to pass the basic skills subtest of the Illinois State Certification Tests.

### *Project Rationale*

The Professional Preparatory Program design is based on the assumptions that retention in higher education and success in a major field is promoted by:

1. Involving students in a learning community that relates to and values their academic and career goals and interests, as well as their lived experiences. Each student in the program has identified a desire to pursue a career in teaching and to enter a preservice education program.

2. Providing quality developmental education services that promote transfer of learning strategies and skills to courses in both the general studies program and the professional sequence. For instance, the reading and study strategies courses are linked thematically to required education courses to provide the context for application and transfer of strategies and skills.

3. Providing a credit-bearing freshman experience seminar linked to developmental education course work, which directly supports entry into a major in education. The seminar is designed to provide students with information about requirements for entry into preprofessional programs and other university requirements impacting future teachers, as well as academic preparation for meeting these requirements.

4. Providing students with foundational knowledge supporting success in professional courses. The linked courses are designed around the theme "Education in the Year 2000." Students examine and explore critical issues and the implications of these issues for themselves and their communities, while developing more sophisticated strategies for the demands of college reading, writing, and studying.

5. Giving students in the first year in higher education the opportunities to develop relationships with other cohort members interested in similar pursuits, faculty, and senior level students.

# Design

Students are enrolled in three linked courses during their first semester on campus: college reading, basic writing, and freshman experience. During the second semester, they enroll in another set of linked courses: college reading and study strategies, general writing, and introductory educational foundations. Students choose to enter the learning community when they attend university orientation. Instructors meet throughout the year to discuss student progress, coordination, curricular revisions, and similar issues.

### Semester One

Students examine critical issues in education through reading, dialogue, reflection, and writing. Students enrolled in the college reading course engage in extensive and intensive reading and responding to four assigned books, a student choice book, and a student-authored book all related to the learning community theme (see Table 1). The forms of discourse of the texts become more complex across the semester. Vocabulary develops through a student-driven generative model, and reading comprehension is enhanced through multiple experiences with texts, or forms of knowledge, that relate to and value the students' lived experiences. The reading and writing connection is strengthened as students collaborate to publish their own critical philosophical and pedagogical beliefs about schooling and education, as well as their own voices in journals, stories, or narratives. Themes are revisited throughout the semester in a spiral design where each exposure and opportunity for collaboration promotes more sophisticated responses and understandings by individual students and the learning community as a whole.

There is particular emphasis on fostering: a) a discourse community where students are empowered as learners through valuing diverse and alternative perspectives, b) a focus on exploring and challenging forms of schooling that seek to limit or marginalize members of oppressed groups, and c) a

**Table 1. Texts Used in Semester One.**

| Assigned Texts | Student Choice |
|---|---|
| *Among School Children* (Kidder, 1989) | *Dangerous Minds* (Johnson, 1992) |
| *36 Children* (Kohl, 1967) | *Amazing Grace: The Lives of Children and the Conscience of a Nation* (Kozol, 1995) |
| *Savage Inequalities* (Kozol, 1989) | *You Can't Say, You Can't Play* (Paley, 1992) |
| *Life in Schools* (McLaren, 1994) | *Always Running* (Rodriguez, 1987) |

valuing of the experiences and voices the students bring to the classroom. Hence, "the discourse of student experience supports a view of pedagogy and empowerment that allows students to draw upon their own experiences and cultural resources and that also enables them to play a self-consciously active role as producers of knowledge within the teaching and learning process" (Giroux, 1989, p. 149).

During the content-oriented freshman experience seminar, students meet weekly with a counselor from Educational Services and Programs. They also meet with an adviser from the College of Education to foster successful orientation and acclimation to the university environment. Specific objectives include critically reflecting on and applying strategies for coping successfully with the academic, social, and cultural demands of the freshman year. The students develop a working knowledge of resources that promote persistence and retention. They also engage in a panel discussion with practicing teachers and are introduced to the maze of institutional and state requirements for general and teacher education.

Both the first and second semester English writing courses are designed to incorporate readings and discussion related to the theme of education. A process writing model with an emphasis on personal narrative and experience serves as the focus of the first semester writing course. Students write extensively with opportunities for multiple revisions, peer editing, and instructor guidance. Students are introduced to word processing activities which were not always available at their secondary schools.

### Semester Two

Coordinated and thematically linked experiences continue through a reading and study strategies course. An introductory educational foundations course provides a context for the application and transfer of strategies and critical reading techniques. Instructors coordinate the strategies and foundations courses to allow greater opportunities to apply strategies in real contexts, which in turn strengthens learning. Students explore the various philosophical, sociological, and instructional components of schooling and education and choose the study strategies that best suit their needs.

Students continue to meet individually with and receive counseling from their freshman seminar instructor/counselor. They also meet more formally with the assigned academic adviser to discuss plans and requirements for entering the teacher education program. Future plans call for peer counseling where senior level students provide new students with insider information gained by successfully navigating the postsecondary system.

Students continue as a cohort into a general writing course, progressing from the personal narrative of the basic writing course to more formal scholarly discourse. Drawing upon the thematic content, students more deeply explore critical issues related to pedagogy as they learn to prepare various types of research papers. Students use traditional library-based resources and references, as well as evolving resources available through the worldwide web.

## Discussion

The instructors have reconstructed the curriculum and pedagogy to promote a community of empowered learners in thematically linked courses. This process has resulted in increased collaboration, sharing of ideas, and planning of coordinated lesson activities and events. The linked course framework fosters innovations that build on students' past experiences, providing rich and meaningful contexts and links through which students construct new knowledge.

The coordinated, multiterm, thematically linked courses bring together students with relevant interests and unique experiences while fostering opportunities for these students to learn from each other. "The classroom space is seen as providing occasions for students to support one another as they test ideas and learn from each other" (Pradl, 1996, p. 88). Through integrated thematic content, students develop, apply, and transfer study skills and techniques in content courses and "real-life" situations. Students build a firm knowledge base using critical issues linked to their past experiences and prior knowledge and bring their own stories or mini-narratives to the learning process.

Teacher education faculty and instructors provide support, advising, and mentoring relationships for the cohort group, while cohort members form a supportive peer group. The community of faculty, instructor, and cohort members appears to have had a positive effect on the students' overall acclimation to social and academic university life. Students' interest, motivation, and continuation in the Preprofessional Preparation Program appear to be high. There appears to be a further benefit in terms of cumulative grade point averages and second year retention rates as compared to the general special admissions population. The culturally relevant experiences and learning opportunities fostered through this collaborative partnership create an empowering educational environment more conducive to the success and retention of people of color in a teacher preparation program, and eventually in the teaching workforce.

# References

Aronowitz, S., & Giroux, H. A. (1993). *Education still under siege.* Westport, CT: Bergin & Garvey.

Boylan, H. R., Bliss, L.B., & Bonham, B.S. (1997). Program components and their relationship to student performance. *Journal of Developmental Education, 20* (3), 2-9.

Delpit, L. (1995). *Other people's children: Cultural conflict in the classroom.* New York: The New Press.

Gay, G. (1993). Building cultural bridges: A bold proposal for teacher education. *Education and Urban Society, 25* (3), 285-298.

Giroux, H. A. (1989). School as a form of cultural politics: Toward a pedagogy of and for difference. In H. A. Giroux & P. McLaren (Eds.), *Critical pedagogy, the state, and cultural struggle* (pp. 125-151). Albany, NY: State University of New York Press.

Jones, V.C., & Clemson, R. (1996). Promoting effective teaching for diversity. In L.I. Rendon & R.O. Hope (Eds.), *Educating a new majority.* San Francisco: Jossey-Bass.

King, S. H. (1993). The limited presence of African-American teachers. *Review of Educational Research, 63* (2), 115-149.

Ladson-Billings, G. (1992). Liberatory consequences of literacy: A case of culturally relevant instruction for African American students. *The Journal of Negro Education, 61* (3), 378-391.

Pradl, G. M. (1996). *Literature for democracy.* Portsmouth, NH: Boyton/Cook Publishers.

Shor, I. (1992). *Empowering education: Critical teaching for social change.* Chicago: The University of Chicago Press.

Tinto, V., & Goodsell, A. (1993). *Freshman interest groups and the first year experience: Constructing student communities in a large university.* (ERIC Document Reproduction Service No. ED 358 778).

Tinto, V., Goodsell-Love, A., & Russo, P. (1994). Building community. *Liberal Education, 79,* (4), 26-29.

Tussman, J. (1969). *Experiment at Berkeley.* New York: Oxford University Press.

Wilcox, K. J., delMas, R. C., Stewart, B., Johnson, A. B., & Ghere, D. (1997) The package course experience and developmental education. *Journal of Developmental Education, 20,* (3), 18-27.

Yopp, H. K., Yopp, R. H., & Taylor, H. P. (1991). The teacher track project: Increasing teacher diversity. *Action in Teacher Education, 13* (2), 37-42.

# Texts Incorporated Thematically in Learning Community Courses

Johnson, L. (1992). *Dangerous minds.* New York: St. Martin's Press.

Kidder, T. (1989). *Among schoolchildren.* Boston: Houghton Mifflin.

Kohl, H. (1967). *36 children.* New York: Plume.

Kozol, J. (1989). *Savage inequalities.* New York: Harper Perennial.

Kozol, J. (1995). *Amazing grace: The lives of children and the conscience of a nation.* New York: Crown.

Lawry, J. (1992). *College 101: A freshman reader.* New York: McGraw-Hill.

McLaren, P. (1994). *Life in schools.* New York: Longman.

Nieto, S. (1996). *Affirming diversty: The sociopolitical context of multicultural education.* New York: Longman.

Paley, V.P. (1992). *You can't say, you can't play.* Cambridge: Harvard University Press.

Rodriguez, R. (1987). *Always running.* New York: Simon & Schuster.

# THE FIELD EXPERIENCE TRIAD: INFLUENCES OF THE COLLEGE INSTRUCTOR AND COOPERATING TEACHER ON THE PRESERVICE TEACHER'S BELIEFS, PRACTICES, AND INTENTIONS CONCERNING LITERACY INSTRUCTION

**Deidra W. Frazier**
**Thomasine H. Mencer**
**Mary Annette Duchein**
Louisiana State University

## Abstract

*This study examines the influences of the college instructor and cooperating teacher on preservice teachers' beliefs and intended practices regarding literacy instruction. Participants included 25 elementary education majors enrolled in a reading, writing, and oral communication methods course, 2 college instructors, and 14 cooperating teachers. Findings indicated preservice teachers' beliefs and intentions were: a) strengthened or changed; b) more influenced overall by college instruction than by cooperating teachers; c) strongly influenced by field experience, specifically direct experience teaching, particularly when their teaching practices were unlike those of their cooperating teachers; and d) influenced most when cooperating teachers demonstrated practices consistent with college instructors' philosophy of literacy instruction. Findings suggest several criteria for field experiences in conjunction with college-based methods courses.*

## Introduction

Researchers (Merseth, 1991; Shulman, 1995) lament the failure of teacher education programs to prepare future teachers to use knowledge gained from college instruction, suggesting that preservice teachers view theory and principles learned in university training as having little application in real classrooms. Preservice teachers' perspectives often conflict with their college training resulting in resistance to new ideas or instructional practices. Researchers (Florio-Ruane & Lensmire, 1990; Perry & Rog, 1992) note these perspectives are based on preservice teachers' past experiences as students. Such influences have been observed in content reading instruction (Bean & Zulich, 1990; Stewart, 1990) and teaching methods at elementary levels (Goodman, 1988; Hollingsworth, 1989). When preservice teachers' perspectives are left unexamined, the result is often resistance against content and practices taught during elementary-level literacy preparation (Herrmann & Sarracino, 1993) and writing methods courses (Florio-Ruane & Lensmire, 1990).

In addition to relying on personal perspectives, preservice teachers tend to turn to cooperating and supervising teachers more than to college instructors for guidance concerning instructional practices. Mencer (1996) and Metcalf (1991) noted preservice teachers' teaching beliefs generally change in the direction of the cooperating teacher.

Richardson-Koehler (1988) similarly noted that within two weeks of field placement, student teachers discount their college instructors' influence, attributing most of their practices to their cooperating teachers. Earlier researchers also found that student teachers seek legitimization of their roles as professionals more from cooperating teachers than from college supervisors (Friebus, 1977) and that cooperating teachers exercise inordinate authority in determining student teacher success (Barrows, 1979). Thus, when preservice teachers encounter conflicts between their training and observed teaching, they may perpetuate existing classroom instruction and superficial learning (Hollingsworth, 1989). In short, research clearly indicates that of the field experience triad members (i.e., the preservice teacher with her personal and educational perspective, cooperating teacher, and college instructor), the college instructor has the least influence on the preservice teacher.

Several reasons may explain the weak role of college training. Florio-Ruane & Lensmire (1990) suggest the short duration of training is insufficient to change views formed over years as students. Also, many preservice teachers find it difficult to apply theoretical, pedagogical, and content knowledge to practice (Weinstein, 1988), particularly when methods or materials differ in school settings (Stewart, 1990). Others note preservice teachers' perspectives of inferior power relations may cause resistance (Britzman, 1991; Stewart 1990).

To address this resistance and understand the complexities underlying preservice teachers' practices, it is necessary to examine their beliefs. Pajares

(1992) suggests that attention to teacher candidates' beliefs should inform educational practice, and that teacher education programs should promote positive change in preservice teachers through reflection on what, how and why something is taught (Pajares, 1993). Kagan (1992) further states that studying the forms and functions of teacher beliefs, as well as their antecedents and expressions, is critical to the success of teacher education programs.

In light of these findings and suggestions the researchers investigated the critical interplay among members of the field experience triad in the context of their own literacy methods course involving field experience. This exploratory study examined influences of individuals in the field experience triad on the preservice teachers' beliefs, practices, and intentions concerning literacy instruction.

## Method
### *Participants*
Participants included 25 elementary education majors (preservice teachers) enrolled in a literacy methods course, 2 college instructors, and 14 cooperating teachers. Two instructors, each describing her philosophy regarding literacy instruction as holistic and interactive, team-taught the course. Fourteen teachers from two elementary schools served as cooperating teachers. Criteria for selecting cooperating teachers were willingness to participate in field experience and flexibility in allowing preservice teachers to use approaches learned in class. With the exception of four teachers described by the college instructors as having holistic beliefs, cooperating teachers' beliefs were unknown prior to field placement. Preservice teachers were assigned in pairs to a cooperating teacher, with the exception of three, who for logistical reasons were placed singly and encouraged to collaborate with peers.

### *Literacy Methods Course and Practicum*
The field experience included an initial 2-week phase of observation and participation followed by the teaching of reading, writing, and oral communication in small group and whole class formats for 10 weeks. Preservice teachers met as a class at least twice weekly to discuss literacy instruction and specific field experiences. Assigned readings included *Classrooms That Work: They Can All Read and Write* (Cunningham & Allington, 1994), *Transitions: From Literature to Literacy* (Routman, 1988); *The New Read-Aloud Handbook* (Trelease, 1989); and *Managing the Whole Language Classroom* (Eisele, 1991). Preservice teachers kept portfolios in which they reflected upon their educational backgrounds and developing philosophies of literacy instruction. The two instructors, committed to fostering positive growth through encouraging reflection on what, how, and why instructional decisions were

made (Pajares, 1993), sought to promote their own holistic and interactive philosophies regarding literacy instruction.

### Data Sources and Analysis

Data sources included a) preservice teachers' portfolios containing lesson plans, lesson reflections, and written observations and analyses of their cooperating teachers' instructional practices; b) preservice teachers' responses to final exam questions requiring discussion of beliefs and intentions in light

---

### Table 1. Criteria for Literacy Philosophies

*Holistic*
- instruction developmentally appropriate and child-centered
- use of a variety of print, including narrative, expository, and environmental
- immersion in children's literature; teacher reads aloud daily
- literature extension activities; shared language activities
- reading/writing instruction linked
- journal writing; inventive spelling encouraged
- student choice considered and encouraged in reading and writing activities
- reading for pleasure encouraged
- emphasis on meaning/comprehension in reading instruction
- phonics, spelling, and vocabulary taught in meaningful context
- variety of activities to promote oral language development (e.g., readers theater, choral reading, echo reading, drama, music)

*Skills-based*
- basal-driven curriculum; excessive use of worksheets
- reading groups based on ability; emphasis on round robin reading
- teaching of spelling, phonics, and vocabulary in isolation
- little or no reading for pleasure
- minimal writing activities; no journal writing
- inventive spelling not encouraged
- little or no group work other than reading groups; little sense of community
- student choice in reading and writing activities not considered

*Interactive*
- combination of holistic approaches and some aspects of skills-based teaching; often combined use of basal and other types of print
- holistic approaches combined with the teaching of skills in isolation
- instruction driven by needs of children as well as state curriculum guide

of their field experience and college instruction, and categorization of their cooperating teachers' beliefs; c) instructors' field notes on class discussions concerning cooperating teachers' beliefs and practices; and d) conferences with and field observations of preservice teachers. Data were collected over the 15-week semester and analyzed via constant comparative analysis (Miles & Huberman,1984). Matrices were developed and triangulated across the three researchers (two of whom were the college instructors and one of whom was an instructor in another section of the same literacy methods course) and data sources to control for bias. Patterns of beliefs and practices among cooperating teachers and beliefs, practices, intentions, and influences on preservice teachers emerged throughout the semester. Final categorization of participants' approaches to literacy instruction was completed when all the data were collected at the semester's end.

The researchers categorized cooperating teachers as having holistic, interactive, or skills-based philosophies if the majority of their stated beliefs and/or observed practices reported by preservice teachers were consistent with one of these philosophies. Categorization of preservice teachers was based on direct observation of their teaching as well as the other data sources. Also, unlike the cooperating teachers who were only asked to discuss their rationale for their teaching rather than categorize their beliefs, preservice teachers were asked to categorize themselves as having holistic, interactive, or skills-based beliefs at the semester's end. Thus, while categorization was done by the researchers, the perspective was primarily that of the preservice teachers. In all cases there was agreement between the researchers' and preservice teachers' categorization of cooperating teachers. The researchers defined holistic, skills-based, and interactive philosophies according to criteria which they developed from their experience as literacy educators (see Table 1).

## Results and Discussion

This study relies largely upon perspectives inferred from preservice teachers' observations, practices, and reports. Findings therefore must be considered in light of the limitations of such self-report data. Hollingsworth (1989) also cautions that preservice teachers tend to mirror ideologies and rhetoric used by those perceived to be in superior positions of power. The possibility that preservice teachers sought to please the researchers, two of whom were their instructors in this course, also must be considered when interpreting these findings.

### *Categories of teaching philosophy regarding literacy instruction*

Based on the operational definitions of philosophies regarding literacy instruction (see Table 1), the researchers categorized 6 cooperating teachers as having a holistic philosophy, 1 as having an interactive philosophy, and 7 as having a skills-based philosophy. Of the 25 preservice teachers, 21 were categorized as having a holistic philosophy, 1 as having an interactive philosophy, and 3 as having a skills-based philosophy. Categorization of teaching philosophies based on portfolios and final exam responses was consistent, with the exception of one preservice teacher who described her beliefs as skills-based, yet demonstrated holistic practices.

### *Beliefs and intentions*

Data analysis indicated preservice teachers' beliefs and intentions were a) strengthened or changed; b) influenced more by college instruction than by cooperating teachers; c) strongly influenced by field experience, specifically direct experience teaching, particularly when their teaching practices were unlike those of their cooperating teacher; and d) influenced most when cooperating teachers demonstrated practices consistent with the college instructors' philosophy of literacy instruction.

Sixteen of the 25 preservice teachers stated their beliefs in holistic teaching strengthened and 9 stated their beliefs changed by the semester's end. Five of the 9 preservice teachers changed from a skills-based to a holistic philosophy, 1 changed from a skills-based to an interactive philosophy, and 3 changed from a holistic to a skills-based philosophy.

### *Beliefs in holistic teaching strengthened (16 preservice teachers assigned to 12 cooperating teachers) (see Table 2).*

These preservice teachers stated their holistic beliefs were strengthened, with college instruction reinforcing the field experience. Preservice teachers' field experiences are grouped according to their cooperating teachers' philosophies.

**Preservice teachers with holistic cooperating teachers.** These cooperating teachers taught lower elementary grades and demonstrated practices consistent with those promoted in college instruction. Preservice teachers described field experiences as extremely positive and cooperating teachers as nurturing, having respect for children, maintaining a warm, inviting classroom atmosphere, and being enthusiastic about their profession. They further stated that field experience allowed them to apply ideas and instructional practices learned in college and that they intended to continue these practices in their future classrooms.

**Preservice teachers with an interactive cooperating teacher.** Two preservice teachers were placed with a kindergarten teacher described as "doing lots of literature, but also lots of worksheets." Although the field experience was positive, both preservice teachers felt their cooperating teacher was a little restrictive (e.g., insisted on children coloring in the lines), and

## Table 2. Preservice Teachers' Beliefs in Holistic Teaching Strengthened

| No. | Grade | Cooperating teacher | Grouping | Partner's beliefs | Field experience | Most influence on beliefs |
|-----|-------|---------------------|----------|-------------------|------------------|---------------------------|
| 1 | K | Holistic | Single | | Positive | College instruction |
| 2 | K | Holistic | Paired | Holistic | Very positive | Field reinforced college instruction |
| 1 | 1 | Holistic | Paired | Holistic | Very positive | Field reinforced college instruction |
| 2 | 1 | Holistic | Paired | Holistic | Very Positive | Field reinforced college instruction |
| 2 | 1 | Holistic | Paired | Holistic | Positive | Field reinforced college instruction |
| 1 | 2 | Holistic | Single | | Very positive | Cooperating teacher |
| 2 | K | Interactive | Paired | Holistic | Positive | Application of college instruction |
| 1 | 1 | Skills | Single | | Somewhat positive | College instruction |
| 1 | 3 | Skills | Paired | Interactive | Negative | Application of college instruction |
| 1 | 4 | Skills | Paired | Holistic | Positive | College instruction |
| 1 | 5 | Skills | Paired | Skills | Positive | College instruction |
| 1 | 5 | Skills | Paired | Skill | Negative | College instruction |

better approaches could have been practiced. The classroom was described as organized and pleasant, and the cooperating teacher as nurturing. Preservice teachers were allowed to implement their own teaching ideas, saw the benefits of more holistic teaching (e.g., the use of more children's literature), and stated their future practices would be more consistent with holistic teaching.

**Preservice teachers with skills-based cooperating teachers**. Most of the skills-based teachers taught upper elementary grades. Overall, field experiences were described as more negative than those of the previous two groups. These cooperating teachers tended to be depressed about the teaching profession, made negative comments about the college teacher education program, had low expectations for their elementary students, and had discipline problems. Their statements included, "I wouldn't teach if I had to do it over again," "The kids are lazy and don't want to learn," "Some students will never make progress in reading," and "Whole language will cause a decrease in reading scores."

Preservice teachers in this group learned "what not to do," explaining that the children's negative responses to inappropriate instruction convinced them of the need for more holistic teaching. Criticisms of instruction included lack of student choice in reading and writing assignments and little or no reading for pleasure. Preservice teachers were allowed to use teaching ideas learned from college even when inconsistent with existing classroom practice. One preservice teacher stated that allowing the children to read and write more resulted in greater enthusiasm and writing improvement. She further stated that comparing her cooperating teacher's approaches with those learned in her own college instruction allowed her to see the benefits of holistic teaching, observing that the previous "three years of skills approaches were not working with these children."

Two cooperating teachers whose curricula were primarily worksheets described themselves as holistic because they occasionally used literature. In both cases, their preservice teachers described them as skills-based teachers who had the desire to teach better, but "just didn't know how." These experiences were considered less negative than others in this group. In one classroom preservice teachers described their field experience as improving after they began constructing and teaching lessons. In this third grade classroom both preservice teachers sympathized with the teacher's plight of having "so many low students" (many of whom could only read and write their names), but held different views about this situation. While one saw this as a result of three years of inappropriate skills-based instruction, her partner agreed with the cooperating teacher's statement that "the kids are so low in skills that they need more instruction in this area."

### *Beliefs changed from skills-based (6 preservice teachers assigned to 5 cooperating teachers) (see Table 3)*

The freedom to apply ideas learned in college instruction had the most influence on preservice teachers who held holistic beliefs. Cooperating teachers had the most influence on preservice teachers who held interactive and skills-based beliefs.

**Beliefs changed from skills-based to holistic.** Preservice teachers reported that field experience allowed them to compare holistic and skills-based teaching and "see how students responded much better when they were taught using ideas from college." One preservice teacher who saw children respond enthusiastically to her literature extension activities and saw her cooperating teacher's "strategies fail," stated, "I'm ashamed to say that I would have been skills-based . . . if not introduced to more literature-based, sensible teaching."

Preservice teachers described their skills-based cooperating teachers as having negative attitudes toward teaching and the college teacher education program. These cooperating teachers were described as being "mean to the

## Table 3. Preservice Teachers' Beliefs Changed from Skills-Based

| No. | Grade | Cooperating teacher | Grouping | Partner's beliefs | Field experience | Most influence on beliefs |
|-----|-------|---------------------|----------|-------------------|------------------|---------------------------|
| *To Holistic* | | | | | | |
| 1 | 1 | Holistic | Paired | Holistic | Very positive | Field reinforced college instruction |
| 1 | 4 | Skills | Paired | Holistic | Positive | Application of college instruction |
| 2 | 5 | Skills | Paired | Holistic | Negative | Application of college instruction |
| 1 | 4 | Skills | Paired | Interactive | Negative | Application of college instruction |
| *To Interactive* | | | | | | |
| 1 | 4/5 | Skills | Paired | Holistic | Somewhat positive | Cooperating teacher/ background |

kids," and as having "given up" on the children. In contrast, preservice teachers described the holistic cooperating teacher as nurturing and respecting her children and as being enthusiastic about teaching. In spite of observing inappropriate teaching practices and being in negative classroom environments, preservice teachers placed in skills-based classrooms considered their field experience beneficial because they could teach using their own ideas and get the experience needed to test these ideas.

**Beliefs changed from skills-based to interactive**. This preservice teacher reported that her college instruction strongly influenced her beliefs, but that the field experience, along with her educational background, had the most influence. The way she was taught as a child ("teach a skill, do a worksheet, take a test") convinced her that "some skills are difficult to teach in the context of literature" and that her preferred approach was a "combination of holistic teaching with worksheets and basal curricula."

The preservice teacher described her cooperating teacher as being "burned out" after teaching 18 years and reported her as stating she "hates to read" and "kids need structure to stay on task and whole language doesn't provide it." The cooperating teacher also refused to allow her preservice teachers to journal with the children explaining that it "wouldn't work" and gave busywork instead. Nevertheless, the preservice teacher described her field experience as somewhat positive because she had freedom to practice her own ideas. Interestingly, even though her practices were consistently holistic (perhaps because her peer partner held strong holistic beliefs), she preferred to teach more like her cooperating teacher.

### *Beliefs changed to more skills-based (3 preservice teachers assigned to 3 cooperating teachers) (see Table 4).*

Preservice teachers reported their field experience and cooperating teachers as having the most influence on their beliefs, describing their cooperating teachers as having negative attitudes toward children and teaching, yet being organized, structured, and in one case, effective. The first preservice teacher, placed in a third grade classroom, reported her beliefs as changing from holistic to skills-based. In spite of these beliefs, she practiced holistic teaching, possibly because she collaborated with a partner who held strong holistic beliefs. She described her cooperating teacher as teaching inappropriately, yet agreed with her statement that the "kids were so low in skills that they needed more instruction in skills because they made D's and F's on many worksheets." She also described the cooperating teacher's attitude toward children and teaching as negative, noting the teacher "yelled a lot," gave spelling tests when many children could only read and write their names, and concluded that many of the children would never experience success. Even though this preservice teacher was critical of such practices and recommended more holistic approaches, she "felt sorry" for the teacher who "desired to teach better, but didn't know how," explaining the teacher was justifiably frustrated because the children "were so low and would benefit from more structure."

Sympathy for the cooperating teacher seemed to strongly affect this preservice teacher's beliefs. It is not clear to what degree other factors such as educational background influenced her beliefs. Possibly, the preservice teacher and cooperating teacher held similar views about the need for control and structure in a classroom. It is noteworthy that while this preservice teacher bought into her cooperating teacher's rationale for inappropriate practice, her peer partner disagreed, attributing the children's poor performance to poor instruction, and noting improved performance and greater enthusiasm when holistic practices were used.

The second preservice teacher was placed in a fifth grade classroom and noted her field experience and "family of educators" background as

**Table 4. Preservice Teachers' Beliefs Changed to More Skills-Based**

| No. | Grade | Cooperating teacher | Grouping | Partner's beliefs | Field experience | Most influence on beliefs |
|-----|-------|--------------------|---------|-------------------|-----------------|---------------------------|
| 1 | 3 | Skills | Paired | Holistic | Somewhat positive | Cooperating teacher |
| 1 | 5 | Skills | Paired | Holistic | Positive | Cooperating teacher/ background |
| 1 | 5 | Skills | Paired | Holistic | Positive | Cooperating teacher |

convincing her of the need for skills-based teaching. She described her co-operating teacher as depressed about teaching and frustrated because "the kids are so lazy and don't want to learn," and as emphasizing worksheets and ignoring the children's needs. She saw the need for better teaching practices, yet described her field experience as positive, explaining that she liked her teacher and sympathized with the predicament of having to teach an "undesirable" group of children. She bonded with her cooperating teacher and could understand her teaching practices.

Before her field experience, this preservice teacher preferred more holistic teaching. Severe discipline problems in the classroom convinced her of the need for skills-based teaching to address behavior and skill deficiencies. When the cooperating teacher's practices were counter to college instruction, the preservice teacher's own background, which supported beliefs consistent with those of the cooperating teacher, had a deciding influence on her perceptions of the appropriateness of these practices. The disparity between her skills-based beliefs and her holistic practices is likely due to the fact that she observed skills-based teaching strongly promoted and modeled by her cooperating teacher, yet planned and taught with a partner who held strong holistic beliefs. Her partner also believed the children's behavior and deficiencies were a result of inappropriate instruction.

The third preservice teacher, also placed in a fifth grade classroom, reported having no particular beliefs about literacy instruction prior to her field experience. She stated that her cooperating teacher taught mostly skills, used lots of worksheets, and did not incorporate recreational reading in her class, yet was "a very effective teacher." Because her cooperating teacher was a very pleasant, nurturing person, the field experience was positive. The preservice teacher stated she "will probably be like the cooperating teacher." In the absence of particular beliefs about literacy instruction and the presence of a pleasant classroom environment, the cooperating teacher's practices had more influence than college instruction. However, as in another case, this preservice teacher's peer partner held opposing beliefs and stated that even though the field experience was positive, she did not intend to use the inappropriate practices her cooperating teacher demonstrated.

## Conclusions

Even though 7 out of 14 cooperating teachers in this study practiced skills-based teaching the majority of preservice teachers (21 out of 25) reported preferences for holistic teaching. Overall, college instruction had the most influence on preservice teachers' beliefs, practices, and intentions, contrary to earlier research indicating personal and academic history (Florio-Ruane & Lensmire, 1990; Herrmann & Sarracino, 1993), cooperating teachers (Hollingsworth,

1989; Mencer, 1996; Metcalf, 1991), and supervising teachers (Barrows, 1979; Friebus, 1977) as having the most influence on preservice teachers.

One explanation for this study's findings may be the nature of the literacy methods course which emphasized reflective practice, collaboration, and networking. Reflective journals likely promoted critical thinking about teaching practices and prevented preservice teachers from agreeing with their cooperating teachers' approach demonstrated "in a real classroom." This explanation is supported in Sampson and Linek's (1994) findings that preservice teachers' beliefs tended to change toward a more holistic view in accordance with that of their instructor. Although participants were limited to teaching mini-lessons to peers and did not teach in real classroom settings, their beliefs shifted and their reflections were valued and nurtured through group interactions, written responses, and class discussions. Sampson and Linek explain that identification of personal theoretical beliefs, cognitive dissonance, (i.e., the attempt to align beliefs and practices), provision of support, and promotion of reflection were all influences in this change process. Such influences were also foundational to the literacy methods course in the current study and emphasize their importance in affecting changes in beliefs.

Pairing preservice teachers to facilitate collaboration also may have strengthened the influence of college instruction. Peers were consistent in their categorization of their cooperating teacher's approach and demonstrated practices promoted via college instruction. However, in spite of this consistency, 5 of the 11 pairs categorized themselves as having different beliefs concerning literacy. It is not clear to what extent peer partners may have influenced each other. But peer partners who held holistic beliefs seemed to have no influence on the three preservice teachers who changed from holistic to skills-based beliefs. Nor is it clear to what extent the three preservice teachers who were placed by themselves were made vulnerable to the influence of their cooperating teachers. One of these preservice teachers espoused beliefs consistent with those of her interactive cooperating teacher. The other two, however, espoused holistic beliefs, which were different from their skills-based and interactive cooperating teachers. Further research is needed to explore the influence of peers in preservice teaching.

Weekly classroom discussions in which preservice teachers were encouraged to reflect upon their field experience and readings also may have strengthened the influence of college instruction. Such networking and collaboration are typically lacking in traditional student teaching and may be lacking in research studies involving methods course practica. Any comparison of influences on preservice teachers in methods courses involving practica and student teachers must be considered in light of different program foci (i.e., emphasis on pairing, collaboration, networking, and reflection).

Findings in this study underscore the powerful influence of field experience in shaping beliefs about teaching. Clearly, when there is consistency between college instruction and the cooperating teacher's classroom, both philosophically and in practice, the preservice teacher is more likely to observe, understand, and apply principles learned via college instruction, even when they conflict with personal perspectives. However, the difference between the influence of *observing* and *experiencing* classroom practices must be noted. In the current study, even when the cooperating teacher demonstrated practices inconsistent with those promoted in college instruction, preservice teachers were more influenced by their college instruction when they were allowed to teach holistically. The self confidence and sense of accomplishment gained after teaching a successful lesson appeared to be a strong influence on the preservice teachers' beliefs and intentions. Most cooperating teachers in the current study gave their preservice teachers a great deal of flexibility, which seemed critical in shaping their beliefs and intended practices.

It is also noteworthy that every preservice teacher who observed and experienced holistic teaching was convinced of its benefits. It would be interesting to challenge the three preservice teachers' preferences for skills-based teaching by placing them in holistic classrooms. For some preservice teachers, observing holistic teaching may have been necessary to convince them of its benefits, while for others, the direct experience of teaching via holistic approaches was persuasive enough.

The cooperating teacher's attitude toward the teaching profession, by no means a small influence, was emphasized by preservice teachers. There were marked differences between reported attitudes of holistic and interactive teachers, and skills-based teachers. Holistic and interactive teachers' attitudes were positive, enthusiastic, and nurturing toward their children. Preservice teachers in these classrooms had exceptionally positive experiences and professed beliefs and intentions consistent with them.

On the other hand, most of the skills-based teachers had negative attitudes toward teaching and the college teacher education program, problems with discipline, low expectations for the children, and in many cases, had given up on the children's ability to learn. While such a dismal classroom atmosphere had little influence on preservice teachers' attitudes, it nevertheless affected their beliefs, practices, and intentions. Many saw the situation as a challenge, attempted to "rescue the children" via more holistic instruction, and saw these efforts rewarded when children responded with enthusiasm and improved academic performance. However, two preservice teachers in such settings reported their preference for skills-based teaching, sympathized with their cooperating teachers, and bought into their rationale for using skills-based approaches, agreeing that the children's misbehavior and severe academic deficiencies necessitated order and teaching via worksheets. These preservice teachers noted a "family of educators" and "teaching the way I was taught" as contributing to their beliefs and teaching intentions. Speculation on how placement in a holistic classroom would have influenced their beliefs invites research in this area.

In summary, these findings illustrate the critical role of college methods courses involving field experience in influencing preservice teachers' beliefs, practices, and intentions. This research challenges the notion that preservice teachers will "teach the way they were taught" and the assumption that the cooperating teacher in her "real world classroom" has the most influence on novice teachers. Findings in this study suggest when preservice teachers receive college instruction along with a strong underlying rationale, examine their beliefs and practices as well as those of their cooperating teachers, and experience success applying what they have learned, they are likely to embrace the philosophy promoted in their college class. In short, if *seeing is believing*, then *doing is convincing*. As one preservice teacher expressed, "I put my philosophy into action and saw it work!" Further research might investigate whether preservice teachers will maintain and refine these beliefs and practices in their future classrooms.

## Implications

Several implications for meaningful, enriching field placements in conjunction with education methods courses are indicated. Members of the field experience triad—the college instructor, preservice teacher, and cooperating teacher—are a network of individuals who form the part of a teacher training program that best simulates the "real world" of the classroom. Findings of this study suggest the following conditions for the best utilization of this network.

- Cooperating teacher practice is consistent with practice promoted in college instruction.
- Communication across all members of the triad is clear and ongoing.
- Preservice teachers a) collaborate with peers and cooperating teachers in planning and teaching, b) observe appropriate instruction, c) have the freedom to create lessons and teach them, and d) reflect on their beliefs and practices.
- Cooperating teachers a) support the college teacher education program and professional development, b) have a positive attitude toward the teaching profession, c) have respect for and a positive, nurturing attitude toward children, d) have a positive, nurturing manner in the role as mentor teacher, e) demonstrate appropriate teaching practice, f) allow preservice teachers flexibility to try their own ideas, and g) give constructive feedback to preservice teachers.

# References

Barrows, L. K. (1979). *Power relationships in the student teaching field.* Paper presented at the annual meeting of the American Educational Research Association, San Francisco.

Bean, T. W., & Zulich, J. (1990). Teaching students to learn from text: Preservice content teachers' changing view of their role through the window of student-professor dialogue journals. In J. Zutell & S. McCormick (Eds.), *Literacy theory and research: Analyses from multiple paradigms* (pp. 171-178). Chicago: National Reading Conference.

Britzman, D. P. (1991). *Practice makes practice: A critical study of learning to teach.* Albany, NY: SUNY Press.

Cunningham, P. M., & Allington, R. L. (1994). *Classrooms that work: They can all read and write.* New York: HarperCollins College Publishers.

Eisele, B. (1991). *Managing the whole language classroom.* Cypress, CA: Creative Teaching Press.

Florio-Ruane, S., & Lensmire, T. (1990). Transforming future teachers' ideas about writing instruction. *Journal of Curriculum Studies, 22,* 277-289.

Friebus, R. J. (1977). Agents of socialization involved in student teaching. *Journal of Educational Research, 70,* 263-268.

Goodman, J. (1988). Constructing a practical philosophy of teaching: A study of preservice teachers' professional perspectives. *Teaching & Teacher Education, 4,* 121-137.

Hermann, B. A., & Sarracino, J. (1993). Restructuring a preservice literacy methods course: Dilemmas and lessons learned. *Journal of Teacher Education 44,* 96-106.

Hollingsworth, S. (1989). Prior beliefs and cognitive change in learning to teach. *American Educational Research Journal, 26,* 160-189.

Kagan, D. (1992). Professional growth among preservice and beginning teachers. *Review of Educational Research, 62,* 129-169.

Mencer, T. H. (1996). *Reflection on teaching: An ethnographic study of preservice teachers' beliefs and practices.* Unpublished doctoral dissertation, Louisiana State University, Baton Rouge.

Merseth, K. (1991). *The case for cases in teacher education.* Washington, DC: American Association of Colleges of Teacher Education and American Association of Higher Education.

Metcalf, K. K. (1991). The supervision of student teaching: A review of research. *The Teacher Educator, 26,* 27-42.

Miles, M. B., & Huberman, A. M. (1984). *Qualitative data analysis.* Beverly Hills, CA: Sage.

Pajares, M. F. (1992). Teachers' beliefs and educational research: Cleaning up a messy construct. *American Educational Research Journal, 2,* 307-332.

Pajares, M. F. (1993). Preservice teachers' beliefs: A focus for teacher education. *Action in Teacher Education, 15,* 45-54.

Perry, C. M., & Rog, J. A. (1992). Preservice and inservice teachers' beliefs about effective teaching and the sources of those beliefs. *Teacher Education Quarterly, 19*(2), 49-59.

Richardson-Koehler, V. (1988). Barriers to effective supervision of student teaching. *Journal of Teacher Education, 39*(2), 28-34.

Routman, R. (1988). *Transitions: From literature to literacy.* Portsmouth, NH: Heinemann.

Sampson, M. B., & Linek, W. M. (1994). Change as a process: A view of an instructor and her students. In E. G. Sturtevant, & W. M. Linek, (Eds.), *Pathways for lit-*

*eracy: Learners teach and teachers learn* (pp. 47-58). Sixteenth yearbook of the College Reading Association. Pittsburg, KS: College Reading Association.

Shulman, J. H. (1995). Tender feelings, hidden thoughts: Confronting bias, innocence and racism through case discussion. In J. A. Colbert, P. Desberg, & K. Trimble (Eds.), *The case of education* (pp. 137-158). Boston: Allyn & Bacon.

Stewart, R. A. (1990). Factors influencing preservice teachers' resistance to content area reading. *Reading Research and Instruction, 29*(4), 55-63.

Trelease, J. (1989). *The new read aloud handbook.* New York: Penguin.

Weinstein, C. S. (1988). Preservice teachers' expectations about the first year of teaching. *Teaching & Teacher Education, 4,* 31-40.

# REDEFINING REFLECTIVE PRACTICE: THINKING FORWARD ABOUT CONDITIONS THAT SUPPORT LITERACY LEARNING

## Jacqueline K. Peck
Cleveland State University

## Abstract

*This paper reports findings of a naturalistic case study of an exemplary teacher's inquiry process, particularly aspects of her reflective practice. Inductive analysis of the data reveals a strong connection between prospective thinking about conditions for literacy learning and reflections on literacy events themselves. The findings also indicate that reflective practice is more systematic than the current body of literature suggests. Implications include a need to engage preservice teachers in prospective thinking about conditions as they plan specific literacy events and to continue research on this component of reflective practice.*

"*Reflect* on the lesson you have implemented. What have you learned about the children? About your teaching?"

"Keep a journal of your personal responses to readings, *reflections* on field experiences, insights gained, further questions you want to investigate."

"Type a 1-page *reflection* of what you noticed and learned about the portfolio process as an assessment tool. You may also want to reflect on any lingering questions you have."

These statements occur in written and verbal assignments for preservice literacy courses that I teach at an urban university. They are invitations for preservice teachers to engage in reflection in the university classroom and in the field as observer and budding practitioner. Although these assignments invite students to reflect on what occurred in their literacy learning and teaching experiences, they neglect to engage them in another dimension of reflective practice, namely the prospective thinking about conditions that support literacy learning.

Although Dewey (1910), in his model of reflective practice, encouraged teachers to consider possible solutions before solving pedagogical problems, prospective consideration of possible conditions for learning is not clearly addressed in subsequent work on reflective practice. Schon (1983) recognized that the complexity and contextuality of educational problems requires thoughtful reflection over time and a willingness to embrace revision of initial ideas. Zeichner and Liston (1987) found reflective practice to be critically important for success in inquiry-oriented programs, and they argued that traditional teacher education programs inhibit the development of reflection. Berthoff (1987) supported reflection by encouraging teachers to "Research" the information they collect in their classrooms. Ross (1987) offered strategies for the teaching of reflective practice. Others found teacher dialogue supported reflective practice by making implicit knowledge explicit (Fox, 1993; Greene, 1986; McDonald, 1987). Hunsaker and Johnston's (1992) collaborative research supported previous findings that teachers can become more reflective given time and support.

The importance of establishing conditions for literacy learning is widely documented. Rich descriptions of environments conducive to literacy learning are available (Edelsky, Altwerger, & Flores, 1991; Goodman, 1986; Vacca & Rasinski, 1992). Carefully established conditions reduced the risks of literacy learning in a study by Allen, Michalove, Shockley, and West (1991). Studies have also shown how inquiry-oriented classroom environments maximize literacy learning and teaching (Peck & Hughes, 1994; Ruddell, 1995). However, these environments do not emerge spontaneously; they are the result of teachers' planful and intentional efforts. In a review of research into teachers' planning processes, Clark and Peterson (1986) reported that studies did not retain distinctions between prospective and reflective thinking. More recent studies embed prospective thinking in a cycle of reflection and contemplation that involves examination of prior instructional acts and projection of future acts (Sampson & Linek, 1994; Walker & Ramseth, 1993). Although these studies focus on teacher planning and raise questions such as "Did I do what I intended to do?", they do not examine teachers' prospective thinking about establishing effective literacy environments.

This paper discusses results of a naturalistic case study of a first grade teacher's inquiry process (Peck, 1995), particularly aspects of her reflective practice. The research question that guided this portion of the larger case study is: How does the teacher establish conditions for literacy learning? Data pertinent to this question comprise the focus of this paper, which concludes with a discussion of the need to redefine reflective practice to include a forward-thinking component. Implications for teacher education and further research are also suggested.

## The Study Design

This study is rooted in the sociocultural perspective that recognizes teachers as legitimate knowledge producers through participation in the social events of their classrooms (Cochran-Smith & Lytle, 1993; Weade & Green, 1989). Its intention is to provide a rich description of an exemplary teacher's inquiry process; therefore, case study (Merriam, 1988) is an appropriate design.

The setting was a first grade classroom in a large urban district. The teacher, Sharon, holds a graduate degree and at the time of the study had 7 years teaching experience, all in the primary grades. She is an active participant in and provider of staff development on topics such as teacher effectiveness and inquiry learning. Her exemplary work is widely documented (Peck, 1996a, 1996b; Peck & Hughes, 1994; Peck & Hughes, 1997) and has been recognized by her principal and central office administrators.

Data collection occurred during the first 10 weeks of the school year and began with an interview using semi-structured, open-ended questions. Each week, Sharon audiotaped think aloud protocols during instructional planning for literacy events. She also audiotaped reflections, first while viewing a videotape of the event soon after it occurred and again several days later in the form of a teacher log. Inductive analysis of the data yielded patterns and regularities (Goetz & LeCompte, 1984; Lincoln & Guba, 1985) that were refined through the constant-comparative method (Glaser & Strauss, 1967).

Because this study seeks to understand the inquiry process of a particular teacher, certain findings will apply to this teacher and classroom only. This limitation is lessened, however, through triangulation of data sources and longevity of the collaboration between the teacher and researcher. For three years prior to the initiation of this study, the researcher was a participant-observer in the teacher's classroom. This long-term collaboration may itself be viewed as a limitation; however, this same longevity engendered mutual trust and respect that resulted in forthright, honest interactions.

## Results of the Study

During the initial interview for this study, I asked Sharon to identify those conditions she intentionally established in her classroom environment. She named four: maintaining high expectations for her students, sharing responsibility for learning with her students, providing a variety of materials and experiences, and integrating literacy processes with curricular content and social interactions. Data segments that addressed conditions for literacy learning supported each of these intentions. They appeared most frequently in think alouds. Table 1 summarizes the domains and categories that were uncovered and refined through the constant-comparative method (Glaser & Strauss, 1967).

Examples follow that define these domains and categories, and moreover, that illustrate the forward-thinking component of teacher reflection.

**Table 1. Summary of Domains and Categories**

| Domain | Category |
|---|---|
| Risk | Challenge |
| | Support |
| Responsibility | Authenticity |
| | Ownership |
| | Independence |
| | Self-evaluation |
| Alternatives | Experiences |
| | Materials |
| | Purposes |
| | Groupings |
| Connections | Integration |
| | Interaction |

### *Risk*

Sharon's high expectations for the children initiate many challenges, but the children are never left to meet them without support. She works to maintain a healthy tension between the challenge and support that moves the children toward greater literacy development. For example, in a think aloud for a group of readers with the least developed literacy skills of the children in this classroom, Sharon stated that the story they were reading "does have limited vocabulary, although very sophisticated concepts are included . . . that help to develop higher level thinking. . . ." Reflecting on a videotape of this lesson, she later commented on the importance of choosing "activities that provide j-u-s-t enough pressure, just enough tension, to constantly move the children upward in their literacy development."

One of the ways to support children's risk-taking is to begin with familiar materials. In a think aloud for a shared reading time, Sharon described how and why she begins lessons with familiar songs, such as "Old MacDonald" or repeated readings of a poem to "encourage the children to loosen up." In a later reflection on that shared reading, she stated that "during this reading time . . . we try to do some songs, some poems . . . the children are familiar with to sort of get warmed up and to make sure that they feel real comfortable with what's going on."

### *Responsibility*

Sharon and the children in her classroom share responsibility for learning—their own and others'. The use of authentic materials and activities is one way this shared responsibility for learning is promoted. Authenticity is demonstrated when the children apply their learning to life situations. Sharon intentionally plans for this in the broadest sense and expects profound outcomes. This is clearly demonstrated in a think aloud for a lesson using *The Little Red Hen*.

> One of my major concerns with teaching my children is that they take the concepts that we cover in the classroom and apply them to their lives outside the classroom. Many of these children live in environments that involve a lot of gang activity. They come from households that are less than friendly. They live in neighborhoods that are less than friendly. So I'm expecting them to, as we talk about this, figure out ways that they themselves can be better people in how they treat each other, the friendship that they show towards other people. And as a result, that'll encourage others to perceive them, to see them as friends.

Reflecting on the same lesson Sharon commented that "after we do the kinds of things that we do, my children seem to want to apply those things in their own lives."

Responsibility is also evident in the children's ownership of their learning. Sometimes this is expressed through their choice of literacy materials, intentionally planned by Sharon and documented in her think alouds. For example, "I'll read the books to the children, put out a sign-up sheet for each of them so that the children can determine which book . . . they'll want to read for themselves." A subsequent reflection on this part of the lesson appeared in Sharon's log. "Each child selected a reading book that they want to read."

Independence is an important condition for literacy growth in this classroom and is indicated in data segments through comments on strategic reading. In a think aloud for a language arts lesson using *The Little Red Hen*, Sharon discussed teaching the /h/ sound. "The children will need to know that sound in order to decode that word 'hen' as they read the story independently." Repeated exposures to text, in this instance *The Little Red Hen*, help children develop strategies to solve problems and think for themselves. Sharon later stated in a reflection,

> I do try to teach reading strategically. There are certain things that . . . good readers do, and those are the things that I try to teach them. . . . You don't get stuck on a word; you look at the context, the meaning of that sentence to figure out what that word is. You use some phonics skills; you don't have to know every sound in the word. . . . You look at the beginning sound, you look at the ending sound. Does the word you pick make sense there? It does? Then chances are good that could be the word. . . .

The strategic reading that Sharon attempts to help her children develop is tied to their ability to self-evaluate. Throughout this study, interview and think aloud segments implied opportunities for self-evaluation, but specific comments addressing evaluation, including self-evaluation, appeared predominantly in reflection and log data. For example, when reflecting on mixed-ability grouping used in a particular lesson, Sharon stated, "The stronger student was there to support and assist the less able student. But on the other hand, the less able student was there to provide many, many concepts for the student with greater abilities. . . . I want children to see the ability within them and the ability within others."

### *Alternatives*

Another condition for literacy learning pervasive throughout the data is providing for alternatives. Instead of viewing some children as not developmentally ready for literacy instruction, Sharon reflected, "What I think we should do is expose children to a variety of experiences. Then they have that as background information. . . . If today they are not ready to do something with that information, then they have that stored away in their memory bank and later when they are more prepared to do it, they use that as a point of reference." In a think aloud for a lesson that occurred during the second week of school, Sharon documented that the variety of experiences offered in her classroom is particularly intended for children often considered to be experientially deficient; a log entry for the same lesson further documented that these experiences are designed to provide "five years of literacy experiences for those . . . children who lack those experiences that we consider necessary for success in school."

The variety of materials used in this classroom also provides alternatives for the children. Sharon provides many kinds of materials that the children may use to gather information. In one think aloud she recorded, "The information will then be looked at through the form of pictures, videotapes, books, audiotaped information that I might share with the children. It'll come from filmstrips. It will also come from, hopefully, various field trips that we'll be taking in the near future." And the children in this classroom do use the resources! A reflection on the same lesson included this statement: "These children are actually using the book [they are reading], not just the book but a variety of books and a variety of materials around the room. . . ." A log entry recorded even later again made reference to the use of a variety of resources: "When we use tons and tons of material the way we do, [the children] have a whole library of resources available to them."

Variety in purpose is evident too. Sometimes it is important to follow explicit directions to achieve the purpose of the literacy event; sometimes it is possible to make choices. Sharon commented in a think aloud for a lesson on habitats, "Now the information that they provide can be either of a general nature, for instance 'They live in the woods' if they pick the bear, or they can say [more specifically] that the bear lives in a cave." In this particular literacy event, some students varied the directions and were still highly successful. Sharon reflected, "There are times when following the directions will get us the result that we need, so you don't have a lot of choice. You have to do it this way. But if you can get to that end result another way, that's OK."

Another aspect of alternatives is the use of multiple and flexible grouping patterns. Sharon elaborated on this aspect in her initial interview.

> The groups often emerge from the variety of materials used. We have individual reading group/literature group books going. Each child has a book bag, which is a collection of books that child can read at [his or her] own level. And then we have a great deal of partner reading, so that two children might be reading the same book. . . . I don't have permanent groups anymore. All of my groups are flexible.

### Connections

In the very beginning of the school year, literacy events in this classroom build upon students' prior knowledge and experience gleaned from their lives outside school and from what they do within the classroom community. Literacy processes and concepts are integrated across curricular areas. Skills are presented and practiced in context. Children also have opportunities to apply what they learn to settings outside school or to subsequent learning experiences.

For example, in a think aloud for a lesson tied to a shared reading of *The Little Red Hen*, Sharon said she planned to ask the students to "think about the ways that friends help each other in various settings. What I want the children to do is to think about how they can help both inside the house and outside the house." Reflecting on the lesson, Sharon explained that the bellwork assignment for that morning asked the students to "think about a time when they were really a good friend to someone and a time when they were not such a good friend to someone." In a log entry recorded even later she continued to reflect on this lesson: "[T]hat whole issue of friendship is a social studies concept that came into play. I was very much pleased with how that fit into this language arts experience."

Integration of curricular areas provides another dimension of connections. Social studies and science are the areas most often identified by Sharon and her students as part of literacy events. In a think aloud Sharon talked about her development of themes based on skills and concepts she needs to teach in each of these content areas; she believes that:

> [Y]ou cannot teach science, social studies, or math in isolation. Otherwise those skills will have no meaning. What I try to do is to tie all those

skills, all those content areas together using my reading/language arts curriculum. I develop . . . my themes as a result of the connections that I see between subject and skill across the board.

In a subsequent reflection she said that establishing these connections is important because "otherwise, you end up teaching skills instead of teaching concepts."

Another think aloud recorded that skills are presented within the context of "a story or a poem or from known vocabulary" because it "gives the children a basis from which to apply that skill . . . If I took an unknown word or if I taught it in isolation, the children would really have no point of reference and as a result would have difficulty understanding. . . ." In a later reflection, Sharon articulated the "advantage to teaching phonics contextually—they know that sound is the same whether it's at the beginning position or at the end. You don't have to teach ending consonant sounds. . . . They'll see the sense of it."

An additional example of natural thematic integration occurred with a group of children who were reading a book about trucks. In a think aloud for one of their lessons Sharon said, "We will continuously connect this trucks theme from this story to our science lesson, 'balls and ramps,' and to our social studies unit that has to do with transportation." As part of this literacy experience, the students kept a log of trucks they observed in their neighborhood for one week. Sharon reflected that they used science processes, such as observing and gathering data, to explore the social studies concept—trucking in their community—in a "reading/language arts environment." In addition, Sharon believed that keeping the truck logs would "have meaning for them as they're looking at trucks in the environment."

Connections in this classroom also encompass social interaction. Often the social interaction resulted in the creation of a collaborative product, such as this instance involving the reading of *The Little Red Hen*, recorded in a think aloud.

The children are going to work together in a small group to create a poster. One side of the poster should talk about ways that friends can help each other inside the house—the inside, indoors—and one way that friends can help each other outdoors. I'm expecting that they talk about these concepts first, and then that they put together a poster that's representative of all of their ideas.

A later reflection documented that Sharon perceived this interaction as a means for building community.

Sharon thoughtfully considers the literacy learning in her classroom before the events take place and repeatedly after they occur. Think alouds predominantly supplied segments pertaining to how she establishes conditions for literacy learning. These intentional plans for particular conditions were implemented successfully; reflection and log segments make that connection.

## Redefining Reflective Practice

The findings reported here indicate that reflective practice is more systematic than the current body of literature suggests. Furthermore, the data demonstrate support for Dewey's (1910) model: Sharon's prospective thinking about conditions for learning is integrally tied to the reflection that takes place after a literacy event. Indeed, one dimension of this teacher's inquiry process is the intentional establishment of conditions. These findings also extend earlier accounts of the importance of setting conditions for literacy learning (Allen et al., 1991; Edelsky et al., 1991; Vacca & Rasinski, 1992).

Attention to the conditions that optimize literacy learning is more important than typically recognized in traditional practice. Forty per cent of all coded segments in the case study made reference to the teacher's intentional establishment of these conditions. This indicates its prevalence in her thinking and suggests the need to join prospective and retrospective thinking in conversations about reflective practice.

This study has important implications for teacher education and continued research. Preservice teachers are frequently encouraged to develop reflective practice through lesson evaluation, journaling, and portfolio assessment. These invitations only partially attend to reflective practice. Preservice teachers need also to be encouraged to engage in prospective thinking—to think forward—about establishing conditions that support literacy learning. This needs to involve more than literacy environments per se. It needs to extend to thinking forward about optimal conditions for specific literacy events as they are planned. Preservice teachers need to document their thinking forward so they have opportunities to self-evaluate their planning. Similar staff development efforts for inservice teachers are also appropriate.

Further studies are needed to continue this redefinition of reflective practice, and it will be particularly important to seek information in appropriate places. Table 2 shows the data segments relevant to establishing conditions as a percentage of the total segments in the data source. In this study, almost three-fourths of the think aloud data addressed establishing conditions. Therefore, it is likely that teacher thinking about establishing conditions for learn-

**Table 2. Percentage of Segments in Each Data Source Relevant to Establishing Conditions**

| Interviews | Think Alouds | Reflections | Logs |
|------------|--------------|-------------|------|
| 39%        | 72%          | 39%         | 27%  |

ing would appear in think alouds more often than in reflective journals. However, collection of reflection data is also necessary so that connections between prospective and retrospective thinking may be uncovered.

In response to this study, I intend to invite my preservice teachers to engage in thinking forward when they plan specific literacy events. It is also my intention to help them explicitly examine their prospective thinking and tie it to the reflections they do after engaging students in literacy events in the field. I also plan to have them share their thinking with others. A new assignment will read:

"*Think aloud.* What conditions for literacy learning are you considering as you plan this lesson for the field classroom? Audiotape your thinking. Bring it to class so you can listen to each others' tapes and dialogue about how you are thinking forward as you plan for literacy learning."

*This work was made possible through the participation of an exemplary professional, Sharon Hughes, the teacher-researcher who opened herself to my inquiry of her process. She has my steadfast respect and gratitude.*

---

## References

Allen, J., Michalove, B., Shockley, B., & West, M. (1991). "I'm really worried about Joseph": Reducing the risks of literacy learning. *The Reading Teacher, 44,* 458-468.

Berthoff, A. E. (1987). The teacher as REsearcher. In D. Goswami & P. R. Stillman (Eds.), *Reclaiming the classroom: Teacher research as an agency for change* (pp. 28-39). Portsmouth, NH: Heinemann.

Clark, C. M., & Peterson, P. L. (1986). Teachers' thought processes. In M. C. Wittrock (Ed.), *Handbook of research on teaching* (3rd ed., pp. 255-296). New York: Macmillan.

Cochran-Smith, M., & Lytle, S. L. (1993). *Inside/outside: Teacher research and knowledge.* New York: Teachers College.

Dewey, J. (1910). *How we think.* Lexington, MA: D. C. Heath.

Edelsky, C., Altwerger, B., & Flores, B. (1991). *Whole language: What's the difference?* Portsmouth, NH: Heinemann.

Fox, D. L. (1993). The influence of context, community, and culture: Contrasting cases of teacher knowledge development. In D. J. Leu & C. K. Kinzer (Eds.), *Examining central issues in literacy research, theory, and practice* (42nd yearbook of the National Reading Conference, pp. 345-351). Chicago, IL: National Reading Conference.

Glaser, B., & Strauss, A. (1967). *The discovery of grounded theory.* Chicago: Aldine.

Goetz, J., & LeCompte, M. (1984). *Ethnography and qualitative design in educational research.* New York: Academic.

Goodman, K. (1986). *What's whole in whole language?* Portsmouth, NH: Heinemann.

Greene, M. (1986). Philosophy and teaching. In M. C. Wittrock (Ed.), *Handbook of research on teaching* (3rd ed., pp. 479-501). New York: Macmillan.

Hunsaker, L., & Johnston, J. (1992). Teacher under construction: A collaborative case study of teacher change. *American Educational Research Journal, 29,* 350-372.

Lincoln, Y. S., & Guba, E. G. (1985). *Naturalistic inquiry.* Newbury Park, CA: Sage.

McDonald, J. P. (1987). Raising the teacher's voice and the ironic role of theory. In M. Okazawa-Rey, J. Anderson, & R. Traver (Eds.), *Teachers, teaching, & teacher education* (pp. 26-49). Cambridge, MA: Harvard Educational Review.

Merriam, S. B. (1988). *Case study research in education.* San Francisco: Jossey-Bass.

Peck, J. K. (1996a, April). *Inquiry pedagogy: Maximizing literacy learning and teaching through shared inquiry.* Paper presented at the Annual Meeting of the American Educational Research Association, New York, NY. ED 396 269

Peck, J. K. (1996b, December). *What can I do?: Inquiry pedagogy as a framework for culturally relevant teaching.* Paper presented at the National Reading Conference, Charleston, SC.

Peck, J. K. F. (1995). *Inquiry pedagogy: A case study of a first grade teacher's literacy instruction.* Unpublished doctoral dissertation, Kent State University, Kent, OH.

Peck, J. K., & Hughes, S. V. (1994, April). *The impact of an inquiry approach to learning in a technology-rich environment.* Paper presented at the Annual Meeting of the American Educational Research Associates, New Orleans, LA. ED 375 796

Peck, J. K., & Hughes, S. V. (1997). So much success...from a first grade database project! *Computers in the Schools, 13,* 109-116.

Ross, D. D. (1987, October). *Reflective teaching: Meaning and implications for preservice teacher educators.* Paper presented at the Reflective Inquiry Conference, Houston, TX.

Ruddell, R. B. (1995). Those influential literacy teachers: Meaning negotiators and motivation builders. *The Reading Teacher, 48,* 454-463.

Sampson, M. B., & Linek, W. M. (1994). Change as a process: A view of an instructor and her students. In E. G. Sturtevant & W. M Linek (Eds.), *Pathways for literacy: Learners teach and teachers learn* (16th yearbook of the College Reading Association, pp.47-58). Harrisonburg, VA:College Reading Association.

Schon, D. A. (1983). *The reflective practitioner: How professionals think in action.* New York: Basic.

Vacca, R. T., & Rasinski, T. V. (1992). *Case studies in whole language.* New York: Harcourt, Brace, Jovanovich.

Walker, B. J., & Ramseth, C. (1993). Reflective practice confronts the complexities of teaching reading. In T. Rasinski & N. Padak (Eds.), *Inquiries in literacy learning and instruction* (pp.171-177). Pittsburgh, KS: College Reading Association.

Weade, R., & Green, J. L. (1989, March). *Action research and the search for meaning.* Paper presented at the Annual Meeting of the American Educational Research Association, San Francisco, CA.

Zeichner, K. M., & Liston, D. P. (1987). Teaching student teachers to reflect. In M. Okazawa-Rey, J. Anderson, & R. Traver (Eds.), *Teachers, teaching, & teacher education* (pp. 284-309). Cambridge, MA: Harvard Educational Review.

# Building Bridges: Designing Project Portfolios to Accommodate the Needs of Beginners

**Joan B. Elliott**

Indiana University of Pennsylvania

**Barbara Illig-Avilés**

Duquesne University

## Abstract

*This classroom research study reports the results of initial and final surveys administered to 60 graduate and undergraduate students as they created their own portfolios while enrolled in Language Arts classes. The focus of the research was (1) to access the background experiences of the students with regard to portfolios, (2) to assess participants' reactions to portfolios as a form of assessment, and (3) to explore students' perceptions and feelings as they worked through the portfolio process. The article also describes the framework and guidelines for the Project Portfolio as it was developed for those courses.*

Portfolios have gained wide acceptance in the educational community during the last decade. They are currently used at all levels of instruction (McLaughlin & Vogt, 1996; Tellez, 1996) and in all aspects of the curriculum. However, the way portfolios are defined varies greatly. Valencia (1990) defines portfolios as "samples of work that exemplify the depth and breadth of expertise" (p. 338). Wolf and Siu-Runyan (1996) provide a more precise definition as they explain that portfolios are:

> A selective collection of student work and records of progress gathered across diverse contexts over time, framed by reflection and enriched through collaboration, that has as its aim the advancement of student learning. (p. 31)

The definition preferred by the authors, and used for the purposes of this study, was developed by Paulson, Paulson, and Meyer (1991). They state that portfolios are:

> A purposeful collection of student work that exhibits the student's efforts, progress, and achievements in one or more areas. The collection must include student participation in selecting contents, the criteria for selection, the criteria for judging merit, and evidence of student self-reflection. (p. 60)

The organization and content of a portfolio depends on its purpose. Jasmine (1992) developed five separate categories of portfolios: working portfolios, showcase or display portfolios, assessment portfolios, cumulative portfolios, and finally, teacher resource portfolios. Later, Wolf and Siu-Runyan (1996) suggested that all portfolios could be classified into one of three groups: Ownership, Feedback, or Accountability Portfolios.

In teacher education, a key to the design and content of portfolios is close articulation with the actual work of the teacher (Tellez, 1996). Stahle and Mitchell (1993) stress the importance of incorporating portfolios into the college classroom in order to more closely align classroom practices at the university with those of the public schools. This view is supported by other experts in the field (Anderson, 1995; Heiden, 1996; McLaughlin & Vogt, 1996). Portfolios, because they encourage divergent ways to assess learning not typically found in more standardized forms of assessment, can capitalize on students' strengths (Ruddell & Ruddell, 1995). They engender student ownership and facilitate the connection between learning and assessment (McKinney, Perkins, & Jones, 1995; Tellez, 1996). Additionally, portfolios can nurture self-esteem (Gillespie, Ford, Gillespie, & Leavell, 1996; McLaughlin & Vogt, 1996); increase critical reflection (Collins, 1991; Oropallo & Gomez, 1990; Wilcox, 1996); and provide opportunities for decision-making and creative thinking (McLaughlin & Vogt, 1996).

Although portfolios are reported to have many positive affects on student learning, several factors may influence their effectiveness. These include time and prior experience with portfolios. For example, college classes typically run for 15 weeks as opposed to the 40 weeks in K-12 classrooms. This abbreviated time period may be critical when the portfolio goal is to provide opportunities for students to demonstrate growth and development in a very broad area like literacy. In addition, the college classroom may be the first place students have been required to participate in creating a portfolio. Therefore, it seems imperative that instructors at the college level be aware of this factor and provide instruction, guidance, and support in portfolio development.

In many instances, the portfolio has become a high-stakes project—a major document upon which grades are based. Tellez (1996) reminds us that evaluation remains an issue separate from the development of a portfolio, and that although portfolios for the purpose of formal assessment have been widely accepted, most research supports the portfolio as a vehicle primarily for self-assessment. Portfolio conferences with an instructor, small group sharing with peers, self-assessment, and a rubric developed collaboratively with the students can make the evaluation process more understandable and consistent (McLaughlin & Vogt, 1996).

## Research in Action

The remainder of this article will focus on a classroom research project implemented by the authors during the Summer and Fall of 1995 while teaching three separate classes, two graduate sections and one undergraduate section of Language Arts. The teacher research was designed to: (1) assess the background experiences of the students in the three courses with regard to portfolios; (2) assess participants' reactions to portfolios as a form of assessment; and (3) explore students' perceptions and feelings as they worked through the process of creating their own portfolios. The authors surveyed each of the classes at the beginning and end of the courses and gathered data from the students' portfolios. The results of the initial survey suggested that the participants lacked background experiences with portfolios. As a result, the classroom researchers structured a "Project Portfolio." In each of the courses, the portfolio was assessed as part of the course grade (40% of the final grade in the undergraduate class and 30% in both graduate classes).

Thirty-six graduate students and 25 undergraduates participated in the study. All undergraduates were second semester sophomores or first semester juniors, and were either elementary or early childhood majors. The graduate students were more diverse. The majority were working toward their reading specialist certification. Others were seeking a second certification in elementary education. Their prior certifications were in business, English, industrial arts, physical education, and special education. Many were inservice teachers working on their master's degrees. A few doctoral level elementary education students were also enrolled.

## The Initial Survey

A survey distributed at the beginning of the course asked the participants to respond to the following statements: (1) Describe your understanding of portfolios (definition, types, content of, uses, assessment, other), and (2) Describe your experiences, if any, with portfolios. Additionally, the graduate classes were asked to complete the following sentence stem: I currently feel that portfolios . . .

Self-report findings at the undergraduate level indicated that although all students had heard of portfolios, most did not appear to have a clear or comprehensive understanding of the process or the product, the portfolio itself. Twenty-three of the 25 students (92%) defined portfolios as collections of student work, and all 25 (100%) indicated that they were used as a form of alternative assessment. Only 14 of the undergraduates (56%) described types of portfolios, and those were categorized according to subject area. Twelve students (48%) listed reading and writing portfolios. The remaining 2 students explained that students could create portfolios in any subject area. Contents of portfolios, when described, included such items as reading lists, responses to literature, pieces of writing, and samples of other student work like tests and homework. Although the undergraduate participants all indicated that portfolios were a form of alternative assessment, they did not appear to have any clear concept of the assessment process. Eight students (32%) indicated that portfolios should be self-assessed or assessed collaboratively with the teacher; the others did not address that issue. One student wrote, "I know students are supposed to self-assess their portfolios with the help of the teacher, but I don't know how it's done. I guess I would ask the student questions about why he put certain pieces in the portfolio." Another wrote, "Students and teachers should look at the portfolio together to see strengths and weaknesses."

Analysis of the data implied that these particular undergraduates had no prior experience with developing their own portfolios. As one student responded, "We only talk about them, we don't do them."

Initial survey results at the graduate level indicated that the majority of the 24 participants (66%) defined portfolios as a collection of student work, but only 10 (28%) described types of portfolios. Common responses included showcase, working, and assessment portfolios, as well as portfolio categories by subject area, i.e. writing, art, math. Less than a third (11 students or 30%) responded specifically to portfolio content. Those who did included such things as writing samples, art work, assessments/tests, video tapes, projects, student self-reflection and teacher observations, conference notes, and checklists. Although the graduate students alluded to the fact that portfolios are assessed by the teacher or in collaboration with the student, they, like the undergraduates, did not indicate how assessment would be accomplished. Three participants wrote that portfolios were assessed with the use of a rubric or checklist, and one reported using a "quantity assessment—8 out of 10 required pieces earn[ed] an 80%."

Graduate responses to the second question asked participants to describe their experiences, if any, with portfolios. Some interesting results were revealed. Ten (28%) of the graduate students indicated that they had some previous experience with portfolios. Another 10 (28%) stated that they had

heard about portfolios through coursework or other professional development, but had no actual hands-on experience with portfolios. Eleven students (30%) had no experience or background knowledge regarding portfolio development or assessment. Five (14%) students chose not to respond.
An analysis of statements that completed the sentence stem (I currently feel
that portfolios . . .) revealed 31 (86%) positive responses.

## The Project Portfolio Framework

Guided by the results of the initial survey and Paulson, Paulson, and
Meyer's (1991) definition, the instructors designed the framework of a "Project
Portfolio." It was hoped that the Project Portfolio would support their students' initial journeys into portfolio development, promote student learning,
and provide a format that would allow comparisons among students. The
Project Portfolio was designed with a narrow focus in order to facilitate a
student's ability to demonstrate progress and effort within an average 15 week
semester or within an abbreviated summer session. The framework was
semistructured to provide a scaffold for students, yet afford students the
opportunity to select content. The Project Portfolio was divided into three
parts:

*Building Your Knowledge*—Students were first asked to choose a
specific area of Language Arts instruction to research. They were given
a list of approximately 15 topics, but were not restricted to those choices.
Examples of areas for student research included Readers' Theatre, newspapers in the classroom, poetry, spelling, etc. The guidelines required
students to complete a search on their selected topic, then to skim the
material to locate a minimum of 5 or 6 pieces that they considered the
most helpful.

After students had read and reacted to the selected articles, they
were required to write a personal belief statement regarding the topic.
Students were encouraged to consider alternate forms of writing, such
as poems, letters, diary entries, and editorials.

*Putting Your Knowledge to Work*—The second part of the portfolio required the students to demonstrate expertise on their topics of
choice by planning, implementing, and documenting an appropriate
individual project. A variety of ideas were provided and the classes
brainstormed additional possibilities. Examples included creating a
teaching video, newsletter or booklet for parents or fellow educators,
learning centers and other hands-on activities, presenting a poster session, or actually documenting work with a group of children.

*Reflection and Self-Assessment*—The final part of the portfolio was
evaluative in nature. Students were asked to reflect upon the actual

process of developing their portfolio in a short narrative. Additionally, the students were asked to write an assessment of their own portfolios using as a guide the rubric developed collaboratively by the class and the instructor.

## Post Assessment Results

All students completed a five question final survey (Figure 1) that incorporated a Likert-like scale during the last week of class. The survey was designed to assess the students' reactions to portfolio assessment. The assessment instrument was an abbreviated format of one originally used by Craig and Leavell (1994).

As can be seen in Figure 1, the majority of undergraduate and graduate students indicated that they initially had positive reactions to the idea of portfolio assessment; however, more graduate students reported a neutral or "we'll wait and see" reaction. An overwhelming majority of participants at both levels indicated positive feelings toward portfolio assessment at the end of the course, and reported that the portfolio provided a valuable contribution toward their learning. The majority of participants indicated a belief that portfolio assessment would be valuable for them as teachers. Additionally, results at both levels indicated that the participants preferred a portfolio structure with a combination of instructor requirements and student choice.

## Qualitative Results

The students' reflections in part 3 of the Project Portfolio were analyzed using Glaser and Strauss's (1967) constant comparative method. Protocols were read numerous times to identify "chunks" of meaning with regard to participants' perceptions of the portfolio process. These "chunks" of meaning were then identified and categorized.

The analysis of the data suggested that the majority of participants perceived that they felt some level of confusion and anxiety as they began the process of developing the portfolios. One student wrote, "I really don't know where to begin. This seems like an awful lot of work for 3 credits." Another remembered thinking, "I just wish[ed] I really understood what you wanted us to do." Other students seemed to take a more philosophical approach. A non-traditional undergraduate stated, "It's obvious I have to start early and get organized. Actually this might be good for me."

At the conclusion of the process, however, all the students indicated that they felt positive about their portfolios and the portfolio process. Three themes emerged as students wrote about the process and the Project Portfolios. One was the framework of the Project Portfolio. Students reported that they liked the narrow focus, as well as the fact that the guidelines provided them with

## Figure 1. Summary of Undergraduate and Graduate Responses to Portfolio Post Assessment

Undergraduate N = 25
Graduate N = 36

My initial reaction to portfolio assessment was:

|  | Negative | | | | Positive |
|---|---|---|---|---|---|
|  | 1 | 2 | 3 | 4 | 5 |
| Undergraduate | 8% | 20% | 44% | 28% | |
| Graduate | 3% | 5% | 39% | 28% | 25% |

My current reaction to portfolio assessment is:

|  | Negative | | | | Positive |
|---|---|---|---|---|---|
|  | 1 | 2 | 3 | 4 | 5 |
| Undergraduate | | 4% | 28% | 68% | |
| Graduate | 3% | 3% | 5% | 33% | 55% |

How valuable was the portfolio assessment in contributing to your learning?

|  | Not Valuable At All | | | | Very Valuable |
|---|---|---|---|---|---|
|  | 1 | 2 | 3 | 4 | 5 |
| Undergraduate | | 4% | 44% | 52% | |
| Graduate | | | 8% | 42% | 44% |

How useful would portfolio assessment be for you as a teacher?

|  | Not Useful At All | | | | Very Useful |
|---|---|---|---|---|---|
|  | 1 | 2 | 3 | 4 | 5 |
| Undergraduate | | | 32% | 68% | |
| Graduate | 3% | | 17% | 25% | 56% |

Which would you prefer? Circle the number of your preference.

|  | Undergraduate | Graduate |
|---|---|---|
| 1. Instructor designated assignment | 4% | 3% |
| 2. Portfolio assessment with student selected assignments | 12% | 22% |
| 3. Portfolio assessment with student and instructor selected assignments | 84% | 75% |
| 4. Other | | |

*Note: Survey adapted from Craig & Leavell (1994).*

support, yet permitted significant student choice and flexibility. One graduate student wrote:

> I liked the portfolio assessment, but need the structure of instructor-selected or suggested assignment[s]. It is fair to have both select the assignment. Guidelines are useful, but student choice is meaningful. I need some guidelines, but it is nice to have flexibility.

The second theme that emerged referred specifically to the assessment aspect. Students reported increased knowledge about rubric development and liked the fact that they had considerable input into the design of the assessment rubric. The following comment summarizes the feelings of both the graduate and undergraduate students. "I learned about the difficulty in assessing portfolios. Learning to do a rubric was really helpful. I liked the fact that WE constructed the rubric." Students also noted that the portfolio "really showed what they knew" about their topic of choice.

Finally, many students made comments regarding the learning that they attributed to the portfolio. A few of the more concise statements are reported below:

> "I learned so much about my topic, more than I would have in a paper or class presentation." (undergraduate)

> "It (the Project Portfolio) helped organize my work and learning. I also learned how portfolio assessment can be used. It gave me an overall view of what I did for the course . . . As a teacher, it is important to actually go through the process. I will better understand what my students go through." (graduate)

> "I'm really into this! Portfolio is finished, but I'm still reading articles." (undergraduate)

> "The most important part was the application. It forced us to move from theory to real classroom teaching. I really learned a lot." (undergraduate)

> "I like the concept of portfolio assessment and have a better understanding because I went through the process. It was a lot of work, but I am pleased with the final product." (graduate)

## Highlights of the Project Portfolios

The projects designed by the graduate and undergraduate students to demonstrate their expertise were innovative and interesting. In many instances, the projects demanded more student time and effort than instructor-created assignments would have required. For example, two undergraduate women, after researching storytelling, volunteered as storytellers for the local PTO.

They provided an hour-long storytelling program for the children while parents were engaged in the PTO meeting. Portfolio documentation included a copy of their storytelling program, a letter from the PTO president thanking them for their time and expertise, and photographs spotlighting both the storytellers and the obvious delight and engagement of their audience. A third undergraduate student worked as an instructor in an after school program. She documented her work with a multiage group of children as they developed their own newspaper. Two other undergraduates volunteered part-time in a local daycare. One documented the planning and implementation of a series of learning centers that focused on developing listening skills, while the other worked with one five year old and documented his literacy progress as it emerged over a 12 week period.

In the graduate courses, there also were diverse projects. For example, a museum educator created a newsletter for parents which included a calendar entitled "Thirty-One Ideas for Summer Fun." The calendar, developed for fifth graders, provided activities that focused on reading, writing, and thinking. A math educator designed and developed a computer software program on emergent literacy, while a substitute elementary teacher developed a series of large posters depicting the stages in the writing process. Another graduate student created a poster session on Readers' Theatre.

## Limitations

A limitation in any classroom research project is researcher bias since the researcher is also the classroom instructor. This study, however, involved two researchers teaching three separate courses. This provided for a variety of data sources while researcher collaboration helped control for bias. Secondly, although the surveys and actual portfolios provided the data, the information was self-reported. Thus, the validity is dependent upon the accuracy with which the information was reported by the participants. It should be noted that the Project Portfolios were assessed as a part of final course grades. Even though students remained anonymous during data collection, the evaluation may have affected participant responses. Finally, as with any classroom research, the results are not generalizable to the larger population.

## Summary and Reflections

At the beginning of the project, the graduate and undergraduate students in this study did not have a comprehensive understanding of portfolios and the purposes for which they can be designed. Additionally, they had limited or no actual experience with developing or assessing portfolios. The results of this classroom research suggest that instructors should consider their students' backgrounds and allot time to build a knowledge base on all aspects of portfolios and portfolio assessment.

Many of the students reported feelings of confusion at the beginning of the portfolio process. These same feelings were reported by students in other studies (McLaughlin & Vogt, 1996; Oropallo & Gomez, 1996). This disequilibrium may have been due to a lack of background and/or the difficulty some students experienced in selecting and/or narrowing their focus. However, once the students were immersed in the process and were provided with appropriate feedback from instructors and peers, they appeared to feel more confident and comfortable with their personal decisions.

The Project Portfolio had a narrow focus (one or two specific topics) which seemed well-suited to the limitation of time in the college classroom. The project did enable the students to investigate the topic(s) in depth and to demonstrate their knowledge in ways they found meaningful.

At the conclusion of the portfolio experience, students overwhelmingly agreed that portfolio assessment was a valuable tool for their own learning and reported that they would consider portfolios as an alternative form of assessment in their own classrooms either now or in the future. Participants also preferred a portfolio structure that provided guidance and support, but permitted student choice. The researchers hypothesize that the flexible structure of the Project Portfolio provided a scaffold for beginners in the portfolio process while at the same time giving them control over the product.

The researchers have learned much about utilizing Project Portfolios, and they continue to change and adjust the portfolio and the portfolio process to meet the changing needs of their students. For example, more time has been scheduled for individual and small group conferencing with peers and for conferencing with an instructor to plan and organize the portfolio project. More time has also been set aside for students to dialogue and share their research and to solve other problems related to the portfolio.

At the undergraduate level, the Project Portfolio has been extended to include several small, formal papers. Students now engage in process writing and peer editing as they summarize and react to four of the articles.

The assessment rubric, because it is negotiated with each individual class, has also continued to evolve. Both instructors plan to continue to use Project Portfolios in their Language Arts courses and will continue to refine the process.

# References

Anderson, R. (1995). *Encouraging all voices to be heard: Constructing collaborative student teacher portfolios.* Paper presented at the 45th Annual Meeting of the National Reading Conference, New Orleans, LA.

Collins, A. (1991). Portfolios for biology teacher assessment. *Journal of Personnel Evaluation in Education, 5* (2), 147-168.

Craig, M. T., & Leavell, A. G. (1994, November). Preservice teachers' perceptions of portfolio assessment in reading/language arts coursework. Paper presented at the 38th Annual College Reading Association Conference, Clearwater Beach, FL.

Gillespie, C. S., Ford, K. L., Gillespie, R. D., & Leavell, A. G. (1996). Portfolio assessment: Some questions, some answers, some recommendations. *Journal of Adolescent & Adult Literacy, 39,* 480-491.

Glaser, B. G. , & Strauss, A. L. (1967). *The discovery of grounded theory.* Chicago, IL: Aldine.

Heiden, D. (1996). *Modeling authentic practice and assessment: Practicing what we preach in reading/language arts methods courses in teacher education.* Institute presented at the 41st Annual Convention of the International Reading Association, New Orleans, LA.

McKinney, M. O., Perkins, P. G., & Jones, W. P. (1995). Evaluating the use of self-assessment portfolios in a literacy methods class. *Reading Research and Instruction, 35,* 19-36.

McLaughlin, M. & Vogt, M. E. (1996). *Portfolios in teacher education.* Newark, DE: International Reading Association.

Oropallo, K., & Gomez, S. (1996). Using reflective portfolios in preservice teacher education programs. In E .G. Sturtevant & W. M. Linek (Eds.), *Growing literacy* (pp. 120-132). Harrisonburg, VA: The College Reading Association.

Paulson, F. L., Paulson, P. R., & Meyer, C. A. (1991). What makes a portfolio a portfolio? *Educational Leadership, 48* (5), 60-63.

Ruddell, R. B., & Ruddell, M. R. (1995). *Teaching children to read and write: Becoming an influential teacher.* Boston, MA: Allyn & Bacon.

Stahle, D. L., & Mitchell, J. P. (1993). Portfolio assessment in college methods courses: Practicing what we preach. *Journal of Reading, 36,* 538-542.

Tellez, K. (1996). Authentic assessment. In J. Sikula (Ed.), *Handbook of research on teacher education* (pp. 704-721). New York: Macmillan.

Valencia, S. (1990). A portfolio approach to classroom reading assessment: The whys, whats and hows. *The Reading Teacher, 43,* 338-340.

Wilcox, B. L. (1996). Smart portfolios for teachers in training. *Journal of Adolescent & Adult Literacy, 40,* 172-179.

Wolf, K., & Siu-Runyan, Y. (1996). Portfolio purposes and possibilities. *Journal of Adolescent & Adult Literacy, 40,* 30-37.

# REDUCING RESISTANCE TO CONTENT AREA LITERACY COURSES

## Lia Maimon

Montclair State University

## Abstract

*This study provided a context to allow opportunity for a change in attitutde related to the value and relevance of a content area literacy course for preservice teachers. The method described was implemented during a 15-week period. Changes in student attitudes and conceptualizations were documented through questionnaires, videotaped discussion sessions, and various artifacts. The students demonstrated a more positive attitude toward literacy and its application to diverse fields of study as a result of the intervention.*

## Introduction

It is well documented that pre-service teachers bring with them a whole host of attitudes and positions which make them resistant to content area literacy courses (Holt-Reynolds, 1992; O'Brien, Stewart, & Moje, 1995). O'Brien and Stewart (1992) studied pre-service teachers and found that the prevalent attitudes were dissent, dismissal, and skepticism. Other studies (Holt-Reynolds, 1992; Ratekin, Simpson, Alvermann, & Dishner, 1985; Sturtevant, 1993) found that practicing teachers don't assume responsibility for literacy instruction in content areas.

Instructors who teach content area literacy courses face considerable challenges because of the resistance of pre-service teachers. Despite this, very little research has been done to see how to address this resistance. In light of the central role that literacy plays in the success of the pedagogical strategy as a whole, it is essential to eradicate the prejudice against content literacy courses in as many students as possible. This study documents methods that have been successful in revising many pre-service teachers' attitudes toward content area literacy. If these methods are more widely implemented, educators have the chance to change the content area literacy portion of the certification program from an unenlightening hurdle to a useful tool.

## Background

Some of the resistance may be due to misconceptions about the nature of content area literacy courses. For example, Rafferty (1990) found that a large number of pre-service teachers believed that content area reading courses were aimed at improving their reading skills, while others resented being asked to serve as reading specialists. These kinds of misconceptions can be quickly dispelled. Other complaints about content area literacy instruction and courses, however, are more substantial.

Part of the resistance to content area literacy instruction may be related to preservice teachers' views of content literacy. O'Brien, Stewart, and Moje (1995) suggest that when content literacy strategies are viewed as supporting traditional educational purposes, such as helping students extract information from text and study for tests, the strategies represent little that is new for teachers. Although teachers might see the potential value of the strategies, they may not see that the strategies facilitated their content area's educational goals. In fact, teachers sometimes view these strategies as time consuming and inappropriate (O'Brien & Stewart, 1992; Stewart, 1990; Vacca & Vacca, 1993).

On the other hand, O'Brien, Stewart and Moje (1995) claim that when content literacy is conceptualized as socially constructed knowledge, it can be considered radical pedagogy that challenges the prevailing notions of teaching. For example, use of the Know-Wonder-Learned (KWL) strategy (Ogle, 1986), requires that students take control of their learning to some extent because they are asked what they want to learn. When KWL is combined with a method like cooperative learning, students are given even more control. This kind of student control is antithetical to the traditional culture that relies on teacher control, which is the only mode in common use in secondary schools (Cuban, 1984; Goodlad, 1984; McNeil, 1988). School authorities including teachers may not want to give up their control (Sizer, 1985) and often students may not want to take control (Myers, 1992). O'Brien et al. (1995) also state that: "Content literacy education seems to be caught in a controversy: by tapping into traditional notions of teaching, the infusion of literacy seems irrelevant to teachers, while strategies based on a socio-constructivist view of learning offer a too-difficult challenge in the seemingly immutable world of high schools (Boyer, 1983; Cuban, 1986)."

Another factor that affects resistance to content area literacy courses is teacher theories. Harste and Burke (1977) found that, despite statements to the contrary, teachers have definite theoretical views on reading instruction, which they define in terms of belief systems or philosophical principles. Belief systems are complex, multifaceted systems of individual beliefs which constitute a major component of teacher theories (Richardson, Anders, Tidwell, & Lloyd, 1991) and have several features (Nespor, 1987). Belief systems convert abstract feelings and ambiguous attributes, such as ability, into distinct, well-specified entities. Belief systems also provide alternativity, in which an individual visualizes an ideal which is significantly different from the existing reality. Because of their personal nature, the components of belief systems are open to debate and controversy (non-consensuality), while an event can be relevant or irrelevant to different people based on their own subjective interpretations (unboundedness). Beliefs carry heavy affective and evaluative loading based on feelings and personal preference.

Beliefs are also organized in networks of episodes based on personal experiences. For teachers, Nespor (1987) contends these episodes are reflections of their experiences when they were students, especially those of particularly significant events. These beliefs are formed early and tend to be difficult to change. In many cases teachers' belief systems guide them to oppose content area literacy instruction (Pajares, 1992).

Belief systems, however, are not the only component of teacher theories. Roehler, Duffy, Herrmann, Conley, and Johnson (1988) assert that it is what the teacher knows and how that knowledge is organized that mediates teacher theories and subsequent actions. This could be declarative knowledge about what needs to be taught, procedural knowledge about how to teach, or conditional knowledge about how to act in specific situations. Kinzer (1989) refers to this type of knowledge as mental models. These mental models often have a knowledge base that limits teachers' options and increases their opposition to content area literacy. Thus teacher theories, reflected in belief systems and mental models, have an impact on teachers' willingness to accept content area literacy as an important issue.

In order to encourage teachers to adopt content area literacy instruction in their respective fields, a course was designed which recognizes that teaching is a social enterprise embedded in the culture of schools and develops a critical awareness of teacher theories reflected in beliefs and mental models. The course was designed to enhance pre-service teachers' ability to reflect on the complexities of school contexts, weigh the personal benefits and risks involved in using content literacy strategies, and increase their empowerment. The purpose of this study was to investigate whether this course would reduce pre-service teachers' resistance to content area literacy instruction. More specifically, the impact of the course was evaluated through the following questions (adapted from Craig & Leavell, 1995):

1. Did pre-service teachers' perceptions of literacy instruction change? If so how?
2. What were pre-service teachers' reactions to specific components of the course?
3. Did pre-service teachers feel that the insight gained in the course was useful in providing future practical classroom applications?

## Method

### Participants

The participants were 24 students enrolled in a required content literacy course for fine arts, vocational education, health education, music, business, physical education, mathematics, and foreign languages majors. All students were seeking initial certification, with only two students having had limited teaching experience.

### Data Collection and Analysis

This study utilized multiple data sources. Summary impressions were written at the end of each session, ten of which were videotaped. An open-ended questionnaire was given at the end of the course (see Appendix). The questionnaire was not administered at the beginning of the course because of the concern that calling attention to the relevant issues could bias the participants. Instead, initial resistance to the course was assessed by informal discussions which were documented on videotape or by summary impressions.

The questionnaires were not anonymous. This was necessary because, in addition to serving as evaluation forms, the questionnaires were used to assess students' ability to critically reflect upon what they learned in the course. In order to rule out a possible bias, other anonymous course evaluation forms were used for comparison. The anonymous evaluation forms addressed the quality of the course and instruction, but they did not directly address change in resistance to the course.

The data from the videotapes and the questionnaires were analyzed by two raters. They were coded and compared to artifacts, such as reflective writing, journals, tests, syllabus, and projects resulting from classroom instructional simulations.

## Procedure

The 15 week course was divided into three sections. The first five weeks were devoted to literacy theories, the next seven weeks to literacy practices, and the last three weeks to applications. During the literacy practice and application sections, the theories were revisited. Each section addressed the interaction between the social nature of the teaching of literacy and teacher theories as well as the development of the reflective abilities of pre-service teachers. However, the emphasis on each of these aspects was somewhat different in each section.

Drawing on a model developed by Mosenthal (1984), a framework that categorized literacy instruction into three broad perspectives was presented. Each perspective presupposes a different socio-political purpose; therefore each has a different emphasis on means-and-ends relationships. The different perspectives are mutually exclusive, although researchers and practitioners are aware that they are incomplete.

First the *traditional* perspective was introduced. The purpose of the traditional perspective is to pass on the values and knowledge that an authority deems important. Reading is viewed as a set of skills to be mastered by the end of elementary grades; hence literacy has no place in content area teaching. This perspective was modeled in the transmission model of teaching by delivering a lecture and requiring students to give quick factual answers. Discussions were discouraged and only teacher-student interactions were allowed. Excerpts from the movie *The Paper Chase*, which portrays a traditional teacher, were shown. The movie excerpts and the instructional modeling were then discussed in terms of effects on the education of children.

Next the participants were introduced to the *student-centered* perspective. The goal of the student-centered perspective is to nourish an individual's self worth, autonomy, and growth. It was explained that it is the transaction model which best promotes this purpose. According to the student-centered perspective, literacy can be integrated into all areas of learning. The student-centered perspective was introduced to the students by presenting excerpts from the movie *Dead Poets' Society*, which portrays a student-centered teacher, and followed by collaborative learning activities. The participants compared the teacher in *Dead Poets' Society* to the teacher in *The Paper Chase*. The relationship between school cultures and teacher perspectives was addressed. Student-to-student interactions were strongly encouraged and the lesson was guided by a series of open-ended questions. An analysis followed, and the student-centered theories were presented in the form of a mini-lecture. Finally the social implications of a student-centered education were discussed.

The *emancipatory* perspective was introduced next. Its goal is to change social inequities by empowering learners through knowledge. Through discussions, inquiry, and lecture, the students were informed that the transformative model promotes this goal by relying on the assumption that learning should be recognized as a socio-cultural enterprise. According to the emancipatory perspective, language and literacy are embedded in power relations. The emancipatory perspective was addressed by discussing the moral responsibility a society has to ensure equal access to the best education possible for all students (Goodlad, 1994). The issue of active intervention in school policy and curriculum was discussed in the context of the possibilities open to new teachers.

In order to enhance pre-service teachers' reflective skills, an additional theoretical framework based on the *Theory of Literacy Complexity* (Maimon, 1995) was introduced. The Theory of Literacy Complexity argues that the elements of the three perspectives described above can be integrated in complementary terms rather than exclusionary ones without undermining desirable social goals and purposes. It suggests that content area literacy instruction should be viewed as a complex system which has several characteristics that make it distinct from simple systems. The Theory of Literacy Complexity argues that different literacy contexts, meaning sources, and meaning processes interact in many ways, allowing the emergent self-organization that is responsible for literacy learning. The framework based on the Theory of Literacy Complexity allowed pre-service teachers to integrate different aspects of the perspectives discussed above.

The pre-service teachers watched excerpts from the movie *The Marva Collins Story.* They then discussed and analyzed it, both orally and in writing, in terms of the Theory of Literacy Complexity. Marva Collins' teaching method illustrates the Theory of Literacy Complexity because she expresses beliefs in the socio-political purposes of education of all three perspectives. For example, she uses fables as sources to pass on values the authority deems important. She also considers as absolutely necessary the student-centered goals of developing self worth, autonomy, and growth, as well as the emancipatory goal of empowering students through knowledge.

Collins' pedagogy combines elements from all three perspectives. She relies on traditional elements such as phonics, drill, and recitation along with student-centered constant praise and development of individual strengths and interests. She encourages critical thinking and taking action to improve the students' lives outside the school, which are characteristics of the emancipatory perspective. The curriculum also combines the different perspectives. Collins uses both classics and contemporary books which have relevance to the students' personal lives. She utilizes standardized tests as "survival" skills to prove that her students are learning, but she also uses authentic assessment, which challenges students' ability to transfer knowledge to new social situations.

Each of the curricular elements, methods, and types of assessment Collins employs can be explained in terms of the three perspectives. All of these elements, however, become agents in a larger, complex system where they interact and respond to many sources of feedback. The rich interaction between the different elements leads to literacy acquisition.

In order to evaluate pre-service teachers' knowledge of the theories and their applications in schools, they observed a lesson and gathered as much information as possible about students, teaching methods, assessment methods, teacher, and school. Next they analyzed the data in theoretical terms. In order to provide the larger picture of learning, the data from the individual observations were then summarized and analyzed collectively in terms of the three perspectives. The strengths and weaknesses of the different types of instruction and their socio-political consequences were addressed.

Next the course was divided into two components that were addressed concomitantly. One component was geared toward using literacy strategies that could be integrated into the different content areas, while the other component was geared toward broadening pre-service teachers' involvement with self-directed reading for personal purposes.

To address the first component, selected literacy-enhancing strategies were introduced. Pre-reading strategies included Prereading Plan (PreP) and Anticipation Guide. During-reading strategies included semantic mapping; Question, Answer, Response (QAR); and KWL. Next vocabulary strategies such as Contextual Redefinition, Preview in Context, Concept of Definition, and Etymology, were introduced to enhance concept development. Both vocabulary and comprehension strategies were connected to relevant theories and practiced by means of various simulations, role playing, workshop activities, and whole group and small group discussions. The pre-service teachers were also asked to adjust these various strategies to their own content areas. Pre-service teachers were frequently given three minutes at the end of a lesson to summarize what they learned and ask questions about the lesson. Those questions served often as introductions to the following lesson. Both naturalistic and objective forms of assessment were addressed by analyzing and critiquing actual forms of assessment as well as their social implications and consequences. The nature of standardized tests was further explored by requiring the students to design and take an objective test based on the course content, and then to critique the test.

The second component of the course consisted of "book searches". The pre-service teachers selected books that were of interest to them, brought them to class, circulated them, shared their opinions, and exchanged ideas. A bibliography was created and distributed for further use at the end of the semester.

The last three class sessions were devoted to application in the form of micro-teaching projects, in which students taught a lesson in their respective fields and reflected on it afterwards. The other members of the class critiqued the lessons, which were videotaped.

## Results

The results of the data analysis are reported following the initial research questions.

### Question 1: Did Pre-Service Teachers' Perceptions of Literacy Instruction Change? If So How?

The students' perceptions of literacy instruction, generally and in the content areas, changed dramatically during the course. Some students also mentioned that their own attitudes about reading changed. One pre-service teacher wrote, "Before the course I didn't think of myself as a reader but through bringing in the books each week I saw how much I really do read." Another expressed a changed attitude about her future students' reading habits:

> Although I love reading, I know that a lot of people do not. This course has provided me with strategies that will encourage reading. Making reading the text interesting and therefore more apt to be remembered by the students is a challenge to any teacher. If I can help anyone have a positive attitude to learning and to reading, I will consider myself successful.

Another student mentioned the importance of an expanded conceptualization of reading:

> I guess my thoughts about reading have changed significantly over the semester. I now realize that reading also involves the students' background knowledge, interests and emotions. I see now how, as teachers, we have to remember that we teach more than reading, we teach *students* reading. Also, reading incorporates more than just reading in the sense of reading an English novel. Instructions to math exercises, PE vocabulary lists and hotel advertisements all constitute reading, and there are reading strategies which a teacher can use to enhance students' understanding of them.

The reason for a changed attitude about literacy and literacy instruction in several instances was related to the fact that students realized that teaching reading is a complex issue which involves multiple contexts, as the following quote expresses:

> I have learned so much about what it takes to read and comprehend. I see how everything comes together: the teacher, the materials, the texts, the students and the environment. I have a greater love for reading and plan on making more time to read more materials. I had always heard that if you were a good reader and read many materials, you would be knowledgeable and smart. This class has proven this statement to me.

One student said, "The class raised a lot of new thoughts and ideas, and it encouraged choice." Another student agreed: "Instead of you giving us the best way of teaching you let us figure out which way is best for us."

Students' perceptions of content area literacy instruction also changed during the course. Most students initially felt that the course was irrelevant to their majors. The following is an example of such an opinion:

> When I first registered for this course, I thought very little—if anything—about reading and reading instruction. The course just represented another hurdle for me to jump over for my certification. If someone had asked me what reading and reading instruction is all about, my first reaction probably would have been to say: "reading is how the

brain deciphers written words and reading instruction is how we teach the brain to do so." I would have said that because the title of this course, "Reading: Theory and Process," made me expect that the scientific aspects of reading would be discussed in this class. Also, when I first registered, I thought that reading and reading instruction were straight forward and play only minor roles in the foreign language classroom, especially on the lower levels. Finally, on the first day, I felt sorry for all of the PE majors who had to take this course. What does reading and reading instruction have to do with their field anyway?

At the end of the course, all but one of the students saw the relevance of the course to their content area. For example, one student wrote: "Now that the class is over I feel that I learned a lot of useful tips that I will not only use in a health class but that I will also use in a physical education class."

Students also mentioned that the course broadened their perspectives about teaching and showed them how to integrate literacy into their respective content areas. This is from a prospective art teacher:

> I have learned how to incorporate reading into an art lesson and hopefully promote interest not only in a specific art work, but in an artist, his or her life, the concerns of the artist, the techniques used to create the art work, the society in which the art work was produced and the historical context of the art work. Through reading, we learn about our world, past and future.

A future math teacher echoed the same sentiments: "I have realized the importance of literacy instruction in mathematics. I also see the importance of students reading effectively so they can take charge of their own learning. I have gained a repertoire of strategies to accomplish these things."

In general, students reported that the course promoted their learning. For example one person wrote, "The course to my surprise did have a great deal of useful and interesting theoretical information and techniques. Very little of it was rehash of my prior knowledge that I could bring to the course, and I was pleasantly surprised by the text which I very reluctantly bought and am now ready to use in the future."

## Question 2: What Were Pre-Service Teachers' Reactions to Specific Components of the Course?

All students expressed the opinion that more than one aspect of the course contributed to their changed perceptions of literary instruction. One wrote, "I feel that all the aspects that we covered this semester were responsible for my new insights and ideas." A majority of students mentioned knowledge of the different teaching perspectives as being instrumental in the change process. For example one of them wrote: "I also learned that effective teaching integrates all the three perspectives in a natural way that empowers students through learning while empowering the teachers with a natural, effective approach to teaching." The students reported that the films provided good examples of the theoretical methods, and the in-class activities helped them apply these ideas. One student wrote:

> I obtained a significant learning experience from this course. The topic which will stick in my head forever is the comparing and contrasting of the three types of teachers: traditional, student-centered, and emancipatory. The charts which we set up in class showing the different goals, contexts, processes, etc., as well as the handouts were very helpful. In addition the movies which we saw (*The Paper Chase, Dead Poets' Society* and *The Marva Collins Story*) really transposed this idea from written concepts to real life. When I observed my high school math class I really felt knowledgeable and confident about evaluating the strengths and weaknesses of the teacher and his lesson.

Several students mentioned the group activities as being instrumental in changing their opinion. As one of them reported: "I felt that our group activities were most productive. Having my peers share their experiences was equivalent of having twenty-four other professors' opposing views, individual statements and constructive criticism allowed me to grow." Several students said the class atmosphere was instrumental in changing their prejudice against literacy instruction: "Another reason the class was successful was the fact that we, as students, felt very comfortable talking and discussing various topics and you as a teacher really tried to promote this type of learning environment. I really learned in this class simply by being there." Others mentioned the importance of modelling student-centered activities. In his journal, one student wrote, "The small group and workshop activities were worthwhile and instructive. In my own experience as a student, I have done little group work. I would like to use group work when I teach." One of the two students who expressed negative feelings about these sorts of activities wrote, "I found it difficult to always participate in class and my interest level was not fully stimulated."

The assignments also had an impact on reducing the students' resistance to literacy instruction. By having to design and take a test themselves, the students' perceptions about assessment became more elaborate. Commenting on the test, one of them said:

> The student-designed test was a terrific assignment because it forced the student to apply the knowledge in two formats that typically become part of the teacher's arsenal of evaluation: the multiple choice test and the true false test. Because we are responsible for creating fair and accurate questions, we were required to comprehend the infor-

mation being tested. It also forced us to be aware of the limitations that these tests place upon students by not allowing any elaboration that would indicate that higher learning has occurred.

One of two students who disliked this assignment wrote: "I understand the reasoning behind making us design a standardized test. . . . However, I feel that most of us have experienced their unfairness and limitedness in our own education."

Other students commented on the micro-teaching assignment. "The micro-teaching was good because it gave us a chance to use the new strategies learned in class to integrate into our discipline," wrote one student. Others expressed similar ideas orally. All but two students acknowledged the book search assignments as pivotal to changing their attitudes toward literacy instruction. This is best expressed by one student who wrote, "One of the greatest assignments was our book searches. Every week after listening to what my classmates said about different books, I found myself borrowing, buying, and using the texts they presented. This was productive and useful." Videotaping was also cited by the students: "The use of the video during our book discussions was helpful in keeping the group on task. At first, I felt self-conscious, but after a while, I forgot about it, and it did not bother me." Journal writing received mixed reviews. Some appreciated it because it allowed reflection, while others thought it was too much work.

The assignments complemented the rest of the course and did not repeat other course material. Several students responded positively: "I actually learned while doing the assignments that is, in many classes the assignments are given just to test what you already learned. In this class the assignments made me apply and expand upon what I already knew when I began them. I gained new knowledge during the entire process of completing the assignment."

### Question #3: Did Pre-Service Teachers Feel That the Insight Gained in the Course was Useful in Providing Future Practical Classroom Applications?

All but one student indicated that the course would help them in the future. One student said that he had already implemented a strategy in his teaching assignment for another class. The students said that the course supplied them with specific strategies which they would use in the future. For example, one prospective teacher wrote, "I believe that reading instruction can be a part of physical education. I could easily incorporate vocabulary and concept comprehension into my lessons. Reading is an important component, which is often overlooked, but which makes physical education a more well-rounded subject." Many students mentioned that they would integrate certain approaches which were modeled.

The students became aware of their own teaching styles. For some, the course also provided a better knowledge of their own strengths and weaknesses. One student expressed the following: "This is important because not every student is motivated or learns the same way. This class and the approaches discussed gave me more options."

Other students found the theoretical aspects of the course most relevant to their future careers. For example, one student indicated:

> The theory section of the course was important because it let out in a systematic way the types of philosophies to education that exist. It is important to develop an approach or philosophy to education before entering the classroom and modify thereafter. This clarity helped me make some decisions about my own understanding of education. Just as importantly, the theory unit also prepared me for the situation in which my approach does not match with the school I work in. I will definitely use this knowledge.

## Conclusions

The analysis of the data reveals that the students' conceptualizations of literacy and teacher theories changed during the course. The prospective teachers gained insight into the complexities of real learning contexts, which broadened their conceptualization of literacy in general and teaching in their content areas in particular. This was possible because the course did not follow the infusion model of teacher preparation in which schools are viewed as neutral settings and teachers are viewed as strategy technicians who implement the advice of literacy educators (O'Brien, Stewart, & Moje, 1995). Instead the course addressed the complexities of schooling and encouraged pre-service teachers to consider how these factors relate to them.

The data also suggest that the participants were able to change their teacher theories. According to Janasek (as cited in Clark & Peterson,1986), teacher theories combine "beliefs, intentions, interpretations and behavior that interact continually and are modified by social interaction" (p. 287). The dynamic that was created was especially conducive to changing the students' belief systems. The data suggest that the different aspects of students' belief systems, such as feelings, alternativity, affective loading, and personal experiences, were affected by the course. Moreover the knowledge the students gained allowed them to alter their mental models because the course broadened their perspectives with regard to declarative, procedural, and conditional knowledge. Finally the course allowed the students to think critically about the benefits and risks involved in using content area literacy strategies.

In interpreting the results one must be cautious, however, because these pre-service teachers have yet to teach their own classes. Though they indicated that they would use the knowledge they gained in the course this remains to be seen. The actual effect of the course on real teaching situations has not been demonstrated; it can only be predicted.

Previously it has been documented that the resistance of pre-service teachers to literacy instruction is hard to change (Holt-Reynolds, 1992; Sturtevant, 1993; Wilson, Konopak, & Readance, 1992). This study supports the idea that such a change is possible despite the difficulties (Deegan, 1994).

---

# References

Boyer, E. L. (1983). *High school: A report on secondary education in America.* New York: Colophon.

Cuban, L. (1984). *How teachers taught.* New York: Longman.

Cuban, L. (1986). Persistent instruction: Another look at constancy in the classroom. *Phi Delta Kappan,* 68, 7-11.

Clark, C., & Peterson, P. L. (1986). Teachers' thought processes. In M. Wittrock (Ed.), *Handbook of research on teaching* (3rd ed., pp. 255-296). New York: Macmillan Publishing Co.

Craig, M. T., & Leavell, A. G. (1995). Pre-service teachers' perceptions of portfolio assessment in reading/language arts coursework. In W. M. Linek & E. G. Sturtevant (Eds.), *Generations of literacy: 17th yearbook of the College Reading Association* (pp. 83-96). Harrisburg, VA: College Reading Association.

Deegan, D. (1994). Literacy in the content areas: Ain't no need to sing the blues. *Reading Improvement,* 31, 177-186.

Goodlad, J. I. (1984). *A place called school: Prospects for the future.* New York: McGraw-Hill.

Harste, J., & Burke, C. (1977). A new hypothesis for reading teacher research: Both the teaching and learning of reading are theoretically based. In P. D. Pearson (Ed.), *Reading: Theory, research, and practice. 26th yearbook of the National Reading Conference* (pp. 32-40). Clemson, SC: National Reading Conference.

Holt-Reynolds, D. (1992). Personal history-based beliefs as relevant prior knowledge in course work. *American Educational Research Journal,* 29, 325-349.

Kinzer, C. K. (1989). Mental models and beliefs about classrooms and reading instruction: A comparison between preservice teachers, in-service teachers and professors of education. In S. McCormick & J. Zutell (Eds.), *Cognitive and social perspectives for literacy research and instruction: 38th yearbook of the National Reading Conference* (pp. 489-499). Chicago, IL: The National Reading Conference.

Maimon, L. (1995). *From exclusion to common ground: A new approach to reading theory and practice.* Paper presented at the 9th European Conference on Reading, Budapest, Hungary.

McNeil, L. (1988). *Contradictions of control: School structure and school knowledge.* New York: Routledge.

Mosenthal, P. (1984). The problem of partial specification in translating reading research into practice. *The Elementary School Journal,* 85, 199-226.

Myers, J. (1992). The social contexts of school and personal literacy. *Reading Research Quarterly,* 27, 296-332.

Nespor, J. (1987). The role of beliefs in the practice of teaching. *Journal of Curriculum Studies*, 19, 317-328.

O'Brien, D. G., & Stewart, R. A. (1992). Resistance to content area reading: Dimensions and solutions. In E. K. Dishner, T. W. Dean, J. E. Readance, & D. W. Moore (Eds.), *Reading in content areas: Improving classroom instruction* (3rd ed., pp. 30-40). Dubuque, IA: Kendall/Hunt.

O'Brien, D. G., Stewart, R. A., & Moje, E. B. (1995). Why content literacy is difficult to infuse into the secondary school: Complexities of curriculum, pedagogy, and school culture. *Reading Research Quarterly*, 30, 462-463.

Ogle, D. (1986). KWL: A teaching model that develops active reading of expository text. *The Reading Teacher*, 39, 564-570.

Pajares, M. F. (1992). Teachers' beliefs and educational research: Cleaning up a messy construct. *Review of Educational Research*, 62, 307-332.

Rafferty, C. D. (1990, November). *From preservice to inservice: Diffusing content reading resistance.* Paper presented at the annual meeting of the National Reading Conference, Miami, FL.

Ratekin, N., Simpson, M. L., Alvermann, D. E., & Dishner, E. K. (1985). Why teachers resist content reading instruction. *Journal of Reading*, 28, 432-437.

Richardson, V., Anders, P., Tidwell, D., & Lloyd, C. (1991). The relationship between teachers' beliefs and practices in reading comprehension instruction. *American Educational Research Journal*, 28, 559-586.

Roehler, L. R., Duffy, G. G., Herrmann, B. A., Conley, M., & Johnson, J. (1988). Knowledge structures as evidence of the 'personal': Bridging the gap from thought to practice. *Journal of Curriculum Studies*, 20, 159-165.

Sizer, T. R. (1985). *Horace's compromise: The dilemma of the American high school.* Boston: Houghton Mufflin.

Stewart, R. A. (1990). Factors influencing preservice teachers' resistance to content area reading instruction. *Reading Research and Instruction*, 29, 55-63.

Sturtevant, E. G. (1993). Content literacy in high school social studies: A focus on one teacher's beliefs and decisions about classroom discussions. In T. V. Rasinski & N. D. Padak (Eds.), *Inquiries in literacy learning and instruction: 15th yearbook of the College Reading Association* (pp. 3-12). Pittsburgh, KS: College Reading Association.

Vacca, R. T., & Vacca, J. L. (1993). *Content area reading* (4th ed.). New York: Harper Collins.

Wilson, E. K., Konopak, B. C., & Readance, J. E. (1992). Examining content area reading beliefs, decisions and instruction: A case study of an English teacher. In C. K. Kinzer & D. J. Leu (Eds.), *Literacy research, theory and practice: Views from many perspectives. 41st yearbook of the National Reading Conference* (pp. 475-482). Chicago, IL: National Reading Conference.

# Appendix

This questionnaire is designed to obtain feedback about the course. I need it to reflect upon the course and refine it. In answering the questions please be as specific and detailed as possible. Use a new page for each answer.

1. Complete the following: When I first registered for the course, I thought that reading and reading instruction . . .

2. Explain how the course did or didn't contribute to your learning and explain why. In your answer you may consider the following:
   a. Activities: formal presentations (more or less), movies, whole class discussion, case study, observations from the field, simulations, small group activities, video taping, scripts and role playing, discussions about articles, workshop activities, etc.
   b. Assignments: observation, student-designed test, projects, reflective writing.
   c. Processes: considering new ideas, raising questions, being reflective, using ideas creatively, contributing to class discussions, maintaining high levels of achievement, considering diverse viewpoints, providing provisions for individual interests, stimulating interest, providing meaningful learning experiences, creating a constructive climate for learning.
   d. Content: understanding different educational contexts, understanding the relationship between reading and your content area, relating theories to practice, using strategies in your field.

3. Now that the course is over have your thoughts and attitudes about reading and reading instruction changed? If so, what factors and processes were involved?

4. Explain how and why you might or might not use what you learned in the future.

# THE UNHEARD VOICES OF STUDENTS IN SCHOOL REFORM: A COLLABORATIVE STUDY WITH CONTENT READING PRESERVICE TEACHERS

**Don Pottorff**

Grand Valley State University

## Abstract

*This collaborative study with middle and secondary preservice teachers enrolled in a reading methods course examined student perceptions of good teachers and characteristics of favorite teachers. It also examined issues involving homework, making a class interesting, tests, and classroom rules. Results showed that students like teachers who have a sense of humor, respect them, listen to them, are fair and flexible, make learning fun, and make sure everyone learns. Students prefer homework that is meaningful, not just busy work and would like teachers to understand that they often feel burdened with homework. In addition, students say they learn best through whole group and small group discussions, prefer multiple choice tests, and want to be involved in making classroom rules. As a result of this study, preservice teachers developed deeper understandings of their students and student perceptions. In return, students were pleased that teachers cared enough to listen.*

Recently there has been renewed interest in school reform, particularly at the middle and secondary school levels. Unfortunately, it appears that students whose education and lives are most affected by these reforms are being excluded from this dialogue. Middle and secondary school students typically are given fewer opportunities for decision making, have fewer personal and positive relationships with teachers, and are subjected to greater teacher control than elementary students (Eccles & Midgley, 1989). This conflict comes at a time when developmentally these students have an emerging need for self-expression, identity, and autonomy (Schlosser, 1992). When setting policy, whether at the school level or in the classroom, educators need to understand that procedures are often perceived dissimilarly by different groups of students and frequently affect diverse groups of students in ways which are not always positive (Wehlage & Rutter, 1996).

Convincing secondary preservice teachers that listening to the voices of students is both worthwhile and empowering (Lincoln, 1995) is often a difficult task, because they have not typically experienced it in their own education (Schlosser, 1992). In fact, several researchers have found that preservice teachers have a tendency to want to be overly controlling of their students (Goodman, 1985; Tabachnick & Zeichner, 1984; Zeichner & Gore, 1990). This tendency can lead to decreased motivation on the part of students and can contribute to increased behavior problems (Combs, 1979; Glasser, 1997). In fact, Deci and Ryan (1985) believe that being in control of one's fate is a contributing factor in all motivated behavior and is a central force for intrinsically motivated behavior. This is consistent with the findings of Damico and Roth (1993), who reported after interviewing 178 secondary students that many school practices, intentionally or unintentionally, hinder students' progress toward graduation. Chief among those practices was the over monitoring of students. Oldfather and McLaughlin (1993) suggest that in order to be motivated, students need to be given opportunities to "find their passions, discover what they care about, create their own learning agendas, and most importantly, experience meaningful connections between who they are and what they do in school" (p. 3).

When student voices are heard, their perspectives on school and learning are remarkably similar to those of teachers (Phelan, Davidson, and Cao, 1992). Teachers want respect. They want to work with students who are enthusiastic, have a sense of humor, are open to learning new things, enjoy their subject-area content, and are considerate of others. Students indicate that their wants and desires from teachers and schools are identical.

In order to help preservice teachers enrolled in *Reading in the Content Areas* begin to listen to and value the voices of their middle and secondary school students, the author decided to take Lincoln's (1995) advice and include them in a research project. For this purpose, an open-ended questionnaire was designed in class, and later refined and administered to their students. Preservice teachers were involved in all phases of the study, including design of the questionnaire, collection of student responses, and analysis of the data.

The purpose of the study was to examine middle and high school students' perceptions of characteristics of good teachers, good teaching, and classroom practices. The hypothesis was that there is much to be learned by listening to students when reforming schools. More specifically, the study asked students to respond to questions about the following areas:

1. Characteristics of a good teacher including personal attributes, classroom management practices, and teaching style.
2. Characteristics of favorite teachers.
3. Issues related to homework.
4. Elements that help make a class more interesting.
5. Test preferences.
6. Issues related to classroom rules.
7. Understandings they wished teachers had about students.

## Subjects

As part of an assignment, 34 preservice middle and high school teachers enrolled in a state-required reading methods course were asked to survey one complete class of students in their major teaching content area in order to better understand their students, their needs, and their thinking. Of these preservice teachers, 24 were assigned to 18 public high schools in 15 different school districts. Another 10 were assigned to 6 public and 1 private junior high schools in 7 school districts. Overall, 946 middle and high school students from 19 school districts in West-Central Michigan were included in the study. The school districts included rural, urban, and suburban populations.

## Design

In preparation for the study a questionnaire was designed to gather data on students' perceptions about characteristics of good teachers, good teaching, and favorite teachers. In addition students were queried on issues involving homework, making a class interesting, tests, and classroom rules. The first questionnaire contained only open-ended questions (see Appendix A) and was administered as a pilot trial to 400 middle and high school students from rural, urban, and suburban schools reflective of the sample in the study. Student responses were evaluated and a second, more refined questionnaire was developed (see Appendix B), asking students to make forced choices. For example, an open-ended question on the pilot survey, "What are the characteristics of a good teacher?" evolved into three questions on the final survey with forced choices in the areas of personal characteristics, classroom management, and teaching style. Similarly, responses on the pilot survey revealed three areas of concern about homework: feelings about homework, preference of kind, and how much is reasonable. Student comments were tabulated for frequency and led to forced choices in the homework questions on the final survey.

Finally, preservice teachers were briefed on administrative procedures, permission was received from school districts to administer surveys, and questionnaires were distributed to students in their classrooms for immediate supervised completion. This provided a 100% response rate from students present on that particular day. All questionnaires were returned for analysis within a two week period.

## Results

### Question #1: A good teacher is one who:

Responses to this question dealt with personal characteristics of teachers. Sixty-nine percent of the students responded in nearly equal numbers to 3 of the 6 choices. These choices were *has a good sense of humor, respects students,* and *listens to students* (see Table 1).

### Question #2: A good teacher is one who:

This question involved classroom management. Forty-seven percent of students responded *is fair* when asked this question, while another 27% responded *is flexible.* Only a very small number of students chose *is an easy grader, doesn't get angry, is strict, or enforces rules* (see Table 1).

**Table 1. Characteristics of a Good Teacher by Percentage of Responses.**

*Qualities involving personal characteristics:*

| | |
|---|---|
| Has a sense of humor | 24% |
| Respects students | 23% |
| Listens to students | 22% |
| Is patient and caring | 16% |
| Is enthusiastic | 10% |
| Is someone you can trust | 5% |

*Qualities involving elements of classroom management:*

| | |
|---|---|
| Is fair | 47% |
| Is flexible | 27% |
| Doesn't get angry | 7% |
| Is strict and makes you work hard | 7% |
| Is an easy grader | 7% |
| Enforces rules | 5% |

*Qualities involving teaching style:*

| | |
|---|---|
| Makes learning fun | 46% |
| Explains and makes sure all learn | 24% |
| Uses a variety of teaching methods | 13% |
| Lets you learn at your own pace | 10% |
| Knows the subject well | 5% |
| Teaches responsibility | 2% |

### Question #3: A good teacher is one who:

For this question students indicated preferences related to teaching style. The overwhelming choice here was *makes learning fun* with 46% of the responses, followed by *explains and makes sure everyone learns* with 24% of the responses. Small percentages of responses were scattered among *uses a variety of teaching methods, lets you learn at your own pace, teaches responsibility,* and *knows the subject well* (see Table 1).

### Question #13: What were the characteristics of your favorite teacher?

Choices for this question included all 18 items from the first three questions to see if personal characteristics, classroom management practices, or teaching style was chosen more often than the others. Although providing 18 choices tended to fragment the responses and lead to low percentages of all choices, two responses stood out from the rest by ratios between 2 and 5 to 1. These were *made learning fun* and *had a sense of humor.* The first choice came from the category of teaching style while the second came from personal characteristics.

### Question #5: My feelings about homework are that I:

Analysis of responses revealed that 38% of students *don't like it,* while 23% *believe that it is necessary* and 21% *believe it is a good way to learn.* Only 6% stated that they *don't do it,* 9% said that they *do it if it isn't too much,* and 3% *believe teachers don't grade it* (see Table 2).

### Question #6: If I have homework, I would prefer it to be:

Thirty-four percent of students responded *meaningful, not just busy work,* 27% answered *easy and short,* while 24% wanted *creative projects.* Only 2% of the respondents wanted homework to be *challenging and difficult* (see Table 2).

### Question #7: How much homework is reasonable?

*Only as needed* was the response of 33% of students, while 21% suggested that *2 or 3 times per week per class* was sufficient. Only 8% of students felt that no homework should be assigned (see Table 2).

### Question #8: If you were a teacher, what would you do to make a class interesting?

Forty-seven percent of students responded that they would *allow students to work in groups.* Thirty-two percent favored having *more whole group discussions.* Two choices with low percentages of selection were *show more films* and *lecture more* (see Table 3).

**Table 2. Issues Relating to Homework by Percentage of Responses.**

| *Feelings about homework:* | |
|---|---|
| Don't like it | 38% |
| Believe that it is necessary | 23% |
| Believe it is a good way to learn | 21% |
| Do it if it isn't too much | 9% |
| Don't do it | 6% |
| Believe teachers don't grade it | 3% |
| *Type of homework preferred:* | |
| Meaningful, not just busywork | 34% |
| Easy and short | 27% |
| Creative projects | 24% |
| Something that forces me to think | 13% |
| Challenging and difficult | 2% |
| *Reasonable quantity of homework:* | |
| Only as needed | 33% |
| 2 or 3 times per week per class | 21% |
| 15 minutes per night per class | 15% |
| 30 minutes per night per class | 12% |
| None | 8% |
| Once per week per class | 7% |
| One hour per night per class | 4% |

### Question #9: How do you learn best?

The favored responses to this question were reversed from those of number eight (see Table 3). Forty-one percent of students felt that they learn best *through whole class discussions,* while 32% reported learning best by *working in groups.* Twenty-one percent favored *reading and working alone.*

### Question #10: What type of tests do you prefer?

Students were given the choices of essay, true/false, multiple choice, short answer, and a mixture of the types of questions. Forty-one percent of students responded that they prefer *multiple choice* questions, while 33% said that they liked a mixture of the four. The least popular types of test questions were *essay* with 4% and *short answer* with 5% (see Table 3).

### Question #12: Who should make classroom rules?

There was a strong consensus among students ( 65%) that classroom rules should be made collaboratively between teachers and students. In contrast, 17% felt that teachers alone should make the rules, 11% felt that students should be responsible for making the rules, 5% believed that it should be the teacher and school principal and 2% believed the principal acting alone should set class rules (see Table 3).

### Question #14: I wish teachers would understand:

Students were given six choices derived from responses to questions on the pilot questionnaire. Choices included *the stress on students, we have homework in other classes, not to punish all when a few disturb, we can't be quiet all day, students can't be perfect,* and *how teenagers think and behave.* Fifty-five percent of students selected either *we have homework in other classes,* or *the stress on students.* In addition, students were given the opportunity to comment about their choices to this question. Analysis of comments indicated that these two responses were often related. Many students at the high school level spoke of trying to juggle the work required to pass six

**Table 3. Responses by Percentages About Making a Class Interesting, Learning Style, Test Preference and Classroom Rules.**

#### How would make a class interesting?

| | |
|---|---|
| Allow students to work in groups | 47% |
| Have more whole group discussions | 32% |
| Have more quiet working time | 7% |
| Show more films | 2% |
| Lecture more | 2% |

#### How do you learn best?

| | |
|---|---|
| Through whole class discussions | 41% |
| By working in groups | 32% |
| By reading and working alone | 21% |
| Through lectures | 6% |

#### What type of tests do you prefer?

| | |
|---|---|
| Multiple choice | 41% |
| A mixture of types of questions | 33% |
| True/false | 7% |
| Short answer | 5% |
| Essay | 4% |

#### Who should make classroom rules?

| | |
|---|---|
| Teacher and students in class | 65% |
| The students in the class | 11% |
| The teacher | 7% |
| Teacher and principal | 5% |
| The principal | 2% |

courses, the necessity of holding a part time job, participating in sports and other extra curricular activities, and having a social life. In addition, students spoke of averaging thirty minutes to an hour of homework in many of their courses which, when multiplied by the number of courses taken, made an inordinate amount of homework. One student wrote, "Doesn't my teacher realize that we have lives beyond her course?"

## Discussion and Conclusions

At the inception of this study, preservice teachers were skeptical about its success. The majority of them expressed an opinion that students would not take the questionnaire seriously, or even respond to it at all. Others felt that students who did respond would likely answer in a frivolous manner or, in their words, "blow it off." These perceptions were supported by many of their supervising teachers, some of whom were apprehensive about giving the questionnaire at all. In actuality, the opposite occurred. Preservice teachers reported that students tended to be very conscientious in their responses and that they expressed surprise and appeared to feel honored to have their opinions heard. In fact, the experience was so positive that a number of the supervising teachers decided to give all of their classes an opportunity to respond to the questionnaire, and in some schools other teachers within departments or teams administered the questionnaire as well. More importantly, a change in attitude became apparent among preservice teachers, who were surprised that students identified qualities of good teachers similar to their own beliefs. These qualities included having a good sense of humor, respecting students, listening to students, fairness, flexibility, making learning fun, and making sure everyone learns. These qualities were similar to those identified by McCabe (1995) and the National Association of Secondary School Principals (1996).

Preservice teachers were unaware that most students are not totally opposed to homework. They learned that it is the quantity of homework, which typically isn't coordinated among teachers within a fragmented school framework, that can become a problem for students.

The preservice teachers took to heart students' requests to more often be allowed to work in groups, and seemed to begin to take more seriously cooperative discussions and projects within their own content reading methods class. Prior to this experience, some preservice teachers had been consistently observed sitting in a circle facing one another with a group problem, yet attempting to solve the problem individually.

Preservice teachers wondered in class why students overwhelmingly preferred multiple choice exams over essay exams, and speculated that perhaps it was because students are often not taught how to answer essay questions. They discussed ways to teach and model essay test taking.

Preservice teachers were impressed by the number of students (76%) who felt that either the teacher and students or the students alone should make the rules for their classrooms. This finding led to renewed interest in Glasser's (1990) quality schools concept where teachers are viewed as lead-managers who work with students to set rules and solve problems, as opposed to the adversarial position teachers often assume with students.

In conclusion, the hypothesis that much can be learned from listening to the voices of students was confirmed in this study. Through this project, preservice teachers developed deeper understandings of their students and their perceptions, feelings, likes, and dislikes. In return, students were pleased that teachers would care enough to listen. As a result, the seeds for mutual cooperation and respect were sown, leading toward an environment where fertile learning could take place. Combs (1979) states, "If a student believes that the teacher is unfair, it makes little difference whether the teacher really is or not. What matters is what the student experiences, not what someone did or intended to do" (p. 195). To fully understand fairness in the eyes of students, teachers need to listen to, connect with, and value student views and perceptions. Education is not something simply to be administered to students; it is a joint venture in learning built around cooperation, respect, enthusiasm, motivation, and good classroom leadership.

# References

Combs, A. W. (1979). *Myths in education: Beliefs that hinder progress and their alternatives.* Boston, MA: Allyn & Bacon, Inc.

Damico, S., & Roth, J. (1993). General track students' perceptions of school policies and practices. *Journal of Research and Development in Education,* 27 (1), 1-7.

Deci, L., & Ryan, R. (1985). *Intrinsic motivation and self-determination in human behavior.* Rochester, NY: Plenum Press.

Eccles, J., & Midgley, C. (1989). Stage-environment fit: Developmentally appropriate classrooms for young adolescents. In C. Ames & R. Ames (Eds.), *Research on motivation in education* (Vol. 3, pp. 139-185). San Diego, CA: Academic.

Glasser, W. (1990). *The quality school: Managing students without coercion.* New York: Harper Perennial.

Glasser, W. (1997). A new look at school failure and school success. *Phi Delta Kappan,* 78, 597-602.

Goodman, J. (1985). Field-based experience: A study of social control and student teachers' responses to institutional constraints. *Journal of Education for Teaching,* 11, 26-49.

Lincoln, Y. (1995). In search of students' voices. *Theory into practice,* 34 (2), 88-93.

McCabe, N. (1995). Twelve high school 11th grade students examine their best teachers. *Peabody Journal of Education,* 70 (2), 117-126.

National Association of Secondary School Principals. (1996). *The mood of American youth.* Reston, VA: Author.

Oldfather, P., & McLaughlin, H. J. (1993). Gaining and losing voice: A longitudinal study of students' continuing impulse to learn across the elementary and middle level contexts. *Research in Middle Level Education,* 17, 1-25.

Phelan, P., Davidson, A., & Cao, H.T. (1992). Speaking up: Students' perspectives on school. *Phi Delta Kappan,* 73, 695-704.

Schlosser, L. (1992). Teacher distance and student disengagement: School lives on the margin. *Journal of Teacher Education,* 42 (2), 128-140.

Tabachnick, B., & Zeichner, K. (1984). The impact of the student teaching experience on the development of teacher perspectives. *Journal of Teacher Education,* 35, 28-36.

Wehlage, G., & Rutter, R. (1986). Dropping out: How much do schools contribute to the problem? *Teachers College Record,* 87, 374-392.

Zeichner, K., & Gore, J. (1990). Teacher socialization. In W.R. Houston (Ed.), *Handbook of research on teacher education* (pp. 329-348). New York: Macmillan.

## Appendix A: Open-ended Student Survey Used in Pilot Study

We value your input. Please take a moment and answer the questions that follow.

1. What are the characteristics of a good teacher?

2. How will this course affect your life? Do you see a connection? Is it important? Will you use what you have learned later on?

3. What are your feelings about homework? What kind and how much would you prefer?

4. How do you think this class should be taught? Do you prefer discussions, lectures, working in groups, etc.?

5. What type of tests do you prefer?

6. If you were a teacher, what would you do to make this class interesting?

7. What classroom rules would you have, or not have? Who should make class and school rules?

8. Please complete the following sentences:

   a. My favorite teacher was _____ because _____

   b. I wish teachers would understand _____

   c. If I were a teacher, I would _____

# Appendix B: Student Survey Used in This Research Project

We value your input. Please take a moment and answer the questions that follow.

1. **Choose only one.** A good teacher is one who:

____is enthusiastic ____has a good sense of humor

____respects students ____listens to students

____can be trusted by students ____is patient and caring

2. **Choose only one.** A good teacher is one who:

____doesn't get angry ____is an easy grader ____is fair

____is strict ____enforces rules

____is flexible ____makes you work hard

3. **Choose only one.** A good teacher is one who:

____uses a variety of teaching methods ____teaches responsibility

____lets you learn at your own pace ____knows the subject well

____explains/makes sure everyone learns ____makes learning fun

4. Do you see a connection between this class and your life? Is it important? Will you use what you are learning later on?

5. **Choose only one.** My feelings about homework are that I:

____believe it is a good way to learn ____don't like it

____believe that it is necessary ____don't do it

____believe teachers don't grade it ____do it if it isn't too much

6. **Choose only one.** If I have homework, I would prefer it to be:

____challenging and difficult ____easy and short

____meaningful, not just busy work ____creative projects

____something that forces me to think about the subject

7. **Choose only one.** How much homework is reasonable?

____one hour per night per class ____once per week per class

____30 minutes per night per class ____2 or 3 times per week per class

____15 minutes per night per class ____only as needed

____none

8. **Choose only one.** If you were a teacher, what would you do to make a class more interesting?

____have more whole group discussions ____show more films

____allow students to work in groups ____lecture more

____have more quiet working time

9. **Choose only one.** How do you learn best?

____through lectures ____through whole class discussions

____by working in groups ____by reading and working alone

10. **Choose only one.** What type of tests do you prefer?

____essay              ____true/false            ____multiple choice

____short answer      ____a mixture of the other four kinds

11. What classroom rules would you have, or not have if you were a teacher?

12. **Choose only one.** Who should make classroom rules?

____the teacher          ____the students in the class

____the principal        ____the teacher and students in the class

____the teacher and principal

13. **Choose three.** My favorite teacher was _____ because he/she:

____was patient and caring          ____was enthusiastic about the subject

____made learning fun               ____had a sense of humor

____was flexible                    ____was strict and made us work hard

____respected students              ____was an easy grader

____didn't get angry                ____used a variety of teaching methods

____was someone you could trust  ____was fair

____enforced the rules              ____let you learn at your own pace

____taught responsibility           ____explained & made sure all learned

____listened to students            ____knew the subject well

14. **Choose only one.** I wish teachers would understand:

____the stress on students

____we have homework in other classes

____not to punish all when a few disturb

____we can't be quiet all day

____students can't be perfect

____how teenagers think and behave

    **Please explain your choice.**

15. If I were a teacher, I would:

# A Collaborative Model for Developing a Children's Literature Pathway into Preservice Methods Courses

## Jane Brady Matanzo
## Marie F. Doan Holbein

Florida Atlantic University

## Abstract

*Two elementary methodology professors collaborate by using and extending children's literature to provide a common pathway among methodology courses and a means to facilitate the transfer and application of learning. The collaboration described herein specifically focuses upon the development of a model containing six elements which was implemented with students taking elementary language arts and mathematics methodology courses. Examples and/or procedures are given for each element of the model including bibliographic card formats, student reflections, children's literature content bibliographic starters, and professional children's literature resources that can be accessed by students.*

"May I use the children's literature bibliographic cards and activity ideas I made during my language arts course to help me with my mathematics project?"

This question was posed mid-semester by a preservice student enrolled in a mathematics methodology course where students were expected to create a partial portfolio that would include projects based on children's literature selections. As the student asked the question, the professor observed that there was a hesitancy and a sense of 'dishonesty' in making multiple uses of materials and ideas developed in previous or simultaneous courses. She also noted that other students in the course were anxious to hear her answer which was, "Yes, do build upon your previous and current projects from other courses and apply them to what you are now doing in relation to mathematics."

The students still seemed to doubt that the use and adaptation of previous or concurrent learning and materials developed would be condoned. The mathematics professor then spoke to other methodology professors who agreed with her and were surprised by the question. Being on a relatively small campus, these professors often articulated and felt that the transfer of strategies, ideas, and materials among methods courses already was occurring and being encouraged. Because the ease and frequency of transfer appeared to be in question, the language arts and mathematics methodology professors agreed to develop a collaborative model for transfer of learning between those two courses. Children's literature was selected to be the "pathway" of transfer because all methodology professors wanted to include children's literature in their courses. Depending on the success of the model. methodology professors in science and social studies expressed interest in joining this effort; thus, their content areas also were included in the planning and development of resources.

## Theoretical Background

The transfer and application of learning gained and combined from various courses, subjects, or themes have been topics of research for almost 100 years (Bransford, Vye, Adams, & Perfetto, 1989; Prenzel & Mandl, 1992; Singley & Anderson, 1989; Voss, 1987). Resnick (1989) defines learning transfer as the "flexible applicability of knowledge (p. 2)." Current thinking from a constructivist viewpoint is that one reconstructs knowledge in order to apply it to other situations. Collins (1990) believes that the learner must develop a global framework before he or she can integrate what is known into new situations. It also is believed that transfer is more probable and longer lasting "where the 'context of use' of the knowledge is obvious to the student" so the student psychologically conceives the possible "range of application" (p.5) for given concepts and processes (Prenzel & Mandl, 1992).

To ascertain how and if such transfer might relate to the methodology training of preservice teachers, Noe (1994) designed an integrative curriculum model based on a 12 hour course that provided strategies and continuity to integrate the various content methodology courses. Sixty-one percent of the students used the integrative strategies learned in this course during their student teaching. Eighteen of the 72 graduates became employed as teachers by the time of this study and completed a questionnaire. The majority of those respondents felt that the preparation they received in this program influenced them to adopt an integrative philosophy. Sixty-six percent of the former students felt they were prepared to integrate and transfer knowledge and skills learned to many aspects and areas of their teaching. Thirty-eight percent of the respondents extensively incorporated integrative strategies learned, while the remaining respondents indicated substantial to moderate use of such strategies in their classrooms.

Various educators working with preservice students (Gordon & Hunsberger, 1991; Moore, 1991; Oropallo & Gomez, 1996; Seaborg, Mohr, & Fowler, 1994) found that preservice journals used alone or incorporated into a larger portfolio encouraged students to reflect on what they had learned, build a more astute awareness of strategies and possibilities for wider application, and consider innovative ways of thinking and applying what was learned to actual classroom situations. Several of the above researchers stressed that feedback from peers, professors, or others resulted in more responsive thinking by the students.

A variety of sources (Burton, 1992; Dynak, 1997; Nevin, 1992; Winograd & Higgins, 1995) have also noted the success of combining language arts and mathematics instruction. Nevin (1992) stressed that, "literature is a natural way to introduce a new concept " and that exposing students to stories urges them to "listen, interpret, and reflect on content" (p. 144). The National Council of Teachers of Mathematics (1991) recommended in its professional standards that "teachers move from traditional text and teacher-centered teaching to empower students to construct their own knowledge of mathematics" (p.2). One way the Council advocates this be accomplished is through wide reading, which can be encouraged by the inclusion of children's literature as an active part of a mathematics curriculum.

This inclusion of literature as a commonality among the various methodology courses was what the professors and writers of this article envisioned when they developed their collaborative model. Support for such inclusion is given by numerous professional sources. Routman (1988) and Norton (1992) both indicate that literature-based learning is taking hold in countries such as Australia, New Zealand, England, and Canada, and is becoming an important vehicle of instruction and means for concept reinforcement in various states. Norton stresses that in order to develop an effective reading program based on literature, "teachers need to know how to select literature and must be skilled in the instructional strategies that highlight the best features of literature as well as excite students (p. 5)." Gunning (1996) believes that students gain proficiency in both their reading and conceptual knowledge by reading books and periodicals related to the content that is being studied. However, Walker and Roskos (1994) warn that ". . . few preservice teachers today have experienced learning within a literature-based classroom, and preservice teachers' early conceptions of teaching are derived largely from their experiences as students themselves" (p.60).

Briggs and Stiefer (1995) decided to act upon this type of challenge by actively incorporating children's literature in their reading and language arts classes with the intention that knowledge and strategies learned would be applied to all areas of the curriculum. Students developed a literature card file, kept response journals, formed book discussion groups, and started personal children's literature collections. Journals gave insight into their reactions to various literature selections as well as into thinking and group discussion processes. The final journal entry was to ascertain if these preservice students would use discussion groups in practice. The students stated unanimously that book discussion was a strategy they would use in their own classrooms. However, as Briggs and Stiefer reflected on the incorporation of literature in their courses, they decided some revision was in order. Among the revisions are: acquiring common sets of children's literature books for course discussion, adding a greater choice in literature response activities, including musical and artistic responses, and accepting and encouraging more variety in terms of response modalities. In light of their experience, they advocate that "the principles and similar activities could be incorporated into any reading/language arts, science, and math courses by elementary faculty collaborating or teaming with content area faculty" (p.206). They contend this collaborative practice enables students to see their faculty members working together and to become more aware of the possibilities of interdisciplinary instruction. This tenet is echoed by Kelly and Farnum (1990) who suggest that "teacher education classes must provide process models that both demonstrate appropriate classroom practice and enhance content learning" (p. 268).

## The Collaborative Model

This university's collaborative model was based on three concepts: a) knowledge and instructional strategies can be transferred across the curriculum; b) student response journals and portfolios can offer opportunities for reflection; and c) children's literature is gaining a growing presence as a base for instruction. This collaborative model features six elements:

1) Exposure to a variety of children's literature and its use in language arts and reading courses;

2) Articulation among faculty as to the importance of and ways to include children's literature;

3) Reinforcement in methodology courses by including children's literature in assignments, strategies, and/or activities;

4) Transfer, application, and extension of experiences related to children's literature among the courses;

5) Philosophical and psychological preparation for effective implementation of thematic units; and

6) Encouragement of reflection among developing practitioners.

### Exposure to a Variety of Children's Literature and Its Use in Language Arts and Reading Courses

At this particular campus, the combined language arts and children's literature methodology course usually is the first methodology course in which students enroll. It must be completed prior to taking two reading courses which are sequenced in subsequent semesters. However, it is becoming more prevalent that students who have transferred may already have completed one or more methodology courses. A number of students also elect to take several content methodology courses at the same time they enroll in language arts. Blocks of sequenced methodology courses are the preference of the faculty; however, this is not yet a program reality. Therefore, consideration for providing an integrative base in the language arts and children's literature course which could be applied to simultaneous and/or future methodology courses is currently needed. The language arts and children's literature course is designed to introduce students to a variety of genres such as realistic fiction, historical fiction, modern fantasy, concept and informational books, poetry, and biography. One feature of the course is that students select a theme such as "Foods Around the World" and find examples of this theme in the various genres. Students are guided by the professor in webbing or clustering the topics and subtopics found in a variety of children's literature selections and other print and non-print resources. In a culminating course activity, cooperative teams of students select a literature book and teach a minimum of four individually prepared lessons relative to the content and skills in mathematics, science, fine arts, and social studies. A recent practice is to have each team of students introduce the core book and teach the lessons to an actual class in grade levels three, four, or five during a half day at a local school. This helps the preservice students ascertain the appropriateness of their chosen book for a given group of elementary students. Preservice teachers also self-evaluate the effectiveness of their lessons in elaborating and extending integrated content knowledge and skills based on that book. Preservice students supplement the core book by introducing students to other related books that will extend the content of the lessons. This requirement encourages the examination of the topic from assorted viewpoints and genres.

Starter bibliographies are disseminated in the language arts and children's literature course for mathematics, science, and social science (see Appendix A). Each of these bibliographies features a variety of literature examples relative to those content areas and leaves five or more blank lines to encourage preservice students to add and share additional literature examples they discover. Students also are given a children's literature bibliographic resource list (see Appendix B) to help them become familiar with resource lists and journals which feature book reviews and other information for locating relevant literature.

### Articulation Among Faculty as to the Importance of and Ways to Include Children's Literature

This faculty was aware and accepting of using children's literature as an integral part of their course materials, objectives, and assignments. The language arts and mathematics professors who piloted the collaborative model began the process of integrating assignments, activities, and materials. Specific strategies introduced in the language arts course included scavenger hunts, graphic organizers, book bags, inquiry reading, literature circles, Brain Feed, and A Fact A Day. These activities provided a sample of the variety of experiences that can be used across the curriculum. Although the faculty members have not formally shared these strategies with their colleagues, it is suggested this be done whenever possible. Students' use of these strategies in their content classes suggests to faculty members that the strategies can be applied in different content areas. The methodology faculty should meet periodically to share content, skills, and assignments they stress in their courses and to discuss children's literature they find applicable.

### Reinforcement in Methodology Courses by Including Children's Literature in Assignments, Strategies, and/or Activities

The mathematics professor implemented the model in a loosely defined sequence. She first presented and modeled how to use math-related children's literature. Students then emulated her and/or the language arts professor by incorporating some of the same activities and strategies for books they were bringing and discussing in class.

As the mathematics methodology course progressed, students were assigned to cooperative groups where they developed and presented lessons which integrated children's literature with mathematics. Specific lesson plans were developed using a format common to methodology professors in all the content areas. The components of the lesson plans included focus, objectives, materials needed, motivation, procedures, evaluation criteria, follow-up activities, a bibliography of related children's literature titles, software suggestions, and any additional resources.

Many of the activities tried by students reflected examples given or developed by them in the language arts and children's literature course. It was not unusual for students during the mathematics course to visit the language arts professor and share how they were applying various strategies learned in her course to their math assignments.

The students also were required to record their literature finds on 4x6 inch bibliography cards. The entries were less formal than those recorded in language arts, but added to already existing files. Card summaries included recommendations for grade levels, mathematical operations identified, and suggested teaching strategies. Figure 1 presents three examples of student-prepared bibliography cards:

**Figure 1. Bibliography Cards for Math-Related Children's Literature**

*The Librarian Who Measured The Earth*
Author:Kathryn Lasky
Illustrator:Kevin Hawkes
A spectacular book with bold and colorful illustrations tells the story of Eratosthenes, a Greek student, who lived over 2000 years ago. This simple text presents a wonderful story and challenging math concepts for the reader. Rec.: Third, fourth, and fifth grades.

*Anno's Counting Book*
Author and Illustrator: Mitsumasa Anno
This book introduces counting and number systems by showing mathematical relationships in nature. The author illustrates each number in a variety of ways and students discover it. There also is an excellent note in the back of the book about ways to introduce numbers and counting. This book would be appropriate for kindergarten and first grade.

*26 Letters and 99 Cents*
Author and Photographer:Tana Hoban
One half of the book features the letters of the alphabet and when you turn the book over and upside down, it's a separate book that features coins—up to 99 cents! The coins are photographs and excellent to use when children are learning the value of money.
Rec.: K-2.

## Transfer, Application, and Extension of Children's Literature Related Experiences Among the Courses

Professors modeled ways to include children's literature across the curriculum. Both the mathematics and language arts professors reminded students that their ideas could be transferred, applied, and modified for any content area lesson. Once students realized they could use the same children's literature selections in a variety of ways for different courses without "cheating", it was not unusual for them voluntarily to incorporate literature in lessons for art, science, social studies, music, and physical education. One student excitedly shared in a hallway how she was using *The Drinking Gourd* (Monjo, 1970) to demonstrate her competency on the ukelele and to teach a song related to an historical event or period in her music methods class. Another student showed three children's literature selections he had discovered on ways to juggle and taught juggling skills gained from the books to peers in his physical education class. Students are more frequently visiting professors to talk informally about children's literature and to seek book suggestions to incorporate with their various projects.

### Philosophical and Psychological Preparation
### Toward Effective Implementation of Thematic Units

An initial impetus for developing the collaborative model was the panic expressed by many students during the beginning of their teaching internships when they were told to develop a thematic unit. The students seemed to have never heard of this concept, although the professors believed that students were being prepared in each class to design lessons and an eventual unit. A conscious effort is now being made to use the term "thematic unit" more consistently across the methodology courses, which has somewhat quelled students' anxiety. In recently completed units, children's literature appears to be the framework of the unit, with many subsequent lessons and activities relating to specific books.

The outline which interns follow in their units incorporates the language arts areas of listening, speaking, reading, writing, and drama. It also is expected that social studies, science, math, art, music and appropriate special activities will be integrated. To plan their units, students complete a graphic organizer which displays the theme with spokes and empty "boxes" for to each area and/or concept to be included. Students first are exposed to this format in the language arts and children's literature course. During the mathematics course, students add their newly acquired mathematics activities and literature titles. The goal is to maintain this organization of ideas throughout the methodology courses. Therefore, as students begin their internships, they are armed with a substantial amount of information and resources which can be modified to accommodate a particular grade placement and the unique needs of specific classrooms.

### Encouragement of Reflection as Developing Practitioners

Students at this campus are expected to develop a portfolio that represents what they know and can do in terms of teaching. The portfolio combines examples of experiences students had throughout their many courses. Photographs and other types of evidence are in the cumulative portfolio which is to be completed by the conclusion of the internship. The portfolio is to be developed as a composite of an individual's prowess and promise. It is considered in the overall evaluation of the internship and is used as an introduction during employment interviews.

One aspect of the portfolio is for students to reflect upon their observations, participation activities, and teaching experiences through journal entries. The journal is a critical component of the required portfolio. According to Keiffer and Faust (as cited in Krause, 1996), three major processes that should be considered in developing a portfolio are 1) collection, 2) selection, and 3) reflection. The reflection entries are viewed as one source of evidence of students' growth process. The journal comments evolved from simple notes with a singular observation to more critical assessments regarding the appropriate use of children's literature and the effectiveness of strategies and activities. A sampling of student journal reflections regarding daily activities includes:

"I enjoyed discussing the children's literature selections pertaining to mathematics."

"It was helpful to listen to other students' findings during our discussions."

"I'd like to keep expanding my list and keep a file of good books because I know I'll refer to it in the future."

Students also were asked to reflect in a positive and constructive manner on their own cooperative group lesson presentations and on the presentations of other groups. As students became more comfortable with this type of evaluative process, the *depth* of their reflections increased gradually as is indicated by one preservice student's journal entries concerning the following lessons.

*A lesson on division* (early in the course)
"The book, *One Hundred Hungry Ants,* was great."

*A lesson on graphing*
"The graphing exercise was eye-catching and children would find it interesting. I liked the display of books put all around the room."
Note: The students who presented this lesson provided a bibliography of literature resources related to the lesson and created a display of selections based on the bibliography.

*A lesson on geometry*
"This group used the book, *Grandfather Tang's Story,* as the basis of their lesson plan on TANGRAMS. I liked the way they had students doing TANGRAMS at their seats. Their extension activity of having students write a story and then use a TANGRAM to illustrate it was good."

## Evaluation of the Model

Just as the students reflected on their experiences, the professors reflected on the collaborative model. After thoughtful deliberation, several elements of the model were identified as strong and others were determined to be in need of modification. The collection of literature and reflection on its uses were successful and clearly met course objectives. Expectations were pleasantly surpassed as professors noted consistent growth in the depth of students' perceptions, reflections, and knowledge of children's literature.

Reflections by the professors unanimously indicated that the model would be strengthened if specific strategies were given for each of the titles or genres.

A Children's Literature Idea Bank Across the Curriculum could be established and periodically updated by students who completed the course(s). The Idea Bank would be available to less advanced students to use as a planning resource to suggest categories of books and a variety of genres to include in lessons. Students created a minimum of 40 titles for the language arts and children's literature course and added 10 more in the mathematics course. Because many students exceeded these requirements, the number of annotations might be increased. Several students noted that the more extensive their card file, the more helpful it was in developing thematic units during their internship.

## Next Steps

The next step is to share the modified collaborative model and the findings to date with methodology professors in social studies and science so they may travel this collaborative pathway to literacy. In addition, an eventual goal is for the students experiencing this model to internalize it and apply it to their own teaching. It is hoped that a student will perceive the elements of the model as 1) *I* need to continue building upon my knowledge of children's literature; 2) *I* need to articulate with my own faculty members; 3) *I* need to include children's literature in the assignments, strategies, and/or activities I plan and implement; 4) *I* need to transfer, apply, and extend children's literature throughout my curriculum; 5) *I* need to consider children's literature as a base for my thematic units; and 6) *I* need to reflect upon the effectiveness of my teaching and the progress of my students. Although this model is in its early stages, students are envisioning children's literature possibilities across their preservice teaching experiences and are using children's literature as one essential ingredient in planning and teaching.

---

## References

Bransford, J. D., Vye, N. J., Adams, L. T., & Perfetto, G. A. (1989). Learning skills and the acquisition of knowledge . In A. M. Lesgold & R. Glaser (Eds.), *Dimensions of thinking and cognitive instruction* (pp.381-413). Hillsdale, NJ: Erlbaum.

Briggs, C., & Stiefer, T. K. (1995). Literature infusion: A shot in the arm for elementary methods courses. In W. M. Linek & E. G. Sturtevant (Eds.), *Generations of Literacy* (pp. 199-208). Harrisonburg, VA: College Reading Association.

Burton, G. M. (1992). Using language arts to promote mathematics learning. *The Mathematics Educator, 3*(2), 26-31.

Collins, A. (1990). *Generalizing from situated knowledge to robust understanding.* Paper presented at the Annual Meeting of the American Educational Research Association, Boston.

Dynak, J. (1997). Structuring literacy course tasks to foster deliberate use of strategy instruction by preservice math teachers. *Journal of Adolescent & Adult Literacy, 40*, 280-285.

Gordon, C. J., & Hunsberger, M. (1991). Preservice teachers' conceptions of content area literacy instruction. In J. Zutell & S. McCormick (Eds.), *Learner factors/ teacher factors: Issues in literacy research and instruction* . (pp.399-407). Chicago, IL: National Reading Conference.

Gunning, T. G. (1996). *Creating reading instruction for all children.* (2nd edition). Boston: Allyn & Bacon.

Kelly, P. R. & Farnum, N. (1990). Practicing what we teach in reading education programs. *Journal of Reading, 33,* 264-269.

Krause, S. (1996). Portfolios in teacher education: Effects of instruction on preservice teacher's early comprehension of the portfolio process. *Journal of Teacher Education, 47,* 130-138.

Moore, M. (1991, Fall). Reflective teaching and learning through the use of learning logs. *Journal of Reading Education* , 17, 35-49.

National Council of Teachers of Mathematics. (1991). *Professional standards for teaching mathematics.* Reston, VA: Author.

Nevin, M. L. (1992). A language arts approach to mathematics. *The Arithmetic Teacher, 40,* 142-146.

Noe, K. L. (1994). Effectiveness of an integrated methods curriculum: Will beginning teachers teach as we have taught them? *Journal of Reading Education, 19,* 45-49.

Norton, D. E. (1992). *The impact of literature-based reading.* New York: Macmillan.

Oropallo, K., & Gomez, S. (1996). Using reflective portfolios in preservice teacher education programs. In E. G. Sturtevant & W. M. Linek (Eds.), *Growing literacy,* (pp. 121- 132). Harrisonburg, VA: College Reading Association.

Prenzel, M., & Mandl, H. (1992). *Transfer of learning from a constructivist perspective* (Research report No. 6). Munchen: Ludwig-Maximilians-Universitat, Lehrstuhl fur Empirische Padagogik und Padagogische Psychologie.

Resnick, L. B. (1989). Introduction. In L. B. Resnick (Ed.), *Knowing, learning, and instruction* (pp. 1-24). Hillsdale, NJ: Erlbaum.

Routman, R. (1988). *Transitions: From literature to literacy.* Portsmouth, NH: Heinemann.

Seaborg, M. B., Mohr, K., & Fowler, T. J. (1994). Preservice teachers' learning processes: A descriptive analysis of the impact of varied experiences with portfolios. In C. K. Kinzer & D. J. Leu (Eds.), *Multidimensional aspects of literacy research, theory, anhd practice* (pp. 440-447). Chicago, IL: National Reading Conference.

Singley, M. K., & Anderson, J. R. (1989). *The transfer of cognitive skill.* Cambridge, MA: Cambridge University Press.

Voss, J. F. (1987). Learning and transfer in subject-matter learning: A problem solving model. *International Journal of Educational Research, 11,* 607-622.

Walker, B. J., & Roskos, K. (1994). Preservice teachers' epistemology of diagnostic reading instruction: Observations of shifts during course work experiences. In E. G. Sturtevant & W. M. Linek (Eds.), *Pathways for literacy: Learners teach and teachers learn* (pp.59-71). Pittsburg, KS: College Reading Association.

Winograd, K., & Higgins, K. M. (1995). Writing, reading, and talking mathematics: One interdisciplinary possibility. *The Reading Teacher, 48,* 310-318.

## Appendix A: Bibliographic Starters

### *Mathematics*

Anno, M.(1975). *Anno's counting book.* New York: Harper Collins.

Carle, E. (1977 ). *The grouchy ladybug.* New York: Harper Trophy Books.

Crawford, J. (1992). *How do octopi eat pizza pie?* Alexandria, VA: Time-Life Books.

Gardner, T. (1991). *Math in science and nature.* New York: Watts.

Giganti, P., Jr. (1992). *Each orange had 8 slices.* New York: Greenwillow Books.

Hoban, T. (1987). *26 Letters and 99 cents.* New York: Greenwillow Books.

Holtzman, C. (1995). *A quarter from the tooth fairy.* New York: Scholastic, Inc.

Lasky, K. (1994). *The librarian who measured the earth.* New York: Little, Brown & Co.

Markle, S. (1993). *Math mini-mysteries.* New York: Atheneum.

McMillan, B. (1991). *Eating fractions.* New York: Scholastic, Inc.

Reid, M. S. (1990). *The button box.* New York: Dutton Children's Books.

Schwartz, D. M. (1989). *If you made a million.* New York: Lothrop, Lee & Shepard Books.

Scieszka, J. (1995). *Math curse.* New York: Viking.

Stanley, D. (1991). *Siegfried.* New York: Bantam Little Rooster Book.

Tompert, A. (1990). *Grandfather Tang's story.* New York: Crown Publishers.

Viorst, J. (1978). *Alexander, who used to be rich last Sunday.* New York: Atheneum.

### *Science*

Arnold, C. (1993). *On the brink of extinction: The California condor.* San Diego, CA: Harcourt.

Brandenburg, J. (1993). *To the top of the world: Adventures with Arctic wolves.* New York: Walker Co.

Brooks, B. (1994). *Making sense: Animal perception and communication.* New York: Farrar.

Brown, L. K. & Brown, M. (1990). *Dinosaurs alive and well!: A guide to good health.* Boston, MA: Little, Brown Co.

Cole, J. (1989-present). *The magic school bus series.* New York: Scholastic.

Cone, M. (1993). *Come back, salmon.* Phoenix, AZ: Sierra Club Books.

Dewey, J. (1995). *Wildlife rescue: The work of Dr. Kathleen Ramsey.* Honesdale, PA: Boyds Mills Press.

Durrell, A., George, J. C. & Paterson, K., (Eds.) (1993). *The big book of our planet.* New York: Dutton.

Elkington, J., Hailes, J., Hill, D., & Makower, J. (1990). *Going green: A kid's handbook to saving the planet .* New York: Puffin Books.

Lauber, P. (1991). *Seeing earth from space.* New York: Orchard Books.

Lauber, P. (1986). *Volcano: The eruption and healing of Mount St. Helens.* New York: Bradbury.

Pringle, L. (1996). *Dolphin man: Exploring the world of dolphins.* New York: Atheneum.

Simon, S. (1994). *The oceans.* New York: Morrow.

Swanson, D. (1995). *Safari beneath the sea.* Honesdale, PA: Boyds Mills Press.

Temple, L. (1993). *Dear world: How children around the world feel about our environment.* New York: Random House.

### Social Science

Aliki. (1993). *Communication.* New York: Greenwillow.

Atkin, S. B. (1993). *Voices from the fields: Children of migrant farm workers tell their stories.* Boston, MA: Little, Brown Co.

Bial, R. (1993). *Frontier home.* Boston, MA: Houghton Mifflin.

Bunting, E. (1990). *The wall.* New York: Clarion.

Burleigh, R. & Wimmer, M. (1992). Flight: *The journey of Charles Lindbergh.* New York: Philomel Books.

Carrick, C. (1993). *Whaling days.* New York: Clarion.

Carter, J. (1993). *Talking peace: A vision for the next generation.* New York: Dutton.

Coleman, P. (1996). *Rosie the riveter: Women on the home front in world war II.* New York: Crown.

Conrad, P. (1992). *Prairie vision: The life and times of Solomon Butcher.* New York: HarperCollins.

Ellis, V. F. (1990). *Afro-bets first book about Africa.* New York: Just Us Books.

Freedman, R. (1994). *Kids at work: Lewis Hine and the crusade against child labor.* New York: Clarion.

Fritz, J. (1987). *Shh! We're writing the constitution.* New York: Putnam Berkley Group.

Giblin, J. C. (1993). *Be seated: A book about chairs.* New York: Harper-Collins.

Hamilton, V. (1992). *Many thousand gone: African Americans from slavery to freedom.* New York: Random.

Hausherr, R. (1989). *Children and the AIDS virus: A book for children, parents, and teachers.* New York: Clarion.

Hoyt-Goldsmith, D. (1993). *Celebrating Kwanzaa.* New York: Holiday.

Hoyt-Goldsmith. D. (1994). *Day of the dead: A Mexican-American celebration.* New York: Holiday.

Maestro, B. (1993). *The story of money.* New York: Clarion

McKissack, P. & McKissack, F. (1995). *Christmas in the big house, Christmas in the quarters.* New York: Scholastic.

Meltzer, M. (1992). *The amazing potato: A story in which the Incas, Conquistadors, Marie Antoinette, Thomas Jefferson, wars, famines, immigrants and French fries all play a part.* New York: Harper Collins.

Monjo, F. N. (1970). *The drinking gourd.* New York: Harper and Row.

Murphy, J. (1996).*The great fire.* New York: Scholastic.

Murphy, J. (1994). *Across America on the emigrant train.* New York: Clarion.

Myers, W. D. (1992). *Now is the time! The African American struggle for freedom.* New York: HarperCollins.

Rogers, F. (1995). *Let's talk about it: Adoption.* New York: Putnam Berkley Group, Inc.

Stanley, J. (1993). *Children of the dust bowl: The true story of the school at Weedpatch Camp.* New York: Crown.

## Appendix B: Children's Literature Bibliographic Resources

*Book links, connecting books, libraries, and classrooms.* (monthly). Chicago, IL: The American Library Association.

Braddon, K. L., Hall, N. J., & Taylor, D. (1993). *Math through children's literature. Making the NCTM standards come alive.* Englewood, CO: Teacher Ideas Press.

Cullinan, B. E. (Ed.). (1992). *Invitation to read: More children's literature in the reading program.* Newark, DE: International Reading Association.

Hickman, J., & Cullinan, B. E. (Eds.). (1989). *Children's literature in the classroom: Extending Charlotte's Web.* Norwood, MA: Christopher-Gordon Publishers.

Kennedy, D. M., Spangler, A., & Vanderwerf, B. (1990). *Science and technology in fact and fiction: A guide to children's books.* New York: Bowker.

Laughlin, M. K., & Kardaleff, P. P. (1991). *Literature-based social studies: Children's books and activities to enrich the K-5 curriculum.* Phoenix, AZ: Onyx.

Moss, J. F. (1994). *Using literature in the middle grades: A thematic approach.* Norwood, MA: Christopher Gordon Publishers.

Thiessen, D., & Matthias, M. (Eds.). (1992). *The wonderful world of mathematics.* Reston, VA: National Council of Teachers of Mathematics.

Tunnell, M. O., & Ammon, R. (Eds.). (1993). *The story of ourselves: Teaching history through children's literature.* Portsmouth, NH: Heinemann.

Whitin, D. J., & Wilde, S. (1992). *Read any good math lately? Children's books for mathematical learning, K-6.* Portsmouth, NH: Heinemann.

Wood, K. D., with Moss, A. (Eds.). (1992). *Exploring literature in the classroom: Contents and methods.* Norwood, MA: Christopher-Gordon Publishers.

Zarnowski, M., & Gallagher, A. F. (Eds.). (1993). *Children's literature and social studies: Selecting and using notable books in the classroom.* Washington, DC: National Council for the Social Studies.

## DATE DUE

|  |  |  |  |
|---|---|---|---|
|  |  |  |  |
|  |  |  |  |
|  |  |  |  |
|  |  |  |  |
|  |  |  |  |
|  |  |  |  |
|  |  |  |  |
|  |  |  |  |
|  |  |  |  |
|  |  |  |  |
|  |  |  |  |
|  |  |  |  |
|  |  |  |  |
|  |  |  |  |
|  |  |  |  |
|  |  |  |  |
|  |  |  |  |
|  |  |  |  |

#47-0108 Peel Off Pressure Sensitive